RAINFOREST

CAPITALISM

RAINFOREST

Power and
Masculinity in a
Congolese Timber
Concession

THOMAS HENDRIKS

CAPITALISM

Duke University Press *Durham and London* 2022

Printed in the United States of America on acid-free paper ∞
Designed by Aimee C. Harrison
Typeset in Minion Pro and Univers LT Std by Westchester
Publishing Services

Library of Congress Cataloging-in-Publication Data
Names: Hendriks, Thomas, [date] author.
Title: Rainforest capitalism : power and masculinity in a Congolese
timber concession / Thomas Hendriks.
Description: Durham : Duke University Press, 2022. | Includes bibli-
ographical references and index.
Identifiers: LCCN 2021018233 (print)
LCCN 2021018234 (ebook)
ISBN 9781478015239 (hardcover)
ISBN 9781478017844 (paperback)
ISBN 9781478022473 (ebook)
Subjects: LCSH: Lumbermen—Congo (Democratic Republic)—Social
life and customs. | Logging—Congo (Democratic Republic) | Lumber
camps—Congo (Democratic Republic) | Lumber camps—Congo
(Democratic Republic)—Management. | BISAC: SOCIAL SCIENCE /
Anthropology / Cultural & Social | HISTORY / Africa / Central
Classification: LCC HD8039.L92 C74 2022 (print) |
LCC HD8039.L92 (ebook) | DDC 634.9/8096751—dc23
LC record available at https://lccn.loc.gov/2021018233
LC ebook record available at https://lccn.loc.gov/2021018234

Cover art: Photograph by the author.

Frontispiece: View of the CTI labor compound's central avenue at
noon.

For loggers, wherever they are

CONTENTS

NOTE ON ANONYMITY

To ensure confidentiality and protect the privacy of people whose lives have provided the basis for this book's argument, I use fictive names for all the men and women appearing in these pages. I also use a pseudonym—CTI or Congolese Timber Industries—to refer to the Congolese branch of the European company that operated the logging concession where fieldwork happened. Yet, notwithstanding my use of generic names for sites that are specifically linked to CTI's presence (e.g., forest camp, river camp), I had no choice but to refer to neighboring villages and towns by their actual names. Undoubtedly, this makes the logging concession identifiable to insiders. A more watertight guarantee on anonymity would, however, make every reference to a wider context impossible and thus create an image of the concession as an isolated world artificially cut off from its specific region and history. Balancing concerns for contextualization and anonymity, the following chapters propose a particularized and concrete ethnography that nevertheless protects people's privacy and respects the trust they bestowed on me.

NOTE ON PHOTOGRAPHY

I am a reluctant photographer, but the images that separate the chapters in this book are mine. I have reproduced them here in seemingly anachronistic black-and-white, which immediately brings to mind the colonial archive and its racialized oppositions. This manipulation is deliberate. It points at the uncanny reappearance of a past in the present. And it visualizes how, for many people in this book, the present itself was felt as always almost over: as a world that could simply disappear overnight.

The aesthetic trick of black-and-white troubles linear temporalities and blurs firm separations between past and present—not, as Johannes Fabian (1983) put it, to deny the "coevalness" between ethnography and what it makes into its object, but to foreground the messiness of history, the ephemerality of the present, and the synthetic nostalgia for a remembered colonial past that pervaded the logging concession.

Moreover, editing to black-and-white is a useful technique for evoking the subdued hues and damped tones of a rainforest world where light is often scarce, as well as for showing the sharp shadows and blinding boundaries that emerge in forest clearings. It is also a device for reproducing the texture of timber and vegetation and for suggesting the poetic force of bulldozers and chainsaws.

In contrast to the portraits of Congolese workers, there are no images of white loggers. Although a substantial part of this book is about them, their visual absence remains problematic. Yet it is the product of a different relationship to photography. Among the European managers, taking pictures was not a common practice. In the labor compounds, however, pictures were everywhere. Workers paid photographers to document their achievements and dreams. And my small camera was merely taken up by what was already there.

Fuel truck on a logging road

PROLOGUE

We suddenly realize that the enormous padauk tree is about to fall down and crash into the surrounding rainforest. People shout and run in different directions. One of the loggers drops his heavy chainsaw on the ground and pushes me forward. I get stuck in thick bushes and creeping lianas. In the heat of the moment, I lose sight of the others. Looking over my shoulder, all I see is a wall of vegetation closing itself behind me. The massive tree loudly groans. I am unsure where it is coming from. A loud rattling of snapping fibers swells into a thundering roar that vibrates through the soil. Within seconds, heavy branches fall from the sky. The air is filled with bees, ants, dust, and organic matter. I cover my mouth and close my eyes. When I reopen them, diffuse sunlight permeates a thick green haze. A couple of meters before me I can just make out Freddy's silhouette as he gets back on his feet. The humid forest smells of gasoline, sweat, freshly sawn timber, and smashed vegetation.

The abrupt silence is eerie. We reassemble and check on one another. The giant tree lies on the forest floor, leaving a huge hole in the canopy. Sap flows and resins bleed from its stump. My watery eyes avert themselves from the light that violently pours in—as if illuminating a crime scene. In its downfall, the padauk has uprooted other trees, dragging along vines and snapping stems. Behind its stump, someone from the logging team has left his lunch in a plastic carrier bag. Cassava bread and tinned sardines stick out from a mulch of rotting leaves. A jerrycan sits next to an abandoned safety helmet. A broken coffee cup lies nearby. In the distance, the hollow hammering call of a great blue turaco and, further still, the faint sound of another chainsaw.

After the visceral crash, the return to routine is impressive. The assistant feller absentmindedly checks the saw blade and adds motor oil to the machine. A logging clerk measures the trunk and records its characteristics in a small notebook. I watch him hammer a production number into the tree's reddish cut surface. Years before I was taught that these numbers form the basis of an accounting system allowing each tree to be traced back to its source. As a forestry student back in Belgium I had also learned to identify this particular tree species as an African padauk or *Pterocarpus soyauxii*— from pictures and textbooks, of course; none of us had ever seen one for real.

The chainsaw operator quietly sips from a small bottle of liquor. "That tree was trouble," he says. "I didn't think it would fall this way." As always, the team had carefully estimated its most probable falling direction. With his machete the assistant feller had opened up an escape route through the undergrowth, opposite to where they thought the padauk would fall. With great precision, the chainsaw operator had carried out the standard procedure of controlled tree felling. First he removed the buttress roots. Then he formed a deep hinge above the base. Next he made one horizontal cut. At the same time, he kept a number of securities in place: spots where the trunk was not entirely cut through. Like this, he said, the tree could remain standing for weeks, even months, without falling down.

We had also inserted thin sticks into the freshly made cut as cautionary devices that would signal any of the padauk's shifts in weight. Halfway throughout the procedure, when the massive tree suddenly came to lean toward us, the sticks immediately translated its turning and warned us to move to the other side. We all knew we had to stay coolheadedly close to the tree until it began its final downfall. But, at this moment, even the experienced chainsaw operator looked nervous. He asked his assistant to open up a second escape route—just in case. Then, another unexpected shift in weight. The tree now blocked the chainsaw in an immobilizing headlock and seemed to hesitate. Its branches were entangled with other trees, making it difficult to predict what would happen. Our team leader picked up the spare chainsaw and cut through the last security. "Run!" I heard. And run we did—in unforeseen directions.

Incidents like this were nothing unusual in the north of the Democratic Republic of the Congo. Workers at the CTI logging concession often described their job as a constant fight between men and trees. They used prayers, ancestral medicines, and practical tricks to protect themselves. New apprentices sought experienced loggers as "work fathers" to help them. And chainsaw operators smoked cannabis and drank strong local liquor in the early mornings on their way to work from the labor camps. It made them see clearly in the forest, they said.

But trees had their own will and character. Some made unexpected turns. Others simply spun out of control. Workers had witnessed terrible accidents. In the forest, unforeseen things happened. Dangers lurked in unexpected corners. In contrast to the village, forest space was experienced as an ambivalent realm of nightly forces. A place of witchcraft but also of healing. Where things were rarely what they seemed and could always turn into something else. To thrive in this shape-shifting world, "You had to be strong," workers told us, "and ready for surprise."

Freddy—a student from Bumba who had joined me as my research assistant—agilely embraced the risk-taking masculinity this world seemed to demand. I, on the other hand, often felt unfit for the task. Although trained as a forest engineer, I was unprepared for the visceral violence of large-scale logging. This book is the product of our unlikely fieldwork: an ethnography of industrial timber production in the Congolese rainforest.

The anecdote above can easily be read as an allegory of the devastating force of global capitalism and its hunger for natural resources. Transnational timber firms indeed create new frontiers in "out-of-the-way" places and violently transform living creatures into tropical hardwood (Tsing 1993). Logging enterprises generate profits that flow to corporate head offices and shareholders but bypass forest residents and national societies (Ferguson 2006). One might therefore take the falling padauk tree as an apt metaphor for the destructive power of chainsaws, timber companies, logging interests, and a profoundly unjust system of extractive capitalism. A world where corporations are powerful economic actors that literally change the aspect of the earth. Where huge chainsaws destroy vulnerable forest ecologies and damage their human and nonhuman inhabitants in an age of large-scale disasters called the Anthropocene.

But the same opening vignette also tells another story, one in which tree felling is not so much a metaphor for the power of timber firms, but rather a scene of vulnerability, precarity, uncertainty, and fear. In the thick undergrowth, where it is impossible to keep an overview, one is often *too close* to see what happens. Claustrophobically near the action, all sight is partial, murky, and oblique. In the messy encounters between men and trees, chainsaws penetrate trunks but are also dropped in panic. Trees fall down but also spin out of control. The standardized procedures of so-called controlled felling are supplemented with alcohol, drugs, magic, and religion. Visceral flashes of excitement feed a macho embrace of danger but also undermine lumberjack performances of strength. Loggers present themselves as tough risk-taking men but also emphasize the physical breakdown of their bodies in a demanding world where better options are scarce. And yet, normality and routine lubricate life on the work floor.

How to weave this second and perhaps counterintuitive story of *experienced lack of control* alongside or within better-known stories about corporate strength, discipline, and surveillance? How to write about the doubts, failures, weaknesses, excesses, and nervousness that loomed large in the industrial production of tropical timber without thereby ignoring its moments and modes of violence? How to relate to forces that were enacted in the company's name without assuming to already know what they are or what they do? And how to think the power of rainforest capitalism from the midst of its undergrowth, through its very surprises and unexpected turns?

Based on ethnographic fieldwork in and around the CTI timber concession in the Democratic Republic of the Congo in the aftermath of the 2008 financial crisis, this book starts from the everyday lives, dreams, fears, and desires of different inhabitants of its logging camps—workers, expat managers, jobseekers, traders, prostitutes, farmers, smugglers. It aims to describe the affective life of power under rainforest capitalism. In order to do so, it will have to stray away from common readings of extractive capitalism. The following chapters deliberately deal with topics—such as popular memories, boredom, game-playing, troublemaking, oneiric displacements, occult realities, racial fetishism, transgressive masculinities, sexual fantasies, and queer dynamics—that might not be immediately associated with timber production. Yet this book shows how and why these aspects must be included as inherent parts of the analysis of capitalist extraction in the contemporary moment. Large-scale industrial logging indeed depends on labor but also on race, gender, affect, imagination, and desire. Hence its strength—and its precarity.

After felling a tree

ACKNOWLEDGMENTS

Writing these pages has been both a pain and a joy. I loved returning to field-notes, some of them almost ten years old, and looking at them with fresh eyes. Recrafting chapters of a dissertation I had kept closed for so long. Listening again to recorded voices that made me laugh and cry. Rediscovering attachments to an ecstatic world of rainforest logging from which I had tried to distance myself. Remembering intense friendships. But also moments of anger, suffering, depression, and violence.

Writing a book on capitalism and ecstasis was itself often an ec-static process. It literally took me, once again, *outside* of who I thought I was. And outside of the dissertation I had written. Revision deployed its own logic as forces I could barely control but which I tried to redirect into new forms. I could never have done this alone. I wish to thank all friends, family, colleagues, and students who have, knowingly or unknowingly, helped bring this book to an end.

This all started as an odd doctoral project. Initially it was merely the desire of a recently graduated forestry engineer to study a professional world he felt reluctant to enter. My forestry professors at Ghent University (Belgium) had taught me a lot about forests, tropical and otherwise, and I am still grateful to them for teaching me how to "think like an engineer" without thereby overlooking the inherent poetics of science. But our training held little place for people who actually live and work in logging concessions. I therefore ventured to study anthropology at the KU Leuven University (Belgium). That decision literally changed my life.

It was in Leuven that ideas started to take some concrete form. I was extremely fortunate to have Filip De Boeck as my supervisor. Filip has been the most generous guide. As vague plans turned into a written project, he was always there to read drafts and provide helpful comments. He also created conditions in which I could grow and gave me the freedom to trace my own paths in the forest of academia. This book is profoundly indebted to his work and support.

My gratitude extends also to my co-supervisor, Christian Lund, who, since we first met in Niamey, took an immediate interest in my research plans and helped sharpen them on the road. And to Theodore Trefon, who had initially hired me as an assistant for a research project on charcoal trade around Kinshasa and Lubumbashi. Theodore's practical advice and rare knowledge of the Congolese logging sector have been indispensable for making this project possible.

I would also like to express my gratitude to Bogumil Jewsiewicki and Steven Van Wolputte for their constructive feedback that eventually found its way into this book, and to Katrien Pype for her advice as both a colleague and a friend as well as for her criticism as an examiner.

A special place is reserved for Johannes Fabian, whose sincere engagement with my work has truly marked its future. It was from him that I first learned about *ecstasis*, and our inspiring conversations and his generous offer to proofread several chapters greatly motivated my writing. The following pages are a belated expression of my indebtedness to his thought.

It goes without saying that this project would have been impossible without CTI—the timber firm in whose logging concession fieldwork took place. Although I cannot reveal its real name, I wish to express my deepest gratitude to its directors and executives. Their courage and openness allowed this study to happen but also made them vulnerable. I am equally grateful to the five European managers who lived and worked in the logging concession. During fifteen months of electrifying fieldwork between 2009 and 2011, we shared joys and laughter but also anxiety, loneliness, and frustration. Affectionate dialogues, angry reactions, harsh disputes, reconciliations, and revisions slowly crafted the argument contained in these chapters. Perhaps the expat loggers will find some pages unpleasant. Or disagree with others. Yet this book is an honest account of the world of rainforest capitalism in which we came to find ourselves together. I can only hope the result will resonate with those in the sector yearning for a different future.

I am equally indebted to the workers and other inhabitants of the CTI labor camps as well as to the villagers I regularly visited. They have been generous hosts, fantastic neighbors, and some have become true friends. They taught me what it meant to live between hope and despair, as we shared the rhythms, possibilities, and sorrows of camp life. It is with them and from them that I learned to think again about what I thought I knew. And it is because of their hospitality, friendship, and humor that, even today, I continue to dream about the colors, textures, sounds, and odors of the forest. I cannot name the individual families, men, and women to whom I would like to bring honor. But I retain their memories with great affection.

Warm and special thanks also go to Freddy Boka Gala for his invaluable work. He has been so much more than a research assistant. Not only did he prove to be a conscientious translator, language teacher, and formidable motorcycle mechanic, he also appropriated my initial research plans and turned them into a collaborative project. I am equally grateful to Marcel Akpala from Bolende and Jules-César Gbema from Bumba for our long conversations about regional history and Mbudza and Bati customs and traditions. Their experience and wisdom have been of great help to comprehend the environment in which CTI came to operate.

My appreciation also goes to Père Carlos Rommel for accommodating me during my visits to Bumba. To Frère Luc Vansina for his logistical support from Kinshasa. And to Françoise Van de Ven, the secretary-general of the Congolese Fédération des Industriels du Bois (FIB), who took an immediate interest in my project and whose outspoken opinions I greatly valued.

I also thank the Flemish Interuniversity Council (VLIR) for granting me a generous VLADOC grant. The KU Leuven for its institutional support. My colleagues at the Institute for Anthropological Research in Africa (IARA) for offering me a warm home. And Kristien Hermans and Ann Weemaes for taking special care of the practical and financial aspects of my project.

Writing about the racist, misogynist, and often violent world of rainforest logging was not easy, and in 2013 I therefore decided to leave that world behind and dedicate my research to a new topic. Only four years later, after intense submersion in the queer worlds of Kinshasa and Kisangani, did the time seem ripe for another look at the timber concession. But the prospect was frightening. So many things had changed. The world had changed—and I with it. Trump, Brexit. Three of my grandparents had passed away. I was offered a teaching position at the University of Oxford. I had divorced and found a new love. We bought a house and welcomed a cat. Then, during writing, COVID-19 happened and Black Lives Matter intensified. The existential vulnerability this book tries to show has never been so obvious—and, I hope, never so urgent.

I am therefore deeply grateful to those who encouraged me in this daunting process. Nancy Rose Hunt has been an enthusiastic and energizing supporter. Elizabeth Ault from Duke University Press has been the most helpful and engaged editor. The anonymous reviewers have been extraordinarily generous, and their constructive comments have greatly benefited these pages.

Also, in Oxford, I found myself in a stimulating environment in which to revise chapters. I specifically thank my colleagues at the African Studies Centre and the Institute for Social and Cultural Anthropology. I am also grateful to both Oxford and Leuven for enabling me to take a one-year writing retreat. In the uncertain job market and harsh academic world, it is heartwarming to find colleagues who show trust, kindness, patience, and flexibility.

Over the years many people have contributed to this book, as commentators on paper presentations or readers of draft chapters and articles. I particularly wish to thank Lys Alcayna-Stevens, Arjun Appadurai, Karin Barber, Hans Beeckman, Florence Bernault, Ann Cassiman, Bambi Ceuppens, Brenda Chalfin, Simukai Chigudu, Carli Coetzee, Muriel Côte, Thomas Cousins, Jeroen Cuvelier, Zana Etambala, Elizabeth Ewart, Mattia Fumanti, Kristien Geenen, David Gellner, Peter Geschiere, Juliet Gilbert, Benoît Henriet, Nancy Rose Hunt, Benedikt Korf, Peter Lambertz, Jerome Lewis, Dominique Malaquais, Hélène Neveu Kringelbach, Insa Nolte, David Pratten, Ramon Sarró, Rachel Spronk, Jonny Steinberg, Jean-François Staszak, Kristof Titeca, Joseph Tonda, and Joe Trapido.

Finally, I cannot but acknowledge my deepest gratitude to my parents, brothers, and sister, who have supported me in so many ways. To my friends for their care, patience, and understanding despite my long absences during fieldwork and secluded writing. And, of course, to my love, for the good-hearted optimism, strength, and enthusiasm that kept me going and with whom I adore building a new future.

Workers on their way back from the forest

Introduction
Thinking with Loggers

THE PROLOGUE'S OPENING VIGNETTE evokes an often-overlooked precarity at the heart of industrial rainforest logging that challenges analyses of extractive capitalism based on taken-for-granted assumptions of corporate strength. This book indeed shows how and why lived vulnerabilities deeply marked and affected the operations of the company I came to call Congolese Timber Industries, or CTI. The following chapters thus trouble critiques of capitalism that remain invested in essentialized conceptions of extractive companies, as if they were always inherently strong actors able to control and dominate the spaces in which they operate. As we will see, CTI rather experienced itself as *out of control* in an environment that constantly escaped its will and undermined its objectives. The ethnographic challenge presented by this observation is to account for CTI's existential precarity and vulnerability without thereby underestimating its actual powers to exploit and extract.

To address this challenge, *Rainforest Capitalism* foregrounds and theorizes a complex dialectic between power and what I call *ecstasis*. Fieldwork in and around the CTI timber camps indeed brought to the fore a recurring relation between ex-traction and ec-stasis—that is, resonances between processes that literally *draw out* material or energy from a certain milieu and processes that make one *stand outside* of one's self or self-control. The following chapters slowly illustrate and unpack this link as a pathway for thinking rainforest capitalism differently. This introductory chapter sketches the theoretical landscape and wider context in which they move.

The first three sections of this chapter introduce central tools and ideas that have been helpful to understand the lived intricacies of power in the logging concession. The first section introduces feminist critiques of capitalism that nuance and destabilize the idea of corporate phallic power and trouble scholarly desires to find a more or less coherent or rational system underneath the messy surface of capitalism. The second section builds on these feminist critiques and supplements them with a recent postcritical turn in the humanities and social sciences that promises new ways for anthropologists to *engage with* what they feel uneasy about. It specifically proposes postcritique as an ethnographic method for tracking the eruptions, experiences, echoes, traces, and effects of vulnerability in the midst of performed strength. The next section then introduces the idea of ecstasis as a key concept to describe and understand existential precarity as an undertheorized dimension of power and control.

The last four sections situate this book in its wider context. Section four introduces the rapidly growing anthropology of natural resource extraction and sketches some important divergences between industrial logging and other industries, such as mining or oil. Section five surveys the scarce literature on timber production and argues for more ethnographic studies that take logging firms seriously as complex actors in their own right. The following section provides a brief oversight of the particular history and legal framework of timber production in the Democratic Republic of the Congo (DRC). The final section introduces the timber firm in which fieldwork took place.

Feminist Critique and the Capitalist Monster

In a recent overview article that situates dominant trends and directions in anthropology, Sherry Ortner (2016) observes that, since the 1980s, a certain "dark anthropology" has dominated the otherwise diverse discipline. Many anthropologists indeed focus on exploitation, inequality, and suffering in an increasingly neoliberal world. This "dark" focus is extremely valuable for explaining and understanding the dire state of the world. Yet this dominant style of anthropology can also lead to a numbing repetition of the same ideas. *Capitalism*, for instance, can easily become an a priori concept that is parachuted into texts, seminars, and conferences as the ultimate cause of what we are trying to grasp (and want to change). In the best critical writing, capitalism is a productive prompt for thinking ethnographically about its conditions of possibility. But it can also operate as a simplifying black box or "big leviathan" that is ritually invoked as an explanation rather than what needs to be explained (Callon and Latour 1981).

In reaction to the implicit essentialization of capitalism as a singular, homogenizing, and monolithic system, several anthropologists have started to rethink its often taken-for-granted logic. In their "Feminist Manifesto for the Study of Capitalism" (2015), for instance, Laura Bear, Karen Ho, Anna Tsing, and Sylvia Yanagisako explicitly call for strategies that "reveal the constructedness—the messiness and hard work involved in making, translating, suturing, converting, and linking diverse capitalist projects." Anna Tsing's work, in particular, has foregrounded the situatedness, openness, heterogeneity, and cultural specificity of capitalist formations—their fragility as well as their effectiveness and violence (Tsing 2005, 2015).

This new anthropology of capitalism draws on longer traditions of feminist critique. In *The End of Capitalism (As We Knew It)* (1996), for instance, J. K. Gibson-Graham—a pen name created by the feminist geographers Julie Graham and Katherine Gibson—famously noted that, in most critiques of capitalism, "the project of understanding the beast has itself produced a beast," that is, "capitalism" as a totalizing system and final cause (1). For this reason, they called for alternative strategies that study the manifold realities of capitalism*s* (plural) without automatically reconfirming or reinvigorating an "abstract capitalist essence" (15). As such, they hoped to "slay the capitalist monster" that many of its self-identified critics have helped feed (21).

The following chapters deeply resonate with this feminist invitation to rethink capitalism as a more fragile, open, and vulnerable configuration rather than as an all-powerful and all-devouring phallic system. Yet, Gibson-Graham and Tsing mainly develop their analyses from a position *outside* of capitalism—the former by thinking from noncapitalist formations, the latter by exploring "peri-capitalist" dynamics that make capitalism possible from its cracks, fissures, and zones of abandonment. This book, by contrast, is firmly situated *within* a capitalist firm. Implicated in and contaminated by industrial logging, it proposes an ethnography of capitalism from one of its contemporary nodes.

Such a position is not unique. Ethnographers increasingly produce accounts of capitalism from its inside. In her remarkable ethnography of Wall Street, for example, Karen Ho (2009) (a coauthor of the aforementioned feminist manifesto) is explicitly interested in undermining the apparent coherence and rationality of global capitalism from within. Yet, despite our similar positions, our methods and epistemologies are quite different. Ho primarily draws from official discourses and private interviews with (former) investment bank employees in order to explain their Wall Street worldview. She thereby argues that, rather than take these employees' thoughts about the global economy at face value, we need to debunk them as products of the *ideology* of globalization if we want to find out what really happens in the world of global finance (Ho 2005, 68).

This book takes a different route. Instead of evoking the hidden forces of ideology to account for our interlocutors' *mis*conceptions and beliefs, it follows their words, thoughts, acts, and feelings in a less suspicious mode of inquiry. This deliberate approach is a consequence of the unexpected fact that, during fieldwork, the CTI loggers themselves were the first to undermine the idea of the multinational timber company as a powerful actor. Their constant complaints about a frustrating powerlessness to "get things done" directly rubbed against official company discourses in which CTI posed as a responsible and rational actor managing the rainforest in a sustainable manner and bringing development to an isolated part of the Congolese interior. As we will see, its European managers indeed portrayed themselves as relatively powerless victims of an environment over which they had barely any control, emphasizing (and almost taking perverse pleasure in) the risk of "losing their minds" in the "crazy" world of logging. Moreover, workers and villagers alike were not so much concerned about CTI's excessive power (though they sometimes happened to be its victims) as about its *in*capacity to make a difference to their lives.

Hence, while Ho deliberately avoids taking bankers and traders "at face value" in order to deconstruct the Wall Street worldview as nothing but a product of its own ideology, I merely had to take loggers *at their word* in order to follow the cracks in the timber company's image. As such, loggers became unexpected allies and guides in the project of troubling the rationality of capitalism—not only the European managers but also, as we will see, their Congolese employees, who often expressed surprisingly similar concerns about experienced powerlessness. If we aspire to understand industrial logging from the inside out, we need to take their stories seriously: not to naively believe our interlocutors, but to fully realize what logging feels like; to think *with* them, as Isabelle Stengers (2003) would suggest, rather than to try catching them in a lie or to demystify their false consciousness by showing what the world is *really* like, if only they could see it for what it was.

Instead of writing off such feelings and perspectives as merely misguided or irrelevant to the analysis of rainforest logging, this book takes them as vibrant starting points for thinking capitalism differently. The following chapters emerge from a moving field of affective fluxes, slumbering moods, barely audible whispers, circulating rumors, and contradictory stories. "Not," to quote Kathleen Stewart (2017, 192–93), "to track the predetermined *effects* of abstractable logics and structures but, rather, to compose a register of the lived *affects* of the things that took place."

Indebted to a feminist heritage but equally committed to thinking with loggers—and their often violent, misogynist, racist, and macho world—this book therefore stretches critical imaginations. Some sections can provoke discomfort, indignation, pain, shame, anger, or resistance. Others will trouble our desire to find fault and blame the capitalist beast we love to hate. All of this was part of fieldwork. I cannot change the racism, misogyny, and bigotry I stumbled on in the CTI concession. But we *can* change the stories we tell. One might even argue we *have to* if we want to really engage the darkness of contemporary life anthropologists so rightly insist on.

Capitalism, Ethnography, and (Post)critique

This book approaches the concrete, messy, and murky realities of rainforest capitalism without assuming to already know *what* it is studying. In order to understand capitalism at work without reducing the world of industrial logging to a mere symptom of—or even allegory for—a larger whole, the following pages complement the still necessary posture of critique with what literary scholar Rita Felski (2015) has called a more "post-critical" ethos that troubles the always already suspicious attitude of the critic as well as the distance toward her object. Rather than repeat the standardized routines of critique that would, yet again, expose ideology or denaturalize truth, postcritique looks for alternative possibilities of reading and writing that are based on intimacy, engagement, trust, love, belief, attachment, possibility, surprise, hope, and restoration.[1]

One might obviously wonder whether the contemporary moment is really such an opportune time to call for a turn away from critique (Foster 2012). Its defenders nevertheless emphasize that postcritique is part of ongoing progressive commitments (Anker and Felski 2017). Postcritical politics can, for instance, be a way of mattering beyond the walls of academia or of allowing for hope in bleak times. Of course, postcritical experiments can always be accused of naivety or wishful thinking, especially when new humanistic modes of reading and writing are smuggled into the social sciences, which are often very proud of *their* critical credibility (Hage 2012). But, at least in anthropology, the implication, vulnerability, and risky entanglement of the writer/reader in what she engages with is nothing new. The ethnographic method is effectively based on attachment and intimacy—and requires a hermeneutics of trust rather than suspicion (Ricoeur 1965).

Yet the intimate implication of the ethnographer in her object of attention does not prevent or exclude critical moments both during and after fieldwork. Indeed, even a deliberately *post*critical ethnography does not, as Diana Fuss (2017, 354) puts it, "have an easy time keeping its hands clean (of ideology, of prescription, or of just bad temper)." In the following chapters postcritique is not, therefore, the absence of critique. It comes only *after* critique—literally—as this book comes after the earlier work from which it has been transformed. When confronted with multinational corporations, the question is not, therefore, whether "to critique or not to critique" (Appel 2019b), but to find a way of *dealing with* structures of power. This book figures many stories of violence, racism, and misogyny that do not need my critical capacities to make their shocking nature apparent. Critique was already there: in thoughts, actions, and everyday experiences of expat managers, workers, and villagers who did not wait for outside critics to dissect their situation. For this reason, postcritical ethnography does not avoid politics altogether or "endorse normativity" simply because of its commitment to people whose lives one has shared (Gilbert and Sklair 2018, 10).[2] It rather tries to carefully attend to what happened and to use its inevitable complicity in a way that "adds reality rather than taking it away" (Love 2017, 66).

For these reasons, this book slows down the habitual fervor of critique to unveil the underlying structures of reality and jump to final causes. Instead of assuming, for instance, that the global timber economy is a powerful "system," or that the logging company is a dominant "agent," it starts from the concrete ways in which people, things, feelings, and ideas come into being with each other; coagulate into moments and lingering moods; make and undo worlds; resonate with and through bodies; produce traces, memories, and lines of flight; and take on the form of seemingly overwhelming forces and desires in always vulnerable processes of assemblage.[3] While it describes the violence and injustice that come with large-scale logging, it does not provide a disembodied critique of its object. Replaying feelings, sentiments, moods, and atmospheres, its criticism is situated *within* its subject matter rather than hovering above it as a transcendent "view from nowhere" (Haraway 1988).

My project is thus a postcritical and stubbornly hopeful attempt to remain open to possibilities in places where one might otherwise forget to look. Places like logging concessions, for instance, where transnational companies and the system they embody are often supposed to show themselves *at their strongest* but where sustained ethnographic attention actually reveals dimensions of weakness that often remain undertheorized. Relaying the anxiety, vulnerability, precarity, and nervousness behind masculinist displays of power and control, the following chapters thereby hope to trouble the "textbook economics view of the corporation" as a strong and rational actor that would be "jacked up with superpowers" (Welker 2016b, 420, 398).

In this book, *capitalism* thus needs to be taken as an invitation for thinking rather than a solution: a dynamic question that emerges from the field rather than a standard answer to our analytical problems; not a closed system that always already explains the power of a transnational firm, but an open field of forces where agencies depend on their capacity to deal with and bend each other and where any position of power is situational, ephemeral, and sometimes self-destructive. As we will see, this conceptualization is primarily indebted to Central African cultural repertoires about wealth accumulation as the outcome of so-called occult practices in which people eat each other's life forces. While capitalism thereby certainly acquires systemic qualities as a generalized ecology of eating and being eaten, this system—so it will turn out—remains fundamentally ambiguous, contradictory, versatile, and opaque.

Making Concessions to Ecstasis

In order to think capitalism differently, we therefore need to make *concessions* to what I call ecstasis. To concede is both to *give away* and to *give in*—to renounce and to yield. As the word indicates, a concession implies both a granted right and a grudging acknowledgment. In its strict sense, a logging concession is a delimited area over which the state has conceded timber rights to a private actor. But in order to understand the affective life of rainforest capitalism, we need to keep the double meaning of concessions in sight. As we will see in the following chapters, the actual and concrete making of the CTI logging concession indeed obliged CTI to *concede to* material, discursive, and affective forces beyond its control: to villagers and roadblocks; to state agents and policemen; to the weight of history, memories of violent extraction, and nostalgia about colonial paternalism; to daydreaming, foot-dragging, and troublemaking employees; to smugglers, mud, rain, and fuel shortages; to racism, boredom, liquor, sex, fetishism, and desire.

This book not only describes the actual power of the timber firm to make its concession—by negotiating, surveying, and prospecting; moving people, money, and machinery; mapping, building, constructing, and maintaining roads; and turning trees into corporate raw material to log, evacuate, and sell. It also tracks how CTI had to *make concessions* whenever it had to acknowledge that its actions were entangled in dynamics not of its own making. The following chapters therefore approach the logging company as a fragile, permeable, vulnerable, anxious, nervous, and insecure assemblage caught in "networks which [were] only ever partly in its control" (Thrift 2005, 3). By doing so, ecstasis will become the name for what we need to concede to—but also for the act of conceding as such.

Etymologically speaking, ecstasis denotes situations in which one *stands* or *steps outside* of oneself. In Western philosophy, reflections on ecstasis go back to the ancient Greeks. Plotinus described ecstasis as a becoming-possessed by a transcendent Oneness by way of an undoing of the self that gave access to total plenitude (Hadot 1993). For Christian mystics, ecstasis was a process through which believers reached beyond their individual bodies in order to participate directly in God. In the twentieth century, French philosophers such as Henri Bergson and Georges Bataille drew on this mystic tradition to write beyond the limits of rationalism.[4] Existentialists also came to mobilize ecstasis for approaching the fundamental openness of human consciousness.[5] And phenomenologists have understood ecstasis as the mutual implication of the Other and the Self, so as to think beyond subject/object distinctions in Western metaphysics.[6]

In anthropology, ecstasis usually describes overpowering moments of rapture and trance-like emotional states that carry one beyond rational thought or self-control. At the same time, Ioan Lewis's (1989) comparative study of shamanism and spirit possession also defines ecstasis as a technique for "mastery" over exacting pressures.[7] Either way, ecstasis seems inherently linked to spirituality, mysticism, ritual, and religion, as it denotes the dissolution of the self and its communion with a greater whole. For Émile Durkheim (1912), the ecstatic transcendence of individuality was indeed central to the "collective effervescence" of ritual.[8]

And yet, ecstasis is more than that. In *Out of Our Minds* (2000), a detailed anthropological account of colonial expeditions in the Congo Basin, Johannes Fabian explicitly mobilizes ecstasis beyond its religious dimension. He describes how and why late nineteenth- and early twentieth-century European explorers were "more often than not . . . 'out of their minds' with extreme fatigue, fear, delusions of grandeur, and feelings ranging from anger to contempt" (3). Through subtle readings of little-known travelogues, Fabian particularly tracks "the effects of alcohol, drugs, illness, sex, brutality, and terror, as well as the role of conviviality, friendship, play, and performance" in the project of imperial exploration (9). More than a religious concept, Fabian takes ecstasis first and foremost as an epistemological notion. As we will see in chapter 1, his striking originality lies in a radical understanding of ecstasis as a *condition of possibility* of, rather than an obstacle to, the generation of knowledge.

The following chapters further broaden the notion of ecstasis beyond its usual focus on spectacular acts of rapture, altered states of consciousness, moments of frenzy, erotic bliss, or overwhelming euphoria. As we follow its manifestations in the CTI logging concession, ecstasis will also come to incorporate more mundane atmospheres, affective waves, and lingering moods that resonate with a broader existential conundrum of *being-out of control*. As such, the following pages connect with philosophical reflections on the human condition as an ethnographic exploration of what Judith Butler (2004, 137) calls the "ek-static involvement" of all selves in others. Illustrating dependency and precariousness where we can—and should—also see "power," ecstasis will thereby become a placeholder for *a set of complex feelings of vulnerability, penetrability, and even impotence in the face of larger forces, structures, and histories—as well as for the frustration, anger, and resistance these feelings generate.*

While this book thus directly draws from Fabian's idea of ecstasis as being out of one's mind, it nonetheless develops his primarily epistemological concept into a more existential direction by illustrating how and why conceding to ecstasis is not just a fundamental condition for knowledge production but also a fundamental reality of (and challenge for) human life. Moreover, as an ethnographic—rather than historical—account, it fleshes out the idea of ecstasis in lived detail and describes its dialectical relationship to power *as the affective and experiential dynamic that is generated whenever people are confronted with the limits of their own actions, realize their capture, and try to take back control.*

To some extent, this take on ecstasis approaches fundamental insights from so-called existential anthropology. Yet, while it flirts with Michael Jackson's (1998, 21) understanding of power and control as first and foremost "issues of existential mastery," it also insists on tracking the *political* effects of this existential dimension in a particularly unjust world of racialized inequalities and skewed life chances. Moreover, while the following chapters effectively illustrate human life as an attempt to overcome existential aporias, they ultimately remain agnostic about the universality of the human condition they thereby imply. Rather than tell "the same story over and over," this book is about the *specific* salience of ecstasis in the particular context of rainforest logging (Lambek 2015, 73). Furthermore, Jackson's anthropology often seeks to reaffirm human agency in an otherwise overwhelming world and understands ecstasis mainly as a way for people to step "outside of the circle of normative . . . life in order to recapture and reconstitute it" (Jackson 1998, 27). The following pages, by contrast, mainly show the *limits* of ecstasis as a way to successfully take back control.

Ecstasis is not, however, merely one thing. In the course of this book, we will encounter ecstatic modes, moments, and possibilities at different occasions and in different guises: in village roadblocks, rumors about an imminent company closure, frustrations about being blocked and getting nowhere, fears of losing it all, heavy drinking, occasional fighting, feelings of nervousness and boredom, abrupt accelerations in time, and sudden panics about missing the moment. But we will also see ecstasis at work in church services, stories about zombie workers, suspicions about white cannibals, or the losing fight against fuel smugglers and illicit squatters, as well as in paranoia, choleric outbursts, transgressive masculinities, colonial nostalgia, racist phantasmagoria, and whirlpools of desire.

Obviously, ecstasis was not not always and everywhere present in the CTI logging concession. Despite the ephemerality and instability of life, people *did* find a sense of security in multiple attachments, and many could attain certain levels of control. Yet, at the same time, all security was relative, all balance was threatened by crisis, and all power was destabilized by excess and delirium. People seemed to move in and out of ecstatic waves—at different times and for different reasons. And, under some conditions, ecstasis became a more "ordinary affect" than others (Stewart 2007).

The question is therefore: What is this peculiar structure of feeling that might explain why, notwithstanding the unequal distribution of vulnerabilities between individuals—expat managers, Congolese workers, and surrounding villagers—and despite the highly segregated worlds in which they lived, many still experienced concession life in such surprisingly similar ways (Williams 1977)? How to understand that, although people obviously felt very different things, individually and collectively (about the company for instance), their feelings were nonetheless affected by an infectious *Stimmung* that attuned us all to the world (Heidegger 1995)? How to approach the impression that, though expressed, experienced, and conceptualized differently by different individuals, there seemed to be something troublingly *alike* for all? And how to give an ethnographic account of this particular "atmosphere" that pushed people together while also driving them apart (Anderson 2009)?

It is crucial to emphasize that foregrounding ecstasis in no way implies underestimating the all-too-real effects of racialized capitalism on the ground. This book does not deny CTI's actual powers to log trees, make money, impose violent measures, or reproduce broader structures of inequality. It merely enables a different relationship to power, one of "implication and entanglement, rather than purity and transcendence" (Stewart 1991, 400). Instead of repeating well-rehearsed critiques of corporate capitalism and its destructive practices of extraction and exploitation that take a bird's-eye view of messy happenings on the ground, the following chapters deliberately "stay with the trouble" (Haraway 2016). They complement the critic's view from *without* with more humble stories from *within*—tales of investment, profit, violence, and desire but also of failure, excess, hubris, impotence, and retreat.[9]

In the conclusion, we will have the opportunity to take stock of the possibilities and limitations of ecstasis for anthropology and to reflect on its usefulness as a tool for understanding corporate power in the context of extractive capitalism. But how far can we *concede to* ecstasis as a device for thinking with loggers and their multiple avowals of powerlessness? What concessions are we, as critical readers and observers, prepared to make? And how vulnerable to, contaminated by, and complicit in the proliferation of ecstasis can any *post*critical anthropology become? These questions will accompany the following chapters. This book does not propose any final answers; it is a queer experiment that inherits, repeats, and mimics ecstatic processes—rather than withdraws from them, as if they were not also about us (Pandian and McLean 2017).[10]

The Anthropology of Extraction

As an ethnography of industrial logging-in-action, the following chapters can build on a growing anthropology of capitalist extraction. If ecstasis is therefore the first pole around which they tell the story of rainforest capitalism, *extraction* is the second. At its most general level, ex-traction can be defined as the process whereby living beings draw out, pull out, or remove material or immaterial elements from a milieu, which is more or less resistant and requires the application of force. As we will see, in the case of CTI, the company not only extracted trees and timber from the forest but also surplus-value and life force from its workers.

Extraction is, obviously, not limited to capitalism. As a basic condition of existence, it is an inevitable aspect of the ek-static dependencies of life. Yet extraction takes on particular forms under specific historical conditions. The *capitalist* extraction of natural resources, for instance, has been increasingly industrialized and invasive. And extraction plays a continuing and crucial role in what David Harvey (2003) calls "accumulation by dispossession" as an ongoing response to crisis. Extraction thus points at capital's inherent relations "with its multiple outsides"—whether literally as "the forced removal of raw materials and life forms from the earth's surface, depths and biosphere" or, more broadly, as processes that "draw upon forms and practices of human cooperation and sociality" (Mezzadra and Neilson 2017, 185, 188).

Extraction therefore always implies a degree of violence. It sits at the center of the destructive power of transnational corporations as they appropriate and expropriate nature, turn over the earth, and sell natural resources as commodities on the world market. Yet extraction also requires the fulfillment of an entire set of preconditions. Natural resources are not simply there; they have to be *made* extractable (Tsing 2003). In practice, extraction implies a long list of activities: exploration, identification, mapping, negotiation over access and control, investment, technical and logistical procedures, and the monopolization of knowledge. Such practices, processes, and procedures are not only vulnerable and fragile in and of themselves. The structural dependency of extractive practices on multiple outsides equally implies their *entanglement* in the very milieu from which they strive to extract value—entanglements that, as we will see, have their own ecstatic effects.

This book brings to the fore how, as a capitalist practice, industrial rainforest logging extracted from and thus depended on an environment it could barely control. As such, this work adds to an expanding literature that paints increasingly complex pictures of the agencies at work in extractive industries. While anthropologists have often foregrounded the agency of subaltern communities (beyond their reductive depiction as victims of extractive companies), recent ethnographic work also focuses on the agency of supposedly powerful corporate or state actors. These nuanced inquiries re-embed extractive practices in social relations—such as kinship ties or moral economies of patronage—and situate contemporary extraction in historical trajectories, cultural registers, and broader relations of power (Gilberthorpe and Rajak 2017, 190).

Rather than simply "displac[ing] agency (and indeed causation) onto 'capital' itself," I thus try to foreground the multiple agencies that made (and unmade) a logging concession (Gilberthorpe and Rajak 2017, 200). As such, I directly follow in the footsteps of other analyses of extractive capitalism. Marina Welker and Alex Golub, for instance, show how big transnational mining corporations need to be "enacted" by different actors and come into being as profoundly *relational* entities (Welker 2014; Golub 2014). Hannah Appel (2019a) also presents offshore oil rigs and oil companies in Equatorial Guinea as *situational* achievements that must be constantly performed and maintained in the face of their material connections with the outside world. And in her ethnography of corporate social responsibility, Dinah Rajak (2011) explores the ongoing dependencies of current extractive processes on lingering continuities with racialized frontiers of colonial empires.

Yet, as David Kneas (2018, 755) observes, most of this scholarship centers on giant companies and big investments, such as massive oil rigs or large mineral deposits. Marginal production sites and smaller firms, on the other hand, are seldomly taken as starting points for thinking extractive capitalism. It is nonetheless especially here that the unsteady making of corporate power can be studied. Hence, when shifting attention from mining or oil to timber production, where the size of companies and their investments is usually of a different scale, new opportunities for researching extractive capitalism present themselves. Very much like junior mining companies, CTI—though a relatively large player in the Congolese logging sector—was a rather "precarious entity" whose presence was threatened, unstable, and sometimes plainly *un*successful (Kneas 2016, 70).

So, although mining and oil continue to receive the lion's share of ethnographic interest and often dominate theorizations about extraction, logging presents particular affordances for the anthropologist of capitalism (Gilberthorpe and Rajak 2017, 186, 188). The divergences in size and scale between logging operations and most mining and oil extraction sites is only one of the differences that needs to be kept in mind when reflecting on—let alone generalizing about—extractive industries. While mining, oil production, and logging obviously share many characteristics in the contemporary moment, a clear understanding of their divergences is needed to grasp the theoretical opportunities and ethnographic possibilities logging concessions offer.

Different sectors and industries differ first of all because of their resource-specific materialities (Richardson and Weszkalnys 2014). The qualities and properties of timber are indeed quite unlike those of minerals, oil, or gas. As material substances, they allow for different affordances, potentialities, and agencies that affect the ways in which they can be engaged (Rogers 2012). For example, because timber is not considered toxic, pollution is of a completely different nature and scale than in many mining and oil operations. And because timber is seen as a renewable resource, it can theoretically be managed in such a way that avoids depletion. Unlike minerals or oil, trees are living, growing, and reproducing beings. Forestry is therefore deeply and historically invested in projects and dreams of sustainability that, though rarely achieved in practice, inform most management models of timber production, which are based on rotation cycles that allow forest areas to regrow in between logging activities.

But resource materialities cannot be reduced to issues of substance alone. At least in the initial stages of its commodity chain, the materiality of timber should also be seen in relation to forest ecologies, landscapes, climate, and geography. These broader material networks indeed constitute the milieu in which extraction has to operate, and they affect what labor practices, levels of technology, surveillance tools, infrastructures, spatial organization, risk management procedures, and health and safety standards are possible and deemed necessary.

The material-ecological specificity of *tropical rainforests* (alongside their historical, political, and cultural particularity) effectively shapes what industrial timber production looks like. For instance, in contrast to forests in temperate or boreal climates, lowland tropical rainforests contain a huge variety of tree species. But due to wood-technical reasons and marketing limitations, merely a dozen or so fetch high enough prices on the world market to make their harvesting profitable. Furthermore, because each of these commercial species is represented by only a handful of fully grown individual trees per hectare, timber companies have no interest in clear-cutting their concessions. Companies therefore only raze tropical forests when they need *land* rather than trees—for palm oil plantations, soybean fields, or cattle grazing grounds. Timber companies, by contrast, generally skim off the most valuable trees and leave the others standing, operating as *selective* harvesters of specific species. Hence, contrary to what mediated images of large-scale clear-cutting often suggest, tropical timber production does not radically transform the landscape in such spectacular ways.[11]

The particular ecology of rainforests has far-reaching effects on the temporality and spatiality of tropical timber production. Because of its selective nature, rainforest logging requires vast areas and work teams that are constantly on the move. In comparison to large mining sites, logging is therefore an inherently mobile and relatively ephemeral activity.[12] Moreover, because of their size, logging concessions are unlikely to be closed off from their surroundings. Whereas it is often impossible to walk into active mining sites or onto oil rigs without passing checkpoints and other forms of control, logging concessions generally remain highly *penetrable* spaces. Of course, as several studies have shown, seemingly secluded mines are also surprisingly permeable despite company attempts to police their boundaries (Rajak 2011; Welker 2014). Even the idea of the offshore oil rig as a friction-free point cut off from national societies requires enormous work to produce and maintain (Appel 2012a, 2019a). But logging concessions are *physically* impossible to seclude as tightly controlled enclaves, and, for this reason, most tropical timber production has to occur alongside—and in partial competition with—other forest residents.[13]

In short, rainforest logging is a form of capitalist extraction that is specific to the rainforest as its material, imaginary, and symbolic milieu.[14] As we will see, it was often the structural mobility and permeability of tropical timber production that created the particular affective circuits in which CTI was confronted with its inability to control what it was supposed to manage. The logging concession was indeed a particularly *ecstato-genic* place where corporate power and its rationalities quickly showed their limits. Foregrounding the precarity and vulnerability of logging, as well as its failures, slippages, and excesses, this book perhaps illustrates affective realities that might very well mark, albeit to different degrees, most if not all extractive practices under neoliberal capitalism. But tropical logging concessions show more *openly* what mines and oil rigs often succeed in hiding (at least until they get dissembled by their critical ethnographers): the ecstasis of extraction.

Timber Firms—An Ethnographic Blind Spot

Because of their particular affordances, logging concessions thus seem interesting places from which to study extractive capitalism in the contemporary moment. Yet, while industrial timber production increasingly affects the lives and worlds of people and forests on our planet, logging continues to remain surprisingly marginal in the quickly expanding literature on natural resource extraction. *Ethnographic* research in particular is remarkably scarce, and concrete insights into the quotidian life of timber industries remain very much limited to studies of lumberjack cultures in North America or Australia.[15] In the global south, anthropologists have mainly focused on artisanal logging rather than industrial timber production.[16] Or they have added to the extensive literature on "community forestry" or "participatory forest management," contributing to debates on land rights from the perspective of forest users and indigenous communities rather than timber firms.[17]

There is considerable scholarly interest in forestry as a science and in forest departments as sites of governmentality. Historians, for instance, have studied the intimate links between forestry, empire, and colonialism.[18] And social scientists have analyzed the role of forestry in contemporary state politics, illustrating the injustice it produces and the popular resistance it often generates.[19] But, also in this literature, logging companies remain below the radar. Even political scientists who look into concrete political economies of timber trade usually have little to say about what goes on inside logging firms.[20]

As long as anthropologists remain reluctant to study logging companies, we risk—as Christian Lund (2006, 679) puts it—excluding "the 'bad boys' from our analytical lens" and developing "tunnel vision" and losing "perspective." While difficulties of access and ethical considerations might explain this reluctance, I also suspect that—particularly in the Congo Basin—a long-standing anthropological fascination for rainforest communities and so-called forest people continues to prevent ethnographers from depicting timber firms as anything more than actors we already think we know. However, in order to understand ongoing social and ecological transformations in rainforest areas, logging companies need to be studied as complex, contradictory, and multiple actors in their own right rather than as black-boxed monoliths on which to screen images from the outside.

A rare ethnographic insight into industrial rainforest logging can be drawn, for instance, from Rebecca Hardin's (2002, 2011) work on the Dzanga Sangha Special Reserve in the Central African Republic. Although Hardin focuses on a *conservation* rather than a logging concession, she approaches timber firms as important actors in the field who, alongside state administrations, NGOs, businesses, and village communities, reinvent old logics of patronage and reproduce what she calls "concessionary politics" (Hardin 2011, S116). Hardin's work aptly illustrates how and why concessions are not just formal acts or legal arrangements but also social processes in which different actors interact and compete.

This book builds on Hardin's analysis of the conflictual politics of making and maintaining concessions and especially on her understanding of timber companies as new "big men" who are "engaged in a form of social contest that was central to their identities, as well as to their territorial control" (S121). But whereas Hardin's ethnography still largely deals with timber companies from the outside, as one of several actors in the field of environmental conservation, the following chapters study one particular company—from within and from its core business of logging.

Industrial Logging in the Congo

As the first sustained ethnographic description of an individual timber firm, this book should be read within its context. The Democratic Republic of the Congo—a huge country at the center of the African continent that was violently created as the Congo Free State, then called the Belgian Congo, later renamed Zaire, and now often referred to as Congo-Kinshasa—is indeed a particular case when it comes to logging. In the following paragraphs, we will therefore have a brief look at the specific history, changing legal framework, and current status of industrial timber production in the country.

Because of its rich mineral deposits, the DRC is frequently called a *geological scandal*—a term coined by a nineteenth-century Belgian geographer that quickly became a colonial cliché. Continuing to today, Congolese and non-Congolese alike effectively refer to the DRC's staggering contrast between "scandalously rich" soils and "extremely poor" people to denounce both colonial exploitation and contemporary extraction in a so-called failed state. In the CTI concession, European managers and Congolese workers indeed asked with similar desperation "why potentially so rich a country could be so poor." Policy makers too consider the presence of copper, cobalt, gold, diamonds, and coltan prime factors of instability and war. And academics continue to debate the complex relationship between armed conflicts and natural resources in the region.

Yet beyond its mineral wealth, Congo is equally known for its vast forests. Ever since Europeans became fascinated with its interior, the Congolese rainforest has sparked fantasies of wild beasts and exotic tribes living in either harmony or mortal strife with their natural environment. For many, Congo's forests also form the backdrop of the red rubber scandals and the extreme violence of concessionary companies, both in King Leopold's

Congo Free State and the later Belgian Congo (Hochschild 1998). From Joseph Conrad's *Heart of Darkness*, to V. S. Naipaul's *A Bend in the River*, and Tim Butcher's *Blood River: The Terrifying Journey through the World's Most Dangerous Country*, the supposedly inaccessible Congo Basin has left its visitors spellbound. Indeed, as a phantasmagoric setting, little seems more generative of ecstasis than the "life, wealth and mystery" of the Congolese rainforest (Trefon 2016, 17).

But, perhaps surprisingly, current Congolese timber production remains rather low in comparison to that of other Central African countries.[21] Its profitability is significantly hampered by high transport and operation costs as well as poor infrastructure (Trefon 2006, 104). The vast majority of timber concessions are effectively situated far from the ocean and remain inaccessible by road. Most logs therefore have to be shipped over long distances to Kinshasa and then driven to the port of Matadi before they can be exported to Europe or China. Moreover, because trees of the right species and dimension are often few and far between, rainforest logging requires careful planning, good logistic organization, and a relatively large labor force to prospect, mark, and map individual trees as well as to create an extensive road grid before trees can be logged, hauled out of the forest, and put on ships. Yet because many companies can only profitably harvest between 0.5 and 3 trees per hectare, most investments produce relatively little return.

For this reason, the macroeconomic importance of the Congolese timber industry remains limited. At the time of fieldwork, industrial timber production accounted for only about 1 percent of GDP, though it represented a vast total area of more than 120,000 square kilometers or 11 percent of the national forest. Whereas in Gabon, for instance, forestry is said to be the second foremost job producer in the country, the entire sector in the DRC employed only about fifteen thousand people. Moreover, although logging companies were supposed to pay taxes—such as area fees, annual cutting permits, logging taxes, export taxes, and income taxes—their actual contribution to the public treasury was modest and arbitrary. And while state services were legally required to retrocede 40 percent of paid area fees to lower administrative entities, tax money rarely trickled down to the area from which it was generated.

To understand this particularity of a country whose extensive forests are omnipresent in global imaginations but whose actual timber industry remains surprisingly limited, we need some history. Timber companies penetrated the Congo Basin comparatively late, and large-scale logging had a relatively slow start in the Belgian Congo. While some colonial timber exploitation already occurred in the Lower Congo region at the end of the nineteenth century—mainly to produce sleepers for the railway between Leopoldville and Matadi—forestry only really took off in the 1930s. It nevertheless remained largely limited to the Mayombe forests in the west of the country, where limba trees (*Terminalia superba*) could be easily exported because of their proximity to the Atlantic Ocean. In the 1950s, some logging firms began moving eastward to the Kasai River and Lake Mai-Ndombe. But it was only in the 1970s, more than a decade after independence, that the richest limba stands in the Lower Congo were depleted and companies had to move into the central basin to look for other commercial tree species.

In the Congolese interior, most large-scale logging therefore dates from the postcolonial period. Yet, in the mid-1970s, industrial logging already started to slow down considerably after president Mobutu's Zaireanization campaign had nationalized most foreign companies. In the course of the 1980s, after most of these nationalization policies were revoked, timber production recovered somewhat but, in the 1990s, many companies suffered from a quickly worsening political and economic crisis. In 1997 rebel leader Laurent-Désiré Kabila overthrew Mobutu's 32-year autocratic reign, and the subsequent Second Congo War from 1998 to 2003 forced timber companies to close down most concessions in rebel-controlled areas. Transport via the Congo River had become impossible, and yearly national production figures dropped to below 50,000 cubic meters—whereas at independence in 1960 the country had produced 575,000 cubic meters.

During this war, several companies nonetheless managed to acquire new and extensive timber concessions illegally at very low prices and speculated on their future value. Concerned about the ecological consequences of a possibly unchecked postwar logging boom, the international donor community therefore urged the Congolese government to establish new forest laws to replace the outdated colonial regulations from 1949. In 2002 a new forest code was published that aimed to put into practice principles of sustainable forest management. All new concession contracts now had to be accompanied by management plans (*plans d'aménagement*) in conformity with the standards required by the code. In theory, all concessions had to be managed according to a rotation cycle that would allow for sufficient regrowth so that, after twenty-five years, harvesting could be resumed in logged-over forest blocks. Due to economic and political uncertainties, however, timber companies were often unable to plan for the future, and most therefore preferred to make all the money they could in a single exploitation round and then move elsewhere.

The new forest code also resonated with a broader post–Cold War push to democratization and decentralization on the African continent. It particularly enforced the formal recognition of so-called local populations as stakeholders in forest management. Although logging companies had always tried to realize customary access to forests via informal gift arrangements with village chiefs, the new forest code formalized these compensations, which significantly gained in financial and political weight. Concretely, the code obliged timber firms to negotiate so-called *cahiers des charges*, or social responsibility contracts, with forest communities and to realize the promises made therein, such as building schools, dispensaries, roads, and other community infrastructure. Yet, as we will see, rather than solutions, such projects quickly turned into sources of more disagreement, conflict, and disillusion. In many regions, relations between village communities and timber firms became particularly tense.

Furthermore, forests remained the formal property of the state and could be acquired only *as concessions* from the ministry in the form of contracts that granted companies the exploitation rights over geographically delimited areas for a period of twenty-five years. To a large extent, the 2002 forest code thus retained the old and notorious concession system that colonial authorities had previously used to grant private companies access to huge tracts of land in return for taxes or a share in their profits.[22] As concession contracts remained the only form of legal access to natural resources, they continued to clash with popular and customary property regimes. Moreover, while concession residents retained the right to hunt, fish, and collect non-timber forest products, agriculture was not allowed in these areas—though, in practice, the legal ban on farming was often impossible to enforce.

The 2002 forest code is often seen as an essential step to regulate what the World Bank had predicted would become an important "post-conflict growth sector" (Roda and Erdlenbruch 2003). After the Second Congo War, industrial timber production indeed increased and reached about 350,000 cubic meters in 2008. But the code's capacity to halt illegal logging, enable the equal sharing of benefits among all parties, and fight corruption in the sector remains deeply contested (Global Witness 2015; Trefon 2006, 2008).

Moreover, in the last trimester of 2008, when the bankruptcy of an American investment bank accelerated what became a global financial crisis, tropical timber prices abruptly dropped by 15 to 30 percent in only a couple of weeks. Between 2008 and 2009, log exports decreased by half. Many Congolese timber firms therefore started to accumulate deficits and had no choice but to close down concessions, laying off thousands of employees. In late

2009, however, the sector was already in full postcrisis reconstruction. The first signs of an economic recovery had emerged on the horizon, and several timber firms were rehiring workers to make up for lost time. It was in this excitable context that fieldwork began.

The Company and Its Concession

When Freddy and I arrived at the concession operated by CTI, the DRC officially counted more than sixty timber firms and around eighty logging concessions. Yet only a dozen or so were operational. Some were smaller firms owned by Congolese businessmen or Lebanese or Portuguese families. Others were subsidiaries of multinational corporations. All in all, four major companies dominated the sector.

CTI was one of the older logging firms in the country. Created in the early 1970s as the Congolese branch of a European timber corporation, it ran a sawmill near Kinshasa and operated several concessions in the interior. In the late 1980s it had for instance acquired an area of more than five thousand square kilometers north of the confluence of the Itimbiri and Congo Rivers. When logging started there in the early 1990s, the concession quickly became the unique provider of formal salaries in the area between the commercial center of Bumba to the west and the old railway town of Aketi to the east. While, as we will see, the Itimbiri region had a long history of foreign companies extracting ivory, rubber, cotton, and palm oil, industrial logging was entirely new. Before independence, timber production had indeed been limited to some small eucalypt plantations that produced firewood for steamboats and a handful of non-timber companies felling trees as building material.

The first mechanical sawmill in the area, for instance, was built by Premonstratensian missionaries for their own construction works. Despite this small scale, in 1933 the Flemish priest Father E. Van den Bergh from the mission post of Lolo already seemed to possess detailed knowledge of the Itimbiri timber resources. In an early (and highly fictionalized) ethnography of the Mbudza people who inhabited the area, he wrote:

> The trees from which the Budja [sic] make their canoes usually produce very fine timber. Do you see that giant tree, with its bronze trunk and its fine-teethed leaves? It is the *mbangi*, the Congolese oak. The *liboyo* is a colossus of strength and leafage, which I would call, although it is not so dark and black, the Congolese walnut. Quite similar to the *liboyo* are the

less rare and brown-flamed *litutu* and *esukumboyo*. Nice furniture timber is produced with *lilongo* and wonderful paneling comes from the *bosanga*. The brown *boliki* and the yellow *boleko* are solid and strong. For hard work, you have the iron *libenge*. The copal tree, the *paka* (*Nacrolobium ceruloides*), is tough and resistant. Rather heavy orange-yellow timber can be obtained from the *boseke*. The *lugudu* is suitable for thick wood. But also the *mokono*, the *mosange* and the *mokawi* are by no means to be ignored. For handles, joints and steels for tools, there is nothing better than *goyave* and orange wood. And you don't need to wonder if there are tall trees in the Congo when I tell you that three hundred boards were sawn from one tree and another giant promises a hundred rafters. (Van den Bergh 1933, 99–100; my translation)

At the time of our fieldwork, the CTI concession was one of the most productive in the country and mainly produced timber such as sipo (*Entandophragma utile*), sapeli (*Entandophragma cylindricum*), padouk (*Pterocarpus soyauxii*), and iroko (*Milicia excelsa*). Every month, between eight and ten thousand cubic meters of logs were shipped to Kinshasa via the Congo River—a journey of fourteen hundred kilometers that could easily take up to three weeks.

In the early 1990s, CTI had built a private port at the Itimbiri River and constructed a road to reach the concession farther north. It had also built offices, a garage, a labor compound for its Congolese workers, and bungalows for its European managers. In 1994 it erected a second labor camp in the middle of the concession as well as extra offices, another garage, a repair workshop, and two more expat bungalows. These two sites had attracted people from the wider region and had rapidly grown into multiethnic communities of, respectively, three and six thousand people.

Both labor camps comprised official workers' quarters but also unofficial squatter neighborhoods and newly created adjacent villages. In these agglomerations, contract employees, day laborers, jobseekers, traders, farmers, hunters, smugglers, bar keepers, and so-called free women all lived on the rhythm of the monthly arrival of salaries that were flown in from Kinshasa. The European expats, on the other hand, lived in colonial-style bungalows that were physically separated from the labor camps. At the start of our fieldwork, CTI had just hired a Danish forester in his early seventies as the new site manager. Together with three Frenchmen in their late fifties and early sixties and a Spanish forest engineer in his early thirties, they formed an isolated expat community.

The number of Congolese employees fluctuated between 230 and 490 over the time of our fieldwork. Together with their families, these men were housed in company-built wooden barracks in one of the labor compounds. About half of them originated from surrounding villages and were hired mainly as prospectors or company guards. The other half came from farther away and occupied more coveted positions—such as truck driver, chainsaw or bulldozer operator, cartographer, or statistician. CTI had transferred many of these so-called skilled laborers from other concessions in the country. Others had grown up in or around old plantation companies in the region. Although people spoke several languages with family and friends, on the work floor workers mainly communicated in the common vernacular, Lingala.

The CTI concession was fairly densely populated in comparison to other concessions. With about ninety thousand people living within its borders, it was home to village communities that subsisted primarily on slash-and-burn farming supplemented by trapping, hunting, fishing, and collecting. Every two or three years, men opened up new fields in the forest where, together with their wives and children, they cultivated such crops as cassava, maize, rice, groundnuts, beans, plantains, and sweet banana. Hunters and trappers provided their families with game, such as small antelope, wild boar, monkey, pangolin, and porcupine. Women and children collected mushrooms, caterpillars, termites, snails, wild roots, and leaf vegetables. Most families raised chickens and ducks, and some also owned goats or pigs. Although the larger villages hosted daily or weekly markets, most people preferred to go to town, where they garnered higher prices for their rice, groundnuts, and bushmeat.

While the nearest commercial center of Bumba hosted the usual set of development agencies and offices of international and local NGOs, the concession area was largely devoid of their presence. Notwithstanding the occasional billboard along the road signaling some sleeping agroforestry or aquaculture projects or the logos of UNICEF or the Red Cross on the walls of dispensaries and schools, forest residents said they were largely ignored. They often blamed their marginal location along the border between the Equateur and Orientale Provinces that ran right through the concession.[23] Moreover, for conservationists, the region was simply too populated to be of real interest. For human rights activists, the area lacked armed conflicts. And for indigenous rights organizations, the absence of so-called pygmy villages seemed to exclude the region from their maps. While, as we will see, international activist groups such as Greenpeace did sometimes engage with (and campaign against) the company, their actions rarely trickled down to the concession itself.

Ethnically and linguistically, the majority of concession residents identified as either Mbudza or Bati. This differentiation was supposed to overlap with the provincial border, but realities were more complex. Many villages harbored mixed populations and maintained oral histories that told of long patterns of migration. Moreover, while most farmers and hunters had a vague idea about the forest area that belonged to their village, clan, or lineage, actual boundaries were quite fluid. Hence, because CTI negotiated all agreements at the level of what were called *groupements* (genealogically related villages), its arrival sparked new border tensions between neighboring communities as well as between "autochthons" and "migrants" (Geschiere 2009).

While the concession was often a tense social environment, people from far and near nonetheless considered the CTI logging camps as highly attractive sites. Although hunters often complained about chainsaws scaring away prey animals and women deplored the increasing difficulties of collecting species of edible caterpillars that preferred big sapelli trees as their hosts, most villagers felt as if CTI's presence created more opportunities than obstacles to their livelihoods. Some of them found temporary jobs as day laborers. Others participated in trading, smuggling, and prostitution. New company roads rendered the area accessible (again) for trucks and regional traders, and logging itself opened up new farming grounds as well as markets for locally produced food.

At the same time, negotiations about the cahiers des charges often broke down, and CTI's inability or unwillingness to keep its promises led to increasingly open conflicts. During our fieldwork, discontented villagers regularly erected roadblocks, several of which resulted in violence. Such tensions added substantially to an already nervous atmosphere. After the 2008 financial crisis, global timber prices were rising again, and CTI managers frantically tried to follow production orders from Europe. But because of the long distance to Kinshasa, the concession's profitability was structurally vulnerable to the slightest perturbation. As we will see, roadblocks, together with exceptionally long periods of rainfall and fuel shortages, caused frustrating slowdowns. As a result, the air was often thick with rumors about a possible concession closure.

In 2012, a year after Freddy and I had left the concession, these rumors suddenly realized. The European mother company sold CTI to a new investor, who decided to close the site. The expat managers insisted that the new regulations had made it impossible for law-abiding companies to follow the

rules and still remain profitable. Civil society people maintained that escalating conflicts with village communities had pushed CTI to withdraw. Some
villagers were glad the company was gone, but others deplored its departure.
For many, it felt as though another period of isolation had begun.

The European loggers had moved to other concessions, within the country or without. Some workers followed. Others dispersed. Farmers continued for a while to cultivate their fields. As I write, the rainforest is once
again reclaiming old logging roads. CTI buildings are slowly joining the
other ruins of foreign capital. And people maintain they are, yet again, "en-
claved" (*enclavé*). Maybe, they say, another company will arrive someday
and reconnect their forest to the outside world. But only if God wills it (*soki
Nzambe alingi*).

Structure of This Book

Rainforest Capitalism describes how and why, for many of its inhabitants, life
in and around the CTI timber camps so often felt like it was out of control. In
order to grasp the affective realities and intricacies of power under rainforest
capitalism, it slowly tracks and illustrates the *ecstasis* that industrial logging
generated in so many striking and captivating ways.

The following pages are broadly structured as a general move from labor,
history, and political economy toward race, gender, and desire. The first
chapter presents the methodological, epistemological, and ethical challenges of doing ethnographic fieldwork across racialized boundaries in the
CTI logging concession. Chapter 2 offers a detailed analysis of the concrete
realities of labor for different work teams in the concession. Chapter 3 shows
how CTI operated in a region that was deeply affected by histories and memories of colonial extraction. Chapter 4 describes the tense relations between
the logging company and neighboring communities. Chapter 5 turns toward
the labor compounds and specifically unpacks the characteristically outward orientation of camp space and time. Chapter 6 evokes everyday expat
life and analyzes the European managers' deliberate construction of their
own so-called dark selves. Chapter 7 revisits the expat quarters from the
perspective of Congolese workers and villagers to map some of the occult
realities that were said to underlie timber production. Chapter 8 presents the
competitive and often transgressive dynamics of masculinity in the labor
camps. Chapter 9 looks into the slippery issue of expat sexuality in a highly
racialized and fetishized economy of desire. The conclusion takes stock of
the accumulated ethnographic material and proposes a theoretical reflection

on the dialectics of power and ecstasis in extractive capitalism. The epilogue ends the book on a more hopeful note.

Rainforest Capitalism gradually unpacks multiple ecstatic dynamics as they manifested in different forms and situations. Yet, while it ties these chapters together, ecstasis is not a strong concept that remains the same as it accumulates examples. Neither does it fully explain rainforest capitalism. It is a device that only obliquely approaches what often remained beyond words. But I believe it allows for a story on industrial logging that is as different as it is necessary.

View of the Congo River in Bumba

Awkward Beginnings

"IT WAS A HARSH PLACE FOR DOING BUSINESS," Bernhard said. From over his desk, the CTI managing director examined me intensely—as if to find out whether I would survive in the rainforest. Although I was terrified that he would mistake me for a Greenpeace spy, his piercing gaze was not really suspicious. Rather, he looked worried, almost unable to suppress a fatherly concern for my well-being. Only an hour ago I had introduced myself as a young forestry engineer on my way to becoming an anthropologist. And I had extensively thanked him for allowing me to do research in "his" concession, more than one thousand kilometers from Kinshasa. But I clearly didn't look like the men he usually sent in there.

Bernhard had given me a tour of the offices, sawmills, and piling areas where logs arrived by boat on the Congo River. The company site in Kinshasa looked neat and tidy. "Order is important for running a business," he said. "Logging is a long chain of activities that are tightly linked together and need to be controlled as much as possible." As I conscientiously took notes in my small notebook, Bernhard sighed. "But in the end," he said, "it all depends on what happens in the forest." He inspected some rafts of floating trunks waiting to be loaded onto the wharf and looked upstream over the river to the horizon. Perhaps he pictured the faraway concession he visited every two months or so by aircraft, and how, in the forest, things seemed a lot less neat and tidy.

A German expatriate in his late fifties, Bernhard had already worked for several multinational companies in different African countries. This was by no means his first confrontation with things spinning out of control. But never had he experienced the stubborn inertia of the world as vividly as he did now. It was November 2009, and hope was slowly rebuilding on the basis of timid signs that the global economic crisis was making way for economic recovery. The fragile demand for tropical timber was climbing again, and the European company to which CTI sold its timber was pushing Bernhard to increase production.

Since the end of the Congo wars, the logging sector had become increasingly competitive. A growing number of small, flexible firms were able to react quickly to changing circumstances and sell timber on the global market without much concern for the new environmental regulations. CTI, on the other hand, was too big to afford itself a bad reputation. Again, Bernhard sighed heavily. He said the company had made significant efforts to have its activities certified according to international standards of sustainable timber production. But nongovernmental organizations had recently accused CTI of excessive logging and ignoring legal obligations toward village communities. Most of these allegations were based on false information, Bernhard claimed. And he added that he was glad I would finally go to his concession so that, once and for all, "objective" scientific research could prove that these nasty accusations were wrong.

A year before Bernhard had replaced the site manager responsible for the operations in the logging concession. Unfortunately, the new manager had only made things worse. Over the past months, conflicts had escalated within several villages over the schools and dispensaries CTI needed to build as compensation for the trees it took. The executives from the European headquarters therefore decided to call upon Jens, the old Danish forest engineer who had successfully reopened the concession in 2003, after it had been closed for five years during the Second Congo War. Jens was an experienced and rigid man. "If there's someone fit for the job," Bernhard said, "it's Jens."

He pulled out a map from his drawer showing the Itimbiri concession demarcated by a thick black line. Thin lines represented roads, and small dots were villages—"more than a hundred-and-fifty of them," he said. He put his finger on the nearby town of Bumba. "While other companies are lucky to have almost empty concessions, our forest suffers from a huge demographic pressure. Bumba is estimated to have a population of more than two hundred thousand inhabitants. Add to that the almost ninety thousand people living within the concession's borders, and you have a rough idea of the problem we face." Every time he visited the concession, Bernard said, he witnessed new houses being built and new fields cut, steadfastly gnawing at precious timber resources.

He then showed me an aerial photograph that depicted in bright red colors the "alarming" rate of deforestation caused by shifting cultivation in and around the logging concession. *This*, he told me, was the real problem of Congo's forests: slash-and-burn farmers, not timber companies. The visually processed satellite image indeed seemed to produce incontestable proof. Every time journalists came by his office, he showed them this map so that they could talk about real problems rather than focus on unfounded Greenpeace accusations. My job as an anthropologist would be the same, he said: looking at realities "on the ground"—*sur le terrain*—unbiased and without political agenda.[1]

Bernhard nevertheless warned me that I would have a hard time. The villagers in the Itimbiri forests, he claimed, were of a particularly hard-headed stock: easily provoked and prone to overreacting as well as hopelessly divided, with corrupt village chiefs who seemed unable to speak for their communities. With whom do we negotiate the agreements required by the new forest code, he asked, if there were no legitimate power structures?

Maybe I could help him solve some of these issues, since the situation was really getting out of hand? Instead of appeasing tensions, building new schools and dispensaries only seemed to make things worse. Villagers had set up roadblocks and sabotaged machinery to stop logging operations. And, as if that was not enough, organized fuel smugglers were causing considerable losses for the company. It was a real mess, he said. "You'll not be short of nice social problems to study," he laughed.

This chapter gives a methodological account of what might seem to be fairly traditional ethnographic fieldwork in a not-so-traditional setting. First, it continues the awkward arrival story begun above to describe how I negotiated access to the CTI logging concession.[2] It then describes my particular position as a young white Belgian forestry engineer/anthropologist doing research among loggers in the DRC. The next section discusses the practicalities and sometimes ecstatic nature of fieldwork and reflects on the ethical and political challenges of studying transnational corporations. The chapter ends by tracing a path between paranoid and reparative writing, which helped build this book as a postcritical account of the often-violent world of industrial rainforest logging.

Negotiating Access

A few days after speaking to Bernhard, I traveled to Bumba in the company of Tim, one of the executives from the European head office, who had been sent to the DRC to follow up on the Forest Stewardship Council (FSC) certification process.[3] We boarded a small airplane operated by a friend of Bernhard's, a Belgian pilot who ran his own aviation business. As we took off, Tim told me that the European market was demanding more and more certified timber but that getting an FSC label was not easy. Certainly not in this country, he said.

To our surprise, three passengers in the front row turned their heads and presented themselves as German Greenpeace activists. They were organizing a workshop on illegal logging in Bumba and must have overheard us. Tim was visibly taken aback. "Really," he asked, "I didn't know about that. Why have I not been informed?" He cautiously tried to start a conversation. But the activists were not eager to chat with a representative of a company they had recently accused of irresponsible practices. Yet they still invited us to their workshop. "Of course," they smirked, "you are *both* welcome to attend."

The ease with which the Germans mistook me for a CTI employee was unsettling. To correct their impression, I emphasized that I was an independent researcher and nervously told them I was indeed about to start long-term fieldwork in the CTI concession but that I was not employed by or bound to the logging firm in any way. They nodded but seemed unconvinced.

An uncomfortable silence installed itself between us. The ethnographic rapport I had started to build with Tim seemed gone. He stubbornly looked out of the fogged aircraft window. The plane began to zigzag between towering thunderstorms. A little later, heavy turbulence made some passengers scream. Others started to pray. Tim seemed unaffected by it. I stoically tried to ignore my fear of flying, maybe to repair our fragile bond. A year later, the small aircraft crashed in Bandundu, killing all but one passenger.

I had met Tim for the first time a couple of months earlier in the headquarters of the European parent company. I was excited. Much to my surprise, CTI seemed willing to grant me access to its concession. Most timber companies were notoriously suspicious of outsiders. I had of course used my qualifications as a forestry engineer to get a foot in the door. And I had written a polite letter in which I described how my research project would nuance and revise the one-sided and stereotypical picture that media and international organizations usually painted. I also indicated that my project would take into account the manifold problems and difficulties logging companies faced, and I pointed to the possibility of finding pragmatic solutions to their challenges.

I had little hope that this approach would work, but CTI replied positively. The company invited me for a talk and even offered to pay for transportation and accommodation. As I had not yet secured a research grant, I gladly accepted the offer.

Yet, when finding myself facing Tim, as well as the general director and personnel officer, I quickly realized I had entered a tricky field of mutual instrumentalization. Much like in a job interview, the executives tried to read my intentions, discover my allegiances, and evaluate my capacities. Literally negotiating my project without much preparation or prior advice, I was overcome by a panic about the possible ethical implications of my choices. Their suspicions about my research amplified my own paranoia about their intentions to control, manipulate, or even censor my future writing. In order to safeguard my independence, I therefore decided to change my negotiation strategy and no longer present my work as potentially useful for the sector. Instead, I overemphasized its strictly academic nature and bluntly stated that my dissertation would "only be of interest to scholars" and not provide any use value for the company itself.

This improvised strategy to deflate CTI's expectations about a problem-solving anthropology worked surprisingly well. But it came at a price. Tim said they would grant me access to their concession only on two conditions. First, they wanted to prevent me from disclosing confidential information. Second, they insisted that, despite its overall academic nature, my presence still needed to be somewhat useful for their day-to-day management. We therefore settled on a formal *access-for-confidentiality* deal and a more informal *access-for-assistance* deal.

The first involved signing a confidentiality agreement in which I promised not to disclose confidential matters to third parties without the company's approval.[4] The agreement also obliged me to send all future text drafts that mentioned the company name and were available to the wider public to the company head office one month before publication. It then required me to take into account CTI's observations and reflect these accordingly in my final publications.

Although clearly a means for exercising control, the confidentiality agreement did not entail direct censorship. It merely formulated a right of response. At the time, I hoped that sharing text drafts would enable fair discussions about my analyses. I had no idea this hope would quickly crumble after I effectively emailed my first article for comments two years later. In his reply, Tim told me my text was not what he had expected. After long discussions over email, telephone, and Skype, it became clear that the company managers not only found my account unflattering, unfair, and biased; they also claimed I had lost myself in vague rumors and irrelevant details. Despite interventions from my university, they continued to question the academic validity and objectivity of my research, and we eventually ended up in a frustrating epistemological standoff (see also Mosse 2006). From that point on I decided to refer to the company by the pseudonym CTI. This not only eased the company's concerns about reputational damage, but it also circumvented the confidentiality agreement, as it applied only to publications that explicitly mentioned the company's name.

The second deal—access for assistance—was not fixed in legally binding terms but was part of the broader give-and-take of negotiations. While I insisted that my future publications would be strictly intended for an academic audience, we agreed that I would also write a separate report for the company. Tim suggested that, as a countergesture to the company's goodwill, I assist in realizing the "socio-economic diagnostic of the concession area," a document the new forest code required all logging companies to attach to their management plans. I agreed and spent the first month of fieldwork conducting a population census and socioeconomic survey. Later I also drafted the required diagnostic itself and added data on regional history, migration patterns, local politics, camp demographics, and the cultural significance of specific tree species.

This second deal spared CTI the cost of hiring an outside expert and allowed me to get to know the area in a fairly short time before focusing on my own research. But it did not make it any easier to claim independence vis-à-vis the company when talking to people in or around the concession—or when justifying myself to Greenpeace activists. On that first flight to Bumba I had not yet fully anticipated the emotional toll that thorny issues of trust, complicity, and (in)dependence would take. But I already felt how mutual suspicions could electrify the air.

Among My Own People

After stopovers in Mbandaka and Lisala, the aircraft pursued its course over thick grayish rainforest. In the early afternoon we arrived in Bumba, a small but bustling commercial town along the Congo River. A white Toyota Land

Cruiser was waiting for us near the airstrip, and two Congolese CTI employees swiftly guided us past the Direction Générale de Migration (DGM). The Greenpeace activists, by contrast, were held up. Uniformed men claimed that their visas were not in order. But we hurried past them. Now there was no more way of hiding the bare fact that I was being taken care of by the logging company and already benefiting from its privileged relationship with local administrations. I tried to reconcile myself with the idea that, in order to study a timber firm from the inside out, I would inevitably be thrown into its complicities and power games.

We drove about thirty kilometers along the Congo River to CTI headquarters. Large trucks carrying enormous tree trunks arrived from the production sites farther north. At the road junction I caught my first glimpse of the labor compound. Behind two lively bars and a motorcycle repair shop, children were playing between wooden barracks, and women strolled to the market. Our vehicle then passed through a guarded gate that separated the river camp from the fenced work site. In front of the main offices I was introduced to the Congolese human resources manager who, after a brief conversation, instructed one of his clerks to take me to what he called the Garden of Eden (*le jardin d'Eden*), where I was supposed to wait until one of the Europeans returned from the forest.

Tired from the trip, I somehow hoped this Eden would be a bar with refreshing beer. As I followed the clerk, we passed garages smelling of oil and gasoline where workers could be heard repairing heavy machinery. On the river side, logs were being loaded on boats bound for Kinshasa. When we came to yet another gate, my guide loudly announced: "This is Eden!"— perhaps to wake up the guard in his small wooden shelter. Before me, five small bungalows bordered the Itimbiri River. Despite the ornamental palm trees and flowerbeds, the place seemed very unlike the Eden I expected. With their scaly whitish walls, the bungalows made a rather shabby impression. In contrast to the busy road junction near the labor compound, the place seemed desolate. "This is where the whites live," the clerk informed me, "and the third bungalow is for visitors; that's where you'll stay."

A smiling man then introduced himself as cook to the Danish site manager who lived in the adjacent bungalow. As he showed me my room, I felt a racialized logic of difference and segregation pinning me down to my proper place. Some minutes later, a jeep stopped on the driveway, and a bony, tanned European man entered the bungalow. He abruptly presented himself as Michel, the forest overseer, and was very curious about my presence. "An anthropologist!" he shouted when I introduced myself. "It's a pity you won't find any Pygmies or other interesting tribes here in the forest; they all lost their traditions ages ago." I clumsily explained I was not looking for traditional tribes but wanted to understand everyday concession life as a way to grasp how global dynamics of capitalist resource extraction manifested themselves. Of course, my reply raised more questions than produced satisfying answers. "Anyway," Michel cut me short, "Welcome to hell!"

At first I thought it a mere coincidence that Michel's cynical "hell" contrasted so poignantly with what the human resources manager and his clerk had earlier referred to as a paradisiacal Garden of Eden. I later came to realize that both expats and Congolese used the opposition between heaven and hell as a metaphorical device for understanding and criticizing the world and discovered how it resonated with widespread racial imaginaries. That night I uncomfortably shared my first meal with the European loggers: Jens, the recently hired Danish site manager; Julien, the French mechanic who had been working at the concession for several years; Roger, the French construction manager who had just arrived from Congo-Brazzaville; and Michel, the French forest overseer who had come to the river site to meet me.

During dinner—tuna salad, rump steak and fries, and vanilla pudding— the expats expressed their concerns about the planned Greenpeace meeting in Bumba. They warned me not to get carried away by environmentalist rhetoric and urged me to form an opinion based solely on my own observations. I again tried to reassure them that I had not come to assess their operations but wanted to understand how extractive capitalism worked by looking closely at a timber concession. Once again I was not sure my words realized their intention.

Yet, against my expectations, it turned out that the European loggers quickly came to accept my presence. Although my shift from forestry to anthropology continued to puzzle them, they somehow took me as one of them. Whereas my university degree, age, and class background set me apart, as a forest engineer I could indeed speak their language.[5] Moreover, as a young white man with a colonial family history—my mother having been born in the Belgian Congo, where my grandfather was a paratrooper officer—our biographies resonated. As such, my whiteness was soon enough drawn into stories I already knew too well.

That first night, however, I worried deeply about how difficult my research might become. Not, as Bernhard had predicted, because of the hardheaded concession residents with whom I was about to become acquainted, but because of my presence among men supposedly of my own kind: single, white, European, expat foresters. It was with lots of doubts and hesitations that I entered the rowdy world of chainsaws and machismo to which I somehow already belonged. This book is profoundly shaped by the emotional challenges, ethical paradoxes, and at times ecstatic nature of doing research in a "field" whose very availability for study was the product of uncontrollable historical and political-economic forces that also made me into who I was.

Friendship, Fieldwork, and Ecstasis

During the fifteen months of fieldwork that took place in the CTI logging concession between November 2009 and July 2011, I spent most of my time joining work teams in the forest, taking rides on bulldozers and logging trucks, assisting prospectors and learning the names of different trees, following everyday activities in company offices, trying to help out in garages and workshops, drinking and killing time in the labor camps, playing games with children, poking fun with youngsters, attending never-ending meetings, praying at church services, mourning at funerals, mediating in conflicts, chatting with farmers, accompanying hunters, meeting village chiefs, dining with expat managers, listening to their stories, and reading novels that allowed me to temporally escape the bleak world of logging.

Over time I came to understand why Johannes Fabian (2000, 280) considers ecstasis to be not just an inherent aspect of colonial exploration but also, more troublingly, an "integral dimension" of ethnographic inquiry itself. In the logging camps, fieldwork indeed included its share of alcohol and drugs, anger and frustration, intimacy and paranoia, moments of danger and excitement, choosing sides and being pulled apart in multiple directions, role-playing and mirroring. On a deeper epistemological level, fieldwork also requires ethnographers to get out of their selves so as to meet others on unfamiliar terrain; it presupposes risk and vulnerability—a being *caught with others* that opens up the possibility of "non-intentional communication" (Favret-Saada 2012, 443).

Yet while Fabian emphasizes the fundamental way in which all ethnography depends on an ecstatic involvement of the self in the other, he equally warns us not to turn ecstasis into a *method* or "mistake conditions and dimensions [of knowledge production] for ways and means" (Fabian 2000, 280). Ecstasis, he writes, is "not something to pursue in the practice of ethnography.... Seeking such experiences ... is the privilege of mystics, perhaps of artists, but the knowledge they are after is not what we seek" (281). In his view, ecstasis is a requirement of fieldwork—not its aim.

Fieldwork certainly had its ecstatic moments but also its quotidian routines: Long hours of participant observation in the labor camps and expat quarters when nothing seemed to happen. Jotting down initially meaningless field notes. Drawing up questionnaires for semistructured interviews that had to be tape-recorded and transcribed. Collecting, copying, and photographing texts and images to discuss with research participants. Traveling to nearby villages and towns to talk to local historians, traders, chiefs, and people from civil society so as to get a better understanding of the broader geographical, historical, and political environment. Engaging in archival research during breaks in Belgium in order to reconstruct regional history.

Freddy, an energetic young man in his early twenties from Bumba, often accompanied me as my research assistant during my time in the forest. When we first met, Freddy had just returned to his father's house after obtaining a bachelor's degree in law from the University of Kisangani. He was planning to continue his studies and was looking for a way to save money. I told him I might need a translator and someone to teach me Lingala. We agreed that he would earn $100 per month—the same salary as most new CTI workers. I found this an appallingly low wage. As a student, I was of course bound by my limited research budget, but the inequality between his salary and mine was something I always wanted to make up for. At least I managed to pay him through a formal contract with CTI that gave him access to free health care.

Freddy and I shared a company-built house in the labor compound in the middle of the concession with two young, unmarried, and recently hired employees. From that house we first undertook motorcycle trips to villages in the area to conduct the census and survey I had promised CTI. During these trips, Freddy's outgoing character and mechanical skills compensated for my initial shyness and technical clumsiness. We also spent hours transcribing and translating interviews and processing data. After some time, Freddy began keeping his own fieldnotes, and we extensively discussed our observations and experiences in what was, for both of us, a new world. Slowly, an intimate friendship grew.

My Lingala improved, and I became increasingly absorbed in the everyday rhythms of camp life. Initially my presence in an otherwise black labor compound generated jokes, frowns, and suspicions—from both Congolese employees and European managers. Rumors circulated that I was working for an auditing company or spying for the World Bank. But who had ever heard of a white auditor eating and sleeping in labor camps, apparently doing nothing and just hanging around? It took quite some time and impression management before my seemingly transgressive presence was taken for granted, though doubts about my motivations periodically reappeared. My colonial family history, however, rarely closed doors. To the contrary, it often created a common background—however painful at times—that opened up possibilities for dialogue, interaction, and understanding.

As more and more people got used to the idiosyncratic idea of having a Belgian neighbor living among them, our house became a meeting place. After a while, Freddy and one of our housemates asked their girlfriends to come and live with us. Two other friends also moved in to help with cooking and daily chores. As such, we became a dynamic and flexible living arrangement—not so unlike others in the timber camps.

Alongside this house in the labor compound, I also negotiated a room for myself among the European expats. I was given a bedroom in the bungalow occupied by Pablo, a young Spanish forest engineer who began working for CTI a couple of months after my arrival. Having a room of one's own was not just indispensable for writing; it was also a necessary condition for achieving my ethnographic objective of simultaneously understanding the lifeworlds of Congolese workers *and* European expats. It was only by living on both sides that I could perceive how they coproduced their respective differences—and realized how they were mutually affected by what I would later come to call the ecstasis of rainforest logging.

In practice, this double objective forced me to constantly move back and forth between racially segregated communities. I often spent my days in the labor compound, had dinner in the expat quarters, and returned to the camp for the night. Or I spent the day with a work team in the forest, after which I took a shower at Pablo's bungalow, had something to eat in the camp, and slept in the expat quarters. Sometimes I was taken up for several days with a family until one of the expats urged me to have a beer in the evening. At other times I confined myself to my room to write, until one of the workers defied the unwritten rules of racial segregation and "kidnapped" me for a night of drinking, gossip, and fun in the labor compound.

While absolutely essential, this mobility was possible only because of my white privilege. The Garden of Eden was indeed off-limits to most Congolese. To our great frustration, it was therefore impossible for Freddy to join me during fieldwork among the expat loggers. This painful situation never stopped provoking unease and occasional conflict, but eventually it also formed a deeper understanding between us.

In fact, it was only by stumbling around racialized power structures that I learned to recognize the abiding force of whiteness. As I viscerally felt the consequences and sanctions of racial transgression, my bodily experiences became data in their own right and formed the reflexive basis from which, perhaps paradoxically, I could develop relationships based on mutual respect. Moreover, it was often by sharing feelings of self-doubt with people around me that we could maintain and repair confidence. Despite, or perhaps because of, my introvert character in a hard environment, profound friendships could develop with very different people in both the logging camps and expat quarters.

Yet, although I thus managed to create fragile relationships of trust, there was always something that bothered me. Because of my wedding ring, most people knew I was married and often asked questions about my wife. I answered them as honestly as I could but also thought it best to cover up my partner's gender and first name. Given the seemingly homophobic world of logger machismo, I believed it was wise to avoid coming out—though admittedly I never really knew whether or not my fears were justified. No longer used to living in the closet, however, my lies and evasions made me feel insincere toward the very persons who were often so open about *their* intimate affairs.

At the same time, however, this closeted queerness also made me find shelter with people to whom I felt an intense but unspoken connection. I believe that some of my most profound friendships were at least partly due to the particular salience of homosocial intimacies in a heteronormative world. And while this specific positionality heightened my sensitivity to the quotidian violence of gender in the logging camps, it also amplified the erotic ambiguity of heterosexual masculinities. Notwithstanding its emotional challenges, this dissimulated queerness therefore brought to the fore dimensions of rainforest logging that might otherwise have remained less tangible. As such, it accounts for the sometimes queer turns the analysis and story will take in the following chapters.

How to Study a Corporation?

I was very lucky to have been given access to a world that often remains off-limits to long-term ethnographic research. But studying *in* transnational corporations also comes with particular methodological challenges. Apart from the problems of access and thorny issues of friendship, trust, and betrayal raised above, this section discusses three practical difficulties that any insider study of corporations must necessarily face.

First, big companies generally find themselves in a relative position of power vis-à-vis the researcher. Ethnographers therefore need to "study up," as Laura Nader (1969) famously described it. Doing so, they are confronted with the limits of ethnographic methods in settings that seem hostile to participant observation. Indeed, although I was allowed to live, work, and study in the CTI concession, my position was precarious. The expat managers could banish me from the field if they wanted to. And while they rarely openly intervened into my movements, I constantly felt the need to protect myself against more subtle forms of company control and find pragmatic ways of looking into sensitive issues without jeopardizing further access.

The power imbalances of studying up therefore raise persistent questions about research autonomy and dependence. In practice, my fieldwork was possible only because of CTI's infrastructure and material resources. Whereas I had bought my own motorcycle, I indeed used company gasoline. And while I occupied a company house in the labor compound, I also had a room in one of the expat bungalows. My closeness to and dependence on CTI therefore inevitably exposed me to risks of moral corruption and political cooptation (Coumans 2011). And yet, accepting dinner invitations, using company services, biting my tongue, and even forcing a smile when racist or sexist jokes were made were essential for lubricating research, notwithstanding the moral and emotional discomfort it provoked.[6] It was only through *participation* that studying up also became a more intimate "studying sideways" *with* the people I was thought to resemble (Hannerz 1998).

Second, studying corporations also presents particular difficulties with regard to the negotiation of informed consent. All during my fieldwork, I explicitly told people how I had arrived in the concession, who was funding me, and what I had come to do. I generally presented myself as a student writing a book on everyday life in a logging company. Most people reacted enthusiastically and consented to participate.[7] The expat managers were glad that a researcher who somehow looked like them would finally describe what really happened in the sector. Many workers were proud that their lives and stories would end up in academic publications. And villagers were generally excited about their largely ignored region being studied by an anthropologist.

Whenever participants raised concerns about the ways in which specific issues might or might not turn up in my writing, consent was renegotiated. But because of my intention to simultaneously understand the lifeworlds of expat managers, Congolese workers, and neighboring villagers, a full disclosure of shifting research topics was not always possible. Much of what was said indeed constituted "hidden transcripts" spoken behind the back of those who lived on the other side of a racialized divide (Scott 1990). Rumors, gossip, stories, and dialogues therefore had to be handled with care. When having dinner with expat managers, for instance, I could not always reveal what I was working on in the labor camps. Neither could I always share these dinner conversations with workers. As a result, the expats often distrusted my closeness to their employees, while the latter sometimes frowned upon my personal relationship with their bosses.

While presenting oneself and one's project differently to different interlocutors might be an ordinary aspect of ethnography (and of life itself), fieldwork in transnational companies also entails more explicitly contradicting allegiances, commitments, affinities, and affiliations (Welker 2016a). Moreover, because half of my fieldwork entailed studying (up) the lives of people who were, in many respects, more powerful than I was, the inevitable issue of choosing sides was difficult. Given the power discrepancies in the concession, it was indeed risky to openly oppose the European loggers. Access to the concession depended on their continuing approval—which, in turn, relied on my apparent avoidance of certain issues. Hence, although the air was often thick with racism, misogyny, and violence, we could rarely, if ever, explicitly talk about these things as legitimate topics for research.

A third practical challenge when it comes to studying big transnational companies is where or what to study. A corporation is indeed multiple, internally diverse, and geographically spread out. In practice, it is not always clear where it begins or ends because its definition requires continuous work and boundary-making processes that are always "flexible and dependent on the situation" (Giskeødegård 2016, 116). Furthermore, different people speak *for* the corporation or *in its place*: owners, managers, directors, workers. Others speak *about* it: subcontractors, shareholders, creditors, suppliers, auditors, neighbors, politicians, activists, critics. For this reason, *the* corporation needs to be constantly performed so as to give it continuity, substance, and identity. As Marina Welker (2014) aptly puts it in an inspiring study of a U.S.-based corporation and its Indonesian copper and gold mine, it has to be "enacted" by different people in different circumstances.

In the following chapters, the acronym CTI must be understood in this performative sense, as an entity created and put together by those who speak for, to, against, and about it (Appel 2019a). Because of this continuous enactment, CTI was different things to different people. As we will see, it was simultaneously employer, owner, concession holder, father, teacher, developer, partner, cannibal, enemy, ally, victim, target, and prey. What it *was* was the outcome of a temporary actualization of a possible relationship. Moreover, in everyday parlance, corporations are often seen and approached as *persons* and thus are attributed with intentionality, agency, attitudes, and opinions as well as rights, entitlements, and responsibilities. Metaphors of "corporate personhood" are indeed widespread and used by companies and their critics alike (Kirsch 2014a, 208). But corporations can only emerge as persons *in relation* to others and come into being in and through struggles and negotiations (Golub 2014).

The ideal ethnographic study of CTI *as a corporation* would therefore entail doing research in multiple locations: in its European headquarters and Kinshasa offices, with its clients and shareholders, in state administrations, auditing companies, and NGOs. It is indeed by applying what George Marcus (1995) calls "multi-sited ethnography" that projects such as Welker's or Appel's reveal the surprisingly fragile processes through which corporations are constructed, performed, and enacted as the strong entities they often seem to be. Yet this book is mainly written from the CTI concession only. Instead of situating the vulnerability of CTI within the quotidian and multisited processes through which it came into being, the following chapters foreground CTI's precarity as an affective reality *of* its experienced powers.

The difference is subtle but important. This book does not try to tackle *how*, given its multiplicity and permeability, CTI could appear as a stable entity at all. Our problem is rather *why*, despite the appearance of CTI as a powerful force, rainforest logging was still lived as such a vulnerable process caught in dynamics that were difficult to control. What it thus misses in reach it compensates for in depth. Rather than a multisited theorization of CTI as a corporation, it tracks the possibilities and limits of corporate power *in* the concession and tells a complex story about what industrial logging felt like for people living closely with its effects.

From Paranoid to Reparative Writing

Fieldwork in and on a transnational logging company clearly comes with particular methodological and ethical challenges, many of which have to do with the unequal power relations between ethnographer and interlocutors. After fieldwork, however, these power imbalances change.

Back home I was indeed no longer dependent on practical company support or restrained by the possibility that CTI might put a premature end to my project. While writing my dissertation, some of the painful issues that had remained hidden during fieldwork could therefore impose themselves, claiming central places in my analysis. The first cathartic months of writing were often characterized by an intense anger, which I struggled to transform into a more productive force. But as I gradually managed to impose the formal and academic conventions of the doctoral dissertation on the emotional turmoil of fieldwork, a distance was created from where I could take control of ecstatic experiences and catch ephemeral realities in seemingly stable concepts and theories. Hence, as an act of interpretation, the entire writing process was very much what Susan Sontag (2009, 7) called "a revenge of the intellect upon the world."

As a result, my thesis could not but reinforce the characteristic paranoia that is so often a generic mark of dissertations. While written to protect itself against an academic world waiting to judge its many flaws, it was also a paranoid reaction against real and imagined company control: a text full of preemptive strikes, defensive trenches, and possible escape routes. Despite the wonderful criticism, support, and encouragement I received from my examiners and supervisors, I was exhausted and ultimately dissatisfied with the result.

Four years later, however, while rereading fieldnotes and revising chapters, a certain mildness began to soften my perspective. The need to establish a critical independence from a world to which I awkwardly came to belong made place for a newfound empathy and even sympathy for the existential drama in which ultimately we were all participants.[8] Without disregarding the politically and epistemologically productive dimensions of anger, repulsion, and suspicion, the following chapters indeed complement paranoia with what queer theorist Eve Kosofsky Sedgwick (2003) would call a "reparative" reading of my earlier writings. For Sedgwick, such readings welcome surprise and remain open to the possible horror of the new that, as a critic, I had often eliminated in an anxious attempt to predict the world and anticipate its ruses (146).

As already noted in the introduction, Sedgwick's call for reparative reading was a crucial precursor to the recent turn to postcritique (Felski 2015). Questioning the paranoia and "hermeneutics of suspicion" that so much characterized the humanities and social sciences, Sedgwick effectively looked for love, hope, nurture, sustenance, affection, and intimacy in the wake of violence, hostility, and depression. As such, reparative readings almost seem to promise redemption *after* critique.[9] Although I remain cautious about this apparent optimism, reparative reading and writing certainly helped me bridge the critical distance that "supposedly successful methods create or presuppose between researcher and researched—a distance through which madness gapes" (Fabian 2000, 208).[10]

The writing of *Rainforest Capitalism* therefore deployed reparative strategies to reconnect to a world I could not leave behind. But, more pragmatically, reparative ethnography also contains the possibility of side-stepping the usual game of critique and countercritique that is often played between extractive companies and their scholars. In fact, like many corporations today, CTI managers often *expected* criticism and even *incorporated* critique into their own narratives (Benson and Kirsch 2010). They were, for instance, very familiar with public accusations and critical press reports, and highly skilled in countering negative points with positive ones to neutralize accusations.

Perhaps a deliberately *post*critical account is less easy to incorporate into business-as-usual. For this reason, this book is not an academy-approved evaluation of industrial rainforest logging. As I see it, postcritique is a way of *not* asking the impossible question of whether or not ethnographers should criticize the corporations they come to know so intimately (Appel 2019b). Or it is a way of not worrying about finding a right balance between critiquing negative and acknowledging positive impacts (Salverda 2019). On the contrary, postcritical reparative analysis can enable *other* descriptions that allow for possibilities of transformation found in the world it encounters.

Hence, instead of merely trying to expose the violent power of a logging company, this book stays a little longer with its murky realities and reconnects to the sustaining ambiguities of the human condition as it manifested itself in the CTI concession. Rather than claim a moral high ground from the sidelines, it slowly wades through the lowland of humanity. And yet, the following chapters do not erase all traces of paranoia or critique. As we will see, paranoid readings and vernacular criticism suffused the world of rainforest logging, where expats, workers, and villagers alike were heavily invested in suspicions, rumors, occult economies, and conspiracy theories. Thinking *with* loggers therefore implies staying with the forces *they* see without presuming that what they see is merely a distorted version of what we see (better).

Staying with loggers requires neither the hegemonic critical stance of the social sciences nor a merely reparative reading that presents itself as a way out of the paranoia that arguably dominates critical theory. Perhaps all anthropological fieldwork and writing automatically takes one beyond Sedgwick's alternatives of critical paranoia and postcritical reparation (Love 2010), or at least nervously alternates between both positions and impulses. Written both *with* and *against* company power, the following chapters foreground the ecstasis of rainforest capitalism as well as the ways in which individuals and communities sutured existential crises of control through reparative and paranoid stories alike—stories this book can only repeat, relay, and recycle.

View of the production camp

Forest Work

IT HAD BEEN RAINING SEEMINGLY WITHOUT END. In the forest, rain is a daily story. But, sometimes, water just keeps falling, not in heavy downpours but in monochrome gray blankets that cover everything in a cold dampness. It makes accessing the forest all but impossible. For four days, CTI workers had remained in the labor compounds. Many had welcomed a much-deserved rest. But yesterday afternoon the sky suddenly cleared up. Later that evening, word came from Jens, the Danish site manager, that everyone was expected back at work the next day.

That morning, I sat on the doorstep of the chainsaw repair workshop waiting for the first workers to arrive at the gathering ground. It was 4:30 a.m. and still pitch dark. Olivier, the mechanic, was already tinkering with a chainsaw. "I wonder whether the trucks will leave today," he said. "The roads are still so muddy." I nodded. Last night, Michel, the French overseer, had strongly disagreed with Jens's decision to send teams into the forest under these conditions.

Olivier was one of the first Congolese workers I had come to know in the forest camp. Being a mechanic ran in the family, he proudly told me. He was born in Kisangani, where his father worked at the port. He later moved to the Lokutu oil palm plantation south of Basoko. Having grown up in a labor camp, Olivier now tried to raise his own three kids in the CTI compounds. But life as a worker was no longer what it used to be, he said. His children were going to the CTI school, but he worried about their future. If only he could send his eldest son to Kinshasa.

A loud metallic drumming interrupted our conversation. Ruphin, one of the company guards, was hitting an old metal bulldozer wheel near the company office. Every morning this rattling sound warned the workers that they were expected to report to their team bosses within fifteen minutes.

A little later, Michel arrived in his jeep from the expat quarters farther down the road. He met with Emile, a Congolese agronomist who had recently arrived from Kinshasa. Michel and Emile knew each other from before, and I could hear them laughing. People called Emile a mestizo (*métis*), and, being of mixed-race parents, he had been given a newly furnished house slightly separated from the rest of the labor compound. Its freshly painted walls starkly contrasted with the adjacent worker barracks.

At the other side of the gathering ground, André unlocked the door to his wooden office. As the highest-ranking Congolese agent at the forest camp, people referred to him as the engineer (*l'ingénieur*). Like most of the Congolese staff, André was a Kikongo-speaking man originating from the area where colonial timber production had started in the 1930s. As in many other timber firms, the highest posts available to Congolese nationals at CTI were occupied by people from the Lower Congo and Bandundu provinces. André lived in a big house on the work site itself, next to the company gate that led to the compounds. On his large terrace he held Sunday prayer services for workers in his entourage. His church, The Way International—a Christian ministry originating from the United States—had the reputation of being a congregation of scientists, scholars, doctors, and "intellectuals."

In the meantime, a group of men had assembled in front of André's office. They were jobseekers hoping to be hired for the day. André was indeed the man to convince. He had a great deal of autonomy to decide whom to employ and whom to reject. As usual, he told the men that no jobs were available. Many would probably try again tomorrow. Some of them would come back in the afternoon and leave "a little something"—a chicken, some bananas, smoked fish—with André's wife in the hope their name might one day appear on a list attached to his office door. Others would accuse him of tribalism. Some would temporarily join The Way.

It was 5 a.m., and more workers trickled through the gate. Their team bosses disappeared inside André's office to receive their instructions for the day. People were quiet, and the mood seemed low. Many of them wore blue work outfits. Some had safety helmets and safety shoes. Others had on slippers. Some wore thick jackets to ward off the morning chill.

Joseph, an experienced tree feller, entered Olivier's workshop. He needed to have his chainsaw repaired. Olivier laughed. "After all this rain, Jens will make you suffer today," he warned. Joseph looked to the floor. "Where is your lunch packet?" Olivier asked teasingly, when noticing Joseph had walked in without his usual rucksack. We all knew Joseph was engaged in a nasty row with his wife over the allocation of his wages. Last week she had even refused to cook for him. "Ah, brother," Joseph said, "that woman . . . she is trouble. I will just have to buy some cassava bread in the forest."

I crossed the grounds with Joseph to look for his apprentice, a young man in his early twenties. His mother—Joseph's sister—had recently sent him over from Mbandaka to stay with his uncle. Joseph let him carry his heavy chainsaw as we climbed into the open container of an old truck. Some villagers were already hiding in a corner, hoping for a free ride into the forest. Freddy also arrived and hopped on. In the meantime, Joseph's nephew quietly sipped from a small liquor bottle. He offered me some. "No thanks," I said, smiling.

Our truck driver suddenly accelerated his motor to signal that departure was imminent. Although several tree fellers were still climbing into the container, he began moving his vehicle. Some workers started running toward us. Joseph laughed out loud at their clumsy moves. Someone hit the truck cabin to make our driver stop and allow everyone to get on board safely.

The truck left the forest camp at dawn and drove east over the main gravel road. In the container we tried to make ourselves as comfortable as possible between chainsaws, machetes, lunches, and safety helmets. Some workers seemed tired. Freddy and others chatted. One man wanted to know whether it was true that the big bosses from Europe were about to visit the concession, adding he had heard they were dissatisfied with Jens's new management. People looked expectantly in my direction. Freddy asked if anyone had news about their salaries. Tomorrow, the twenty-fifth, was payday. But, as usual, the money would be considerably delayed in arriving from Kinshasa. Someone said the secretary had told him that the cash had not even arrived in Bumba, and, in any case, they were still waiting for last month's work bonuses. Joseph pointed out that their premiums were bound to disappoint anyway, given all the heavy rainfall.

On the drive, several workers dozed off, but we were shaken up by the truck stopping abruptly. We had entered a temporary exploitation road that was extremely muddy. The truck moved on, but because of all the slipping and bumping, it became quite painful to remain seated on the metal floor. We stood up and tried to hold on to each other and to the container walls.

After a slippery one-hour drive, the truck arrived at the production camp deep in the forest. As we approached, a policeman and two company guards started running behind us, asking for cannabis. A worker threw them two brown parcels of weed. When we came to a halt, Joseph got off quickly to buy some cassava bread (*kwanga*) and a small piece of meat from a woman who had temporarily set up shop there. The others tried to convince our driver to proceed a little farther. The tree-felling sites were up the road, they said. It was too muddy, the driver claimed. So we all had to get off.

———————

The number of employees working and living in the CTI concession fluctuated significantly over time. In April 2009, in the wake of the financial crisis, the company had drastically downsized its workforce and laid off more than two hundred workers. Six months later, half of them were already reemployed. During the first year of my fieldwork with Freddy, the number of employees more than doubled in a postcrisis acceleration of production: from approximately 230 workers in October 2009 to almost 490 in October 2010. Yet, near the end of our stay, their numbers had already started to go down again. They truly plummeted in early 2012, after the concession was sold.

This chapter evokes the bare realities of labor in the CTI concession and provides a first ethnographic basis for approaching the ecstatogenic lifeworld of industrial logging. By putting employment first and central, it partially returns to an earlier focus on labor in classic ethnographies of capitalist extraction, trying to accommodate for a remarkable "dearth of attention to the rank and file in current anthropological analyses of extractive corporations" (Rolston 2013, 584). Yet, while focusing on the experiences, practicalities, and materialities of labor, this chapter simultaneously foregrounds the gendered connotations, racial realities, and affective dimensions of work in the rainforest. Gender, race, and affect are indeed of primordial importance in understanding how and why (as we will see in subsequent chapters) labor played such an important role in popular memories of connection and disconnection, as well as in performances of masculinity.

What forms of labor did industrial rainforest logging produce? What did these kinds of work actually feel like? How did loggers frame their experiences on the work floor? How did the company try to control its employees? And how did the latter attempt to take back some degree of control? The chapter starts with a brief description of salaries, contracts, and work bonuses that foregrounds the sharply racialized pay gap in the concession. It then provides an insight into more technical aspects of work and zooms in on five specific stages of industrial logging—prospecting, tracking, roadbuilding, tree felling, and skidding/loading. It thereby shows how these different stages produced different work rhythms and gendered atmospheres but also created different possibilities for evading company surveillance. The final section takes a closer look at how CTI tried to monitor its production process and why it was largely able to maintain worker output *without* tight regimes of discipline and control.

"$100 Is a Lot of Money"

Like most older CTI employees, Joseph and Olivier had been hired under an indefinite-term labor contract. They both proudly remembered the day they had received their personal identification number (*numéro de matricule*), which formalized their status as a fully salaried worker. Several of their colleagues, on the other hand, were only employed under fixed-term contracts that were renewed only when needed. They still awaited the moment when, as the law required, they would be granted a permanent position. Yet, since the financial crisis, changes in contract status had become rare.

The wages of CTI agents generally depended on their category and so-called skill level. About one-third of all contractual workers—prospectors, guards, and trackers, for instance—were paid according to the lowest wage grade and received an average monthly salary of $53. Mechanics and chainsaw and bulldozer operators earned between $61 and $82 per month. Accountants, statisticians, and cartographers were paid $94 to $108. Team overseers received $117 to $125, and Congolese staff earned between $356 and $402 per month. In reality, however, actual salaries were somewhat higher because most teams had to work ten to fifteen hours overtime per week. All salaries were also supplemented by medical allowances.

In addition to these salaries and allowances, contract workers also earned monthly work bonuses (*primes de production*). At the beginning of our fieldwork, CTI calculated these premiums on the basis of the overall amount of timber produced during the previous month. But, in 2010, Jens partially transformed these collective bonuses into a more individualized motivation system. For all forest workers with a direct link to timber production, work bonuses were then to be calculated on the basis of their actual output. The expat managers believed this would boost production. But because confusion reigned over their actual calculation and distribution, this new system had only limited success. Workers compared their bonuses and often wondered why some colleagues with similar outputs earned more. Failing to perceive a clear link between their efforts and income, workers suspected that the CTI bosses were handing out bonuses arbitrarily.

Individual bonuses nevertheless reached between $50 and $90 per month during months of full employment and good production levels. Added to wages, an average contract worker could thus earn about $175 per month. In practice, however, wages and bonuses were unpredictable. Weather conditions, fuel shortages, and roadblocks erected by discontented villagers regularly limited the number of working days. In normal months, the majority of CTI employees therefore earned anywhere between $100 and $150 total.

In comparison to the low-cash income of most villagers in and around the CTI concession, this was a substantial amount. The monthly arrival of fresh money indeed made the logging camps into attractive sites for farmers, hunters, traders, barkeepers, and free women to develop their commercial activities. Scarce cash also enabled loggers to create and maintain a distinction from others on the basis of the performance of a certain urbanity in the middle of the rainforest. Olivier, for instance, often said the camps were more like a little town than a village. At the same time, however, many workers bitterly complained about their low wages—especially because, due to its isolated location, life in the labor compounds was so expensive.

Their complaints nevertheless fell on deaf ears among the European managers. The expats often repeated that "$100 is a lot of money out here" and asserted that the locals should be "really thankful to the company because they are making much more money than they would make otherwise." Similar refrains can be heard in mines, oil rigs, plantations, ranches, and timber concessions all over the world. Again and again existing poverty is used as a reason, excuse, and justification for low wages (Appel 2019a, 194). The CTI managers indeed took low pay for their workers as a simple fact of life, disregarding how these salaries were actually a legacy of colonial and imperial histories that still affect racialized distributions of wealth and poverty, inequalities that to this day operate as conditions of possibility for natural resource extraction (Jobson 2019).

For many workers, these locally high but globally low wages were a source of frustration. Joseph, for instance, often said his salary might enable him to "live today" but did not allow him to "save for the future." Whenever he heard his expat bosses tell his colleagues that they "should be happy to have a job at all," he angrily contrasted his own situation with the Europeans' own "astronomical" wages and "luxurious" living conditions. Across the Congolese timber sector, labor was indeed profoundly racialized. In many concessions, a glass ceiling prevented Congolese from attaining higher positions. Even Congolese staff, engineers, and agronomists were paid less than nonnationals who held similar positions. CTI often defended its wage policies by emphasizing that it simply paid its employees according to their "skill level" and "appropriate category" (Appel 2019a, 62). But to its workers, racial inconsistencies revealed how salaries were actually determined by pigmentation.

CTI workers particularly complained about the lack of opportunities to advance through the pay scale. Blaise, for instance, a young business school graduate from Kinshasa, admitted that, even after several years at the concession, he was still at the level of trainee (*stagiaire*). "The absence of promotion truly depresses me," he said. "They keep us at the level of blacks [*nègres*] although I know my job better than anyone!" The structural racism that constantly thwarted his aspirations contributed to his drinking habits. Indebted to several barkeepers, he was eventually arrested and lost his job.

This feeling of being stuck and unable to take control of one's future significantly contributed to the ecstatogenic atmosphere of work at the CTI concession. The starkly racialized inequality of pay, living conditions, and promotions indeed confronted workers with a situation in which they were constantly put and kept "in their place," despite their dreams and ambitions. Together with expat managers' racist remarks, misplaced jokes, and fits of anger, the racialized absence of prospects made the CTI concession into a place that could viscerally throw workers out of themselves (Fanon 1967). Many expressed their anger and frustration but usually only behind their bosses' backs. Rarely did it lead to revolts, work stoppages, or strike actions. In a milieu of scarce opportunities for earning a salary, the threat of being sacked was enough to make most workers bite their tongues.

Moreover, many of these men were happy to have a contract at all. Others, working only as day laborers, were in an even more precarious position. Whereas contract workers were often skilled or semiskilled workers who had already worked in other concessions farther away or grown up in labor camps of other companies, day laborers were usually men from the immediate environment of the logging concession. For the expat managers, day labor was a way of "absorbing some of the massive demand for jobs" coming from the local villagers, many of whom were put to work as temporary guards for the time CTI operated in forest blocks belonging to their communities.

But the company also relied on day workers on a more permanent basis. They were indeed an attractive option because they were substantially cheaper than contractual workers and, also, could be easily discarded. During our fieldwork, their number fluctuated between 30 and 120, according to immediate labor needs. Yet because Congolese labor laws allowed day workers to work for only a maximum of twenty-two days over a period of two months, CTI had resorted to a rotation system in which one group worked while those in another group were furloughed (put to "rest") for two months. Hence, although these men were paid the legally guaranteed minimum salary of sixteen hundred Congolese francs ($1.70 per day), their average salary was actually only about $16 per month as a result of these obligatory resting periods. Expat managers often claimed that day workers could easily return to farming while they were laid off, but, in practice, combining farming and work for CTI was extremely difficult due to their absences during key stages in the agricultural season.

The actual hiring of both day laborers and contractual workers was the direct responsibility of senior Congolese staff who acted as gatekeepers and brokers in recruitment processes. The European expats, on the other hand, kept a relatively low profile in the messy business of offering jobs to abundant candidates. As a result, Congolese staff members like André, the forest camp engineer, or Mbadu, the chief of personnel from the river camp, wielded considerable power in distributing employment opportunities and often acted as patrons for the men they hired.[1] Olivier, for instance, still ceded Mbadu, who had employed him, part of his salary in return for his continuing protection. Most new CTI employees also entered into hierarchical training relationships with a more experienced work father (*papa ya mosala*). This work kinship, which could last for several years, implied a regular exchange of gifts and money for skills, advice, and support. In this way, team overseers could, for example, generate extra revenue by claiming a part of the salaries of workers whose names they had introduced to their bosses.

Yet, job trading was only one of many opportunities for making extra money on the side. Truck drivers, for instance, could easily increase their income by secretly transporting people and goods in return for cash or forest products. Prospectors, trackers, and tree fellers developed networks for buying meat from hunters and selling it in the camps, despite CTI's efforts to prohibit the trade in "bushmeat" (*nyama ya zamba*). Mechanics and warehouse employees set up private businesses in spare parts, often with the help of their superiors. And, as we will see in chapter 4, many forest workers sold petrol, diesel, and motor oils to smugglers. These opportunities for making illicit money were at least as important as regular compensation to render work for CTI attractive. Moreover, these tricks and schemes to con their European bosses were also a way of taking back control from a company that was extremely unwilling to assume its responsibilities toward its workers

(Li 2019). As a risky means to partially redress racialized injustices, they too were part of the ecstatic realities of rainforest logging.

Rhythms at Work

Industrial timber production in tropical rainforests requires a series of different activities. While operators wielding enormous chainsaws are often taken as paradigmatic loggers, their work actually depends on—and feeds into—that of other work teams and only forms a relatively minor part of the overall productive and logistical process. Companies that work according to a selective felling model, wherein only the most commercially valuable trees are cut down, first need to have a good knowledge of the distribution of tree species and their dimensions so as to abstract and separate these trees from the forest. Moreover, in order to align and control the activities of different labor crews, they need to geographically standardize their concessions.

For CTI, timber production therefore really started when *prospecting* teams created a geometrical grid of paths in the forest and identified, measured, marked, and mapped all harvestable trees. They were succeeded by *tracking* teams that opened up small tracks between marked trees and the nearest by logging roads, which were themselves built and maintained by *road construction* teams. *Felling* teams then cut down the tracked trees so that *skidders* from the production team could drag them out of the forest toward the road, where their coworkers *loaded* them onto logging trucks. The *transport* team then transported these logs from the forest to the company site on the Congo River, where people from the *beach* team unloaded the logs and piled up until they were put on barges or made into rafts to be towed by boat to Kinshasa.

Other CTI employees remained at the work sites near the labor compounds. The mechanics of the *garage* team, for instance, repaired chainsaws, bulldozers, skidders, trucks, and jeeps. The extensive *general services* team comprised office clerks, telephone operators, company guards, and so-called forest management workers who had to ensure the sustainability of logging operations and take care of relations with surrounding villages. This team also included cartographers and statisticians who generated maps, graphs, charts, and numbers that enabled managers, engineers, and team bosses to keep track of changing realities. Finally, there was the *construction and sawmill* team, whose carpenters and masons were responsible for building health centers and schools in villages where CTI had agreed to realize community projects.

The following sections take a closer look at five specific stages of industrial rainforest logging: prospecting, tracking, roadbuilding, tree felling, and skidding/loading. As we will see, the practical, material, and technical differences between these phases made for rather different work experiences, rhythms, and disciplines. Moreover, although there was some employee movement between crews with similar levels of technical skills—such as prospectors and trackers or skidder and bulldozer drivers—many workers nevertheless specialized over the long run. As such, different work teams carried specific identities and had reputations based on occupational distinctions beyond their common identification as forest workers (*basali ya zamba*).

Logging was also widely seen as a job for men only. It was no coincidence that, with the exception of four company nurses and one female assistant mechanic, all the CTI employees were men. Just like hunting or the initial stages of farming (when new fields are opened up), finding, cutting, and moving massive trees was indeed considered an inherently *male* activity in a forest that was itself symbolically thought of as a predominantly *female* space. Moreover, because different activities had different connotations of risk, danger, and violence that were differently gendered, CTI workers often competed among each other for the status of the real forester (*vrai forestier*) or logger who could best embody or "enact" the corporation (Welker 2014).[2]

PROSPECTING

Prospectors formed by far the largest group of workers in the CTI concession. Unlike their colleagues from other crews, they stayed deep in the forest for weeks on end without returning to the labor compounds. Usually each prospection round (*campagne*) took about three weeks and was alternated with a one-week resting period. The entire prospection crew consisted of two *counting* teams and four *trailing* teams, each of which comprised sixteen workers: a team overseer, thirteen prospectors, a cook, and a hunter. Because local villagers often worked as temporary aides, prospection camps also produced a relatively secluded social space where workers (*travailleurs*) and villagers (*villageois*) operated side by side, in contrast to other labor teams further down the production chain. Concession residents indeed provided much of the local knowledge CTI needed to log the forest, while workers standardized this knowledge into lists, maps, and numbers.

Every morning at about 6 a.m., the prospection teams left their makeshift camp in the forest and walked to their respective working areas, where, after a quick breakfast, they started their activities. The trailing teams were the first to enter the forest. They were responsible for materializing the rectangular tracks that constituted a geographical reference for the entire production process. Teams of six trailers thereby cut open tracks of different widths in the undergrowth, creating a standardized grid of trails. First, a compass holder directed two cutters along straight lines to make initial openings. Then, three cleaners followed and further opened up the trail. Together they laid out the main east-west tracks that separated one thousand–hectare forest blocks. Interior tracks then divided these blocks in two rows of ten smaller forest plots, which were traversed in the middle by an intermediary track from east to west, a secondary track from north to south, and a supplementary track every 250 meters. Along these tracks the trailers planted numbered poles in the ground to mark regular intervals, thus creating a reference system in which each tree could be mapped.

After the trailing teams completed their tasks, their colleagues from the counting teams started to find, identify, mark, and record all exploitable trees in the thus created forest blocks. Ten counters systematically moved forward in each plot along a straight line, cutting their way with a machete and looking for trees in their path. On either side of the plot, two pointers moved along with them on the forest tracks created by the trailing teams. As they moved, the counters shouted to one another to keep a constant distance of twenty-five meters between them while the pointers monitored the overall pace, echoing their shouts with orders like "put yourself on a line" (*alignement*), "look for the tree" (*luka nzete*), "eyes up" (*miso na likolo*), "eyes down" (*miso na nse*), or "let's go" (*toleka*).

When a counter perceived an exploitable tree, he loudly called, "Tree!" (*nzete*), and the entire team stopped for it to be measured. He then shouted its species, diameter, and estimated quality to the nearest pointer, who recorded this information on an exploitation card. The pointer then shouted back the tree's prospection number, which the counter painted on the trunk base. The pointer thereupon planted a marked stick in the forest track to indicate the tree's position.

In the evening all pointers carefully checked their exploitation cards, which indicated the position of all prospected trees in squares of twenty-five by twenty-five meters. These small maps were indispensable to the company because they allowed for the transmission of updated geographical information to subsequent work crews. Possible errors made during the prospection phase could therefore severely hamper activities further down the line. In this sense, prospection was effectively the prime basis of logging. And prospectors often emphasized that, without them, their colleagues would be lost—literally.

Prospectors also considered themselves indispensable in another sense. Ntema, for instance, the overseer of one of the counting teams, often stated that "prospection is the field school [*école de terrain*] of forestry." Prospection was indeed where many CTI forest workers started their careers and became loggers in the first place. "But," Ntema added, "only some are really strong enough to stay with us." For many, the isolated life in the forest away from their family was an undeniable challenge. Yet workers who had not spent time in the secluded prospection camps were often considered not to be real foresters at all. In this sense, prospection was, literally and metaphorically, an initiation into logging.

Ntema had effectively trained many workers in the secrets of tropical dendrology. An experienced man in his late forties from Mai Ndombe, he had arrived at CTI after the war in 2003. He was extremely proud of his detailed knowledge of different tree species, which he mostly recognized by the color, texture, and smell of their bark. Having worked for several logging companies, he knew the names of trees in many local languages as well as in French and Latin. During our trips in the forest he often pointed out subtle ecological variations in the vegetation and accurately predicted the occurrence of specific species. As part of the inner circle of experienced prospectors, he also had served as a work father to several newcomers.

Despite this distinction between old and new workers, the prospection camps were nonetheless spaces of remarkable freedom and camaraderie in which work hierarchies often seemed rather relaxed. Like other team overseers, Ntema, for instance, insisted on having a spot in the large communal huts made out of sticks, leaves, and plastic canvas where workers and villagers slept side by side on makeshift beds. Only Paul, the general supervisor, erected his private army-colored tent in the middle of the camp. As the only Congolese staff member present, he enjoyed considerable autonomy within CTI and was often referred to as "the king of the forest" (*le roi de la forêt*).[3] But although he often urged his workers to keep up the speed in order to meet monthly targets, Paul was also a quiet, soft-spoken person who was greatly respected by his men.

The relatively egalitarian atmosphere of prospection really motivated its workers. While Paul was served his food separately from the rest, his team overseers practically shared the same life as their crew. Together they formed a close-knit group of men who spent most of their time away from their families. Notwithstanding the harshness of life in the forest, many prospectors indeed seemed to enjoy their jobs—in particular, the fresh meat provided daily by their hunters and the drinks shared around small fires at night. "After work, we can relax because there's no trouble here," one of the prospectors told me. Many also intimately knew each other's lives and covered for each other's secrets. It was, for instance, widely known that forest wives (*basi ya zamba*) accompanied prospectors from one campsite to the next, cooking food and selling liquor. But whenever the men's actual spouses dared travel to the forest to chase away their rivals, the prospectors closed ranks.

The striking commensality and sexual license of the prospection camps accounted for a particular sociality that somehow set these forest spaces apart from the labor compounds. Literally away from family responsibilities and village moralities, the camps offered a space of relative freedom in which a close brotherhood could be created. Moreover, as whites rarely visited, oversight from expat managers was rather distant. As such, prospecting allowed for a "liminal" atmosphere of temporary escape from racist structures and for a "communitas" of workers under the guidance of respected and experienced teachers (Turner 1969). Furthermore, unlike in subsequent production phases (discussed below), there was no fuel to be traded with smugglers, no spare parts to be sold, and no machines, chainsaws, or batteries that villagers could loot or sabotage. Life in the prospection camps was therefore fairly easy and conflict-free, and many talked about it with remarkable warmth. Armand, for instance, an office clerk who had originally started as a prospector, told me that "back there in the forest, we were our own bosses. But here [in the office], we are only machines."

This relative freedom explains why, in the labor compounds, prospectors were often viewed as troublesome (*ya mobulu*). But the forest also seemed to require men with specific skills to deal with its dangers. Widely associated with the night, the forest was indeed considered a pre-social space of morally ambivalent forces against and upon which diurnal village life was built. Prospectors were therefore always a little suspect. How could they stay in the forest for so long? And what deals did they strike with the villagers in their midst? Moreover, when prospectors returned to their families for a week of rest, they were believed to reemerge from the bush (*la brousse*) with increased sexual potency. As such, it seemed as if they physically introduced a queer transgressive element of forest sexuality and sociality into the already vulnerable domesticity of the labor camps.

Working as a prospector therefore came with particular gendered and sexualized connotations. But what is more, because prospecting was felt to be the initiatory field school of forestry, *all* loggers were in the end somehow associated with the real and imagined freedom of forest life. Yet the specific ways in which their identities and practices were gendered nonetheless differed between work teams.

TRACKING

The first crews to enter forest blocks after prospection were the tracking teams that had to relocate all mapped trees and open up clearly signed tracks toward them so that tree fellers and skidders would be able to find them easily. Trackers also color-marked special areas and individual trees that needed to be protected from possible damage—such as hunting camps, zones close to waterways, tree species with a cultural value, important fruit species, and so-called future trees that were too small to fell. At the time of our fieldwork, the tracking team consisted of twenty-two workers: sixteen cutters, four pointers, one overseer, and one assistant overseer. Like the trailers and counters from the prospecting teams, cutters were often men from the immediate environment of the CTI concession, whereas overseers and pointers were usually from farther away.

Trucks brought the tracking crews to their work sites in the morning and picked them up in the evening. In four groups (of four cutters and one pointer each), these men walked along the forest tracks the prospection teams had created. Guided by the exploitation cards, the pointers looked for marked poles that indicated the nearby presence of one or more exploitable trees. Upon encountering such a sign, one cutter stayed behind on the main track while his colleagues moved inside the forest block to find the specific tree. To keep contact with one another, they shouted the name of its species and number, often as if over a radio—for instance, "tola, tola, tola number 51, 51, 51 . . . over?"[4] After finding the tree, the cutters double-checked its measurements and opened up a new path. To find the shortest way to the main track, they shouted to their colleague who had stayed behind. Then they planted a new pole along the road that indicated the number of trees found at this location. Finally, the overseer updated the exploitation card.

In contrast to the prospection teams, who advanced at a relatively quick pace, trackers usually operated more slowly. It was, for instance, not uncommon for them to stop working around noon and linger in the forest until the truck came to pick them up at around 4 p.m. In the meantime, some of them cut sticks or leaves as construction material to sell. Others bathed in a clear river or dozed off. For their managers, it was extremely hard to control and check their use of time. Like prospectors, trackers were indeed difficult to track because they were hidden in the forest without making noise or leaving material traces along the roads. For this reason, and perhaps paradoxically, the work floor seemed a space of relative freedom from direct oversight. While the team overseer obviously needed to make sure his men finished the job they had been assigned, together they actively maintained the illusion that they needed more time to reach their targets than they actually did.

This relaxed rhythm was also reflected in the often-provocative songs trackers sang in order to remain in contact with one another in the thick undergrowth. In some of these songs, they for instance playfully replaced the names of women and girls with those of commercial tree species they were looking for. Simon, a young day laborer from Mombwassa and one of the team's cutters, once sang this version of "Malewa," a popular song by the well-known Congolese musician Werrasson:

> Mwana natikaka moke sima ekoli.
> Oya oye eee, sima ekoli.
> Tola nalonaka moke eee, sima ekoli.
> Oya oye eee, sima ekoli.

> The child I left small, the buttocks have grown.
> Oya oye eee, the buttocks have grown.
> The small tola tree that I planted eee, the buttocks have grown.
> Oya oye eee, the buttocks have grown.

As the original song and accompanying dance refer to a young girl who has grown up and whose buttocks now capture the attention of men, the trackers' version explicitly describes the trees they were looking for *as girls*. This striking feminization is not a coincidence. It brings to mind the ways in which local hunters also gendered their prey. The hunters from Yambili, for instance, whom we occasionally accompanied on multiple day trips in the forest, explicitly referred to the animal they were tracing as "my wife" (*mwasi na ngai*). And they sang seductive songs that lured the animal into making itself visible. In its seducing, gendering, and eroticizing dimension, tracking was therefore surprisingly similar to hunting. Unlike prospectors, who systematically combed through the forest in straight lines without knowing what they would find, trackers—just like hunters—followed trails and traces that had been left in the forest. These signs operated as landmarks or blazes that, as Victor Turner (1967, 48) famously wrote about Ndembu hunters, connected "the unknown to the known." Both hunting and tracking therefore appeared to call for similar seductive capacities to find and capture what was not yet seen.

Moreover, it seems that trackers thereby drew from central African cosmologies in which the forest itself is considered a female space, in opposition to the village as a male space (e.g., De Boeck 1991, 123; Turner 1969, 58). Male farmers indeed literally *penetrated* the forest, that is, they opened up, cut down, and burned vegetation so that their wives could cultivate new fields. Hunters feminized and seduced their prey to provide their families with meat. And trackers sang about the growing buttocks of trees, as if hunting for girls and following their traces.

ROADBUILDING

With the next stage in the production process, we leave behind the quiet atmosphere of singing and walking through the forest and enter a noisy world of heavy machinery. Indeed, what the prospectors and trackers did manually, the road construction team did mechanically: open up the (female) forest and create the infrastructure that transformed trees into "natural resources" ready for the taking (Richardson and Weszkalnys 2014). As we thus move from relative silence to noise, we will see how seduction ceded to destruction and love songs made room for war magic. At the same time, the number of local villagers employed in the forest teams dropped significantly.

Jean-Louis was one of the four bulldozer drivers who, together with a grader driver, four chainsaw operators, and their overseer made up the road construction team. He was born in 1962 in Mokaria, a rubber and cacao plantation to the south of the CTI concession, where his father was a carpenter. He told us how his self-described turbulent character as a boy had caused him problems in the missionary school he attended. He quit school and, unable to find a job, left the Itimbiri region to try his luck in the artisanal gold mines along the Uele River to the north. He only returned when CTI opened its logging concession and was hired as a day worker to build the new labor camps. Later he was promoted to assistant driver on a large bulldozer in the road construction team, where his work father taught him how to drive. When Jean-Louis received his own *numéro de matricule*, he was reassigned to a smaller machine on the road maintenance team. Two years later, however, after his work father was fired because of supposed fuel theft, Jean-Louis took his place.

Like his colleagues, Jean-Louis had a very personal and intimate relationship with his bulldozer (see also Rolston 2013). Because he knew his machine so well, he claimed he had become irreplaceable for CTI. Indeed, nobody knew the capricious engine and idiosyncratic gears of his Caterpillar as well as Jean-Louis did. And he was always eager to show me his skills. Every morning he found his vehicle along the road where he had parked it for the night. As the most experienced driver, he was usually the first to push his machine through the forest along lines set out by his overseer. After this initial penetration, the other bulldozers joined him to broaden the track by pushing aside trees and removing roots and stumps. In the process, the conductors frequently had to drive their machines to their limits when attacking (*kobunda*) the biggest trees, which made them shake and tremble in their reinforced cabins.

As soon as the road was sufficiently opened up, a grader machine evened out the surface and chainsaw operators felled adjacent trees on both sides of the new road so as to illuminate its surface and speed up its drying. Most of these roads were temporary exploitation roads and would thus disappear as soon as logging activities moved on. But some were permanent logging roads that needed to be covered with laterite to avoid erosion. These roads also had to be permanently maintained in order to keep the always encroaching forest at bay.

Like other CTI workers, bulldozer drivers liked to describe themselves as strong men. They specifically said they were the ones who really knew how to enter virgin forest (*kokota na forêt vierge*). While this act of penetration can be read as a violent opening up of a feminized forest space, the gendered symbolism of roadbuilding was nonetheless ambivalent. Rather than seduce feminized trees or violate a female forest, road builders usually talked about *attacking* strong and resisting trunks. They thereby seemed to mobilize a logic of combat and war rather than love and seduction. And with it, the gender of trees began to shift.

FELLING

Although their chainsaws often symbolize the violence of logging, the CTI felling team was surprisingly small in comparison to other crews. Its overseer coordinated only six trios of chainsaw operators, assistants, and clerks. Every morning the clerks walked their groups toward the mapped trees on their exploitation cards, while the operators carried their chainsaws and the assistants dragged along five liters of motor oil, ten liters of gasoline, an extra saw blade, a sharpener, and a machete. At the foot of each tree the operators sharpened their machine, and the assistants cleaned the tree trunk of plants and mosses. Then they started the standard procedure for controlled tree felling described in the prologue: they estimated the tree's most probable falling direction, opened up escape routes through the undergrowth, and carefully cut the trunk until the tree fell down.

Just like the trackers, felling teams operated deep inside forest blocks. But the far-reaching sound of their chainsaws easily betrayed their positions and gave CTI managers a crude indication of their progress. For this reason, their work rhythm was less relaxed. Yet fellers also knew that Jens and Michel returned to their bungalows for a nap during the hot afternoon hours. Many therefore tried to complete their share of ten trees per day before 1 p.m. and then took a rest. "It simply doesn't pay off to continue working," one of them told Freddy. "Last month we logged thirteen or fourteen trees per day, but our premiums were still the same." In theory, the system of individualized bonuses should have motivated them to continue working, but most fellers did not feel the difference and often assessed that the extra money they could make did not compensate for the associated risks.

Despite the precautions taken and the technical trainings provided, tree felling indeed remained a dangerous business. Chainsaws often blocked and kicked back, trees suddenly changed direction, and heavy branches fell without warning. Trees, as fellers often said, seemed to have their own will. Because of these dangers, Joseph—the chainsaw operator we met at the opening of this chapter—explicitly described tree felling as a fight (*etumba*) between loggers and trees: "When I see a tree before me . . . that is to say, when he stands upright, he behaves like a man. So, you fight. When you cut him and he falls, you have won. But he can also get back at you, and then you are gone. You never know."

Many tree fellers therefore reinforced their bodies and spirits with alcohol or cannabis and protected themselves with prayers, signs of the cross, or ancestral medicines (*nkisi ya bakoko*). Joseph, for instance, often bought protections from a specialist (*nganga nkisi* or *féticheur*) from Yandjombo who claimed to use old Mbudza war magic to produce new combinations that protected loggers in their daily battles. Although many tree fellers were men from outside the region, they nevertheless consumed and mobilized local mystical forces provided by experts who knew the forest, its spirits, and history.

At this stage of the production process, logging was thus clearly spoken of as *war*: trees fought back, and chainsaw operators saw themselves as fighters protected by war medicine. This logic is strikingly different from the hunting, farming, and growing metaphors we encountered earlier. The image of the growing tree as a young girl in the song of the tracking teams indeed seems directly opposite to the tree as a male opponent in the stories of chainsaw and bulldozer operators. Sawing down trees or crushing them under caterpillar tracks were masculinizing acts of aggression whereby the body of an opponent-tree was eliminated, falling down from its erect combat verticality to a harmless horizontality.

The gender of trees was therefore flexible, relational, and context specific (De Boeck 1994).[5] While prospectors and trackers could mobilize ideas and metaphors of seduction that resonated with the transformative, and ultimately reproductive, practices of hunting or farming, tree fellers and road builders understood their activities through an ecstatic logic of combat and destruction whereby they killed and took down body trees while protecting themselves with medicines, prayers, and intoxicants.

SKIDDING AND LOADING

The next stage of industrial logging is called the production phase and consists of *skidding*—dragging trees out of the forest to the road—and *loading*—putting these trunks on logging trucks. The men working for the production team frequently asserted that, while previous stages were "mere preparation," they were the only ones "who actually *produced* something." Hence, the name of their team. Ignoring the labor time spent by previous work crews, they strategically positioned themselves as the unique producers of value (Marx 1990, 129). Indeed, as long as a tree, whether prospected or logged, stayed in the forest, its value—as a product of labor—remained dormant. But as soon as it was moved out of the forest toward the road, and thus toward the market—where trees were eventually commodified as tropical timber—the frantic run for profit could begin. Hence the nervousness that generally accompanied this time of so-called production.

Every morning the skidding and loading teams were dropped off at the production camp, which, depending on the progress of work, moved to a different place every two weeks. At its center was a large tent where a radio operator communicated with his colleagues from the river camp and forest camp. Around this central tent, company guards and policemen erected shelters and women sold food from makeshift constructions. Moreover, as a hotspot for the fuel trade, smugglers also always loitered nearby because of the presence of heavy machines and vehicles. Hunters and farmers also often visited. When CTI staff and expat managers were not around, many used the radio to chat with family, friends, and business partners in regions without cell phone coverage. As a lively and mobile place with its own group of habitués, the production camp had a real frontier feeling—a mixture of impatience, freedom, and risk.

After breakfast all team overseers assembled in the central tent to discuss the day's work with Benjamin, the general production overseer, and André, the engineer from the forest camp who received daily radio instructions from Jens. There were three skidding teams, counting six men each: two skidder operators, two assistant drivers, a clerk, and a chainsaw operator. And there was one loading team, consisting of two loader operators and two clerks. As in the previous mechanized phases, the skilled drivers were usually migrants from beyond the Itimbiri region, but in comparison to road builders or tree fellers, they were often younger men.

Skidding was perhaps the most visceral of all logging activities. Skidder drivers had to push their powerful vehicles into the forest toward recently logged trees, guided by their clerk's directions and trying to evade wasps' nests and termite hills. Their huge wheels thereby ran into a wall of greenery, smashing smaller trees and pushing others aside. Upon arrival, they maneuvered the logged tree so that their assistants could attach the skidder's cable around its trunk. Pulling the cable toward the machine, they then dragged the tree to the road. In theory, skidders had to follow the tracks their colleagues from the tracking teams had created and thus avoid damaging the surrounding forest. In practice, however, skidding was a messy activity. Cables came off, trunks got stuck, and biting insects made drivers want to proceed as fast as possible.

Once the skidding teams had brought a number of trees to a landing along the road, the loading team could start its activities. Its chainsaw operators first removed the ends of each trunk. Clerks then marked the trunks with individual numbers and a code corresponding to the logging permit of the forest block where they had been felled. The trees were then carefully measured, their volumes calculated. Then they were loaded onto big logging trucks. At the time of our fieldwork, loader operators had to work in two shifts so as to assure a continuous capacity for the trucks that arrived all day from the river camp. Once on the truck, tree trunks were fastened with metal cables, and a clerk filled in a waybill form. The driver then drove his truck to the company port, where his colleagues from the beach team unloaded the trunks on a pile ready for transport to Kinshasa.

Skidders frequently described their work with the same combat and war metaphors as tree fellers and road constructors. Their job was indeed extremely violent in nature. Loaders, on the other hand, considered their work more like a game. Jules, a young man from Basankusu, for instance, took great delight in showing off his agility in moving trees while playfully driving his loader backward, dropping heavy tree trunks on trucks from dangerous heights, "accidentally" blocking the road for others, or having his machine make as much noise as possible.

In his classic ethnographic study of factory work, the sociologist Michael Burawoy (1979) described such behavior as the game of "making out." Yet, while for Burawoy playing was ultimately a mechanism for "manufacturing consent" among factory workers, Jules's game was as much about bending and breaking the rules as about playing along. Rather than generating consent, his playfulness indeed produced and confirmed a sense of independence and control. A notorious drinker, smoker, and womanizer, Jules had been fired several times by previous employers, but he claimed he never had to look for work. He asserted to have "his own ways" of making sure jobs mystically came to him. As long as they did, he could conceive of both his job and his life as a game, which enabled him "to renegotiate the given, experiment with alternatives [and] countermand in [his] actions and imagination the situations that appear[ed] to circumscribe, rule, and define [him]" (Jackson 1998, 28–29).

Production teams were nevertheless subjected to strict company control. While managers and engineers often left earlier production stages relatively unsupervised, so that trackers or tree fellers could loiter in the forest, skidders and loaders usually had to continue their jobs until dusk. Congolese and European managers were also often physically present around the production camp and monitored statistics daily. Under continuous supervision, skidders and loaders therefore experienced considerable stress. Some, like Jules, took this pressure as a challenge and tried to remain on top of it. Others slowly suffered.

Yet provocations and challenges to white authority remained possible. One story in particular never failed to have workers burst out laughing when it was retold behind the backs of their bosses (Scott 1990). Workers from different crews told of an assistant skidder driver who, one day, arrived at the production camp too drunk to work. When Jens turned up to give his orders, the young man climbed on top of a truck cabin and started dancing with a chainsaw as if embracing a woman for a rumba. His colleagues tried to stop him from playing the clown (*faire le fou*), but the driver ignored their calls. Irritated, Jens turned around and shouted in his heavy Danish accent something that sounded like *deucendeu*—broken French for *descendez* (get down). But to everyone's amusement, the dancing worker, undisturbed, replied in Lingala "What? What does he mean? 'Descendez' or 'deux cents francs'?" and put out his hands to receive the imagined two hundred Congolese francs. According to bystanders, this made the old Jens so angry that he almost lost his balance and had to grab the door of his jeep to get back to his feet.

Discipline and Control

In *Outline of a Theory of Practice* (1977, 7), Pierre Bourdieu argued that power is often about "playing on the time, or rather the *tempo*, of the action." The preceding snapshots of work indeed illustrate how, as surveillance increased along the production process, the tempi of successive labor teams accelerated accordingly. While earlier work crews could afford to slow down or get away with extensive foot-dragging and daydreaming, later teams were subjected to more frantic work rhythms. Many also had to make up for money lost due to rainfall, roadblocks, and fuel shortages. Under the nervous conditions left by the 2008 financial crisis, these accelerations, as well as the playfulness and masculine bravura they generated, were palpable manifestations of the ecstatic temporalities of timber production.

Making workers accelerate is obviously a common aim in industrial processes. But why did CTI not invest more in controlling and disciplining some of its scheming, playing, sleeping, and procrastinating work crews? And how did it, at the same time, make others work so hard? This final section shows how the company was able to largely maintain sufficient worker output *without* elaborate or expensive regimes of discipline and control. As such, it provides a first grounded reflection on corporate power—and its limits.

We have already seen how and why CTI's system of individualized work bonuses largely missed its aim. Yet to fully understand the ways in which Jens and other expat managers tried to increase output, we need to take a look at the overall monitoring of the production process. Industrial logging does indeed need daily monitoring because it is a chain of activities wherein the actual output of each level immediately determines the input of the next. In the concession, this monitoring was largely achieved through the continuous production and updating of maps and figures through which managers tried to read the actual state of production, identify bottlenecks, and take action accordingly. Cartography and statistics were thereby indispensable. A brief description of the everyday production of numbers, graphs, charts, and maps will therefore help to see the level of control CTI was able to exert over its workers.

Two offices in the forest camp generated, processed, and packaged different kinds of data. The first was the statistics office, where, every morning, team overseers dropped off standardized forms that indicated the output of their teams from the previous day. Laurent, the assistant statistician, double-checked these forms and then handed them over to Marcel, the database manager, who brought these data together in a single chart that summarized the daily output figures of all forest teams. He then manually imported these output statistics into a monthly table, filling in the line below the statistics of the previous day. Through this table he calculated the so-called advances or number of logs waiting in between two production levels.

Because Jens always insisted on seeing these advances before he left for the forest, Marcel had to transmit the updated figures via radio to the office near the Congo River each morning before 9 a.m. These daily advances allowed Jens to keep track of the actual work done, estimate delays, and target those teams that seemed to be slacking during his inspection tours. Yet it was not always easy to discover the reasons behind apparent bottlenecks. Because of his limited French and practically nonexistent Lingala, Jens could only talk to team overseers, who often came up with what he called "easy excuses" for low outputs. Moreover, as the story about the drunken skidder illustrates, Jens was notorious for his fits of anger. Frustrated by his inability to communicate, he often shouted and hurled epithets at his workers—who usually underwent these insults in silence, fearing possible sanctions, transfers, or dismissals if they talked back. In the wake of such outbursts, team overseers made sure their men worked harder. But, after a while, work rhythms tended to slow down again, and new inspection visits became necessary.

Beyond calculating daily advances that allowed for on-the-spot control visits, the statistics office also monitored the production process on a longer term. Marcel indeed transcribed all data into computer software specifically designed for keeping track of activities. At the click of a mouse he could produce colorful graphs and neat tables that reflected specifically requested summaries. Moreover, this software also recorded the movement of each individual log throughout the entire production process. It ultimately referred to the physical numbers that clerks from the felling and production teams hammered into individual tree trunks as well as into the stumps left in the forest. In theory, this tracking system guaranteed the traceability of all timber originating from the concession. In practice, however, inconsistencies, incorrect numbers, doubles, and disappearing trees were a constant headache that undermined the purportedly scientific basis of sustainable forestry.

Alongside statistics, mapping was equally fundamental for keeping track of a production process that was scattered over a large area. Two cartographers constantly produced maps. Désiré, the oldest, drew his daily maps by hand, while Dieudonné, the youngest, digitalized spatial data in a geographic information system on his computer. On the wall of their office hung a large map of the concession area; frequently updated, it showed the positions of past work sites as well as the location of current work teams. On the other wall, six chalk paper maps provided a more detailed view of the present state of activities in the various rectangular forest plots where work was taking place. These were crucial spatial references for Jens, Michel, André, Emile, and the different team overseers who, by a single look at these hand-drawn maps, could see what was going on in the concession.

To a certain extent, cartography and statistics had to enable company control and surveillance on the work floor. But elegant graphs, precise charts, and colorful maps did more than that. They conveyed an ideal of scientific and rational order that had to prevail over the disorder that the expat managers so often felt to be lurking around the corner. Maps and tables therefore became matters of "deep personal concern" (Fabian 2000, 203), and much effort was put into finding exactly the right colors and graph types that most immediately conveyed the traceability and accountability of sustainable forestry.

At the same time, however, CTI managers were painfully aware of the constructed nature of their cherished data—and hence of their inherent fallibility. Errors and inconsistencies had to be dealt with on a daily basis, and numbers often did not add up. Cartographers and statisticians were adept at cleaning up messy data and compensating for gaps, so as to evoke a soothing reality of order and control. But staff often worried about the lack of fit between realities on the ground and their representation on paper (Harvey and Knox 2015). Maps, charts, figures, and statistics were indeed not as trustworthy as they were reported to be. Efficient inspection rounds on the work floor were therefore not straightforward, and the number of logs that were overlooked and forgotten in the forest functioned as an annoying reminder of the practical limits to dreams of panoptic surveillance.

Furthermore, because work teams were dispersed in inaccessible places, actual control was frustrating, ephemeral, and sometimes illusionary. Workers also knew very well how to strategically maintain output levels high enough to avoid attention but low enough to spare their bodies. Many CTI employees were experts at what James Scott (1985) called "everyday forms of resistance": sabotaging machinery to get extra days off, pretending to be sick, deviating from standard procedures to finish the job more quickly, or taking a friend or relative along for help. The quotidian struggle over the length of the working day, a battle Marx (1990, 352, 432) identified as the motor of class dynamics, was thus not so easily won by their employers. Because CTI was felt "not to take good care of its workers" and often literally intruded on their moments of rest—by requiring its employees to work after normal hours or on Sundays, for instance—workers effectively tried to reclaim some of this "stolen" time by sleeping in the forest, arriving late, or hiding when being looked for (Li 2019). The boundaries between work and leisure, and weekdays and weekends were therefore contested and frequently transgressed in both directions.

For these reasons, CTI seemed largely unable to impose a strict capitalist time regime on its workers. In itself, this is not surprising (Cooper 1992). In his masterly account of time and work discipline under industrial capitalism, E. P. Thompson (1967, 76) recognized that, even in strictly controlled factories, actual work rhythms often remained irregular. Notwithstanding "the supervision of labour; fines; bells and clocks; money incentives; preaching and schoolings," he wrote, everyday work patterns contained "alternate bouts of intense labour and of idleness, wherever men were in control of their own working lives" (90, 73). An ethnographic insight on work in the CTI concession however reveals that such control of one's life is not, as Thompson suggests, merely conditional on one's control over the means of production. It can also arise out of the very unpredictability and opacity of the labor process itself. Because of material, practical, and technical reasons, tropical rainforest logging indeed generated various forms of labor, some of which were highly mobile, autonomous, and relatively invisible and, therefore, prone to slip between attempts at company control and surveillance.[6]

Nonetheless, even without extensive control mechanisms or well-oiled technologies of surveillance, CTI was usually able to realize its targets. Jens's surprise visits, his anger, and the sheer threat of being sacked largely did the job. Although expat managers complained about laziness and a lack of discipline among their employees, workers continued to turn up and produce timber. In the end, CTI could count on the bare fact of regional poverty to motivate its workers. In a largely post-labor landscape where, as we will see in the next chapter, stable salaried work was scarce while memories of it still inspired the desire for distinction and urbanity, more elaborate disciplining mechanisms were simply unnecessary. CTI effectively realized its profits on the cheap, outsourcing the otherwise costly task of motivating its employees to a historical conjuncture in which it happened to find itself, to a labor market that was controlled by demand, and to a lingering legacy of colonialism and imperialism.

———————

This chapter kickstarted the ethnographic tracking of small events and larger structures, and of feelings and desires that contributed to the ecstatogenic atmosphere of rainforest logging. As announced in the introduction, ecstasis is a broad name for experiences and situations—such as vulnerability, penetrability, impotence, and precariousness—that arise when people are confronted with larger forces in their lives. As an existential *being-out-of-control*, it suggests how we are all entangled in dynamics not of our own making—a realization that, in turn, drives us to attempts to win back a sense of control. Attempts that always partially fail.

For the CTI managers, ecstasis lurked in constant irritations about failing work bonus systems, heavy rainfall, missing trees, cooked numbers, and the impossibility of effectively controlling and surveilling many of their work teams. Among their workers, ecstasis was palpable in frustrations generated by locally high but globally low wages, the impossibility of saving for a better future, fears of being sacked, stress about accelerating work rhythms, anger and humiliation in the face of racism, the use of intoxicants, the visceral excitement and masculine bravura of forest work, and competitions for the status of the real logger. It was also at work in risky schemes to make money on the side—in daydreaming, foot-dragging, and game-playing, and in joking and gossiping.

These examples show how and why ecstasis not only manifests itself as an experienced powerlessness whenever one finds oneself to be the plaything of seemingly uncontrollable forces. It is equally a dimension of the very *assumption* of power—as the joy, excess, and delirium that is temporarily generated when one is able to outwit circumstances. Feelings of control and loss of control indeed lie surprisingly close to each other. And, as we will see, the power one assumes can also be the power that pushes one aside. On that account, ecstasis is a tool to describe the affective dimension of the lived ebb and flow of relative power and powerlessness that seems to characterize the human condition.

Shell of a railroad passenger car in Bolende

3

Remembering Labor

EYENGA STILL REMEMBERED THE DAY IN 1988 when a small airplane kept flying back and forth over his campsite in the forest. He had just returned from the village of Yambili, where he sold his latest caterpillar harvest. For months people had been talking about the imminent return of the whites. It was a difficult time. The roads were overgrown, and most companies in the area had long closed their doors. Money was scarce. Small conflicts and witchcraft accusations characterized village life. Eyenga much preferred the forest: hunting, fishing, and collecting caterpillars. He had settled down at the exact place where his father had grown up before the Belgians forced the people from Yambili to move out of the forest and build a new village along the administrative road. Banana groves still indicated where they had cultivated their fields, and a majestic *eleko* tree symbolized their ancestral power.[1]

From the airplane, Michel looked at the hunting and fishing camps below. It would be a perfect place to build the future labor compound, he thought. CTI had sent him to Bumba for an aerial survey of the area where the company intended to start a new concession. The initial results were promising: vast stretches of relatively untouched forest and a good number of tree species that would fetch high enough prices for export to Europe. Apart from these campsites, the area seemed mostly devoid of human habitation. How he loved the ethereal beauty of the rainforest! In 1969, after military service and as a nineteen-year-old, he had left France for Côte d'Ivoire (Ivory Coast). Ever since, he had explored and mapped forests on the African continent. He had started working for CTI in 1977, and until that day in 1988, he could not imagine a better job—the forest had become his life.

Michel and Eyenga's paths would soon cross again. On his first prospecting trips, Michel often slept in Eyenga's hut. Eyenga sold him antelope and porcupines for dinner. Michel had also promised Eyenga a job. In the evenings they shared stories about the forest. And yet they spoke about very different worlds. For Eyenga, the forest had fundamentally changed—it was full of abandoned villages, colonial plantations, and deserted labor camps, where roads were overgrown and people, news, and memories now traveled over a network of old footpaths (*nzela ya bakoko*) that dated back to the time of the ancestors. For Michel, on the other hand, the forest was a relatively unspoiled wilderness, where farmers and hunters still lived in largely the same way as their forefathers. He regretted that the forest would now be "opened up" by his own doing, but he said the region badly needed investments, jobs, roads, schools, and hospitals.

While Michel hoped that CTI was about to bring development to a region stuck in time, for many villagers the logging company was merely the latest addition to a long series of foreigners who had extracted slaves, ivory, rubber, palm oil, cotton—and now timber—from the region (Giles-Vernick 2002). For them, history went far beyond the moment when Michel and Eyenga first met and CTI started its activities north of the Itimbiri River.

––––––––––

This chapter draws from popular memories and oral history, combined with archival research and references to scholarship, to sketch the history of the Itimbiri region.[2] It shows how, rather than an untouched relic of a primeval age, the rainforest in which CTI came to operate was marked by a long and violent history of extraction as well as by alternating experiences of connection and disconnection (Ferguson 1999). The first section provides a brief sketch of politico-economic transformations in the area from the seventeenth to the early twenty-first century. It shows how, after fierce initial resistance against colonial penetration, such unpopular measures as coercive labor recruitment, compulsory cultivation, head taxes, and obligatory road maintenance forcefully integrated the forest into a colonial economy. It then describes how, despite initial resistance, wage labor slowly emerged as a new ideal of modernity and masculinity for an influential minority of residents and newcomers to the region.

The second section shows how, for CTI workers, this old ideal of wage labor, though made precarious under postcolonial conditions, was still central to their performances of social distinction. It describes the 2010 Labor Day parade in Bumba to illustrate how salaries generated strong emotions that constituted the affective context in which loggers constructed self-respect. Then, to further historicize these feelings, the final section revisits places in the rainforest where past labor was still materially present in the landscape as traces left by colonial companies. What stories, memories, and countermemories did their physical remains trigger? And how did they shape contemporary performances of labor in a milieu of chronic unemployment, where salaried work was, for most, a distant memory?

A Brief History of (Dis)connection

The Congolese rainforest has always attracted people from distant lands. Long before European explorers sailed up its rivers, the area was already firmly integrated into a regional network of flows and transformations. Over several millennia, Western Bantu speakers had migrated from the Cameroonian grasslands to the Central African rainforest in search of what historian Jan Vansina (1990, 35) called "a mythical land of plenty." By the seventeenth century, horticulturalists densely populated the Itimbiri region alongside hunter-gatherer populations. The former adopted and developed new patrilineal kinship ideologies, which accompanied the growing inequalities of political power and military strength between villages (106–9). In the region, these villages came to be known by the name of their ancestral founder—prefixed by *ya*, meaning the children of—and were led by so-called big men (110).

In this context of nascent ethnic belonging, strengthened by new cults of ancestral skulls and relics, the people around the Itimbiri River became widely feared for their military force and war magic (117–18). Vansina also specifically mentions how "oral traditions from the Itimbiri Valley and eastward as far as . . . the Aruwimi tell of a vale of Bokombo, west of the middle Itimbiri, in Mbuja land" (118). This mythical vale, strongly associated with the later Mbudza ethnic identity, was "a seventeenth-century land of innovation and prestige, from which the new military, political, and religious style spread out northward and eastward and to which leaders all over the area wanted to be linked" (118).[3]

At the time of our fieldwork, Mbudza elders still told us stories about Wo-kombo, a small rivulet about ten kilometers from the CTI port. According to their accounts, this vale was named after the Mbudza ancestor Wokombo (a name also signifying the umbrella tree, *Musanga cecropioides*), who had migrated southward from the Ubangi region. During his travels Wokombo's first son, Dunga, settled down on the banks of the Mongala River, while his second son, Mbudza, crossed the river and moved farther east. Arriving in the Wokombo valley, Mbudza's four sons—Ndongi, Zamboli, Alua, and Salaka—occupied most of the region. By the end of the nineteenth century, these Mbudza groups had developed into "three major stable confederations, each tens of thousands strong" (119) that gradually solidified into militarized chiefdoms.

This militarization under *bankumu*, or village chiefs, was mainly a reaction against pressures from neighboring peoples like the Bati, who, themselves fleeing from Zande armies, regularly attacked the easternmost Mbudza villages (Vansina 1966, 62). But Mbudza military forces also grew because local big men could increase their spheres of influence by exchanging salt and metal objects with Bangala and Bapoto trading firms along the Congo River (Vansina 1990, 211–18, 227). In the nineteenth century, the lands around the lower Itimbiri River indeed found themselves at the eastern fringes of a new Atlantic trading system that had gradually penetrated into the Congo Basin. European demand for slaves and ivory along the Atlantic Coast had sparked wide-ranging economic specializations that profoundly affected political structures (Harms 1981). Moreover, from the 1880s onward, Itimbiri residents were also confronted with Arabo-Swahili raiders arriving from the east, looking for slaves and ivory to transport to the Indian Ocean. These traders often met with fierce resistance, and Mbudza chiefs who captured Swahili firearms could further expand their own military power.

Around the same time, European soldiers arrived at the Itimbiri as part of the expedition of Henry Morton Stanley, the Welsh American journalist-explorer whom the Belgian king Leopold II had sent to negotiate trade treaties with local chiefs. In 1885, the Itimbiri area became part of Leopold's newly created private domain, the État indépendant du Congo (Congo Free State). But Mbudza armies successfully resisted further penetration, and by 1890, white presence remained limited to the foundation of a provisioning post in Ibembo.

It was only toward the end of the century that the number of Europeans began to increase. In 1898, Premonstratensian missionaries from the Belgian Tongerlo Abbey built their first mission post in Ibembo, thereby laying the foundation of the later diocese of Lolo. Private company agents also arrived to look for ivory and natural rubber for the new warehouses along the Congo River, which were essential nodes in King Leopold's notoriously violent concessionary system (Vangroenweghe 1985).

At its foundation in 1885 the Congo Free State had indeed declared itself the only rightful owner of all so-called vacant lands. Yet, lacking the capacity and resources for their exploitation, the state conceded the right to harvest products and levy taxes to private companies as "concessions" in return for half of their shares (Stengers 1989, 100). As such, a company called Anversoise, founded in 1892, obtained the monopoly over all ivory and rubber sales in the Mongala Basin. While most of its activities were concentrated in Ngombe and Mbudza lands to the west, Anversoise agents from the rubber factory of Ndundusana along the Dua River also sporadically reached the Loeka and Itimbiri valleys. Yet their violent and abusive practices of forced labor led to widespread resistance, and on several occasions Mbudza armies directly fought the rubber collectors. In 1908, when the state sent Force Publique soldiers to suppress ongoing revolts against rubber taxes, they faced no fewer than five thousand Mbudza spearmen (Ambwa et al. 2015, 113–14; Stengers and Vansina 1985, 332–34, 356–57).

The interviews that Freddy and I conducted show that this fierce resistance was still very vivid in popular memory. For instance, villagers talked about the heroic Mbudza chief Dikpo, who reigned over a wide area around Yaliambi, which included the mythical vale of Wokombo.[4] As an infamous "sorcerer" and "man-eater," Dikpo inspired great fear, and his warriors were notorious for killing European agents and their Congolese auxiliaries. While most Mbudza resistance had been broken by the time Leopold II transmitted his private territory to the Belgian government in 1908 (in order to calm international outrage provoked by the red rubber scandal), Dikpo continued to fight the implantation of foreign companies until his death in 1936. During the first decades of the Belgian Congo, corporate interests therefore largely bypassed the Itimbiri area, which was initially merely used as a gateway to the Uele region farther east, where companies had set up oil palm, cotton, and cacao cultivation (Nelson 1994; Northrup 1988; Stengers and Vansina 1985; Stengers 1989).

The Bati lands to the east and north of the Itimbiri region, for instance, had already become the focus of obligatory cotton cultivation in 1919 (Likaka 1997). Villagers were forced to produce a targeted amount of cotton and sell it at a fixed price to the Compagnie Cotonnière Congolaise (Cotonco), which had opened offices in the new railway town of Aketi and built several factories in the region. In the late 1930s, after Dikpo's death, the colonial administration would also force a similar system on Mbudza villagers, who had to grow rice for Greek and Portuguese traders in Bumba. Moreover, in 1938 the Huileries du Congo Belge (HCB), an influential enterprise founded by the British Lever Brothers in 1911, started an extensive oil palm plantation in Yaligimba. In turn, these activities attracted smaller plantations and firmly integrated the region into the wider colonial economy.

Given the recent experiences of rubber collection and violent state penetration, however, villagers were initially very unwilling to work for these new firms. Companies had to enlist workers by force, often through private recruitment firms and assisted by soldiers and state agents who had to make sure village chiefs transferred their assigned quota of men to the new plantations. In order to ease labor recruitment, the state also deliberately imposed head taxes that were payable in cash, which villagers could obtain only through wage work. And to further facilitate tax collection, entire communities were obliged to resettle along the newly built roads, which were themselves constructed and maintained by forced labor.

During the first decades of colonial rule, harsh work regimes, appalling living conditions, and meager salaries made wage work very unpopular, and workers therefore often attempted to escape from their labor compounds (Seibert 2011). After World War II, however, many companies tried to reduce their high worker turnover rate. Several plantations, for instance, followed the example of the Union Minière copper mines in Katanga Province, where better housing, food rations, medical care, and schooling had "stabilized" the labor force as part of a colonial policy to create and control a healthy Congolese "working class" (Bernault 2003, 14; Higginson 1989).[5] In the Itimbiri region the Yaligimba oil palm plantation in particular became an example of new paternalist policies, with clubhouses for its skilled workers, hygiene lessons for their wives, and mission schools for their children.

For many, these places also created new aspirations. Indeed, even at the time of our fieldwork, the 1950s were still largely remembered as a golden age of wage labor. Formal contracts and monthly salaries had effectively become new conditions for a "civilized" masculinity that only a privileged minority of colonial workers could achieve (Ferguson 1999). Perhaps unlike in other parts of the African rainforest, where colonial regimes stimulated peasant production and men aspired to become independent *planteurs*, in the Belgian Congo the promise of modernity was tightly linked to the paternalist ideal of the wage-earning male breadwinner (Jewsiewicki 1976).[6] Cash-crop cultivation, by contrast—at least in the lower Itimbiri—could never shake off its coercive connotations. And as long as the colonial administration made migration to urban areas difficult, it was mainly in and around labor compounds, where private companies, missionaries, and state agents coproduced a grand paternalist ideal, that villagers could taste a new urban "ambiance" (Hunt 2016, 248).

World War II, therefore, is often viewed as a turning point in regional experiences and memories of labor. Whereas before the war salaried work had been highly unattractive, after the war and the spread of paternalist labor policies, wage labor became a coveted pathway to modernity. And, although regular salaries were a reality for only an absolute minority of forest residents, the cultural and social influence of plantation workers to set dreams and aspirations continued to inform gender and identities for a very long time.

On June 30, 1960, the Belgian Congo became an independent nation, but most companies along the Itimbiri initially continued their production relatively undisturbed. Soon, however, revolutionary movements originating from Orientale Province started to affect the region as well. In early 1961, for instance, the former HCB—now PLC (Plantations Lever au Congo)—had to temporarily withdraw its European personnel from the Yaligimba plantation after Lumumbist soldiers from Basoko had arrested its managers.[7] Three years later, in 1964, the same personnel had to flee again due to rapidly advancing Simba rebels from Stanleyville (today's Kisangani).[8] Aketi and Bumba quickly fell to the rebels, whose reputation for war magic and violence often preceded them. Although the Congolese army soon recaptured both towns with the support of Belgian, French, and Rhodesian soldiers and mercenaries, for several years the Itimbiri and Loeka forests remained the scene of continuing clashes between rebels, soldiers, and mercenaries. The last Simbas were only captured in 1966, and it took the new Mobutu regime another year to push back mercenary factions that had, in the meantime, turned against it.[9]

During our interviews, people still remembered the mid and late 1960s as the period when a "real" rupture between the colonial and postcolonial era took place. But rather than celebrate the Simba promise of a true "second independence," popular memories invariably foregrounded killings, disappearances, and the settling of accounts that left behind a broken and terrorized country (Ndaywel è Nziem 1998, 615). For the companies in the region, the times had changed as well. Heavy damage caused by rebels and looting soldiers forced many plantations and factories to close their doors. After peace returned, some of them tried to restart their activities. But, in 1973, they were confronted with Mobutu's decision to nationalize all foreign-owned businesses. Ordinary Congolese in Bumba and Aketi hoped this "Zaireanization" would produce tangible opportunities for taking over the companies and shops of Greek and Portuguese traders in town. Many quickly realized, however, that these enterprises were reserved for Mobutu's political allies, most of whom simply emptied the cash registers and disappeared (Young and Turner 1985).

In 1977, recognizing its failure, the Zairean government tried to "retrocede" several nationalized companies to their former owners, but by then most had already left the country and others were simply unwilling to make the necessary investments. Along the Itimbiri, their departure announced a long period of economic decline. In Bumba, only one Greek rice company remained, but quickly deteriorating roads made it increasingly difficult to send trucks to farmers. In the rainforest, most labor camps and plantations were abandoned. Only Yaligimba continued its activities—now under the name of PLZ (Plantations Lever au Zaire). But it, too, was unable to prevent a dramatic decline in production. With most companies gone or in a permanent state of inactivity, and with state roads reduced to bicycle tracks and erosion gullies, everyday life became increasingly disconnected from the national economy. Many people resorted to farming and hunting. Others migrated to Kinshasa or Kisangani.

In 1988, when CTI first expressed interest in the Itimbiri forests and sent Michel to conduct an aerial survey of its timber resources, rumors quickly spread that the whites (*mindele*) had returned and would soon be hiring many of the region's unemployed. In 1990, when CTI built its first labor compound near the mouth of the Itimbiri River, these new hopes resonated with expectations of democracy engendered by Mobutu's acceptance of a multiparty political system. By 1994, when the company built its second labor compound in the middle of the concession, it had effectively reemployed people, reopened state roads, constructed or repaired a number of schools and health centers, and promised to build several more. "We thought CTI would finally disenclave the region [*désenclaver la region*]," a middle-aged woman from Yambili told us.

Two years later, however, the specter of "enclavement" reemerged. In 1996, Laurent-Désiré Kabila and his Alliance des Forces Démocratiques pour la Libération du Congo-Zaïre (AFDL) had started a war against the Mobutu regime in the east of the country. With the help of Rwandan and Ugandan forces, AFDL soldiers quickly advanced and looted a logging concession on the eastern shore of the Itimbiri. CTI therefore decided to discontinue its operations and only resumed them when Kabila brought Mobutu's rule to an end in May 1997. A year later, however, Jean-Pierre Bemba's Mouvement pour la Libération du Congo (MLC) took control of large parts of Equateur Province. In November 1998 the town of Bumba fell, and timber transport over the Congo River became impossible. CTI therefore had no choice but to close its concession, revoke its expat managers, and furlough its Congolese workers for reasons of "technical unemployment."

This time it took almost five years before the company could start working again. In July 2003 a new transitional government was installed in Kinshasa, thereby ending the Second Congo War. Because many workers had lingered around the labor camps to farm, fish, and hunt, CTI could easily reemploy them. It also cleared the overgrown roads and repaired offices and expat bungalows that had in the interim accommodated rebel officers. Yet continuing support for the MLC created a tense political atmosphere. In the 2006 presidential elections, those in Bumba and most of the Itimbiri region sweepingly voted for Bemba. And, after his arrest in 2008, local politics were characterized by sharp political tensions between the MLC opposition and president Joseph Kabila's Parti du Peuple pour la Reconstruction et la Démocratie (PPRD).

This regional opposition to the Kabila government was also expressed in increasingly ethnic terms. As the self-declared autochthonous inhabitants of the region, many Mbudza felt sidelined by PPRD-appointed non-Mbudza state administrators. In the late 2000s a nationalist youth group, the Lihongela Mbudza (Mbudza family), was founded explicitly to counter the influence of foreigners—especially the Anamongo, an organization of twenty-six ethnic groups claiming descent from a common Mongo ancestor. While ethnopolitical rivalries between so-called Bangala—such as Mbudza from Bumba or Ngombe from Lisala—and Mongo—usually from Mbandaka—dated back to the late colonial and early postcolonial period, they reemerged in a new guise. In the run-up to the 2011 national elections, MLC-supporting intellectuals, politically marginalized Mbudza dignitaries, and impoverished youth organized protest marches in Bumba that tapped into widespread discontent with the region's rulers.

In this context, local opposition to perceived and actual foreign influences took the form of an increased critique of foreign-owned companies. Lihongela Mbudza physically attacked the remaining Greek rice-trading firm in Bumba for its unfair price policies. And, with renewed Mbudza nationalism becoming an explicit register for expressing popular frustrations, CTI was also confronted by increasing conflicts with villagers claiming their autochthonous right to the forest. Moreover, in Bumba, civil society organizations seemed to emerge out of nowhere and criticize CTI for what they alleged was illegal or excessive logging. For the timber company, however, it was clear that international environmentalist organizations were financing and instrumentalizing local groups in an attempt to smear the company's reputation.

It was in this mixture of paranoia and nervousness that CTI had to make up for the precious time it lost during the 2008 financial crisis. Local power games polarized conflicts between the company and particular villages and became political fuel on a regional and even national level. For its expat managers, renewed anti-white feelings revived collective memories of postindependence violence and horrifying stories about mutilating Simba rebels. For villagers, new critiques against foreign companies expressed urgent claims to finally get their rightful share.

For CTI workers, however, the escalating troubles only confirmed that things were no longer what they had been. Strong companies and corporate paternalism were a long-gone reality. Yet, as we will see in the next section, workers still built their self-respect on the basis of an increasingly contested ideology of wage labor. If nothing else, their salaries at least allowed them to *perform* a worker identity that distinguished them from ordinary villagers and the large majority of town dwellers. Every year on May 1, for instance, they could make their social distinction clear during the formal Labor Day parade in Bumba.

Marching *after* Labor

May 1, 2010. The yearly celebration of International Workers' Day in Bumba. Policemen had cordoned off the main street that connected the former white quarters along the Congo River with the colonial *cité indigène* behind the Mobutu roundabout. The street's reddish unpaved surface had been carefully swept clean, and an honorary tent had been erected to shelter town administrators, politicians, and union delegates from the sun. Freddy and I took a place a little bit farther down the road, looking at the old facades of the Portuguese trading companies that once dominated the regional rice trade. While their faded names could still be deciphered, most buildings now served as shops for Lebanese wholesalers, money transfer agencies, cell phone providers, liquor stores, and small boutiques where businessmen from Butembo sold colorful wares "made in China."

A couple of weeks earlier, CTI had received a *note de service* from the labor unions, asking the company to start preparations for the parade and to pay the registration fee of $32.50. But Jens, the Danish site manager, had angrily thrown the piece of paper away. In his stern opinion, "one had to *labor* on Labor Day"—especially with the orders from Europe piling up. Yet participating in the parade was not voluntary. The unions threatened sanctions, and workers protested, forcing Jens to give in. Some employees were finally given permission to leave for Bumba in the back of a company truck, but Jens refused to pay for their parade uniforms. Unlike in previous years, his workers would have to march in their ordinary blue work outfits. Most tried at least to have their wives wash them. But many left for Bumba in low spirits. How would they be able to keep their heads up next to much smaller companies that would, without doubt, dress their workers in specially made uniforms?

The parade was late. A local journalist tried to entertain the assembled crowd through a cracking megaphone. Finally, the *administrateur du territoire* (the highest-ranking state agent in Bumba) arrived. Three white-gloved policemen saluted the flag, and people softly mumbled the lyrics to the national anthem performed by the band of the Kimbanguist church.

The first marchers in the parade were civil servants and government personnel. A lady next to me started laughing. "When have these men really seen their last pay checks?" she asked. Next came office clerks in oversized suits who marched behind banners of such terminally ill state companies as ONATRA (public transport), SONAS (social insurance), SNEL (electricity), REGIDESO (water), or CFU (railways). The irony of their stately performance was not lost on the onlookers. "Where is our electricity? Where is our water?" they shouted.

Then it was the turn of the CTI workers. As they had predicted, their performance was indeed low key. Not only were they largely outnumbered by smaller Lebanese and Chinese trading firms who had dressed their employees in colorful uniforms made of wax cloth that proudly displayed company logos. The workers from the Greek rice-trading firm had even brought along equipment and machines to perform brief sketches for the audience. And employees from several money-transfer agencies threw small bank notes onto the street. The public loved it. Many rushed forward to grab the money while policemen tried to beat them back in line.

After the private companies came people working for local rice mills, NGOs and political parties. Lihongela Mbudza had also sent a delegation. Then came independent shopkeepers, bar owners, hairdressers, street vendors, bicycle taxi drivers, members of the Boy Scouts, and a karate club. Even the elderly, the poor, and the disabled obtained their place at the end of the parade, courageously marching by and pushing wheelchairs. Some performed as fools—again much to the delight of the laughing audience.

Parts of the parade seemed like a grotesque carnival. Others resembled a funeral march. Either way, it showed the exact opposite of what was intended. Although the parade was trying to celebrate labor, it could not help but emphasize the striking scarcity of wage laborers. Workers earning a regular salary were indeed a rare sight, and the majority of participants rather displayed a variety of *non*-labor strategies in a harsh, small-town survival economy. Even those who marched for new Lebanese or Chinese trading companies were usually mere day laborers. Their wages were so low, inconsistent, and unpredictable that people did not consider them to be real salaries.

When the parade was over, the local president of the Intersyndicale—the association of labor unions—gave a speech that praised formal wage labor in such alienating terms that it only made things worse, leading the administrateur de territoire, a Lebano-Congolese politician from Kabila's PPRD party, to try to save the situation. Although few people in his territory were formally employed, he said, we were all laborers nonetheless and should work hard to develop the country. Yet, when Freddy and I later met parade participants in bars across town, they strongly disagreed with their administrator. Godefroid, for instance, a CTI truck driver, insisted that being a true worker meant having a contract, a regular wage, work bonuses, and access to health services. Labor (*travail* in French; *mosala* in Lingala), his colleagues agreed, was proper labor: *wage* work. All the rest was false labor (*faux travail*).

True work had become so much an exception that people sometimes referred to those who still had a precarious job as the non-unemployed (*non-chômeurs*). Hence the desire of CTI loggers to display their exceptional status as salaried workers. The *performance* of labor was indeed of utmost importance to create and emphasize a worker identity that was distinct from the supposedly nonlaboring masses. That year it was therefore deeply humiliating that CTI—by far the largest company in the region—had simply been outperformed by smaller firms known for their lower salaries.

The Labor Day parade reproduced, imperfectly and artificially, an ideology of wage labor that had very much come to frame the idea of the good life but that seemed unreachable for most. As a public spectacle, it offered ways to "remember the present" that commented on the here and now (Fabian 1996). It was indeed an occasion to reflect on and negotiate the weight of a contemporary world where wage labor had not just become precarious but was often redundant (Barchiesi 2011). For many, the absurd performance of labor in a largely *post*-labor environment of chronic unemployment provoked laughter, frustration, nostalgic recollections, anger, irony, and cynicism. Complex affects circulated through the audience as onlookers moved forward and were pushed back by police and as people joked, shouted, provoked, or shook their heads in shame. Yet while the bodies marching before the eye of state power were embarrassing to many, the parade also conveyed old dreams and messages of hope: contradictory feelings that resonated, as we will see, with a much broader affective landscape.

Traces in the Landscape

It was indeed not only in towns like Bumba that current realities and memories of wage labor evoked strong emotions. The landscape in which CTI found itself was literally scattered with the material remains of colonial companies. Old plantations, broken down railroads, and deserted labor camps reminded people of the comings and goings of foreigners, of bygone lifestyles and possibilities, sudden deaths and stretched-out failures, past futures and lingering possibilities (Geissler et al. 2016). CTI's presence reactivated stories about violence, exploitation, flight, and resistance but also about money, electricity, bicycles, and sewing machines. Such memories and countermemories still sculpted the experience of work in the logging concession, where workers tried to live up to the idea(l) of wage labor *after* a reconstructed paternalist past.

This last section takes a look at the ruination of infrastructures that triggered a shared but complex and multilayered "collective memory" (Jewsiewicki 1986). Four particular sites, situated within or close to the CTI concession, illustrate the affective complexity of memory work: an oil palm plantation no longer producing oil, a railway station without running trains, a rubber company that was bombed after the Simba rebellion, and a cotton factory that had been eerily abandoned. Whether still inhabited or left to decompose, such sites generated affects that structured the memory of work for those who lived among the tangible remains of past labor. Rather than suggest one dominant interpretation, the ruinated landscape of the logging concession triggered specific, dynamic, and partly contradictory memories, feelings, stories, critiques, and desires that formed the affective-historical "imperial debris" in which CTI had to operate (Stoler 2013).

The huge oil palm plantation of Yaligimba stood as a monument to past worker identities in a postpaternalist environment. With mixed feelings of pride and sadness, George, a retired palm nut cutter, showed me the neat avenues of his labor compound, indicating the office where he used to receive his monthly salary—as well as the soap, tissues, buckets, plates, rice, sardines, and smoked fish that were regularly distributed to employees. He melancholically pointed at the bar where he used to drink beer with his mates after work and at the *foyer social* where his wife took housekeeping classes. "Life was good back then," he sighed.

Heir to the famous HCB (Huileries du Congo Belge)—and colloquially still referred to as the PLZ (Plantations Lever au Zaïre)—the PHC, or Plantations et Huileries du Congo, exerted an enormous influence on popular historiographies in the Itimbiri region. Unlike other colonial companies, the plantation had indeed managed to continue some production until fairly recently, and memories were still fresh. Situated along the southern limit of the CTI concession, its endless rows of palm trees, labor camps, factories, workshops, expat quarters, laboratories, hospitals, football fields, and clubhouses constituted the most visible testimony of paternalist labor policies in the region (Loffman and Henriet 2020).

In its early years, however, the Yaligimba plantation was not at all the paradise George tried to depict for us. After its creation in 1938, the HCB had to use force to enlist people to cut down the thirty thousand hectares of (what the company viewed as) unused forest for which it had paid local chiefs with bicycles, whiskey, and cigarettes. Many Mbudza farmers therefore fled the makeshift labor camps as soon as they could. But for administrative staff and more skilled workers—most of whom were transferred from already existing HCB plantations in other parts of the country—fleeing was not always an option. George's father, for instance, had been made to leave the company town of Leverville (now Lusanga in Kwilu Province) for Yaligimba. And it was only when working and living conditions improved after World War II that he started to earn a salary that enabled him to marry a Mbudza girl from a nearby village.

In the 1950s, Yaligimba indeed became the smoothly run operation that George, like many children born and raised on the plantation, remembered with affection. After independence in 1960, however, the plantation could not prevent its output from dropping. As the general state of the economy declined, necessary investments and repairs to the factory had to be postponed. Managers were often absent, and workers faced increasing delays in receiving their salaries. In 1995 the last European director finally left the plantation. During the following decade, the Mobutu-Kabila and Kabila-Bemba rebellions slowed down work to an almost complete standstill. And although production somewhat resumed after the Congo Wars, the oil mill had become so dysfunctional that it was shut down in 2008. Still, the plantation housed more than ten thousand people—among whom were 1,250 employees whose salaries had vanished into thin air.

In 2009, PHC workers heard rumors that the company was being taken over by a Canadian investment fund that seemed intent on giving the plantation a second life. A year later, new Congolese managers arrived, but they fired a large portion of the workforce. Those who remained were employed in a replanting program for wages that barely covered living expenses. To make ends meet, many were forced to illegally harvest palm nuts from the Elaeis trees and produce their own oil for sale. "Life has become so difficult," George said. "Even the water pumps have broken down. Because there are no rivers in the entire plantation, my children have to walk for more than an hour to fetch water. But the Canadians don't care."

For older plantation inhabitants, the neoliberal present was indeed very different from the good old days of corporate paternalism. Yet those who shared nostalgic memories about the colonial past could *also* highlight the violence, injustice, and everyday racism of plantation life. One of George's former colleagues, for instance, criticized the luxury in which European directors and technicians used to live and recalled how their segregated living quarters were strictly off limits to Congolese. "And they were very severe," he added. "As blacks, we were not allowed to leave the plantation without a document. And we even couldn't provide accommodation to visiting family members without prior authorization." Discourses about the past were therefore rarely monolithic, and people effortlessly switched from romanticizing to more accusatory modes.

Given the history of violence, racism, and exploitation, memories of the colonial era as a good time (*tango malamu*) might perhaps seem surprising or willfully blind. But their nostalgia needs to be taken seriously (Angé and Berliner 2014). George and his colleagues endlessly emphasized how, despite their toughness, their European bosses "took care" of their employees. "They assisted us with food rations, and there were often extras at Christmas," they said. "The company even helped out with bride wealth payments and donated coffins to bereaved families." As on other HCB plantations, they sometimes contrasted their British managers' goodwill (*bonne volonté*) with the more violent and cruel attitude of Belgian state agents (see also Henriet 2021). In their recollections, paternalism suffused everyday life to such an extent that salaries were almost presented as merely additional to other and more substantial personalized benefits—as if their hard work was not a justified counterpart to salaries but to the maintenance of a *relationship* between employer and employee. Popular memories of white "kindness" and celebrations of "close" relationships with European bosses therefore contained strong moral demands addressed to the new Canadian investors, who were called upon to assume their responsibilities in providing for workers *beyond* the strict labor contract.

Furthermore, some memories and narratives by former PHC workers took an explicitly racial tone. "In the time of the whites," one of the palm cutters told us, "life was different. Today black folk have taken over. [But] the whites listened to people; they knew their workers and their problems. . . . Our own brothers don't want to see our worries. They make us work like machines. They don't know the value of a person. They're only preoccupied with their own situation." Such statements, while making me uncomfortable, were a common refrain that, though idealized, contained an urgent critique of the here and now (Bissell 2005).

As a dimension of popular memories, nostalgia thus seemed the result of contradictory but sincerely experienced feelings. Reenacted in the present to make a point about contemporary life, it operated in a selective fashion and was as much about forgetting as remembering (Fabian 2003). Yet, while it criticized others for the current situation, it also contained a more self-critical subtext about imagined collective responsibilities for the course of history. "Is it not us, blacks, who have chased the whites away?" someone kept asking. Popular historiographies indeed attributed the general decline of the country to its willful "abandonment" by former colonizers but also pointed at anti-white feelings and violence as a cause of that decline. After each period of rebellion and instability, European plantation managers returned in fewer numbers than before. And as mutual distrust increased, the reportedly close relations of paternalism withered away. As such, a growing nostalgia enabled the expression of grief and regret over the disappearance of a largely reconstructed and fictionalized past.

RAILWAY PRIDE AND SHAME

North of the PHC plantation a narrow-gauge railway traversed the CTI logging concession from east to west. Because trains had long become defunct, its tracks were overgrown with lush vegetation. In the early 1990s some railway workers had converted a truck so that it could run on rails, but at the time of our fieldwork it had been more than fifteen years since the last camion rail had crossed the concession. Along the tracks, a small but well-trodden, meandering path was used by *kwamutu* traders to transport barrels of liquor from north of Lisala to the diamond mines near Bondo and Baye. Pushing their heavily loaded bicycles along the old railway, these young men literally carried most of what remained of long-distance trafficking. But fuel smugglers, too, were keen on transporting their goods along the railway. Too narrow for CTI jeeps to pass along, the tracks were indeed a relatively safe way to evacuate stolen or illegally bought fuel.

Halfway through the concession, the railway passed the small station of Bolende, where eighteen CFU (Chemins de Fer des Uele) employees still lived in company-built concrete houses that stood in sharp contrast to surrounding huts. Most of these men had been there for at least two decades. CFU was the latest manifestation of the old Vicicongo company (Chemins de Fer Vicinaux du Congo) that was established in 1924 and which had built an extensive railway network in Orientale Province. It mainly transported coffee, cotton, tobacco, palm oil, and rubber from the Upper and Lower Uele regions to the town of Aketi, where its main station and company headquarters were located. Initially goods were then loaded onto boats that traveled on to Léopoldville. But already in the time of the Belgian Congo, decreasing water levels on the Itimbiri River made it difficult for boats to reach Aketi. In the late 1960s, Mobutu therefore decided to realize old plans for extending the railway to the commercial center of Bumba.

Yet the station in Bolende, completed in 1971, had never really seen the traffic people had expected. During the 1970s and 1980s, agricultural production in the east slowed down and company earnings plummeted. Moreover, in 1998, the war cut off the eastern part of the country from Kinshasa and activities came to a complete standstill. Until the time of our fieldwork, and despite various promises, no train had passed Bolende. And, for more than a decade, the company had been unable to pay the almost eight hundred employees still on its payroll.

Raymond was one of them. As *chef de cantonnage*, he theoretically had to direct seventeen other employees to maintain the railway tracks and keep them clear of vegetation. As their work leader, Raymond occupied the former CFU dispensary where Freddy and I regularly spent the night. Seated on his porch, we often looked at the rusty shells of abandoned railway carriages between the high grasses in front of the old station. Raymond and his colleagues then told us about the past. About people loading rice and maize on trains to Bumba. And about long railway travels to Isiro in the east.

During the Congo Wars, different rebel groups had occupied the station and significantly damaged it. On its walls, child soldiers (*kadogo*) had made charcoal drawings of violent scenes. In order to make money in these difficult times, villagers had removed the large metal rivets and clinch bolts from the railway tracks to fuse them into machetes. "We simply couldn't stop them," Raymond said. "And what remained was eaten away by the forest." But notwithstanding the soldiers and occasional threats from villagers when CFU employees tried to prevent the railway's further destruction, Raymond's men had remained at their post. Their salaries evaporated, but they hoped transport activities would resume after the war.

For this reason, the CFU men stubbornly clung to their former status as salaried workers and jealously guarded their letters of employment. Until the long-awaited sound of trains returned, they said, "we have no choice but to work uselessly [*inutilement*]." Yet many had lost hope. Raymond knew that a solution to their problems was not around the corner. Forced to cut his fields along the rusty carriages and dilapidated railway tracks, he said he felt shame (*nsoni*) in front of other villagers. His wife had recently left him and gone to Bumba, and he had no money to send her. As brothers in suffering (*bandeko ya mpasi*), the CFU men had no choice but to share memories of better times by downing cheap bottles of liquor bought from the kwamutu traders, drinking away shame and despair.

A BLOWN-UP RUBBER FACTORY

Approximately ten kilometers north of the railway station of Bolende lay the village of Mombwassa. It was created in 1944, when a Belgian administrator, known by the name of Ambaliwani (literally, the one who does not take advice), had forced Bati families to settle along the new administrative road near the isolated home of Egbundu, a marginalized leper who had been recently converted. The Lolo missionaries hoped to use this new settlement as an outpost for their activities in the as yet un-Christianized areas to the north. But it was also the site where, stimulated by the rise in rubber prices during World War II, a rubber plantation was created. While, as part of the colonial government's war effort, villagers had initially been forced to collect wild rubber from creepers in the forest, the plantation of *Hevea* trees announced a new chapter in the rubber story.

To cut the forest, plant the trees, and build the rubber factory, the small Comaco company had first recruited Bati farmers from Mombwassa. Five years later, however, when the trees were ready to produce their first latex, a group of Mbudza men was forced to move to its labor camps. The Mombwassa village chief could still point out to us where the new Mbudza workers were housed. Despite their earlier resistance against colonial penetration, which had earned them the reputation as troublemakers, he said the whites considered the Mbudza to be more intelligent than the local Bati. The former therefore took the posts of labor overseer or factory worker, while Bati usually worked as rubber tappers and transporters.

According to the chief's mother, Comaco was run by a handful of French ex-convicts employed by a lady (*Madame*) who rarely visited the site. As far as we could tell from people's recollections, working for Comaco was extremely hard but relatively well paid and certainly less strictly surveilled than jobs in the Yaligimba oil palm plantation. Workers were paid twice a month according to a production premium system, and some were able to save enough money to buy a bicycle or sewing machine. In the 1950s, Portuguese traders had opened several shops, and Mombwassa developed into a small commercial center where people from the region came to buy soap, salt, and clothes. One of the Portuguese shopkeepers even had his own gramophone, and the chief's mother could still hum the tunes from some of his jazz records.

In 1964, however, Simba rebels captured the French Comaco managers and took them to Bunduki. Like most workers, Alexis fled into the forest with his family. For some days it was quiet. But then, he said, he heard an airplane approaching. From his hideout he claimed he saw a bomb drop that completely destroyed the rubber factory. He told us it was probably a mercenary airplane trying to scare back advancing rebels. Others believed it was the Frenchmen themselves who had bombed the factory out of revenge. Some later admitted they doubted whether such a bombing even happened. But Alexis and others stood firm on their story. For them, the apocalyptic self-destruction poignantly marked the end of rubber production.

At the time of our fieldwork, traces of old buildings were still visible along the small river where people now pressed palm oil by hand. The rubber plantation itself had hardly changed. Children now played among the rows of trees and sometimes tapped latex to make footballs. Women took the artificial forest as a shady shortcut to the river. Farmers, however, complained that the remains of insecticides or medicines (*nkisi*) and thick layers of suffocating *Hevea* leaves prevented all growth. For this reason, they had to farm much farther into the forest. Older people still believed the site had to be protected in case the French bosses returned. Younger villagers objected and said the plantation no longer belonged to foreigners. Alexis knew that the spectacular bombing had destroyed all hope for a company resurrection.

Whatever one's views, the rubber plantation imposed itself as material proof of the vulnerable and unpredictable nature of capitalist investment. When CTI arrived in the early 1990s, the inhabitants of Mombwassa proved to be particularly difficult negotiating partners, as if they feared history would again play the same trick and leave them with nothing but memories of bombed futures. For this reason, the demands they made of CTI officials were voiced with particular insistence and urgency. New opportunities represented by the logging company did indeed need to be seized before it was too late.

A BAD WIND BLOWS FROM THE COTTON RUINS

The last site that illustrates the affective ambiguity of regional memories on past labor is the old cotton factory of Bunduki. Situated on the western shore of the Itimbiri River, approximately thirty-five kilometers south of Mombwassa, Bunduki was the administrative seat of the Chefferie of Bodongola. It controlled a series of Bati villages that, like others in the Lower Uele region, had been obliged by the colonial administration to grow cotton since the 1930s.

It is difficult to overstate the hatred people still expressed against this past system of forced cultivation. Even younger villagers relayed stories about Belgian agronomists and their Congolese *moniteurs agricoles* who measured, monitored, and controlled the standardized cotton fields all households had to create and maintain. "If we didn't follow their instructions," a young man in his twenties told us, "we were fined, flogged, and imprisoned." Growing cotton also resulted in hunger, as its cultivation was so time-intensive that it kept many families from producing sufficient food (Likaka 1997).

In all of Bodongola, cotton had to be sold at a fixed price to the Compagnie Cotonnière Congolaise (Cotonco), which had acquired a regional buying monopoly. In each village the company built metal sheds and temporary warehouses where farmers had to bring their cotton after harvest. Cotonco workers then transported the cotton to the Bunduki factory, where it was processed and shipped to Léopoldville. Several former factory workers told us it was difficult to meet production targets. Every harvest season, they said, a European descended from Aketi to run the factory. One of these men was a notorious drunk who had taken to smoking cannabis. Another boss brought his wife and children but had to flee after she discovered he had made a local girl pregnant. Yet despite the hard work, they said, workers were paid decent salaries, and the company had built them relatively comfortable houses. "In a section of the labor compound there even was an electricity grid," a former employee mentioned, a rare sight that gave the village an attractive urban feel.

Like many companies in the region, however, the Cotonco factory was heavily damaged and looted during the 1960s' rebellions. Despite a French takeover, it slowly withered away until its closure in 1986. Its labor compound and worker houses were abandoned. While village chiefs and elders initially managed to preserve the factory and warehouses in case the company would return, local inhabitants began collecting and selling corrugated sheets, metal doors, and other building materials during and after the Congo Wars. At the time of our fieldwork, the company site had become an overgrown ruin. Although the old houses were still standing, not a single family had moved back into them. People said a bad wind (*mopepe mabe*) blew from the factory, and most villagers circumvented it. At nighttime, they claimed, witches gathered in its ruins, where they met up with their colleagues from Kinshasa.

Perhaps even more than other sites, the abandoned Cotonco factory seemed haunted by unwelcome invasions from the past. Was the bad wind a materialization of the pain and hunger associated with obligatory cotton cultivation? Or was it an effect of guilty memories welling up from a labor compound cannibalized by its former occupants? Once again, memories and feelings were contradictory. People hated cotton but missed the urban atmosphere. Some regretted their own role in provoking, amplifying, or simply allowing processes of ruination. "It's our fault," an older man sighed. "We took away all the scrap metal we could use or sell. The company is no longer a corpse. Just a skeleton." Others blamed the French for abandoning them. But whether blowing with guilt and regret or anger and reproach, the malevolent winds of history effectively seemed to prevent people from rehabiting the gloomy remains of the bygone cotton economy.

Moving along sites where the past of rainforest capitalism was still palpable, the memories we encountered were always ambivalent. Ethnographic attention to the multiple feelings they evoked brings to the fore the complex ways in which remains from the past produced and reproduced narratives that oriented people's attitudes and aspirations in the present. The material detritus of capitalist extraction indeed brought into circulation pain, regret, nostalgia, resignation, resentment, hope, despair, anger, guilt, pride, and shame. While old factories, plantations, and railway stations certainly generated stories that significantly differed between individuals and sites, they also triggered nondiscursive intensities and affects that traveled beyond their tellers.

When spoken, these memories produced what Yael Navaro-Yashin (2009) calls an "affective space" that discharged emotive energies and connected people. Yet, while littered with traces of a violent past, the affective Itimbiri landscape cannot be reduced to the single aftermath of an all-devouring trauma (Hochschild 1998). Memories were, rather, as Nancy Rose Hunt suggests, crisscrossed with multiple and partly contradicting afterlives that, though shared, did not add up to one monolithic story (Hunt 2016).

Popular memories and vernacular historiographies also affected how concession residents reacted to CTI. The ruinated infrastructures of long gone businesses indeed produced tangible moral yardsticks to evaluate the loggers' actions. Many villagers, for instance, nostalgically referred to a golden age of wage labor when criticizing the company for *not* reaching the paternalist standard of earlier plantations (Li 2019), while stories about colonial violence and exploitation fed feelings of continuing injustice. In addition, recollections of looting rebels and pilfering villagers made chiefs try to convince CTI that, despite all their claims, they still very much wanted the company to stay. Yet past experiences with broken promises about company returns and reinvestments made everyone suspicious.

Memories thus generated a particular affective context that constrained and channeled the logging company's scope of action. Stories provided vernacular criteria in reference to which CTI could be judged—and was often found wanting. As such, they contributed significantly to the ecstatogenic atmosphere in which CTI had to operate. Histories of past encounters constituted a "mimetic archive" of potentialities waiting to be reactivated in the present (Mazzarella 2017): a memory scape full of early warnings, dead ends, and bygone futures as a fertile milieu for the transmission, amplification, and proliferation of energies that were simply beyond CTI's control. As we will see in the next chapter, this nervous sense of unfinished history sustained an ecstatic mood that strongly affected the collisions, frictions, and dealmaking between loggers and village communities.

CTI workers building a school in Mombwassa

4

Sharing the Company

IT WAS EARLY IN THE AFTERNOON, and a new school building had been officially opened. After a decade of broken promises and renegotiations, the village of Mombwassa could finally showcase its own brand-new building.

Like other recent CTI constructions in the concession, the school was painted in blue and white—the signature colors of Roger, the sturdy Frenchman from Brittany who had been hired as CTI's construction manager. Part of his job was to attend opening ceremonies in which village chiefs and state officials elaborately thanked the logging company for the gift. But Roger did not like it a bit. He was not a man to sit down and listen to others. It was all a big show anyway, he told me. An artificial performance of gratitude. Not a genuine expression of recognition for his hard work. During the entire ceremony he looked visibly bored, and he left as soon as he could.

The utter dependency of these people disgusted him, he later said. Everything had to be done *for* them—they were even unable to maintain the school buildings and health centers he so carefully designed. "And, imagine . . . these are the same people who took me hostage!" he added.

Building the school had indeed been a nightmare. The headmaster had long tried to force Roger to buy the white sand he needed from a nearby sand pit controlled by his family. Roger didn't understand. "How could this guy try to make money for himself from a community project?" he asked.

Roger stubbornly refused. One day, during an inspection trip, he found himself surrounded by a group of angry villagers. A young man got hold of the keys to Roger's Toyota Land Cruiser. It took the police more than two hours to arrive and set him free. "Assholes, hypocrites, liars, and profiteers—*all* of them," Roger said as he finished his story.

After they watched Roger speed away, the assembled Mombwassa residents finished the palm wine CTI had bought for the occasion. I had traveled to the village with papa Mbondo, a Mbudza farmer in his late forties from Quartier Mobutu, a hamlet bordering the CTI forest camp. Mbondo was married to a Bati woman from Mombwassa and had taken the occasion to visit an in-law. "Thom's?" he asked, "why do only *some* villages get CTI schools and dispensaries while others do not?" As a new settlement, Quartier Mobutu had indeed not been able to claim the same rights as Mombwassa. For the logging company, it was not a real village, but an illegal settlement that could easily be bypassed in its community projects.

Mbondo had tried to find a job for his eldest son on a CTI work crew, but all he got were excuses and vague promises. Kikongo-speaking managers and team leaders were now pulling the strings in the company, he said. And skilled Ngombe and Mongo workers from downriver had taken most of the coveted jobs. Unless they had the money to buy a goat and bribe the chief of personnel, local people were unlikely to get hired. "The CTI people only hire their own brothers," Mbondo complained. Like many forest inhabitants, he felt ignored on his own land.

"They take our trees and we get nothing!" a young man confirmed, joining the conversation in front of the new school. Earlier on I had spotted him amid a group of youngsters who were carefully listening in during the opening ceremony. As usual, youngsters and women had not taken part in the meeting with CTI. Many felt their voices were not heard.

"Animals are rare because the chainsaws chase them away," the young man said, "and their trucks kill our goats. They make tons of money, and all we get is an empty school building."

"But it *is* a beginning," the headmaster said, interrupting him. "From now on, even when it rains, we will—"

A plump woman moved forward from behind her market stall. "But what will this new school do for us? Pupils have no books; our children are hungry. What we need is money! Just money. But no one here has a job in that company. Only strangers."

Papa Mbondo agreed. "We see truck after truck leaving full of trees. Where are they going? We don't know. But they make lots of money." He straightened his back. "The elephant needs to be shared [*Il faut partager l'éléphant*]," he finally said. "When hunters kill an elephant, the meat is shared among all. But with CTI only *some* people benefit."

We all nodded in agreement.

The presence of CTI was a rare opportunity to be taken and shared. But foreign companies had become reluctant to accept their assumed position as providers. Single compensatory gifts, like school buildings, could not make up for a staggering lack of concern, care, and assistance toward those who owned the forest. As such, even though they had just experienced the opening of a new school, people claimed—without contradiction—that they "received nothing" (Gardner 2015). For many villagers, CTI indeed tried to sneak out of long-standing moralities of patronage and to avoid the traditional role of the nurturing father-chief into which they tried to maneuver its managers (Schatzberg 2001). In fact, people said, by ignoring its social responsibilities and only caring for itself, the company behaved like a witch (*ndoki*). Some even claimed that CTI made its money through occult deals. During the previous year, the village chiefs from Mombwassa had signed a contract with the company, but few people had seen the document. What had they really agreed to? And why had their dignitaries sold the forest so cheaply?

In this climate of suspicion, communities loudly claimed their rightful share of the company's profits—real or imagined. In return for logging trees they demanded schools, health centers, and, above all, roads that would reconnect them to the wider world: projects they wanted *today* because the loggers might move elsewhere tomorrow. Much to CTI's frustration, villagers thereby tried to trap the company in a moral economy of gifts, demands, claims, and shares. As illustrated in chapter 3, this nervous climate was largely a by-product of history—of popular memories of bygone paternalism and patronage and of new hopes for connection after decades of lived enclavement. As Katy Gardner (2015, 495) shows for the American oil and gas firm Chevron in northeastern Bangladesh, CTI had no choice but to operate "in a specific moral terrain which pre-date[d]" its arrival and which "profoundly affected how their development goods [were] perceived, utilized and contested."

This chapter starts with the 2002 forest code and shows how this new legislation created and shaped expectations of material returns for village communities within the concession. It specifically describes how, during and after difficult negotiations, CTI's managers often felt overwhelmed by forest residents' demands for seemingly never-ending assistance. The chapter then shows how village communities used such tactics as roadblocks, sabotage, and theft to make sure they got their rightful share from a company that was otherwise reluctant to engage in relationships of patronage. It then zooms in on a widespread trade in stolen company fuel to illustrate how, also on a more regional scale, popular actions partially repaired moral economies. It concludes with a reflection on the vulnerable openness of logging to people, fluxes, and dynamics beyond its control that put into question the idea of the neoliberal enclave as a spatial model for thinking extractive capitalism. Why indeed was it so difficult to seal the concession off from its surroundings? And why were the CTI managers unable to avoid the moral and practical entanglements in which they had to operate? They indeed tried very hard to distance themselves from a murky field of politics in which multiple and contradictory voices spoke for local populations, factions allied with or against the company, and gender and generation fractured communities.

Demanding Airports

Although the 2002 forest code was mainly born out of international concerns over the possible ecological costs of a postwar logging boom in the DRC, its aspiration to provide sustainable development also entailed explicitly socio-economic objectives. It specifically obliged timber companies to sign formal contracts with local communities and to realize infrastructural projects that would provide social benefits for forest residents. These *cahiers des charges* were primarily known for their lists of socioeconomic obligations (*clauses sociales*) that had been negotiated with representatives of village communities. Invariably these lists contained promises to construct or repair road sections, health centers, and school buildings as well as to provide special services, such as the free transportation of people and farming products on logging trucks, or the donation of wood coffins to bereaved families.

At the time of our fieldwork, negotiations were generally organized at the level of the *groupement* in whose territory logging operations were taking place. As the second-lowest administrative level in the country, groupements consisted of several villages or *localités* and were part of a wider *secteur* or *chefferie*. Although *chefs de groupement* were official state agents, they also supposedly reflected customary power structures. For this reason, CTI and many other timber firms negotiated their cahiers des charges at this level.

New social responsibility contracts were, however, only the latest iteration of an older logic of gift giving. The cahiers des charges indeed formalized older practices of informal and ad hoc financial and in-kind transfers
between companies and village communities. As soon as CTI arrived in the
Itimbiri region, for instance, it needed to establish access to a concession it
had, legally speaking, already acquired from the then Zairean state. To this
end, it negotiated *protocoles d'accord* consisting of long lists of goods and
money along with promises to build schools or health centers, as well as
houses and offices for village chiefs. These voluntary contracts temporarily
lessened friction between the legal reality of state ownership of all land and
the countervailing reality of ancestral and community ownership of the forest and its trees.

The new cahiers des charges made obligatory what until then had been
merely voluntary. Initially, however, they retained the old methodology of
negotiating deals with local chiefs as legitimate spokespersons of resident
populations. Yet this format was far from representative. Not only did it
exclude large sections of village communities—women, youth, and immi-
grants—it was also a poor reflection of actual power structures. In many
cases rival lineages disputed the authority of officially recognized chefs de
groupement. Also, politicians and local notables, who often preferred to remain behind the scenes, manipulated *chefs de localité* in local and regional
power games. Villagers therefore often mistrusted their own representatives,
accusing them of "eating" the money and gifts they received from logging
companies.

To make up for these shortcomings, a 2008 ministerial decree imposed
a new methodology for the negotiation and realization of socioeconomic
projects. While, until then, they were the outcome of ad hoc agreements, the
new regulation made the amount of money reserved for community projects
directly dependent on the number of trees logged in each groupement. In
practice, logging companies now had to pay between two and five U.S. dollars
per cubic meter extracted from the forest—a variable price that was fixed for
each timber species according to its commercial value. This money was then
to be deposited in a local development fund (*fond local de développement*)
that was managed by a management committee (*comité local de gestion*)
consisting of a delegate from the logging company, five representatives from
village communities, and an observer from the civil society.

In reality, however, problems of embezzlement, overbilling, theft, and fa-
voritism remained. Also, in this new model the same people usually represented village communities. Many logging firms nevertheless hoped these

new structures would put a halt to what they often described as an escalation in compensation claims (see also Kirsch 2006). At least, they said, the price to be paid was now regulated and fixed.

It was indeed a running joke among company managers that unknowing forest residents naively claimed "airports in return for trees." As in other extractive industries, the idea that forest communities had utterly "unrealistic expectations" as to any feasible compensation for logging was a widespread cliché in the Congolese timber sector (Trefon 2016, 25). Julien, the long-haired French mechanic, for instance, once lectured me that, in the past, "the Congolese could be satisfied with pieces of glass and mirror. But now they ask for highways, airports, and universities." He thereby referred to a time when local chiefs, as stories had it, sold their land, ivory ("and even their women") for only a handful of colorful beads and trinkets. But even today, he implied, they still don't know the *real* value of things (Pietz 1985). While they had once given resources away "almost for free," people now believed they could "sell them for astronomical prices."

In effect, the European loggers were frustrated by what they perceived as villagers' stubborn, outrageous, and unrealistic demands. Yet the only time I actually heard a village chief ask for airports during negotiations was when he criticized the staggering differences in levels of development (*niveaux de développement*) between his region and the countries most whites in the room came from. What for many had merely been a rhetorical comparison, the expat managers took as proof of the sheer "irrationality" of their negotiation partners.

While stories about "highways, airports, and universities" thus served to reproduce old stereotypes about the naive emotionality of a racialized other, the CTI expats nevertheless agreed that, at some level, they *did* have a responsibility to develop the region. Yet, the company could not, they often repeated, compensate for a Congolese state that was largely absent or deficient, building roads and infrastructure the administration was incapable of building or unwilling to provide. Whereas their superiors in Kinshasa and Europe sold seductive stories of sustainable development, the concession managers knew that—*sur le terrain*—these were impossible to achieve.

Ever since it began operations in the Itimbiri region in the early 1990s, CTI had encountered difficulties working with village communities. The company had finished its first construction projects in the mid-1990s, but more than a decade later, many had already fallen into disarray. Others had been deferred because of the war, which had led to a five-year closure of the concession between 1998 and 2003. Afterward, everything had to be renegotiated.

New promises were made but difficult to realize. Delays therefore accumulated and tensions with village communities mounted.

During the favorable economic climate of the mid-2000s, the then French site manager was able to lavishly distribute cash to village chiefs and calm anxieties. But with the onset of the 2008 financial crisis profits evaporated, and Jens was called in as the manager who would get a grip on a deteriorating situation. Yet his decision not to hand out easy sweeteners to buy off "fake social calm," led many village representatives, accustomed to long and well-mannered negotiations, to experience his stern bluntness as deeply offensive. Some of them turned their backs on the company. Others took their place. In the end, Jens was unable to break away from the strong moral pull of gift giving. All he did was replace one beneficiary with another, thus swelling the ranks of disappointed officeholders and frustrated regional elites.

Jens had nonetheless arrived at a moment when CTI had begun to take its responsibilities toward concession inhabitants more seriously. Impelled by the European head office and its discourse of corporate social responsibility (CSR), the company indeed erected its new community buildings in concrete rather than wood. And it had hired Roger as construction manager in order to speed up the building process. CTI had also taken steps to certify its logging activities by an external auditing company, thereby hoping to access a market of so-called green timber. As part of this exercise, it had formed a social management team to better communicate with village communities, monitor the implementation of existing agreements, and negotiate new cahiers des charges. But despite these efforts, accumulated construction delays and broken promises remained a permanent powder keg. Roger's accelerated building in one village provoked others to demand similar timescales. And several villages wanted their deteriorated wooden buildings replaced with more durable brick constructions.

Structural flaws in the negotiation process also asserted themselves with new vigor. People contested the composition of official village delegations and accused their chiefs and councilors of withholding information about company meetings, monopolizing insider knowledge, and claiming a disproportionately large share of company gifts. CTI had therefore tried to work with a mediator (*promoteur social*) who was hired from one of the bigger villages in the concession. But the man had been ousted by his own neighbors after they discovered he had sold several bikes the company had donated to the community.

Moreover, as residents started to receive benefits in proportion to the amount of forest they could lay claim to, the exact location of historically fluid boundaries between their often-overlapping territories became a hotly contested issue. In areas where neighboring villages belonged to different language groups, such conflicts gave rise to new forms of ethnic exclusion, as autochthonous politicians and urban elites instrumentalized negotiations in the run-up to the 2011 national elections. As such, rather than resolve tensions, the construction of schools, health centers, and roads only provoked further escalation.

It must be noted that, unlike transnational mining or oil corporations that often engage in high-profile CSR programs and fancy development projects in order to procure a "social license" from surrounding communities, CTI had only modest sums to spend on community infrastructure and so had no choice but to deal with the frustrations these generated (Dolan and Rajak 2016). Moreover, while managers in Europe or Kinshasa had started to speak the language of CSR to the outside world, it had not yet trickled down to the concession. There were no ethical training sessions for its managers, no explosion of local NGOs as partners, and virtually no discourses on empowerment or entrepreneurialism that so often characterize CSR as a neoliberal technique of power.

As such, the CTI concession presented a rather different reality from Dinah Rajak's (2011, 73) characterization of the CSR programs of Anglo-American—a well-known mining corporation in South Africa—as a new "moral regime" that *reinforced* corporate power and authority by allowing the company to become a "corporate citizen." Rajak indeed shows how CSR is central to neoliberal capitalism and argues that, rather than serve as mere moral camouflage covering up business-as-usual, it is "profoundly bound up with the survival, the reproduction and adaptation of corporate hegemony" (89). While recognizing the messiness and failures of concrete programs, Rajak maintains that CSR "serves to empower the corporation" because it significantly extends neoliberalism's "capacity to command consent, silence dissent and co-opt support to its project" (213, 239–40).

The situation in CTI was strikingly different. It resembled instead the "impulsive, misplaced, and rather amateurish" CSR program that David Kneas (2016, 80) describes at a junior mining company in Ecuador. As we will see below, rather than sites for extending company agency and control, CTI's community projects were places of frustration, potential violence, and ecstasis. CTI discourses therefore explicitly identified and constructed the *so-*

cial as the source of its problems. As Penny Harvey and Hannah Knox (2015, 202) put it, for the expat loggers, the social indeed "emerge[d] as quite external to [their] technical framings, and [was] associated with a nontechnical, recalcitrant, or ignorant people who [did] not understand their own actions impede[d] the progress they . . . campaigned for." The social was therefore experienced as a site of failure: it not only stood for what engineering could *not* solve but also for what it was *unable* to disentangle itself from.

Roadblocks, Gifts, and Patronage

When Jens substantially accelerated production after the 2008 financial crisis, Roger's construction projects were unable to follow. Logging activities therefore moved more quickly through the concession than the building of promised community infrastructure. Several villages had their forest logged long before the first brick of a school or health center could be laid. More and more inhabitants grew frustrated with the continuous rescheduling of planned activities. Promises were not kept, and people feared their village would, once again, miss another opportunity. In this atmosphere of impatience and distrust, many openly criticized CTI's practices during meetings and negotiations. But anger also made some resort to more confrontational tactics.

Such popular protest often took the form of roadblocks (*barrières*) that spread throughout the concession in successive waves.[1] Usually they started a few days after village chiefs returned from another CTI meeting about the cahiers des charges. In one particular village, for instance, people had been promised that company workers would rebuild their school, construct a new health center, and surface the marketplace.[2] Yet, when their representatives returned from negotiations apparently empty-handed, villagers suspected they were hiding the actual deal. One schoolteacher demanded that the signed documents be shown to everyone. A man said the village chief and his allies had taken money from CTI in return for not putting their demands on the table. A woman openly accused the chief of cowardice.

"We therefore realized we needed to have *direct* negotiations with the company," the schoolteacher later told us. "Our chiefs did not speak for us." Although different factions in village politics held different opinions, more and more people called for cutting the road (*kokata nzela*). In previous months they had indeed seen how other villages had been able to get what they wanted after erecting a roadblock that forced CTI back to the negotiation table. And because all logging trucks had to pass through their village on their way to the company port, a blockade seemed a potent and effective device to make their discontent known.

One morning, the schoolteacher assembled relatives, friends, and neighbors to cut down a big tree over the road. They reinforced it with bamboo and heavy branches. Then they brought out chairs and a table to wait at the blockade—as an "official delegation" they said—for the first logging truck to arrive. Others assembled at the roadside to see what would happen. Some youngsters danced in anticipation.

The barrière was erected at a strategically chosen place that made it impossible for logging trucks to turn around. When the first driver arrived, he had no choice but to stop his vehicle. He knew that any accident would get him into serious trouble. Young men forced the driver to hand over his keys. "They were drunk and intoxicated with cannabis," the driver later told us, "and armed with machetes and spears." He thought he had even seen a gun. Some of his colleagues had been held hostage in other villages. But, luckily, he was allowed to go. Leaving his truck and the valuable logs behind, he walked back in the direction he came from. Half an hour later, another truck arrived, and the first driver stopped his colleague and told him to turn around. Together they drove back to the forest camp so they could radio the concession manager and tell him what had happened.

When the news arrived in the river camp, Jens exploded. He shouted he would never negotiate with "criminals" and "terrorists" and would not be "blackmailed." The radio message from the forest camp had mentioned that people were waiting for Jens to personally come to their village and renegotiate. But a deal is a deal, he said. They simply must accept what their chiefs had agreed on.

Jens therefore called the administrateur de territoire, who immediately deployed police agents and intelligence people to the chef de secteur of the area in which the "rebel village" was situated and asked them to mediate the conflict. Yet, for many villagers, these state agents and higher raking chiefs were allied to the same people they were trying to circumvent. The attempt at mediation therefore failed and led to a standoff that continued for several days. Growing impatient, Jens then urged the administrator from Bumba to send extra police and military to break (casser) the blockade by force—though, as past events had shown, such interventions could easily turn violent. The next day a group of policemen and naval force soldiers arrived. As they removed the barrière, they indeed destroyed belongings, looted livestock, and maltreated and extorted villagers, many of whom fled into the forest. Twenty men were arrested as instigators and taken to Bumba.

For weeks the village looked eerily abandoned. At first sight, the villagers seemed to have lost their gamble. The injuries, arrests, and material losses were indeed a heavy price to pay for a strategy that did not produce the direct negotiations they had hoped for.

Yet, in the long run, they partially succeeded. After two months of imposed calm, CTI organized a reconciliation meeting where the village chief was made to publicly apologize for the "irresponsible" action of "his people." In return, CTI promised to look into the refashioning of the village school after they had finished other building projects. And it symbolically sealed the renewed contract with extra gifts. This time, the machetes, bicycles, goats, and fuel were distributed more equally among families.

The schoolteacher later recognized that these new gifts were indeed a promising sign. Although the roadblock had not been able to force CTI into realizing all the building projects people had listed, it *had* reconfirmed the continuing relationship between the company and a village that had fallen out of a previous deal. Beyond their immediate and often violent consequences, roadblocks were therefore often surprisingly successful strategies for re-entangling CTI into moral economies from which it would otherwise disconnect (Gardner 2015).

In fact, whereas the company generally tried to reduce the negotiation of a cahier des charges to a one-off deal and simple compensation, most forest inhabitants considered these arrangements as part of an ongoing social contract that had to be kept alive. Repeated commitments and regular gifts were therefore essential. As Rebecca Hardin (2011, 119) suggests, gift giving is an important gesture in making and maintaining logging concessions because it positions the concession-holder as "a kind of big man" in relation to village communities. Jens and Roger indeed had no choice but to (reluctantly and cynically) *perform* the generosity, assistance, and corporate responsibility people expected from them. Hence, although CTI was largely unwilling to play within the rules of a moral economy, it was equally unable to resist its reproduction. Unable to stop giving, it could not but sustain the fiction of itself as a new patron in otherwise postpaternalist times.

Dinah Rajak (2011, 177) shows how, even in companies with more elaborate CSR strategies, concrete projects and programs often "re-invent older relations of patronage and clientelism" despite their neoliberal discourses about self-help, empowerment, and entrepreneurialism. Yet again the CTI logging concession showed a somewhat different reality. While Rajak emphasizes how the gift-like nature of CSR, no matter how much companies try to deny it, always creates highly "coercive bonds" that leave "the receiver in a position of indebtedness and vulnerable to the whims of the donor" (177), in the CTI concession it was the receivers, demanding more gifts, who pushed the donor into continuing moral obligations. Moreover, rather than generosity extending corporate power by commanding compliance and co-opting elites, CTI's reluctant gifts mainly provoked nervousness, impatience, and frustration.[3]

For this reason, the logic of "the gift" is not the only analytic with which to understand the tense relationship between CTI and village communities (Mauss 2012). While roadblocks effectively helped reproduce moral economies of patronage, they were also more direct avenues for demanding what concession inhabitants considered theirs and for actively claiming their share. As previously described, sharing the elephant (*partager l'éléphant*) was indeed an often-used phrase to express the entitlement of forest residents to a *rightful share* in CTI's profits (Ferguson 2015).

While the power of the gift does coerce the receiver, demanding one's "share" transgresses the rules of gift giving and coerces the donor (Rajak 2011, 220). As James Ferguson (2015) argues, *shares* are indeed neither gifts nor market exchanges: they already belong to owners and do not entail debts or expectations of a return. In contemporary Africa, Ferguson writes, many citizens effectively consider themselves "the *rightful owners* of a vast national wealth . . . of which they have been unjustly deprived through a historic process of racialized dispossession" (26). Particularly for the younger generation in the logging concession, memories and stories about past extraction only reinforced their current claim on whatever money CTI was making. Yet, for the European loggers, their incessant demands only reconfirmed racialized ideas about what they saw as the dependency, laziness, opportunism, and brutality of forest communities.

Surely such popular actions as roadblocks could acquire only relatively short-term benefits and goods already on offer rather than change structural problems, such as land dispossession or fiscal injustice, in the unequal relationship between the company and village communities. As such, they "mainly serve[d] to extend the provision of patronage, rather than to provoke structural change" (Edmond and Titeca 2019, 144). One should however be careful not to smuggle in normative ideas about what good politics should look like in a given context. Rather than automatically consider patronage as something always already unfavorable and suspicious, one might also try to understand the dependency it reproduces as a *desired* state without reducing such desires to merely false consciousness (Ferguson 2015). Most villagers indeed combined explicit critique of CTI's practices with a longing for its continued presence as a patron. As such, they were neither unambiguous supporters nor clear opponents of resource extraction (see also Kneas 2018).

But roadblocks were not the only strategy used to reopen negotiations or claim one's share. One night, for instance, armed men and hunters ambushed the company guards at the production camp in the forest to sabotage bulldozers, steal batteries, and empty fuel thanks. When workers arrived the next morning, the ambushers also forced them to hand over chainsaws, machetes, motor oil, petrol, protective helmets, and even shoes and work outfits. "We really had no choice but to obey," one of the skidders said. "The hunters were armed and dangerous." Moreover, because villagers were thought to possess occult medicines to mystically block (*kokanga*) the forest, provoke accidents or snakebites, and make workers get lost, one did what they asked.

Just like roadblocks, such acts of theft and sabotage tried to force the logging company back to the negotiation table. Yet, on the whole, they largely failed. In these cases, CTI indeed directly appealed to the police to recuperate what had been stolen. But it was often extremely difficult to track down saboteurs and find their loot. Several police officers, village chiefs, and politicians actively protected assumed perpetrators and helped sell stolen company fuel and equipment. For CTI managers, this complicity was a sure sign that the "whole population" was against them. "Nothing has changed," Roger once said; "they would still cut our throats if they got the chance." With their warrior-like attires and ecstatic behavior—real or imagined—young ambushers indeed resuscitated horrible postindependence stories of intoxicated Simba rebels mutilating Europeans that reproduced racial stereotypes of violent black masculinities.

In the end, roadblocks, theft, and sabotage became a serious financial concern for CTI. Jens estimated that every roadblock immediately made production costs increase by $10 per cubic meter—a rise of 15 to 20 percent. During our fieldwork, when roadblocks occurred once every three months or so, they were indeed a major obstacle to reaching required production targets. Moreover, conflicts were highly unpredictable and could suddenly intensify. Sometimes tensions in different villages clustered, resulting in a cascade of roadblocks that prevented any logs from arriving at the Congo River for more than a week.

As they undermined the already vulnerable profitability of timber production, it is not unthinkable that roadblocks and sabotage were important reasons why CTI executives and financial directors eventually decided to sell the company in 2012. Relations with village communities—and the violence they triggered—indeed generated such negative press that the European head office feared considerable reputational damage. But a concession closure was not what most villagers envisioned when they blocked logging roads, ambushed production sites, or mystically tied up the forest. They simply wanted their fair share and to make sure the company fulfilled its obligations. Yet, while their actions, claims, and protests did not directly aim for CTI's departure, the course of events was always difficult to control.

Fuel Smuggling

Roads were perhaps the major reason why most concession inhabitants did not want the company to leave. As soon as CTI arrived in the early 1990s, it had indeed built an extensive road grid to reach timber resources and reopened several overgrown state roads to evacuate logs. For the first time in decades, trucks were therefore able to pass through villages without getting stuck, enabling people to easily sell their bags of rice, maize, or cassava in Bumba.

For the expat managers, the well-maintained red gravel roads were a source of great pride. When receiving visitors from Kinshasa or Europe, they often took them on a tour to show the results of their never-ending "fight against erosion." Among themselves, they also discussed the state of "their" roads in great detail. No wonder that roadblocks and the sabotage of road-building machinery were experienced as such visceral attacks on their presence.

Yet the roads that reconnected isolated parts of the rainforest to a regional trading network also significantly opened up the concession. They brought with them new migrations that, as both foresters and environmentalists agreed, were an unwanted side effect of industrial logging. The concession, for instance, attracted professional hunters selling bushmeat (*nyama ya zamba, viande de brousse*), such as antelope, monkey, and pangolin; farmers selling beans, peanuts, and chickens along the roadside; and traders selling soap, salt, sugar, batteries, and cigarettes in logging camps. Mobile entrepreneurial women also specialized in following work teams through the forest to sell them drinks and meals, as well as intimacy and love. Some of them developed long-standing relationships with employees. Jeanine, for instance, often joked that "all the CTI workers were her husbands" when serving them liquor in the production camp.

The same roads also attracted professional fuel smugglers who bought and sold fuel in the wider region between Bumba and Aketi. The CTI concession was indeed a particularly attractive source of stolen diesel, gasoline, and motor oil. While some smugglers acquired their fuel from villagers selling their loot in the wake of roadblocks or ambushes, most of it was bought directly from CTI workers. Their lucrative activities were therefore a constant headache for company managers.

Fuel traders were widely known as *kaddafis*—a name that explicitly drew on the status of colonel Muammar al-Gaddafi, who, at the time of field-work, was still the national leader in Libya. Although some of these trad-ers were members of a recognized tax-paying association—the Association des Revendeurs des Produits Pétroliers de Bumba (ARPPB)—most kaddafis in the CTI concession operated outside the official syndicate. While ARPPB leaders condemned the latter as outlaws or *Arabes sauvages* (wild Arabs), they nonetheless recognized their illegal activities as the main source of fuel for all retailers in the region. In fact, ever since soldiers had pillaged the SEP Congo fuel company during the war, Bumba was without an official fuel supply. Kaddafis thus literally kept the region (and its generators) in motion. As a result, many city dwellers, traders, and businessmen considered fuel smuggling a justified activity. Trading—a substantial part of which occurred on motorbikes—would indeed have been much more difficult were it not for CTI's presence.

Literally siphoning off energy from the concession and rechanneling it toward markets, towns, and trading centers, many kaddafis had effectively become respected citizens. Some of them were even celebrated in local songs. Ousama, for instance, was often loudly applauded in Bumba's bars. His style, money, and mobility were also very popular among the girls of the CTI labor camps, and his nickname reflected his headstrong reputation. Everyone admired the brand-new motorcycle he had bought and appreci-ated the spectacular way in which he used to overload it with yellow plastic barrels of stolen fuel.

Like most kaddafi traders, Ousama usually made his deals with individ-ual bulldozer and skidder drivers in the CTI labor compounds. He prepaid them for a certain amount of fuel and then traveled to the production sites in the forest to gradually acquire what they had agreed to produce. In the early mornings, before European managers arrived, he could often fill some of his jars while skidders, bulldozers, and loaders were being fueled from the tank truck that daily brought diesel into the forest. The CTI pump attendant then simply noted down the liters Ousama tapped as if they were added to the vehicles. At the end of each workday he generally received a second round of fuel during the *remise-reprise*, when drivers handed over their machines to company guards for the night. During this operation, company clerks had to keep record of the amount of fuel that remained in each parked machine. But in determining fuel levels, they used a forged measuring staff that made it appear that more fuel was left in the machines than was actually the case. They could therefore sell the difference between both measurements without leaving any traces in the official consumption statistics.

Usually Ousama stayed in the production camps for two weeks on end, sleeping under a blue tarpaulin tent alongside the company guards and drinking coffee with the CTI radio operator. When Congolese staff or expat managers arrived, he simply disappeared into the forest. Every morning and evening he filled his jars and poured the fuel into bigger containers hidden nearby. During one such stay, he easily collected between two and three hundred liters of diesel, which netted up to $300 when sold in town.

At the time of our fieldwork, the scale of fuel smuggling was truly impressive. Jens claimed that no less than ten to twenty thousand liters of fuel were stolen each month. Not only did it cause considerable financial losses, it also generated frustrating shortages and delays. On his arrival, Jens had therefore declared an outright "war" on the kaddafis. But while he announced that CTI would financially compensate all policemen arresting fuel dealers, the dealers were notoriously difficult to capture. Most smugglers paid protection money to police commanders, army officials, and state agents who were only too eager to receive a percentage of their lucrative business. Some traders even had their own official documents (*feuilles de route*) to shield them from controls. And, even when arrested, many kaddafis simply escaped or were released.

Moreover, CTI workers and staff were themselves also heavily involved in the fuel trade. Some team overseers were known to turn a blind eye in return for receiving a part of the money their workers made. And even though the company promised financial rewards to employees denouncing their colleagues, a generalized silence reigned. At one point, CTI tried to install a paper control system for keeping watch over the fuel consumption of individual truck drivers and machine operators. Sometimes it withheld production premiums from conductors whose fuel consumption was suspiciously high. But cunning accounting mechanisms largely evaded company control. And skilled conductors were scarce. "We are literally leaking on all sides," Michel, the bony French forest overseer said. "But there isn't much we can do. We can't fire everyone!"

For CTI it was thus extremely difficult to take effective measures against widespread trafficking. Buying and selling stolen fuel was simply too deeply integrated into regional economies and local tactics of enrichment. Its ineradicable and always moving network as well as the complicity of CTI staff made fuel smuggling a particularly charged problem. For some expat loggers, the losing war against kaddafis became a personal obsession. Jens, for instance, sometimes took legal matters into his own hands when he "arrested" fuel smugglers on the road and drove them to the forest camp for interrogation, trying to obtain the names of the employees with whom they had collaborated. As such, the uncontrollability of the fuel trade pushed the company toward measures that were themselves beyond the law.

The war against kaddafis was therefore symptomatic of the frustratingly *permeable* nature of rainforest logging. Traversed by roads and constantly leaking fuel, the CTI concession was indeed profoundly open to its surroundings: literally perforated by the combined action of smugglers whose appropriation of stolen property was celebrated in local bars as a legitimate act to develop an otherwise fuel-deprived region.

The Impossible Enclave

Village roadblocks and fuel smuggling illustrate how deeply CTI was entangled in economic dynamics, moral logics, and sociopolitical arrangements over which it had limited control. Both can be understood as forms of popular action that allowed ordinary people to capture a part of what they considered their rightful share. Roadblocks were indeed erected to remind CTI managers of distributive obligations and to reestablish a violated moral economy of patronage and assistance. Fuel theft was widely justified for enhancing otherwise deprived mobilities and for allowing the region to benefit from CTI's presence.

Roadblocks, sabotage, theft, smuggling, a losing war against kaddafis, and the occasional violent arrests of villagers broke every illusion of a smoothly running logging operation. Through them, CTI managers indeed experienced a frustrating dependency on the outside world—intrusions of the social into the technical. Moreover, the physical presence of free women, informal traders, professional hunters, and bushmeat sellers were experienced as *threats* to the ideal of ecologically sustainable forestry. When photographed, their bodies made for bad press and became ammunition in environmentalist campaigns against the very legitimacy of industrial timber production in tropical rainforests.

This chapter effectively illustrates how and why the CTI concession was crisscrossed by people, stories, memories, affects, dynamics, and interests that remained frustratingly beyond corporate reach. The company was fundamentally *entangled*—morally, practically, economically, and politically—in the environment from which it so much desired to distance itself. These entanglements undermine the popular idea of an always already strong company able to impose its will on relatively powerless people by excluding unwanted populations from its activities.

In an influential analysis, James Ferguson, for instance, argues that transnational capital increasingly creates "investment enclaves" on the African continent that are "tightly integrated with the head offices of multinational corporations and metropolitan centers, but sharply walled off from their own national societies (often literally walled, with bricks and razor wire)" (Ferguson 2005, 379). As such, these neoliberal enclaves would form a transnational network of "hopping" global capital that is largely separated from the state and lacks the "social thickness" that characterized late-colonial paternalist investment (379; see also Ferguson 2006). Operated by expatriates, secured by private companies, and providing little or no benefit to the wider society, such enclaves are thought to be profoundly *dis*connected from their immediate environments (Harvey 2003; Sidaway 2007).

Yet one cannot take the tightly secluded neoliberal enclave as the unique spatial model for thinking about extractive capitalism. This ethnography indeed shows a different reality. The CTI concession was profoundly open, porous, and vulnerable to its surroundings. Rather than walled off from its environment, it was traversed by roads and regionally traded commodities; crisscrossed by smugglers, hunters, policemen, and free women; in the grip of stories, rumors, claims, and memories; and generating frictions and occasions for capture and violence. Moreover, instead of lamenting the "enclaving" of their forest, residents often mentioned how CTI "*dis*-enclaved" a marginalized region.[4]

To some extent it is the inherent permeability and mobility of rainforest logging that prevents the tight enclaving of tropical timber concessions. As argued in the introduction, logging companies usually have no choice but to share their space with farmers, hunters, traders, and smugglers. While many mines or oil sites, by contrast, are intensely surveilled with checkpoints, badge systems, and elaborate health and safety regulations—logging concessions often have to operate without such levels of control. Only a wobbly bamboo barrier, for instance, crossed the main access road to the CTI concession, but it was rarely staffed and usually left open. And while expat managers sometimes patrolled the roads in their ongoing fight against fuel smugglers or bushmeat traders, an extensive network of ancestral footpaths, old railway tracks, and abandoned logging roads made effective control of people and goods practically impossible.

Moreover, in contrast to Ferguson's highly secured and secluded enclaves, logging concessions are not generally carved out from a national territory. On the contrary, the CTI concession intensified rather than hollowed out state presence. Seventeen policemen, two police commanders, six naval soldiers, and eight officials working for the immigration, intelligence, and river transport services were permanently stationed in its labor camps and work sites. And inspectors from the forest administration and health department regularly visited its premises. Notwithstanding the regular gifts of money and petrol these state agents received, their relationships with CTI were often tense. Immigration officials, for instance, sometimes threatened expat managers with visa regulations, and policemen, soldiers, and intelligence agents, though directly paid by the company, remained whimsical allies at best. In the Itimbiri region, where state presence was patchy, the concession was therefore not so much an enclave outside the law as an uneasy reclamation of space *by* the law where "politics thickens, rather than thins out" (Côte and Korf 2018, 467).

Unlike larger corporations that can often count on in-house security agents or private security firms, CTI indeed had to rely on state police and military for its protection, but the latter were notoriously unreliable. Corrupt police commanders stationed their pawns in the concession to benefit from lucrative fuel deals. And forces that were called in to break roadblocks often committed abuses that, though under the direct responsibility of the administrateur de territoire, severely damaged CTI's reputation. Human rights and environmentalist organizations effectively accused the company of actively contributing to an atmosphere of violence, an accusation CTI could hardly refute as long as it paid motivation bonuses to policemen and soldiers, lent out company trucks for their transport, or lodged their commanders in company housing.

Hence, the neoliberal enclave is, at most, an imperfect model for a far more complex reality. Recent ethnographies of contemporary resource extraction indeed show how and why enclaves are permanently unfinished, fragile, and partially failing. Alex Golub (2014) and Marina Welker (2014) in particular describe how big mining corporations are constantly sucked into moral responsibilities toward local communities and remain, despite their actual powers, vulnerable to, rather than shielded from, their environments. Even offshore oil platforms—those very formations from which Ferguson theorizes neoliberal capitalism—cannot be taken for granted as simply existing enclaves. Studying an oil rig in Equatorial Guinea, Hannah Appel (2012a, 2012b) indeed describes the "offshore" as a vulnerable product of difficult processes of disentanglement that require work, effort, and massive investments. Although she ultimately provides an example of the relative success of enclaving, her analysis starts from thick webs of proliferating relations and sticky entanglements to show why detachment and separation is a rare and costly achievement that is constantly threatened by what it excludes (Appel 2019a).

While enclaving might very well be an increasingly common spatial strategy for attracting and securing foreign capital in a neoliberal world, actually existing enclaves are, in practice, only ever partial realizations of their own project. Close ethnographic attention to ongoing processes of entanglement is thus necessary for understanding how multinational corporations unfold in regional dynamics from which they often try to "detach" or "disconnect" with various degrees of success (Cross 2011; Gardner 2015).

This chapter describes the CTI concession as an open and porous space entangled in assemblages not of its own making. Incapable of living up to popular expectations sustained by memories of a paternalist past, but equally unable to disentangle itself from their repeated expressions, CTI had to operate from a position of frustrating *im*possibility in an unpredictable milieu that profoundly shaped its actions.

To a large extent, the enclave model could affect the Congolese logging sector only as an unattainable dream. When they talked about oil rig or mine managers they knew in other African countries, for instance, the European loggers often admitted to being jealous of the apparent tranquility and secluded and luxurious lives of these colleagues. In the forest, by contrast, they said they felt "overwhelmed" by concession residents whose physical closeness they experienced as threatening. For this reason, they tried very hard to keep their bungalows and living quarters as essentially white and segregated from their black neighbors. Yet, as we will see in chapter 6, the material and symbolic walls and fences they drew around themselves were also constantly negated and transgressed. Haunted by what Florence Bernault (2003) calls a "politics of enclosure," the impossibility of their desire for distance, quietness, and separation thereby became one more catalyst for ecstasis.

The violence described in the previous pages needs to be understood from this existential position of experienced impotence (see also Henriet

2021). The abuse that accompanied breaking up roadblocks or arresting fuel smugglers was not merely a display of the logging company's force. Unable to control the policemen and soldiers who were supposed to protect its operations, CTI was literally drawn into physical violence and taken in by its consequences. More than a sign of corporate strength, violence appeared as a symptom of weakness (Kneas 2016). Together with the stubborn insistence of popular demands, the constant re-spinning of webs of patronage, and the ineradicable nature of fuel theft, unpredictable violence indeed added substantial layers of uncertainty to an already fragile production process. Escalating conflicts maneuvered the company into an aggressive state that was a serious liability in the long run.

Violence was therefore another face of ecstasis. Roadblocks, theft, sabotage, and smuggling were indeed ecstatic moments and activities—not only for those who tried to stop them but *also* for those who participated in or collaborated with them. The nervousness about building projects slipping away, the anger about broken promises and corrupt village chiefs, the anticipation of a direct confrontation with the logging company, the liquor- and cannabis-induced courage, the fear experienced when policemen descended on villages, the risk of being caught, the quickness of escape, the thrill of success, and the possibility of betrayal all added to an ecstatic atmosphere—a contagious mood that, as the next chapter illustrates, also affected life in the CTI labor compounds themselves.

Photo studio in the labor compound featuring affiches, *colorful Chinese posters*

Out of Here

MARCEL ESIBO WAS A 45-YEAR-OLD CHAINSAW OPERATOR originating from a village north of Bumba. As such, he was one of the few skilled Mbudza men in his work team. For this reason, he and his family occupied a house in the central camp, alongside his colleagues from the felling, road-building, and production teams. Most other Mbudza workers, by contrast, lived at the far end of the labor compounds, as they were employed as prospectors or trackers.

An Embudza-speaking family, the Esibos were indeed considered locals or *autochtones* (that is, native to the region). But Marcel's village was quite far from the CTI concession. The forest camp was situated at the easternmost fringe of Mbudza-dominated territory, and the land on which it had been built was claimed by both the nearest Mbudza village (ten kilometers to the west) and the nearest Bati village (thirteen kilometers to the east). Families from both villages however constituted only a small minority of those actually inhabiting the camp agglomeration. Like many of his neighbors, Marcel therefore maintained that "in the camp, we all come from elsewhere."

There was nevertheless a clear social distinction between people working for the timber firm and villagers (*bavillageois*). This demarcation was immediately visible in the camp layout as a stark difference between company-built wooden barracks and self-constructed, mud-and-stick houses. The former constituted seven official camp quarters, while the latter formed five illicit squatter neighborhoods where a significant number of farmers, traders, jobseekers, and so-called free women had built houses since the camp was erected in 1994. This demarcation between workers and villagers overlapped, albeit only partially, with emic differentiations between autochtones and foreigners (*bapaya*). Local Embudza-speaking and, to a lesser extent, Kibati-speaking families mainly inhabited the unofficial neighborhoods as well as two adjacent new settlements. Official camp quarters, on the other hand, were home to a multiethnic community of workers in which no fewer than twenty-three household languages were spoken—among them, Embudza, Kibenza, Kibango, Mongo, Kibati, Kikongo, Kimbesa, and Ngombe.

This diverse worker population was the direct result of CTI's past hiring practices. Whenever the company closed down older concessions, its managers transferred their most valuable and skilled workers to new locations. But the camp's diversity also reflected broader path dependencies within the wider timber sector, as different logging firms employed workers who had been laid off by their competitors. Over the past decades, the sector had thereby given birth to a highly mobile and ethnically mixed population of self-identified *forestiers*.

Yet despite these material differences, spatial boundaries, and socioethnic specificities, the forest camp was a tightly interwoven agglomeration in which everyday life was marked by mutual dependencies that transcended existing divisions. Creditor-debtor relationships, for instance, brought staff members, ordinary workers, traders, and bar owners together. Workers and smugglers met over fuel deals that could lead to long-term partnerships. CTI employees depended on neighboring farmers and hunters for food. And bars, churches, and boutiques, though sometimes catering to people from particular social or ethnic backgrounds, were often popular socializing places for all. Most if not all camp residents also spoke Lingala as a common vernacular.

Moreover, it was often assumed—but difficult to prove—that many if not most of those who had settled in and around the CTI labor compounds had done so because of tensions with and in their villages of origin. Camp residents effectively talked about themselves as a community of outsiders: people who were attracted by the opportunities the place afforded—and who stayed for as long as its promises outweighed its hardships. Hence, although the labor compounds offered clear pathways for social distinction, they also pushed their residents into a lived commonality.

_____

This chapter looks into everyday life in these timber camps. How did people experience their peculiar living environment? How did they navigate its opportunities and pitfalls? And how did company managers interact with and try to control those who inhabited "their" camps? As generic spaces, camps are often imagined as sites of strict discipline and surveillance. To some extent, the CTI labor camp—with its neat rows of wooden barrack-like houses, architectural anonymity, utilitarian infrastructure, modular organization, and generic placelessness—seemed to lend itself to panoptical control. Haunted as it was by a racialized and violent history, it certainly reminded me of a world I had hoped no longer existed. But the camp was also a place of freedom and escape, hope and possibility: a place that attracted people and oriented them outward. This chapter therefore describes the violence, boredom, and difficulty of everyday camp life as well as its attractions and seductions. Both aspects were part of the timber camps' characteristically ecstatic and ecstatogenic atmosphere.

To understand this particular environment, this chapter starts with a portrait of the Esibo family and describes how camp inhabitants aspired to urban forms and selves while making their lives through largely rural pathways. It then shows how, despite the multiple opportunities and mobilities the logging camps generated, many inhabitants felt trapped in a nervous state of immobility. As a result, they devised strategies for accelerating the rhythm of camp life, for instance through game playing, troublemaking, or drinking. The chapter then looks at workers' homemaking practices to illustrate how quotidian experiences of camp space and camp time were deeply oriented to an outside, as if they were stretched by centrifugal forces that largely propelled desires and imaginations outward. The final section describes everyday camp management and investigates the scope of corporate power when it came to actual interventions in the labor compounds—foregrounding violence as well as relative neglect as further aspects of ecstasis.

Living In Between

At first sight, the CTI logging camps rematerialized an old tradition of camp architecture in the region (De Meulder 1996; Rubbers 2019). But although the identical houses built alongside a rectangular road grid resuscitated memories of late-colonial plantations, the timber camps offered none of their characteristic social provisions and services, subsidized shops, clinics, clubhouses, flowerbeds, organized leisure activities, or educational programs that people often remembered from the heydays of paternalism when "model camps" were thought to be laboratories for a "new welfare society" (De Meulder 1996, 34). Instead, the CTI camp seemed undressed to its older, naked, ugly core—offering only the minimal necessities for survival and producing "bare life" rather than "good life" (Agamben 1998). And yet, life in the camps was still surprisingly attractive. A closer look at the Esibo family illustrates this paradox.

Notwithstanding Marcel Esibo's unique position as an autochthonous worker with a permanent labor contract, his house and household were fairly typical for the timber camp. Apart from Marcel, it consisted of Monique, his 43-year-old wife, their two sons and four daughters, as well as Monique's younger sister, Marcel's older brother, two of Marcel's younger brothers, and two of his paternal cousins. Marcel's younger brothers had arrived in 2003 to look for work after the second Congo War. They had promised to build a house of their own but had been stuck with their brother ever since. Their older brother had recently divorced and, at the time of our fieldwork, was hiding from his in-laws. The two cousins used to be long-distance *kwamutu* traders who had started to transport rice from villages in the concession to Bumba by bicycle.

As with most families, the Esibos had extended their two-bedroom house with additional constructions. Marcel, Monique, and their youngest son slept in one of the rooms in the main house, while their three youngest daughters slept in the second room. Their eldest daughter and her maternal aunt occupied a tiny room in the kitchen hut. Marcel's three brothers and two cousins each shared a self-constructed outbuilding (*annexe*). Together, these buildings surrounded an open space, at the center of which was a half-open hut (*paillote*) that was used to receive visitors. Every morning Monique meticulously swept clean the entire fenced-in family plot (*lopango*) to remove dirt and keep out snakes. By thus eliminating all "matter out of place," she kept the surrounding forest at bay and carefully reconfirmed the spatial and conceptual separation between the plot and the bushy areas that separated the camp from the forest beyond (Douglas 1966).

Like one in two worker households, the Esibos also cultivated their own field. Two years before, Marcel had paid two young men from Quartier Mobutu to open up a patch of primary forest at the other side of the Mamoissa rivulet. Together with her daughters, Monique daily visited this field to sow, plant, weed, and harvest cassava, spinach, maize, and plantains. She was very proud of her agricultural skills. Rare were the days, she said, when she had to buy cassava from farmers. Every afternoon one could see her grating boiled cassava roots with that characteristic Mbudza knife on a long handle to prepare a lightly textured *libulia*—her signature dish of cold cassava mash. Other worker families, she said, had to rely on local villagers because, having spent most of their lives in labor camps, they "lacked the skills, knowledge, and courage" to successfully undertake cultivation. But Monique had not grown up in a labor camp. She was the daughter of farmers.

For running the family, the Esibos had agreed that, each month, Marcel would hand over his entire salary to Monique. In return, Marcel's monthly production premiums were for his own use. "But I often have to beg Marcel for more money," Monique laughed. One of their daughters, for instance, needed regular treatment for a gynecological problem. Their youngest often needed money for school, which required paying off teachers. And their oldest son's girlfriend turned out to be pregnant, which meant Marcel and Monique would probably have to pay the girl's family.

For this reason, while they all depended on Marcel's wage work, most Esibos also generated incomes of their own. Monique owned a small kiosk where she sold basic household articles such as salt, sugar, coffee, milk powder, canned sardines, matches, cigarettes, and—at least until Marcel's older brother, a notable alcoholic, arrived—locally produced liquor. Together with her sister she also farmed a second maize field and sold its produce via Marcel's cousins in Bumba. Her oldest daughter made her own money by assisting a neighboring seamstress. She also regularly received gifts from two suitors (whom she strategically kept at a distance with sweet promises that rarely seemed to materialize). Monique's oldest son had recently bought a digital camera with money borrowed from his sister and constructed a photo studio next to the market area where people paid him to take their portraits. And he had struck a deal with one of the CTI cartographers to print these pictures after office hours.

All extra money was very welcome. Because of its isolated location, the cost of living in the forest camp was relatively high, and the prices of many imported goods were up to three times higher than in town. Many lamented their living conditions. There was no electricity or running water, company-built houses had leaking roofs and rotting walls, schooling was difficult, medicines were often in short supply, and mobile phone contact with the outside world was impossible. Hence, although most camp inhabitants devised inventive schemes for generating money on the side, they still maintained that

the forest camp essentially lacked real opportunities. Many were also indebted to neighbors, traders, and payroll managers who illegally advanced
money by charging monthly interest rates of up to 20 or 30 percent. As a
result, cash seemed to evaporate all too quickly.

Furthermore, Marcel often bitterly complained about family members
turning up to demand money. Refusing them was difficult, he said. For this
reason, most of his colleagues preferred to work in concessions farther away
from their places of origin. Others chose to spend their money immediately—
on liquor or women, for instance. Yet, as a devout Christian, Marcel claimed
he had to "resist these temptations." The little he managed to save was used
for gradually constructing a modest house on the outskirts of Bumba. Other
workers invested in small plantations. But nobody invested in the camp itself. Money was either spent or evacuated. Haunted by memories of past
interruptions and rumors about imminent company closures, the CTI camp
was indeed no place for investing. Many believed the camp had no future,
only a fleeting present. The future was always already elsewhere.

And yet, the same logging camp was also a site of strong regional attraction. A place to construct new livelihoods and where lucrative deals were
in the air. Villagers knew that CTI workers, despite their complaints, had
money to spend. And, in comparison to the surrounding villages, the forest
camp generated a palpably urban-like atmosphere. Some workers had their
own generators, played loud music in the evenings, and turned their plots
into popular bars. Team overseers and Congolese staff sold beer kept cool in
refrigerators powered by electricity tapped from the work site. Fuel smugglers cruised the camp on new motorcycles. Traders showed off their latest
Chinese-made smartphones. And no fewer than seventeen churches catered
to the camp's population. As such, the forest camp also embodied a certain
"elegance and sophistication" that, as described by Nancy Rose Hunt (2016,
15), has a long history in the region: an atmosphere that was not limited to
cities and towns but that also "moved along rivers and streams," stitching the
labor compounds into a nationwide fabric of urban ambiance (248).

The CTI logging camp might therefore best be understood as a profoundly "heterotopian" site—a contradictory *other* place that mirrored,
sometimes in reverse, several other places at once (Foucault 1984). Neither
village nor town, the compound indeed defied the division between urban
and rural, bringing the urbanity of the city (*la ville*) into the rurality of the
forest (*la brousse*)—as both promise and mirage. For many, the camp offered
temporary freedom and escape from kinship relations and pressing village
moralities. For others, it merely attracted scum, criminals, drunkards, and

witches. The camp also resembled the ruins of older labor compounds, plantations, and factories, reflecting an image of what they still might be—but never attaining what they once were. As such, it sustained the attraction of the salary in a largely post-labor environment while also disclosing its largely illusionary nature.

The labor compound was indeed lived as an ambiguous in-between site wherein things were in constant flux and yet also in a strange state of stasis (Masquelier 2019, 26). The camp generated aspiration and anticipation but rarely lived up to its promises. In this place of contradictory injunctions and double binds, people were always on the move and yet felt stuck. Surfing on the rhythm of industrial logging, with its accelerations and disruptions, it was a place that could simply disappear overnight but that probably looked exactly like the next. A place that captured mobile workers in their chase for the good life and reproduced a "cruel optimism" that promised urbanity, work, distinction, and development (Berlant 2011). A place where many nervously stayed because they feared that, if they left, they would miss what they had waited for. As such, real and expected mobilities could always turn into lived *im*mobilities, and a particular kind of boredom invaded everyday life.

Playing against Boredom

It was an afternoon like many others. Workers had not yet returned from work. Women had gone to the river or were puttering around their kitchens. Many teenagers had gone to school, and smaller children were sleeping.

Freddy and I sat in plastic chairs under our neighbors' paillote taking shelter from the sun. At this time of the day paillotes were popular places for young men to hang out, chat, sleep, dream, or just sit (*kofanda kaka*). Martin, our neighbor's son, discreetly talked to a visitor about a new business deal or "coop"—shorthand for *coopération*. Like many camp residents, Martin was always looking out for opportunities to mediate between possible buyers and sellers of all kinds of goods and services—from goats, radios, rice, and diamonds to sex or a CTI job. Yet, despite his many deals and collaborations, he stubbornly maintained that he "did nothing" and "made no progress in life."

Our conversations ebbed and flowed between Martin's complaints and everyday gossip. Martin's cousin, who had recently come to live with us, slowly rearranged his stock of cannabis in what looked like a lady's purse. His inseparable friend slept on a low bamboo bed, snoring on top of a small radio under his head. Time slowed down. There was nothing to do. Martin stretched out on a thin matrass. He closed his eyes. But his leg nervously quivered up and down. Sometimes he seemed to drift away, but the sound of each passing motorcycle or barking dog alerted him.

During my stay in the forest camp I came to enjoy the relative boredom of these afternoons. My companions, on the other hand, often seemed to be waiting for something to happen. Longing for action, their boredom was not like mine—a melancholic weltschmerz from which I drew some pleasure—but a restlessness generated by frustrating experiences of immobility and feelings of being "stuck in the compound" (Hansen 2005). A continuing alertness to make deals while doing nothing. A staying awake while dozing off.

To express these feelings of restlessness, camp inhabitants used words for which "to be bored" can only be an imperfect translation (Musharbash 2007). *Kotungisa*, for instance, meant to irritate, irk, bother, or trouble; *kolembisa*, to discourage, fatigue, and slow down. Although boredom was rarely named as an abstract feeling, people sometimes used the noun *mpi* for describing a situation of generalized dislike. But mpi was not the passive ennui or existential resignation that historians have described as the "privilege" of modernity in the recent West (Svendsen 2005). To feel bored (*koyoka mpi*) was to feel unease, to have too many preoccupations (*mitungisi*) taking up one's heart, and to constantly worry over one's future (Mains 2007, 2017). Hence, mpi denoted active irritation and impatience rather than detachment: the nervous quivering of a leg rather than the empty gaze of apathy, pointed restlessness rather than indulgently doing nothing (Masquelier 2019, 47). In my friends' words, "warming up" rather than "cooling down."[1]

Suddenly Bibiche turned around the corner, abruptly waking me from my slumbering thoughts on the situatedness of boredom. "What news, you useless bastards?" she asked in her familiar high-pitched voice. Bibiche was the flamboyant cousin of another family in our neighborhood. She provocatively pulled a chair from the kitchen toward the paillote, consciously pushing against unspoken gender norms of who could sit where. Freddy tried to ignore her and mimicked an air of disinterest. We all knew about their on-and-off flirtations. I asked Bibiche what *she* had been up to. "Nothing much" she said, deliberately reflecting back to me the answer young men so often gave.

"Why don't we play another game?" she said, asking for the wooden *jeu de six* board Martin kept in his room. In the forest camp, jeu de six—a Ludo game played by four players with pawns on a board—was a favorite game of the unemployed (*jeu des chômeurs*). Bibiche was one of the few women who occasionally measured herself in this game of luck. She put the game board on a small table and encouraged us to join. We agreed and took a small plastic cup used for throwing the dice as well as six pawns made from different colors and materials. These pawns—our children (*bana*)—had to go around the board and enter their home (*kokota ndako*) before other players caught them and sent them to prison.

We first threw the dice to decide who would go first. After Bibiche rolled the highest number, she put the dice in her cup, shook them in front of her forehead, loudly shouted "sixo," and threw them on the board with great force. A six and a one. "Merci," she said, and smiled, because a six brings another child into circulation. Martin was next: a four and a three. "Pirate," he said, as if someone had stolen (*koyiba*) or falsified (*piraté*) his luck. Freddy's turn: another six and a three. He moved one of his pawns on the board, gladly chasing Bibiche's child. My turn: two fives. "Bad luck," I said.

With each round, the pace of the game increased. We often threw our dice before the others had moved their pawns, so it became quite unclear where exactly all the children were on the board or whose turn it was. Pawns that seemed to be somewhere were already somewhere else. And players captured children before the latter were in their true position. Such deliberate accelerations were part of the game: they created new possibilities but also led to accusations of cheating. Sometimes, sessions were simply aborted in bitter but short-lived fights.

Like the card games played by tea-drinking young men in Niger and studied by Adeline Masquelier (2019, 55), jeu de six brought "intense, excessive delight as well as a sense of liberation to [its] participants." Such games were indeed instances of what Clifford Geertz (1972) calls "deep play" and what Masquelier (2019, 54–55) describes as an "all-absorbing form of competitive engagement and a high-stakes venture during which masculinity and social status [were] reaffirmed." Continuing one after another as a tactic to temporarily enliven the passage of time, games could go on for hours. The high tempo, moments of suspense, and sudden eruptions of anger effectively accelerated time not only for the players but also for its onlookers. In this sense, jeu de six was a common device for creating a contagiously ecstatic *playtime*—a "heterochronic" other time that somehow broke the monotony of camp life (Foucault 1984, 48).

The outcomes of such games were not determined by mere chance or accident, however, but rather depended on the inner strength and personal luck (*elikiya*) of their players. People sought to influence their throws by engaging in particular shaking movements, by blowing their breath of life (*mpema ya bomoi*) into the plastic cup, or by exclaiming such things as *kindoki* (witchcraft), *Gécamines* (name of the largest copper company in the country), or

Maison Blanche (the White House). Players also switched pawns that stayed in prison for a suspiciously long time with others, hoping they might respond better to their techniques. Some simply grabbed the plastic throwing cup of a more successful player and thereby tried to steal (*koyiba*) his luck.

As such, games opened up another temporality where, in principle, everybody could win, even though real life was full of failures and obstacles. Repeatedly winning at jeu de six was an indication that, despite being unemployed or lacking money, a man—and, less often, a woman—disposed of a powerful force or agency to intervene in what might otherwise appear as mere coincidence beyond control. Throwing dice was indeed like firing a gun: both are expressed by the same verb, *kobeta*. Rather than a passive idea of luck, it expressed the active taking of a carefully prepared opportunity. Something that was always uncertain, but never aleatory, since it depended on the experience, agility, mental state, and inner luck of the player in question. As devices for ecstasis, games thus reestablished "purposeful temporalities" in which new and stronger selves could be performed beyond the limitations of the here and now (Masquelier 2019, 31). As such, they illustrate how closely related losing control and taking control can be: it was indeed by *losing* themselves in games that players *took* control over the passage of time.

Accelerating the World

Ludo board games were not the only means of accelerating time or manipulating the *tempo* of action (Bourdieu 1977, 7). Camp inhabitants also had other strategies at their disposal to revolt against boredom. As we will see in chapter 7, church services, for instance, offered ecstatic escape routes out of the present moment—especially if and when people prayed and danced for hours, spoke in tongues, or trembled when visited by the Holy Spirit. And residents also used alcohol or drugs to explicitly change, as they put it, the rhythm of the world (*le rythme du monde*).

While many workers secretly smoked cannabis (*mbangi*) while at work in the forest, others discreetly shared their "relax" in huts at the outskirts of the labor compounds. But while drugs were used in relatively private settings, alcohol, by contrast, was usually consumed in public, often in one of the camp's bars (*nganda*) or under a neighbor's paillote. Those who could afford it bought bottles of beer to show off their social distinction and urban style in contrast to more rural drinking habits (Ferguson 1999). But the choice of drinks was also a matter of individual tastes that differentiated one from another. One of the bulldozer drivers, for instance, swore he only drank Turbo

King, a rather expensive brand of dark beer that, as its commercial had it, was *une affaire d'hommes*—something for men only.

Others went for cheaper, locally distilled liquors (*munzelenge, agene, arak, bobo*) sold in soft drink or beer bottles that were often filled from vessels also used for fuel smuggling. As a result, it was not uncommon for liquor to taste like diesel—a mixture that many workers claimed had particularly fortifying qualities. In contrast to individual beer bottles, liquor was usually shared between friends, who passed around one small drinking cup in a clockwise direction while the glass bottle remained in the middle. As such, alcohol provided an avenue for performing individuality as well as for reinforcing social bonds (Van Wolputte and Fumanti 2010).

Bars were therefore places that simultaneously reproduced and broke social boundaries and norms, where job seekers, smugglers, workers, and staff mingled *and* claimed their differences. Moreover, especially for unmarried workers and those who stayed in the compounds without their families, they also provided ample sexual opportunities. Their music, dancing, and free women indeed produced an erotic "ambiance" that signaled the camp's desired urbanity (Biaya 1996). For some, they even opened up possibilities for gender inversions, sexual transgressions, and queer experiments (see also Hendriks 2016).

But drinking or getting stoned (*kolangwa*) was mainly a way for camp residents to forget about their problems. Local liquor in particular was seen as a drink of consolation and relief (*masanga ya libondi*) that chased away the camp's hardships. Cannabis, on the other hand, warmed up (*etokisi*) life, produced the strength to work hard, stimulated the appetite for food and sex, and made one "see others as smaller than oneself." Moreover, like a game of jeu de six, it literally changed time: accelerating heartbeats but also slowing down thoughts. Sometimes it "killed" time altogether (Ralph 2008).

Beyond game playing, praying, drinking, and smoking, some camp inhabitants also deliberately changed the rhythm of the world by creating trouble (*mobulu*) as a welcome interruption of the monotony of camp time (Jervis et al. 2003). Trouble indeed gave people something to watch and talk about. Several young men, workers and nonworkers alike, were specifically known as troublemakers (*bana ya mobulu*, literally, "children of trouble"), whose skills in looking for (*koluka*) or stirring up (*kopelisa*) trouble were simultaneously disapproved of *and* admired. While trouble was a constant possibility some places and moments were nonetheless more troublesome than others. Bars were obvious sites where fights and jealousies easily erupted. But, perhaps surprisingly, funerals also were events where trouble was expected—and even required (Biaya 1998; De Boeck 1998a and 2005).

Funeral wakes or *matanga* were multiday gatherings in which people paid their respects to the deceased and their family, participated in religious services, chitchatted, ate, drank, and caught up with visitors. On average, one or two matangas were organized every month in the forest camp—sometimes for relatives who had passed away in a different part of the country. As such, they were a common part of life. Usually, camp inhabitants gathered in the parcel of the bereaved family to listen to pastors and church bands. But at night, prayers and religious ceremonies gave way to worldly music and (supposedly immoral) *ndombolo* dances. Rumors then also accelerated about possible witches (*bandoki*) who had eaten away the life force of the deceased. And accusations increased in volume.

In this atmosphere of grief, anger, and insult, alcohol and drugs sped up time at the very moment death had brought it to a standstill. As more and more visitors arrived, small quarrels often erupted. And although pastors and elders generally tried to smooth tensions, young men deliberately stirred up the flames. One night, Carlo, one of our neighbors' sons, took off his clothes to face his opponents in his battle gear (*tenue ya etumba*). The next day he proudly told me that he had only taken advantage of a diabolical spirit (*esprit diabolique*) that was already there.

In contemporary DRC, funerals have been described as potentially Bakhtinian events during which social norms can be reversed and life itself contested (De Boeck 2008). But while in urban contexts burials have become prime sites for political contestation and generational conflict, in the forest camp, their antistructural dimension seemed to have been largely accepted as an almost unavoidable and even necessary aspect of heterochronic matanga time. Rather than youngsters explicitly taking over the organization from their parents, funeral wakes alternated between paying respect and performing transgression—to such an extent at times that transgression seemed to temporarily *become the norm* (see also Hendriks 2021). As such, matanga nights, when troublemaking alternated with quieter hours of dozing off around smoldering fires, aptly illustrate the otherwise more implicit normalization of ecstasis.

Dreaming "Otherwheres"

The forest camp was not only a profoundly hetero*topian* space that trapped people's aspirations for a better life but also, as we have seen, a strikingly hetero*chronic* environment where time got stuck until people actively shifted its rhythm. Yet even in this inherently ephemeral and temporary site, residents still managed to create more or less stable homes and attachments. Rather than a transient "non-place", the camp was indeed a site thick with human relations, social networks, and collective memories (Augé 1992; Tonda 2005). It was a place where friendships were formed and romance was born, where churches and prayer groups created community and work-kinship structured socialities, and where people also turned their bare company houses into more livable, colorful, and meaningful dwellings.

Many of these relationships were nonetheless precarious, temporary, and uncertain. People came and went. Logging camps opened and closed. Timber companies moved elsewhere. Compound residents therefore had the feeling that true attachments and investments always lay beyond the camp. "It's hard to make real friends here," one of the trackers said. "In the end, we're all here for one reason only: money." In this section we will therefore look at how CTI employees nevertheless managed to make a home in the timber camps *despite* their hostility to durable emotional and material investment. Loggers, we will see, made their homes especially through objects and images that *referred to elsewhere*. A brief visit to their living rooms indeed illustrates how practices of homemaking largely oriented their occupants to a world *beyond* the camp.

Like most CTI families, the Esibos had transformed their company house into a meaningful home by stuffing their living room with modern objects (couches, cupboards, cabinets) and electronic devices (televisions, DVD players, hi-fi sets, radios). Though the devices usually remained switched off due to a lack of electricity, a well-equipped living room or salon was a prime marker of an urban worker identity, but it was a notable exception in the region.

The history of living rooms goes back a long time. Bogumil Jewsiewicki (2003, 103) shows how, in late colonial cities, Congolese salons were ceremonial spaces for monogamous Christian families to affirm their modernity through "fetish-like objects that were not so much used but signified the status of the person who has bought them with his salary" (my translation). Also in the early *post*colony, Jewsiewicki suggests, salons very much remained a preferential space for claiming petit bourgeois adulthood. But with the evaporation of wages in the 1980s and 1990s, living rooms "exploded" and were replaced by other spaces—empty plots, bus stations, churches, bars—where unemployed men could build new subjectivities (Jewsiewicki 2008, 113). And yet, the striking role of living rooms in the CTI labor compounds suggests that, despite its generalized crisis, the modern ideology of wage labor and its logics of distinction *did* survive in an otherwise largely post-labor milieu—and still materialized in workers' houses.

The specific role these salons played was nevertheless significantly different from that of their postcolonial predecessors. While Jewsiewicki (2003, 103) shows how earlier living rooms were very much "like a museum" because they were "visited rather than lived in" (my translation), the parlors in the logging camp were, surprisingly, neither visited nor lived in. Visitors, colleagues, and friends rarely entered these spaces because most social life took place outside, under the paillote. And only a few families had turned their salons into extra bedrooms or used these rooms for actual living. Hence, while in Jewsiewicki's analysis the parlor was the paradigmatic place for receiving visitors, the logging camp's living rooms had lost much of their semipublic character. Although still museum-like, they had become largely private collections without a public. Indeed, those who needed to testify to and confirm workers' social distinction rarely laid eyes on the modest signs of modernity displayed inside.

So, if not used for living in or receiving visitors, what were these salons used for? For a possible answer, we must turn to a particular kind of object—or, better, image—that was omnipresent in workers' houses (Hendriks and Malaquais 2016). The walls of most living rooms were indeed adorned with *affiches*, colorful Chinese posters imported to Bumba from Butembo, Nairobi, or Guangzhou. Wholesalers sold these posters to boutique owners from the forest camp, where CTI workers bought them for a little more than the price of a beer (US$2.20).

These posters generally depicted one of five common subjects: photoshopped skylines of composite or generic global cities; luxurious Western houses and their interiors, often with profusely decorated tables, food, and wine; lavish flower and fruit arrangements; Congolese and international football players and musicians; or Christian icons depicting Jesus or Mary. Workers made their selections of these posters from what was available at the local market. But because what was on offer was rather limited, the same posters appeared in many living rooms and thus constituted a largely shared repertoire of images.

People had different reasons for buying these posters. Some, stressing their aesthetic qualities, said posters made their rooms "look nicer." Others emphasized their "distracting" role as objects to be looked at when one needed to "relax" or "unwind." Sometimes it was said that posters "made people think." But most workers stated that they "made them dream." Posters indeed allowed for dreams about things, cities, and houses that were "physically impossible to see" but whose image could nonetheless be brought into the home. As such, camp inhabitants very much stressed the agentive or causative capacity of posters above and beyond their representational function (Lambertz 2018, 104). Rather than mere images, they were devices that *did* things to people.

For these reasons, the Chinese posters were profoundly different from the remarkable form of popular art that earlier generations of workers often displayed in their salons. The work of Johannes Fabian (1978, 1996, 1998), T. K. Biaya (1988, 1996), and Bogumil Jewsiewicki (1992, 1995, 2003) indeed describes how local Congolese artists used to mass-produce a limited repertoire of "genre paintings" for urbanites aspiring to a petit bourgeois lifestyle. Fabian (1998, 51) in particular emphasizes that Swahili-speaking families in urban Katanga appreciated these paintings for their *ukumbusho*: their "capacity to activate memory and reflection." Yet, unlike the Chinese posters, which were also sometimes seen as "think-pieces," urban genre paintings were primarily *conversation* pieces, their purpose being "to occasion talk, to prompt stories" (51). Moreover, because paintings often depicted scenes of colonial violence and terror, the public narratives they stimulated contained "a form of resistance to colonial symbolic power" and created "moments of freedom" in which overt critiques of the colony allowed for hidden critiques of the Mobutu regime (69).

Notwithstanding their similar places inside workers' homes, the older popular genre paintings and the more recent posters thus played profoundly different roles. First, while earlier salons were spaces for exhibiting and discussing objects and paintings among visitors, the living rooms in the forest camp were rarely visited, if at all. As a result, the Chinese posters on display did not belong to the same public sphere in which urban paintings took on their meaning. Second, the affiches did not depict the past or present, but rather a future and faraway world that seemed very much beyond the workers' immediate grasp. Third, the posters were not so much bought to "remember" or "reflect"—both expressed through the verb *kokanisa*—as to "make one dream"—expressed through the verb *kolotisa*. And, finally, the Chinese posters did not depict violence, terror, or humiliation but wealth, beauty, and social standing.

Hence, while the former paintings were about *publicly remembering a painful past*, the contemporary posters seemed about *privately dreaming a beautiful future*. Although both constituted what Jewsiewicki (2003, 51) calls a shared iconographic "repertoire of frames that gives a credible form to one's experience," these shifts from public to private, from remembering to dreaming, and from a painful past to a longed for future, might therefore appear to largely dissolve the overtly *political* nature of popular art into a merely oneiric practice.

Yet dreams are powerful devices too. They open up a utopian mode of politics and recycle transnational desires for other worlds into a here-and-now critique of exclusion (Weiss 2009). Dreaming in front of mass-produced and globally consumed commodities indeed allowed workers and their families to see themselves in "otherwheres" (Malaquais 2006). As object-signs in what Arjun Appadurai (1996) calls the "work of the imagination," the posters insistently—and ecstatically—pointed to a distant yet palpable and vibrant Technicolor world.

Monique Esibo, for instance, had bought plastic flowers that made her salon look more like the one on her poster. And her son had his hair cut in the style of his depicted football idol. People also told us that the personnel manager was building a house "just like" the villa in one of the recurrent Chinese posters. As such, these images illustrate how "ordinary lives today are more often powered not by the givenness of things but by the possibilities that the media . . . suggest are available" (Appadurai 1996, 55). Rather than serve simply as simulacra of modernity, the aspirations these posters produced contained a "powerful claim to a chance for transformed conditions of life" and asserted one's right of inclusion in a globalized world (Ferguson 2006, 19).

At the same time, CTI workers of course realized these posters depicted a world from which they were radically excluded (Gardner 2012). Rather than a different tomorrow, the images made them dream about a faraway future "that one wants to enjoy, but to which one will never have material access" (Mbembe 2002, 271). In such a context, Achille Mbembe argues, the "powers of imagination are stimulated [and] intensified by the very unavailability of the objects of desire" (271). Doubly mimicking Western interiors in Chinese reproductions, the posters indeed projected an inaccessible domesticity on the walls of actual living rooms that remained cruelly removed from their depicted ideal.

It was perhaps this combination of the *accessibility* of globalization's mass-produced images and the *inaccessibility* of its material benefits that accounted for the nervous restlessness from which camp inhabitants tried to escape. One of their escape routes was exactly to capture (*kokanga*) the world from which they were excluded. The Chinese posters literally introduced an outside world into one's home and appropriated what came from elsewhere—almost like a hunter returning from the forest with an animal

(Jewsiewicki 1991). Transforming a global image into a local resource for ecopoiesis, this "extraversion" did not diminish but rather relied on the sustained exotic nature of the faraway (Bayart and Ellis 2000).

CTI living rooms and their Chinese posters thus reveal a surprising *displacement* at the heart of homemaking practices. The posters indeed materialized a *decentering* at the heart of ecopoetic practices that are otherwise supposed to "center" life around a stable home (Lovell 1998). In this relatively isolated corner of the Congolese interior, where residents actively reproduced and emphasized their own "remoteness," homemaking practices effectively referred to *other* places and *other* times beyond the here and now (Harms et al. 2014). This incessant mind wandering, which escaped the apparent emptiness of camp life where "nothing ever happened," profoundly speaks to shared oneiric repertoires that not only run through Congolese cities but also capture some of the country's more out-of-the-way places (De Boeck 2011; Tsing 1993).

These displacements point at what one might call the characteristic "centrifugality" of everyday camp life: its outward-propelling force.[2] In the CTI labor compounds, thoughts, desires, ambitions, projects, and trajectories were indeed mainly outwardly oriented. Despite the temporary attachments its inhabitants created, dreams were effectively directed *beyond* the camp, and the little money workers could save was invested *elsewhere*. Perhaps all homemaking practices—as attempts to create stable axes of belonging—generate some centrifugal forces, which draw rotating bodies away from their center of rotation. But, in the logging camps, centrifugality *opened up* the very possibility of a home rather than impeding its stabilization. As such, the Chinese posters suggest how ecstasis was a paradoxical condition of homemaking rather than its limit. They particularly illustrate how the realization of control was, again, dependent on a certain loss of control: on daydreaming and oneiric displacement.

Camp Trouble

The CTI logging camps pushed people outside of themselves. Time and space exploded beyond the here and now. Past and future were always elsewhere. People waited for things that rarely realized. Boredom rubbed against the limits of patience. Drinking, playing, and troublemaking offered ecstatic devices for a way out. Even homemaking and self-making were profoundly outwardly oriented.

Yet this centrifugality did not annihilate the labor compounds' countervailing centripetal attractions. The logging camps were indeed places that simultaneously attracted people and put them off. Centrifugal and centripetal dynamics therefore existed side by side, creating nervous double binds. As such, the camp resembled Giorgio Agamben's (1998, 96) "place of exception"—where "[w]hat is excluded . . . is, according to the etymological sense of the term 'exception' (ex-capere), *taken outside*, included through its own exclusion." This tendency of the camp to produce itself as an exception, to constantly take itself outside, and to include what it excludes, was a fundamental aspect of its ecstatogenic nature.

This peculiar combination of centrifugal and centripetal forces produced desires, trajectories, and mobilities that, though a direct consequence of CTI's presence, largely operated beyond its reach. The camps were indeed difficult to grasp, and European managers complained about their lack of knowledge of what happened inside "their" labor camps. Moreover, the apparently "unclean" and "disorderly" appearance of the forest camp, its "illegal" occupants, and "criminal" activities seriously troubled the picture CTI was trying to get across. At the same time, however, the camp was not its immediate concern. As long as workers showed up for work and production targets were met, managers did not really care about how things sorted themselves out in the labor compounds.

In practice, this ambivalent attitude produced rather messy camp management. Everyday issues, such as the allocation of houses, the reparation of infrastructure, or the organization of collective garbage collecting (*salongo*), elicited quick decisions and ad hoc improvisations that were frequently contested between different managers and more often than not simply postponed. In 2005, the then-French site manager appointed Ibrahim, a man from Maniema Province, as official *chef de camp* in the forest camp. But Ibrahim was a sickly man who, after a truck accident, had taken to excessive drinking. As a result, camp inhabitants often went to see André, the Congolese forest engineer. But André's proposed solutions were often overruled by Jens, who, for camp matters, largely relied on Michel, who generally asserted that his workers, as "true foresters," were used to living in basic conditions and could very well fend for themselves.

Divesting rather than investing in their employees, the European loggers therefore preferred to reduce camp management to a bare minimum. As a result, the compounds were generally sites of relative company neglect rather than surveillance. There were no proper health and safety procedures, no maps of the different camp quarters, no register of its houses, and no population survey. Compound life simply happened outside the company gaze. Although there was a camp hygiene committee, its bimonthly meetings were largely ineffective. Jens rarely listened to the complaints that André, the human resources manager, the secretary, the CTI nurses, the team boss of the company guards, Ibrahim, or his colleague from the river camp were supposed to transmit. And he was simply uninterested in camp safety and hygiene.

Camp issues did become a more pressing matter of moral and hygienic concern, however, once CTI started the procedure for obtaining a green label for sustainable forest management. At one point during our fieldwork, the prospect of external auditors visiting the concession really induced anxiety about the camp's dirty and chaotic outlook. As Jens did not want to give the auditors a "wrong impression," he particularly vented frustrations during camp hygiene committee meetings about so-called illegal squatters who had settled in and around the labor compounds without permission.

These unemployed men and their families, most expats agreed, were a direct threat to the camp's living conditions because they were thought to encourage drinking and prostitution. Also, their makeshift constructions were seen as sources of infection, pollution, fire risk, and overpopulation. And their neighborhoods, bars, and boutiques would be hiding places for fuel smugglers and criminals. As a result, the European loggers started talking about "imposing order," "taking back control," and "cleaning up" the labor camps. One area in particular thereby came to stand out as the paradigmatic squatter neighborhood corrupting CTI workers: Camp Mabaku.

Camp Mabaku was one of the five unofficial neighborhoods in the forest camp. In Lingala, *libaku* means obstacle, and *mabaku* (in the plural) refers to stumbling blocks that literally and metaphorically prevent one from walking upright (*kotelema*). Yet, mabaku also meant challenges, opportunities, and adventures. People for instance stated that one could only reach full adulthood by dealing with the obstacles along one's life path (*nzela ya bomoi*). Stumbling stones were therefore both a problem and a possibility. Moreover, in the Itimbiri region, mabaku were also foretelling signs. Hunters considered stumbling over a stone (*kobeta libaku*) with one's right foot a sure sign of success, while stumbling with one's left foot was taken as an omen of failure.[3]

For these reasons, Camp Mabaku's name aptly described the ambivalent nature of its ambiance as both obstacle and adventure, temptation and ordeal. Adjacent to the unused airstrip and inhabited by a reserve army of potential day laborers, it was built around a popular bar owned by Mamu, an outspoken Luba woman who had settled there after the Second Congo War. Every night she and her twelve-year-old son served a large group of men next to a motorcycle repair workshop. Among them was André, the engineer, who enjoyed free drinks and preferential treatment. Mamu's bar also had a reputation for serving high-quality arak and featuring free women (*bandumba*). Unlike local women, Mamu's ladies were said to be independent urban girls who traveled back and forth between Bumba and the CTI labor camps. But Mamu was also known to mediate between company workers and kaddafi traders, providing the latter with shelter, food, and care in return for a share of their profits.

For the expat managers, the neighborhood was therefore a source of trouble. In 2007 CTI had already appealed to the court to evict its illegal residents in order to make space for new company houses. But many decided to stay. And those who had initially fled to the other side of the logging road—outside the official camp perimeter—returned as soon as they realized the company was not going to build new houses. Hence, Camp Mabaku continued to grow until, when faced with the prospect of a possible company audit in 2010, Jens decided to call in a magistrate from Bumba and give its inhabitants a twenty-day notice to clear the area once and for all.

Although most inhabitants initially ignored the magistrate's order, it became clear that this time things were more serious when eight policemen and a court clerk suddenly appeared one Monday morning with Mbadu, the chief of personnel. Assisted by the policemen, Mbadu and André forced two reluctant bulldozer operators to start their engines and destroy the squatter neighborhoods. Yet, as there were no written records of their occupations, it was not easy to distinguish between squatters' houses and huts erected by CTI workers (who also inhabited Camp Mabaku because of the chronic shortage of company housing).[4] As a result, Mbadu and André had to identify the occupants of each house on the spot. Feigning ignorance, André was thereby able to save several families who had bribed him for obtaining a plot on CTI land. But he was ultimately unable to prevent Mbadu—a staunch Pentecostal Christian—from having Mamu's notorious bar destroyed.

Afterward, Jens provocatively boasted that "the operation had been a success." Bulldozers had run over houses and crushed belongings. Several squatters had been arrested, and five were sent to prison in Bumba. In the short term, the action indeed appeared effective: a large area had been cleared of illegal habitation, and order seemed to have been restored. Yet, again, all this was only temporary. In 2011, near the end of our fieldwork, new mud-and-stick dwellings had already appeared, and many evicted residents had returned to their former plots. Mamu, however, was "too proud to return." As an act of defiance, she built an even larger bar on the other side of the road. Without her, Camp Mabaku was never the same. But her drinks and free women still attracted smugglers, workers, and travelers from near and far. And she could still count on André's protection.

This last episode calls for an analysis of worker camps that goes beyond the mere divination of companies' "political rationalities" and "power strategies" (Rubbers 2019). The CTI labor compounds were indeed not another panopticon under close surveillance or a materialization of biopower (Foucault 1975, 1997). To the contrary, CTI seemed rather unable to produce a coherent camp policy. Its expat loggers shifted back and forth between older ideals of hygiene and social engineering, neoliberal attitudes of disengagement from their labor force, and new incentives produced by certification mechanisms. The violent destruction of Camp Mabaku certainly shows how corporate power could suddenly harden its grasp and take back control. But as evicted families settled down on the other side of the camp perimeter and bulldozed areas quickly attracted others, CTI managers eventually had to acknowledge that they were unable to durably impose their will in the face of larger demographic, economic, and social forces.

While the very materiality of the labor compounds certainly allowed for dreams of reactivating the disciplinary potential of the camp as an architectural form, everyday life generally went on *beyond* CTI's desires and intensions (Hendriks 2015). In fact, the company's rare, violent, and messy interventions seemed more symptomatic of the ecstatic condition of corporate power than of its effectiveness. As Hannah Arendt (1969, 155) suggests, violence indeed showed itself to be the "opposite" of power. Moreover, expat managers' concerns about hygiene and criminality produced only temporary illusions of order and resulted in grotesque explosions of action that, rather than evoke memories of colonial discipline, resonated with a more *post*colonial mode of power (Mbembe 1992). As a sudden overreaction to the prospect of a future audit, the violent destruction of Camp Mabaku contradicted the idea of the company as a calm and rational actor. And, ultimately, it undermined the image of sustainability and corporate social responsibility CTI wanted to convey.

The forest camp was therefore a profoundly ecstatogenic site for many of its inhabitants, whether European or Congolese. It was a place that could, literally, take one outside oneself. This chapter has shown how, for

Congolese workers and seekers of a better future, the labor compounds produced possibility as well as immobility—a double bind that generated heterochronic escape routes, oneiric displacements, and centrifugal forces. The next chapter shows how, also for its expatriates, the concession was a place of both freedom and frustration, breeding boredom as well as ecstatic lines of flight.

Approaching the expat quarters along the Itimbiri

A Darker Shade of White

THE EUROPEAN LOGGERS MANAGING THE CTI concession lived in two clusters of bungalows that were separated from, but adjacent to, the labor compounds. Congolese workers invariably referred to these expat spaces as the Garden of Eden (*le jardin d'Eden*). But for the Europeans, the Edenic quality of their living quarters was hardly apparent. Had Michel, on my first day in the concession, not welcomed me—with some pleasure—to a living "hell"?

At first glance, these contrasting metaphors seemed to speak to two radically different appreciations of a shared reality coming from opposite sides of a racially segregated world. The expat loggers effectively appeared to experience as hell what, for their workers, seemed like paradise. Upon closer inspection, however, these metaphors turned out to be easily reversible and not without their own ironies. Indeed, as a pair of vernacular opposites mobilized by workers and expats alike, heaven could always turn into hell, and vice versa.

While chapter 7 looks at how and why Congolese workers and villagers considered the expat Garden of Eden as simultaneously an attractive place of affluence and a troubling site of occult violence, this chapter shows why its European inhabitants experienced their work environment as both a "paradise" of freedom and adventure *and* a "hell" of stress and frustration. It therefore needs to paint a more intimate portrait of the small and isolated group of expatriate managers in the CTI concession. Who were these men? Where did they come from? What were they after? How did they try to build a home in the middle of the rainforest? And how did they perceive themselves?

To answer these questions, this chapter investigates whiteness as a set of racialized subjectivities but also as an ideology and everyday mechanism of domination (Hendriks 2017). In the CTI concession, where white faces were an extreme minority, "whiteness" was often explicitly brought into the open as a topic for discussion, contestation, and deliberate reconstruction. As such, it was both a violent mechanism of privilege and a source of lived insecurity.

By foregrounding the paradoxes of everyday expat life, this chapter thus stumbles into the inevitably muddy waters of *race* as a slippery signifier (Hall 1996). Indeed, although a biologically disqualified and analytically dubious concept, both Europeans and Congolese openly used race as a vernacular common sense to grasp the world (Appiah 1990; hooks 1992; Miles 1993; Posel 2001). I have kept certain attitudes and events as disturbing and shocking as I found them. But I have also tried to write from a more compassionate or reparative stance—not to explain away violent behavior or excuse blunt racism by referring to a context but to reconnect to a vulnerability we all share and to weave the European loggers back into a larger tapestry from which they felt and thought themselves excluded.

I can only hope this chapter brings to life an ecstatic world in which cynical comments like Michel's "welcome to hell" hold together otherwise contradictory feelings and experiences—such as freedom and boredom, fear and desire, irritability and detachment, love and paranoia, autonomy and dependency, excitement and depression, grandeur and self-doubt. To do so, I had no choice but to write from the shadow of a certain "darkness," an idea the expat managers themselves regularly used to describe their experience—a metaphor with a long and troubling history on the African continent, and especially in the DRC.

A Garden of Eden

Michel was perhaps the first of the five European loggers at the CTI concession to accept me as a fieldworker in their midst. Perhaps he felt some connection to the rather shy and bookish young man who had unexpectedly turned up in his life. I had indeed not expected to find an old Frenchman with whom I could talk about Claude Lévi-Strauss, the famous anthropologist who had passed away in Paris a couple of days before my arrival. I quickly grew fond of our conversations, and we developed a somewhat queer relationship based on largely unspoken resonances.

Unfortunately, as forest overseer, Michel lived in the middle of the concession, while I had initially been given a room in the Garden of Eden alongside the Congo River. During those first months I grew closer to Roger, the construction manager who had recently arrived from Congo-Brazzaville. Although I never felt comfortable with his boastful masculinity, I appreciated his funny stories and sincere advice. I also enjoyed the motorcycle lessons he gave me on the CTI airstrip. Julien, on the other hand, the company mechanic, was very much on his own and spent most of his time in the garages. The ice between us only broke when two Belgians from a concession near Lisala stayed over for a weekend and invited us for dinner. With Jens, however, I never got along. The Danish site manager's authoritarian character frightened me, and the utter disdain he showed toward his workers disgusted me. Nonetheless, over time, we grew accustomed to each other, and near the end of my fieldwork, we were able to have frank conversations.

It was therefore quite a relief when, after two uncomfortable first months, I could finally arrange a house for Freddy and myself in the forest camp and get away from Jens's controlling behavior. At that time I also ended up sharing a bungalow with Pablo, a forestry engineer from Madrid, who had started working for CTI just after my arrival and who occupied a house alongside Michel's in the second, smaller Eden near the forest camp. Pablo and I were of similar age and had a lot in common. We often joked about the old loggers desperately wanting to "initiate" us in rainforest life and complained about Jens's fits of anger. But, most of all, we looked forward to the evenings when Michel invited us for a beer on his terrace overlooking the nearby Mamoissa River.

Listening to Michel, I quickly realized the contradictory nature of his initial welcoming. While framing our small expat community as a hell, he also frequently sang the praise of the beautiful forest around us. As an old *soixante-huitard*, he had left France after the 1968 student protests to look for "something else." Africa, he said, was "something out of the ordinary, a beautiful place that not many Europeans get to see." He adored the tranquility of his isolated life, the exotic mystique of the country, and what he called the "simple and pleasant" character of its people. Leading a rather ascetic life, he looked at the world with some detachment. Far away from social obligations and conventions, he only had himself to account for.

To a certain extent, the older loggers all shared Michel's romantic attitude and experienced the rainforest as a primitive space wherein one could live far away from the vices of civilization and be "closer to nature" (Harrison 1992; Slater 2002). Coming from working-class or lower middle-class backgrounds, they had all left Europe in the 1960s and 1970s, sometimes through military or mercenary pathways, to escape from what they called "social conformism" or "Christian hypocrisy." Julien, for instance, when looking back at his long career, framed his journey through different African countries as a deliberate departure from Western consumerism. And even Jens declared his "love for Africa," admitting that he could no longer function in Europe, as he had become "unaccustomed" to its norms and conventions.

The younger Pablo, on the other hand, had a somewhat different story. He described himself as a "leftist" who had the ambition to change capitalism "from the inside out" and who wanted to save the rainforest through ecologically sound forest management. But he also shared his colleagues' drive and search for adventure. Although they were all paid double or triple what they could earn with similar jobs in Europe, they firmly denied being after money. Instead, they said they were looking for freedom. Roger claimed it was "only in Africa" that one could be "completely free" because "here, you can do whatever you want, without having others looking over your shoulder." In the logging concession, the expat managers could indeed make their own decisions and plan their work without much control or oversight from experts or executives. In the forest they were largely their own bosses.

Yet these romantic narratives and exoticizing tropes were only one aspect of expat discourses and existed alongside bitter complaints about the difficulties of their isolated lives. Roger often contrasted the expat bubbles he had known in African cities with his current life of shit (*vie de merde*) and impatiently counted the days until, every three to six months, he could take a break for a couple of weeks and "leave it all behind." He said concession work was exhausting and threatened to "devastate" one's mind. Even Michel agreed that working in the rainforest was often frustrating because it lacked tangible and durable results. "Nothing ever works here!" Julien also told me. "Everything you do just breaks down and disappears forever." The expatriates' will "to change things" indeed seemed to collide with a world where "nothing ever changes": the roads they built disappeared as a result of erosion, bridges collapsed, and machines broke down. Fuel always arrived too late, and people blocked "their forest" for nothing. Even the profits they made seemed low and insignificant in comparison to that of other sectors.

This experience of ephemerality and futility frequently led to frustrated reactions against an all-encompassing "black" world that the expat loggers held responsible for the "chaos" in which they tried so hard "to create some order." "How can we do our job," Roger asked me, "when those backward imbeciles do all they can to make it impossible?" Sometimes, they nostalgically remembered the 1970s and 1980s as a "good epoch", when villagers were more "docile" under Mobutu, as there was less leeway for protests from below. Sometimes, the decades of authoritarian rule even appeared as a fictitious time when "blacks and whites worked peacefully together"—after the disruptions of the 1960s.

But times had changed. Racial tensions and blunt racist accusations were a constant reality. Villagers were depicted as irrational "brutes" or, at best, "children." And Congolese employees were invariably blamed for the many failures and difficulties on the work floor. The European managers effectively read their workers' strategic foot-dragging and low-key resistance as "laziness" and "stupidity." In practice, their expat freedom was therefore often a freedom to shout, insult, threaten, and humiliate: a white privilege they simply took for granted as "how things work" or, at most, as "what one needs to do." Although they knew little or no Lingala, shouting simple commands seemed part of the job. At the same time, they explicitly *denied* being racists and often defended themselves against imaginary accusations. "I am not a racist," Roger often repeated. "Actually, I *love* them. Otherwise, I wouldn't even be here." Still, the air was thick with what Achille Mbembe (2019, 59) calls "nanoracism," a racist culture whose "banality and capacity . . . infiltrate[d] into the pores and veins" of concession life.

As a result, expat discourse shifted from one extreme to another. Even the paradise-like forest in which the European loggers claimed to live out their dreams of freedom could easily transform into an inferno. Sunshine, heat, and humidity provoked skin rashes. Swarms of biting insects could drive one crazy. And "beautiful savages" turned out to be "irresponsible" slash-and-burn farmers who "degraded" the forest. Instead of a textbook case of a tropical rainforest in "equilibrium," the CTI concession indeed seemed infested with impenetrable underlayers of *Marantaceae* plants, which were thought to indicate "human disturbance." For Pablo, the quest for patches of "true" primary rainforest became a botanical obsession. Every time prospectors entered a new part of the forest, he hoped it would finally meet his ecological criteria. But the forest usually remained second-rate—botanically, financially, demographically, existentially.

To remain sane, the older foresters often told Pablo and me to "keep busy" and "focus on our work"—an old colonial recipe (Fabian 2000, 56). Starting at around 5 a.m. and ending after sunset, work effectively occupied the major part of our days. Pablo liked to take refuge in its tiniest details and could work on Excel spreadsheets or maps until late at night. "In any case," he said, "there isn't much else to do." Roger also often complained about the boredom that nested itself in life. Tired from work, he spent most evenings watching satellite television, surfing the slow internet, or chasing friends on social network sites before an early night's sleep. The next morning he would get up and start the same routine. It drove him crazy, he said. From time to time, he needed to "clear his mind." Together with Julien, he engaged in 4×4 racing contests on bumpy dirt tracks. Sometimes he invited a woman from Bumba to lose himself in her arms.

Every month or so the expat loggers met for a Saturday night dinner where they found some comfort in food, drinks, and stories. Most of the time, however, they simply confined themselves to their own bungalows. While depression and alcohol addiction loomed large, they pretended to know how to "sort out their own problems." Moreover, by deliberately portraying their life as an everyday ordeal, they nurtured the idea of their existence as "hard," "lonely," and "dangerous" so as to depict themselves as tough, self-made men who could survive the most difficult of circumstances—a discourse CTI further bolstered by paying them "hardship allowances" that financially compensated for their "exposure" (Leonard 2010, 69).

In short, the European loggers perceived their environment in deeply ambivalent and contradictory ways. While imagining the rainforest as an Edenic place for free spirits and belated romantics, they also experienced its realities as a living hell they nonetheless "loved." As self-declared outlaws, they claimed to have a "passion for Africa" and to be "addicted" to an isolated life they nonetheless also constantly complained about. And while the concession was a place to "get things done" without annoying oversight, it was equally an environment where attempts to "make a change" always failed because of the region's seemingly entropic "black" nature. As a result, the expat quarters, the concession, the forest, the country, and even the entire continent constantly flickered between heaven and hell—a flickering that indexed the ecstasis of their existence.

Bungalows and Cuisiniers

At the river camp, a fence and a guarded gate separated the Garden of Eden from the labor compounds, company offices, and private port. At the forest camp, however, the expat quarters were simply separated by a stretch of rainforest. But both areas were palpably constructed and lived as *white* spaces where black bodies were always out of place.

Although CTI officially denied that racial logics informed the spatial segregation of its expat quarters, residence in the Garden of Eden was overwhelmingly reserved for whites and Europeans only. I soon enough learned that company workers and compound inhabitants could not visit me while I was at Pablo's place. My Spanish friend had indeed taken over his older colleagues' racist attitudes surprisingly quickly—an involuntary transformation that was truly frightening, not least for himself. Even Freddy, who often came to help me out with transcriptions in the relative calm of the expat quarters, was not really welcome. After much insisting, Pablo had nonetheless agreed to let us to work outside on the covered terrace. When he was out, Freddy and I sometimes went inside anyway. But as soon as we heard Pablo's jeep approaching we had no choice but to move outside again.

The Europeans considered their living quarters as "safe havens" of peace and quiet in which they could retreat after long days of work, hiding from villagers and their "unreasonable" demands. The expat houses were also positioned so as to assure a panoramic view on the nearby forest or the Congo River—untroubled by black bodies, except perhaps for some picturesque fishermen throwing their nets in the distance. Especially on Sundays, whiteness was carefully maintained, and Congolese were strictly kept out. Fences, gates, guards, imaginary lines, unspoken rules, looks, words, and gestures all contributed to create and maintain a segregated space where every transgression was experienced as a deliberate invasion of white privacy and privilege and taken as an occasion to redraw racial boundaries.

Yet, although the borders between white houses and their black surroundings were continuously monitored, complete segregation was impossible. Guards did control the entrances to the expat quarters, but some visitors nevertheless negotiated their way through, hoping to find one of the expats in a good enough mood to listen to their requests. And whenever the Europeans were away at work or taking a nap, women and children were allowed to hurry through the Garden of Eden as a shortcut to the river or a cassava field. Moreover, CTI often accommodated visiting Congolese managers from Kinshasa in a small cabin at the edge of the expat quarters for the duration of their stay. And high-ranking state agents occasionally spent the night in the mess hall, or canteen, near the river camp.

At one time during our fieldwork, the mess also became the temporary home for Rodrigo—a Congolese Portuguese man from Kinshasa who had come for a couple of months to help out with truck mechanics. Although he did not occupy a fully equipped house, Rodrigo's stay immediately tainted the exclusively white character of the expat quarters. Some of the European loggers started to avoid the mess altogether because—or so they claimed— "stinking" Congolese food had "turned the place into a pigsty." As such, the canteen was simply cut out of white space until Rodrigo returned to Kinshasa and the temporary aberration could be restored.

Such Congolese visitors and "intruders" clearly revealed the power of whiteness as a regime of exclusion. Yet, at the same time, their physical presence also troubled its actualization. Whiteness was indeed both a violent reality *and* a surprisingly vulnerable construct that had to be constantly repaired and reaffirmed. Moreover, the concrete maintenance of white space was directly dependent on black labor. Whenever water pumps or satellite dishes broke down, for instance, Congolese technicians were called in. And all European managers had male cooks (*cuisiniers*) who spent their days cooking, ironing, housekeeping, and cleaning expat bungalows only to return to the labor compounds at night.

The racially marked presence of these cuisiniers was indispensable to enabling the practical re-creation of European-esque homes. As central figures who embodied the racial contradictions of white homemaking, they were also subject to intense surveillance and criticism. The expats constantly complained about their cooks "messing up" expensive Western food that arrived from Kinshasa.[1] Or about how they seemed unable to "respect" modern household items—such as microwaves and coffee machines—or "treat stuff with proper care"—such as computers, televisions, DVD players, tableware, cupboards, and couches, all imported by boat or airplane. Because of these tensions, most cuisiniers skillfully made themselves as invisible as possible and carefully tried to avoid confrontations by literally hiding the labor that went into homemaking. Moreover, when not cleaning rooms, making up beds, or setting the table, cuisiniers were largely confined to their kitchens and storage rooms, which were physically separated from the expat houses so as to keep them out of sight.

The spatial segregation of the expat quarters and the physical presence of cuisiniers accounted for the remarkably colonial atmosphere that the Garden of Eden reproduced. But the expat homes were also built according to an old bungalow plan that used to characterize colonial houses in the area. Their quick assembly methods and physical setup—with a raised plinth, detached kitchens and storage rooms, piers, veranda, and obligatory bar—resembled an international bungalow style that had spread from India throughout the colonial world as a "tool of empire" (Headrick 1981; King 1984). Yet in the CTI concession, this bungalow model had merged with a certain chalet-type architecture typical of the European Alps, as heavy roof beams, wooden wall coverings, and dark furniture tried to evoke a coziness that was supposedly reminiscent of the logging company's homeland.

It was in these chalet-bungalows that the expat loggers tried to re-create a sense of home in their largely vagrant existence. Not unlike their own Congolese employees in the labor compounds (see chapter 5), they deliberately stuffed their houses with objects and devices to create a certain Europeanness in the middle of the forest. But *home* was, again, a profoundly paradoxical notion. During rare social gatherings and dinners, homes were for instance nostalgically remembered in stories about favorite dishes and places—stories that often evoked particularly rural forms of belonging. At the same time, this idealized home was unreachable and frustratingly resistant to being reproduced in African settings. To ease this tension, the European loggers deliberately *exiled* themselves, their original homes becoming lost places to which there was no return. Jens, for instance, described himself as an "exile by choice," Julien claimed to "belong nowhere," and Michel found the idea that he would soon retire utterly horrifying. As such, they all claimed to no longer fit into their home societies, as forest life had irrevocably changed them.

Smash It Up

As a practice of racialized separation, expat homemaking was thus "an inherently fragile social achievement [that had to] be maintained carefully against various kinds of odds" (Appadurai 1996, 179). But no matter how hard the loggers tried to re-create Europeanness in the rainforest, their attempts seemed largely doomed to failure. Notwithstanding basic technologies of surveillance and control, unwanted Congolese visitors managed to stubbornly sit and wait in front of expat bungalows. Housekeepers were unable to live up to their employers' standards. New curtains quickly molded because of high humidity. Recently arrived food rapidly spoiled. And notwithstanding the colonial commensality they evoked, the wooden bungalow bars frequently remained sad places for lonely drinking.

Even the quotidian stuff needed to manufacture a homely European atmosphere carried within it a potential for failure. One night, for instance, after a long evening of getting drunk and complaining about life, three expat loggers suddenly began destroying furniture, tableware, curtains, and even a radio. It had begun simply with a glass breaking on the ground. And then the deliberate breaking of another. Before I knew it, I found myself in a violent revolt against the world. It was as if a dam had broken. They calmed down only after one of them threatened to smash up his computer, his link to the outside world. Literally out of their minds, they physically destroyed the very stuff they so protectively cared for, as though they were angry with the objects themselves for their inherent failure to re-present.

That night, instead of continuing the daily struggle of ecopoiesis, the expat managers seemed to violently force it to an end in a catharsis of liquor-induced self-mutilation—a spectacular destruction of wealth that liberated violent energies. Yet unlike the competitive consumption of a potlatch, smashing up their interiors was not a "constructive" form of loss or sacrifice (Bataille 1967). Although it temporarily made dissident masculinities, it did not produce status or honor. Ultimately, the incident was only painful: a self-defeating expression of despair and a sign of "a life got down" (Stewart 1996, 41).

Although an extreme case, this unexpected violence aptly illustrates the limits of white homemaking—as if the expat loggers were momentarily overpowered by the futility of their own actions, and as though all they could ever achieve were merely a ghostly resemblance, an *Entstellung* of an unattainable "European" original (Bhabha 1994). The apparent familiarity the loggers had painstakingly constructed effectively revealed its foreign face, breaking the fragile metonymic link between their white bungalows and a re-presented Western world. Everyday life was interrupted by what Freud calls the uncanny, or *das Unheimliche*: what had seemed so homely was transformed into its very un-homely reverse.[2] In a flash the familiar indeed "turned on its owners" and became "defamiliarized, derealized, as if in a dream" (Vidler 1992, 7).

This event again reveals the profound *centrifugality* that characterized homemaking in the logging camp. The expats' attempts to reproduce a semblance of a European home in their colonial-style bungalows effectively reflect—perhaps uncannily—their own workers' attempts to create modern living rooms in generic houses in the labor compounds. But whereas Congolese employees dreamed in front of Chinese posters that depicted unattainable objects of desire; the expats destroyed real stuff. Each in their own way dealt with the stubborn centrifugality of life in the shadow of rainforest capitalism. As such, and despite their manifest differences, they were part of a seemingly shared ecstatogenic world.

The Last of Their Kind

Notwithstanding habits of keeping to themselves and spending much time alone, the European loggers still constituted a small "expat community." The common constraints of physical isolation, their difficulties on the work floor, their positions of command in the concession's power structure, and the effect of just being together produced similar motivations, frustrations, fears, and desires among them. It also nurtured a distinctively masculine and individualistic style of logger camaraderie. Moreover, while identifying as Europeans, they equally claimed to belong to a disappearing "tribe of African whites" and sometimes explicitly introduced themselves as the "last specimens of the white man in Africa." Thus tribalizing themselves, they even jokingly urged me to take an ethnographic look at them "before it was too late."[3]

This remarkable and perhaps cynical call for a salvage ethnography of their own kind is akin to what literary scholar Ali Behdad (1994, 75) calls "self-exoticization": an old colonial strategy whereby the self deliberately becomes an exotic other who can then be observed and talked about. The expat loggers indeed talked about themselves *as if they were others*. And this peculiar reflexivity allowed them to keep some distance between their everyday acts and a self that objectively examined and excused their behavior. For instance, they confessed to each other—and to the anthropologist in their midst—"incredible" stories about how they had to "improvise" in difficult situations and had *no choice but* to temporarily forget social commands or accepted morality. "I am quite an interesting case," Jens once told me while taking me to town in his jeep. "I am not proud of all the crazy stuff I did . . . but I did what needed to be done. You won't find people like me anymore. These days [CTI] has a lot of trouble finding the right men for the job."

Although there was a great deal of self-aggrandizing rhetoric at work in these stories, their significance primarily lies in the expats' narrative evocation and production of "dark" secrets. The European loggers essentially considered themselves different and exotic because of an *interior darkness* they claimed to share: a rare difference they thought necessary for surviving in the rainforest. Tellingly, this dark production of white selves resembles a literary trope that used to characterize colonial fiction. Indeed, as Anjali

Arondekar (2003, 76; my emphasis) puts it, self-exoticizing narratives in colonial literature often manufactured a masculine self that was "defined, valued and understood *not* through its brazen gestures of conquest, *nor* through its mastery over the native landscape, but instead through an uncovering of its own dark secrets." The CTI expats similarly shared dark stories in order to construct their own autobiographical characters as tough guys who were "crazy" enough to work in places like logging concessions (Hendriks 2014a).[4] Moreover, as we will see in the next section, they often backed their claims to "belong" to the African continent with literary references and cultural tropes that referred to the white (mad)man in the so-called heart of darkness.

Self-exoticizing statements and stories thus produced a self-consciously darker shade of white. But it was a whiteness that was, by definition, performed and framed *as a masculinity*. In effect, by presenting themselves as tough, no-bullshit men trying to bring development against all odds, or as "forest whites" who, in the manner of tragic heroes, confronted the harsh circumstances of the "real Congo," the European loggers deliberately created a distance between themselves and, for example, "soft-minded" development workers or "effeminate" environmentalists. The latter were often ridiculed for criticizing CTI's hard work from behind their desks while not being "man enough" to leave the comforts of their expat bubble and "live in the interior." *Real* rainforest work, they said, entailed "jumping into it" and "making one's hands dirty." As such, dirty hands and dark secrets proved membership in an almost extinct tribe of men strong enough to face the African rainforest exactly because of their supposed darkness within.

Yet, unlike the mercenary self-image that development professionals sometimes use to mask moral anxieties (Stirrat 2008), the expat loggers did not cover up their doubts and frustrations. On the contrary, they explicitly mobilized these difficulties as the very basis from which to forge a new white self. "Of course, it's not right," Julien told Pablo during his first week of work at the concession, "but the world is an ugly place. We need to be strong and do our job. Even when we know it doesn't make a difference." Their self-imposed darkness transformed an experienced powerlessness into an eagerly confessed craziness that paradoxically rebuilt self-confidence—and ultimately saved the white self as a controlling, autonomous, male agent in an environment over which he otherwise felt he had little say. Surprisingly, it was often by confessing to *lose* control that the European loggers tried to regain it, telling themselves stories to "bring an overwhelming and incomprehensible experience 'under control'" (Jackson 1998, 24).

At the same time, this carefully nurtured and, without doubt, exaggerated darkness equally *destabilized* standard ideologies of the white, male, autonomous self. During visits to the logging concession, superiors from the European head offices, for instance, often complained about their expats no longer being "white enough" to operate according to the rules of responsible forest management and CTI's best practices. The visitors' unease with the racism, bigotry, misogyny, and violence they often encountered indexed a gnawing moral discomfort about the ways in which the company's own activities repeated and reproduced earlier colonial power structures whose racialized aspects now seemed out of tune with official discourses on social responsibility and sustainable development. But while visiting managers accounted for the "contamination" of whiteness by way of an excessive "exposure" to an African world, the expat loggers themselves suggested it just took a particular kind of man to do the job: a white man who was *already* sufficiently dark within.

During fieldwork, several stories, jokes, and sarcastic comments about white men seemingly losing themselves in the supposed darkness of the rainforest abounded. Unbeknownst to their expat narrators, however, these anecdotes mirrored tellingly similar narratives that originated from the labor compounds and surrounding villages. Older Congolese inhabitants indeed frequently identified the expat loggers not so much with former Belgian colonial agents—supposedly "real" whites (*mindele ya solo*)—but with Greek and Portuguese traders who used to operate small businesses in the area and were often characterized as "false" whites—or, literally, "pig" whites (*mindele ya ngulu*).[5] Like these traders, they said, the CTI expats were content with living standards "below" their racial status, slept with Congolese women, and did not behave as "real" Europeans. Their rude racism, unkept appearance, and violent outbursts were effectively taken as signs of a "darker" kind of whiteness.

Hence, unlike in majority situations where whites do not usually self-represent *as whites* and where whiteness is thus a form of structural invisibility, whiteness in the CTI concession was an explicit concern—and disputed question—for workers, villagers, expat managers, and their European superiors alike (Dyer 1997). One cannot therefore grasp the affective life of industrial logging in contemporary Africa without fully apprehending whiteness as a structure of privilege and mechanism of control that was *visible* to everyone. With some notable exceptions, most scholarly analyses of neoliberal capitalism in Africa nevertheless remain surprisingly race averse and thus, as Jemima Pierre argues (2013), color-blind.[6] Notwithstanding the growing presence and activities of black businessmen in extractive industries, whiteness effectively remains a structural fixture of large-scale extraction on the continent and was, as we will see in the next chapter, regionally understood as a determining factor in the unequal distribution of wealth (Jobson 2019).

Yet, rather than reify whiteness as an unchanging structure, close ethnographic attention to its quotidian construction and contestation foregrounds both its historical endurance and reinventions (van Zyl-Hermann and Boersema 2017). As an empirical study of whiteness in a particular context, this chapter illustrates how, as a dimension of subjectivity, whiteness was itself a contradictory and unstable construct. On the one hand, expat homemaking practices created and maintained a "black" world against which whiteness could be erected as a fragile and threatened essence that had to be protected and bolstered. On the other hand, the expats deliberately produced a self-exoticized darkness as a paradoxical resource to rebuild and reclaim white authority. Presenting themselves as the last true rainforest whites, the European loggers thereby foregrounded a darker shade of white that re-coined failure and frustration as an ecstatic source of masculine strength and endurance.

Conrad, Again

But what exactly is this interior darkness that so insistently appeared at the center of white self-making, if not the tired old trope of Congo as the so-called heart of darkness? What is this darkness, if not Joseph Conrad's trite double entendre: a supposed characteristic of a racialized world outside *and* a hidden secret within.

Although the expat loggers often invoked darkness as a familiar trope from a broader Western cultural repertoire, at times the more specifically Conradian reference was made explicit. Michel, for instance, who had read *Heart of Darkness* several times in its French translation, was very aware of the ways in which he seemed to repeat old stereotypes of the isolated white man in the rainforest. And Pablo, referring to Francis Ford Coppola's remake *Apocalypse Now* rather than Conrad's novel, often entered his bungalow after a long day of work ironically shouting Kurtz's words, "The horror, the horror!" to simultaneously parody his older colleagues and express his own growing frustrations. More generally, the European managers eagerly used widespread imaginary of "the" Congo as the most "African" and "darkest" place on the continent. As such, they reproduced widely mediatized discourses about the DRC as "the world's most dangerous country" (Butcher 2008), or as a "failed state" characterized by corruption, war, rape, Ebola, mismanagement, and lack of basic infrastructure (Dunn 2003).

Such invocations of Conradian darkness in a contemporary Congolese context obviously pose serious challenges for the ethnographer worried about the involuntary reproduction of colonial stereotypes (Kabamba 2010). As Sara Ahmed (2014, 212) notes, darkness is indeed "a word that cannot be untangled from a racialized history." Whenever I talk to friends and colleagues about my stay with European loggers they frequently bring up *Heart of Darkness*—both seriously and ironically. No matter how much I insist on the ordinary aspects of everyday life in the logging concession, the mere idea of a small group of white men making money in an isolated place faraway in the Congolese interior seems to trigger Conradian imagery. But even more disturbingly, no matter how hard I resist telling the European loggers' stories through a darkening framework, my efforts to de-exoticize expat life were turned upside down *by their own desires* to re-exoticize themselves whenever they posed as special "specimens" of a rare and disappearing breed.

As I see it, their self-imposed darkness needs to be taken seriously as a "metaphor to live by" (Lakoff and Johnson 1980), a striking image through which expat loggers tried to situate, understand, and craft themselves in a present that very much repeated earlier extractive logics. The old trope of darkness indeed seemed to promise, once again, to make some sense of experienced anxieties, and it operated as a self-making device that captured lived emotions of fear and desire. Without inflating Kurtz's words into an essential truth created by the ever-repeated mantra of horror, I take this darkness as a constructed but nonetheless real and affective aspect of expat life in a specific time and place, and as a symptom of the uncanny repetition of earlier days of colonial extraction in the current neoliberal and postpaternalist moment.

In her recent history of violence in colonial Congo, Nancy Rose Hunt (2016, 6; my emphasis) also shows how and why "Conrad's diagnostics *endured* in fact and fantasy, with images of lone, nervous white men who lost it." It thus seems I have no choice but to write *from* Conrad's dark shadow and to try to make the past visible as a disturbing presence. While we should not uncritically accept the power of Conradian imagery, the opposite and voluntarist act of simply imagining oneself as free from its enduring magic seems naive at best. *Il faut faire avec*, Michel would say. One has to stay *with* the trouble, Donna Haraway (2016) later taught me. Ethnographically, there is no safe outsider position of innocence. We can only retell the stories in which we played our part. So that they might perhaps become something else.

The question is therefore not just how to keep these pages from being read as simply one more *Heart of Darkness* story but also how to refrain from complacently congratulating oneself for *not* writing such a story—as if the simple avoidance of the trope of darkness would offer a clean solution out of a murky situation. As we have seen—and will further develop in the conclusion—Johannes Fabian (2000) shows one possible way of doing so, making creative use of the archive to carefully contextualize how and why early colonial explorers in the Congo basin so often felt "out of our minds." Michael Taussig (1987, 5) suggests another possible method: thinking *through* horror with all the risks that such a method entails.

In his magistral study of violence and colonialism, Taussig indeed explicitly identifies "Conrad's way of dealing with the terror of the rubber boom" as an instructive but ultimately insufficient example for his own project (10). For Taussig, Conrad's artistry specifically lies in the way his work helps to "see the myth in the natural and the real in magic" (10). Yet, at the same time, this "mythic derealization of the real" can only be a first step as it always "run[s] the risk of being overpowered by the mythology it is using" (10). Conrad's writing indeed almost seems to desire the greatness of Kurtz's horror and to beautify terror (10). Hence, despite his textual subversions, modernist style, and overt criticism of imperialism, Conrad stands accused of a dehumanizing primitivism and racism that "reduc[es] Africa to the role of props for the break-up of one petty European mind" (Achebe 1977, 788).

And yet, the "mythic subversion of the myth," Taussig (1987, 10) argues, also "requires leaving [such] ambiguities intact." In Conrad's text, Taussig writes, "the myth is not 'explained' so that it can be 'explained away,' as in the forlorn attempts of social science. Instead it is held out as something you have to try out for yourself, feeling your way deeper and deeper into the heart of darkness until you do *feel* what is at stake, the madness of the passion" (10–11). Taussig's own writing deliberately repeats this Conradian strategy but with a postmodern difference as it investigates the political fictions that create the real. Taussig, moreover, specifically foregrounds the "narrative mode of the Indians themselves" (134–35), which is so starkly absent from colonial literature; not, however, by simply "rescuing the 'voice' of the Indian from the obscurity of pain and time" (135)—as anthropology often tends to do—but by foregrounding how *both* colonized and colonizers were and are bound together.

Rainforest Capitalism inherits from and continues Taussig's political and epistemological gesture as it insists on the *similarities* between two racially segregated worlds—expats and workers—that were often imagined as two very different realities. This chapter and the previous one foreground the uncanny commonalities of boredom, displacement, ephemerality, and centrifugality among workers and expats alike. As such, they illuminate the surprisingly shared affective touch of places like logging concessions, despite, beyond, and alongside the structural inequalities they reproduce. Learning from Conrad through Taussig but using a different scale, this book thereby hopes to retain the "hallucinatory quality" of rainforest capitalism without fully succumbing to its power (Taussig 1987, 10). Rather than sing about the greatness of violence, it foregrounds its uncontrollability. And rather than assume corporate power, it reveals ecstatic short-circuits that, among other things, incorporate a dark other within the white self.

The European expats effectively rebuilt their autonomous selves from a stubborn myth of darkness that ran through the concession. But their heroic stories never covered up their self-doubts, existential anxieties, and inabilities to "get things done." Their self-exoticizing stories indeed transformed experienced impotence into a paradoxical resource for self-making. And yet, this same darkness also signaled a powerlessness to resist the very myths and structures the expat loggers reproduced. "You cannot think about this too much," Roger admitted, "the morality of it . . . it stinks." Although rarely spoken, seeds of (self)critique were already there as a possibility that uneasily moved beneath practices and discourses. Conrad's injunction of being "men enough to face the darkness" (2006, 6) therefore also implied an ecstatic confrontation with the expat loggers' own racist and sometimes violent selves. Vulnerable to mythical forces they could not control, the European managers poignantly embodied and reproduced a long and disturbing history that continued to haunt the forest in new iterations: an ecstatic history of which this chapter "cannot be but its latest extension" (Taussig 1992, 10).

The Cercle Vicicongo in Aketi

Cannibals and Corned Beef

SUNDAY, MAY 2010, 8.30 in the morning. Thirty-four forest camp inhabitants assemble in a thatched hut serving as a new church at the other side of the logging road. Most attendants are in their twenties and thirties. Many do not have a regular job at CTI. Women take their places on the left-hand side of the aisle leading to the altar. Men sit on the right-hand side. Tree trunks serve as benches. I stand at the back, but people push me to the front. A white visitor is a rare event that cannot be left unused.

I dance to the rhythm of clapping hands. People sing a song. A woman lifts her arms and starts to pray. Another woman joins her. More and more people close their eyes. A swelling volume of words. A man asks Jesus to deliver him from evil spirits and protect him from witchcraft. "In the name of Jesus!" (*na nkombo na Yesu*), he shouts. People pick up words and phrases, improvising variations on a theme. I see that the young man next to me has tears in his eyes. Rhythms clash and resonate. I cannot help but rock with them, moving my lips as I try to remember a prayer. Some people loudly speak in tongues. I feel the ecstasis without understanding. Affects circulate as glossolalic words coagulate. Fervor infects.

The volume drops. The pastor rises from behind the altar dressed in a shiny, bright green cloak. On the wall behind him is a photograph of a black man with a beard in a white-and-red gown standing on top of a globe with his right arm raised and two fingers pointing to the sky. It is a picture of Mbala Tudikolela, the new Christ from Kinshasa. Two weeks before, the pastor began spreading his message, calling Tudikolela the tabernacle in whom God had taken residence to speak to the Congolese people. Most attendants knew the pastor as the former leader of the Assemblée Chrétienne du Message du Temps de la Fin (Christian assembly of the message of the end times), one of three Branhamist churches in the forest camp. However, following a conflict among Pentecostals, he had left the concession three years earlier. Recently he returned from the capital with a long beard, presenting himself as Ngoli Molangi, an apostle of Tudikolela.

Standing before us with his right hand pointing toward the photograph, the pastor starts talking. He vividly depicts a cosmic battle between God and the Devil. People alternate with a song: *C'est la fin, c'est la fin, c'est la fin de toutes choses* (This is the end, this is the end, this is the end of all things). He then raises his voice and testifies how he has seen, with his own eyes, Mbala Tudikolela healing the sick in Kinshasa, and how he became a follower of Mbala's new church, the Royaume des Cieux sur la Terre (Kingdom of heavens on earth).

On the blackboard next to the photograph he has written today's theme in white chalk: *La dispersion providentielle de Dieu dans la race noire et l'avènement du Royaume des Cieux au Congo Kinshasa, Afrique* (The providential dispersion of God in the black race and the coming of the kingdom of heavens in Congo Kinshasa, Africa). His passionate sermon warns us never to forget that evil and death originated in paradise, where Satan tempted Eve to eat from the Tree of Knowledge. "So, what you here call the 'Garden of Eden,'" he says in Lingala, "is nothing but the birthplace of sin. This Eden here, this Eden where the whites live, just at the other side of the camp, *is a place of evil.*" He obliquely looks in my direction. "It is in Eden that men fall, where Eve made Adam fall." Because of this sin, he continues, the world is doomed.

Turning to the blackboard, he then sketches an overview of the history of humankind after the Fall. He talks about Noah and the deluge. About Abraham leaving his house and family to follow God to an unknown destination. And about how we, too, must look for God. He explains that people like Jacob or Moses could physically "see" God but that when Jesus was born nobody acknowledged him. Only three "men of science" recognized the star. "Today, two thousand years later," he says, "another revolution will take place; the rhythm of the world will change once again through the new tabernacle of God in Kinshasa, Mbala Tudikolela, also called Kei Souverain. Few recognize him, but Mbala Tudikolela's arrival has been signaled by a bright star, and he has been identified as the new messiah. White magicians from Reverend Moon in Korea identified him. Tibetan monks identified him. A European phenomenologist recognized him. And Simon Kimbangu has already announced his coming in 1935 as the liberator of the black man!"

The pastor moves from behind his altar. His rhetorical mode changes from a scholarly lecture to a political speech. "Isn't it true?" he asks, "that the black race is burdened with the curse of Ham, son of Noah? Isn't it true that we only bring forth witches, cannibals, thieves, and imbeciles? That all good things come from white people?" Again, he looks in my direction. I shuffle uncomfortably on my tree trunk. "Just look at the state of the DRC," he continues, "tribalism, poverty, egoism, terrorism, genocide, AIDS, sexual violence, torture, corruption. . . . *But*," he asserts, "things will change because God has now chosen an African man as his tabernacle and will redeem the black race." People loudly shout "Amen!" "Unfortunately," he continues, "white people still come to steal our trees and destroy our forests. Our nation abounds in natural resources, but foreigners take them away." A wave of approval rises from the audience.

Stepping forward he proclaims: "Congo will soon become the New Jerusalem, and when the apocalypse comes, Africa will be saved as the sixth continent. God will return to Africa, and we will no longer need the white man. Because, in the coming Third World War, we—blacks—will guide the entire world. Did not pope John Paul II kiss the earth of the Congo?" People murmur in agreement. "The whites did great injustice when they divided the continent in the Charter of Imperialism in 1885. But soon they will no longer exploit our forest, our lung of the earth." He continues, "Congo-Kinshasa is the promised land, the torch of the world, a paradise on earth, a holy land, the light of the nations, the home of God's divine word, the trunk of divine majesty, hosting the perfume, giving birth to the son of light, and sheltering a great shepherd."

After a long silence he returns to his blackboard. Picking up the drawing chalk, he starts yet another lecture. He cites from the Old Testament to point at the supposed "blackness" of the devil and the contrasting "whiteness" of angels. He draws from "medieval myths" to talk about black cannibalism. And from tales by sixteenth- and seventeenth-century European explorers to prove the "bestial" nature of Africans and their "wild" sexuality. He quotes eighteenth-century Enlightenment thinkers who defended slavery and lamented the "laziness" of black workers, nineteenth-century social Darwinists to describe black underdevelopment, and twentieth-century paternalists to foreground the "childish" nature of Africans. He talks about state-of-the-art genetics to prove "black intellectual inferiority" and about psychological theories to draw attention to "black neurosis."

I am no longer sure whether his dazzling genealogy, shifting between deconstruction and reproduction, actually criticizes or reconfirms racist stereotypes. It seems as if he somehow agrees that black people are indeed "doomed," as if "white science" has given unshakable proof of black inferiority. And yet, after another long silence, he announces again that the black race will be saved by Mbala Tudikolela. "All this will come to an end," he says, "because God has chosen to settle down in the DRC, the new paradise." Lifting his hands to the sky, he concludes: "The old Eden of sin will soon disappear, and a new *black* Eden will rise." Again, people confirm with an amen.

After the sermon the atmosphere is excited. People shake my hand. I feel out of place, yet grateful to be there. We start singing again. A plastic cup goes around to collect money for repairing the church roof. A woman calls for harvesting cassava leaves to raise money for a sick child. Another song starts, and we go outside dancing. Ngoli Molangi, the pastor, approaches me. How delighted he is that a "son of the Belgians" attended his service. I reply that *I* am the one who is grateful. The next day, Ngoli invites me for a long conversation on racism and other things. After that, he became an avid and critical commentator on what I was trying to accomplish by being where I was. This chapter is written for him.

The Royaume des cieux sur la terre was not the only church or movement preaching a radical message of a coming racial revolution in the CTI concession. The idea of a black assumption of power and restoration of balance is an old promise of prophetic movements in the region (Eggers 2015; Jewsiewicki 1976; MacGaffey 1983; Mélice 2012). But Ngoli was one of the more outspoken voices when it came to the importance of race as an eschatological matter. His message sparked vivid debates among men of God in the forest camp—some preaching racial equality and others foregrounding difference. Yet Ngoli's explicit reference to Eden as the "birthplace of sin" particularly resonated with the ambivalence many experienced in the presence of timber production. While most camp inhabitants eventually rejected Mbala Tudikolela as a false prophet, his message clearly struck a chord of deeply felt hopes and anxieties.

Structural racism was indeed a painful reality in the logging concession. The previous chapter already revealed the importance of race from the vantage point of the European expats. This chapter turns to the perspective of their

Congolese workers. The following sections therefore need to plunge into a set of stories, rumors, and suspicions that hint at what in African studies is often qualified as "the occult." Focusing on popular hermeneutics and modes of analysis that were widespread in the Itimbiri region, they offer what Stuart Kirsch (2006) calls a "reverse anthropology"—an anthropology of capitalist extraction *through the perspective of* local residents as they analyzed and interpreted its realities. But this so-called occult analytics of rainforest capitalism should not be taken as simply an "indigenous" mode of reading the world. The occult is itself the product of entangled histories and complex encounters between Central Africans and Europeans (Bernault 2019).

As such, this chapter unfolds another "dark" underside of white presence in the region: not the self-exoticizing trope we have encountered thus far, but a troubling *occult* reality that seemed to account for starkly racialized extraction. For inhabitants of the labor compounds, race was indeed a quotidian reality structured by hidden truths with a long history that manifested again in the present moment.

This chapter first revisits the expat Garden of Eden to show how camp gossip and speculations presented white space as simultaneously a "paradise" and a "place of evil." The chapter then moves beyond the hidden dimension of the European living quarters and reproduces rumors about mermaids, cannibals, and zombies that signaled a much wider "occult economy" that supported and explained the racialized exploitation of labor in the region (Comaroff and Comaroff 1999). As a collective form of social action, these rumors and stories expressed a profound moral critique of extractive capitalism and contained a vernacular theory of accumulation that incorporated CTI in a generalized economy of eating and being eaten. The chapter concludes with a sustained reflection on the ambiguity of cannibalism and reweaves popular conspiracy theories and suspicions about occult forces into a more *post*critical account of power and ecstasis. Its aim is not to expose any final truth behind mere rumors but to retell the paranoid by opening up its reparative potential.

Eden Revisited

Whereas the European loggers generally showed little or no interest in the everyday life of their workers, the latter, by contrast, were deeply fascinated with expat living standards. Whenever Pablo and Michel were on holiday, for instance, friends from the labor compounds insisted on visiting the expat quarters. When I sat with them in Pablo's salon, they invariably commented on how the bungalows, flowerbeds, lawns, and furniture were really just like Europe (*lokola mpoto*). We drank cold beer from the fridge, watched films on satellite television, and enjoyed the freshness of the air-conditioning. Sometimes Pablo's cuisinier brought us something to eat. But, above all, most visitors wanted to "learn internet." These visits always made me a little uneasy, but I insisted on reciprocating the hospitality I so often received in the labor compounds.

It was not for nothing that CTI workers called their bosses' living quarters the Garden of Eden or, simply, Eden—a popular designation their European occupants seemed largely unaware of. In many ways this Eden indeed looked like a paradise. In comparison to the labor camps, which did not have electricity or running water and where, as its inhabitants often said, life was hard (*bomoi eza makasi*), the expat bungalows suggested tranquility (*bopemi*), peace (*kimia*), and the absence of trouble (*mobulu*). They seemed a world of affluence and connectivity, indexing a desired modern lifestyle: a good place (*esika malamu*) where it was agreeable and beneficial to spend time.

At the same time, however, this fascinating place also provoked suspicion. People talked about how a European had beaten his cook and how another one had abused a young girl. Older rumors alleged that a murder had occurred. And some whispered that the expats indulged in sexual "abominations." Stories like these resonated with church sermons about Eden as the birthplace of sin (*esika ya lisumu*) or source of evil (*source du mal*). Several pastors indeed explicitly mobilized the ambivalence of the biblical metaphor as both a paradise *and* the place where Original Sin brought about suffering, hunger, illness, pain, labor, and death. In the dominant eschatological discourse of the compound's churches, this fall of man was at least as important as Eden's prelapsarian innocence: it set in motion the world's moral degradation toward a satanic present, an apocalyptic interlude preceding final salvation (De Boeck 2005).

One day, a Branhamist pastor from the forest camp, a charming man in his early fifties, gave me booklet that was aptly titled *L'Eden de Satan* (Satan's Eden). It contained a French translation of an oral message delivered by William Branham on August 29, 1965, in Jeffersonville, Indiana, and was printed by Shekinah Publications in Kinshasa, a publishing service of Branhamist Shekinah Gospel Missions (Branham 2004).[1] The pastor, who was visibly concerned about my mental and spiritual well-being as a regular occupant of Eden, urged me to carefully read the booklet and then return to him for guidance.

When we met a couple of days later, the pastor patiently explained Branham's message for me. After God had created paradise, he said, Satan took over the world. Reading from the booklet, he then told me that the devil "had six thousand years to build up his Eden, as God had six thousand years to bring His Eden to a close. And by deceit . . . he established his own Eden in this earth, *in sin*" (Branham 2004, 11).[2] Therefore, the pastor continued, today's so-called Eden is really a place of sin where "Satan is taking the throne, as the antichrist" (11). Moreover, he said, this satanic Eden was an "intellectual, educated, scientific Eden" that was "built upon knowledge, [and not] upon faith" (15–16). He warned me that, as a scientist, I should not dismiss God's truth. Neither should I ignore Satan's reign. I thanked him for his advice and wanted to return the booklet, but he told me to keep it and hide it under my bed in Pablo's guest room as a defense against evil.

I had already heard several rumors about white men's magic (*magie ya mindele*) and the "hidden sources" of expat power. Compound residents usually remained vague about its details, but many agreed that the white man is usually a witch (*mundele azalaka kaka ndoki*), implying that whites had access to occult knowledge. Moreover, as the pastor's tutorial made clear, my own research was also vulnerable to being read as a form of apprenticeship in occult sciences (West 2007).

For this reason, researching and writing on what anthropologists often call the occult is never straightforward. The following sections reproduce stories and rumors that, geographically, spread out from the expat Garden of Eden to the wider area around the concession. Their intention is not to exoticize or Africanize what is a global phenomenon, but to carefully situate the occult as a dimension of contemporary industrial timber production (Ranger 2007). In the context of work for CTI, these rumors and stories were indeed produced for a *specific* audience and spoke to *particular* experiences of capitalist extraction.

The River and the Mermaid

In his talk about Satan's Eden, the concerned pastor also emphasized another surprising aspect of Branham's message. The booklet indeed contained an explanation of the doctrine of the serpent seed (*la sémence du serpent*), according to which the devil had sexual intercourse with Eve in the Garden of Eden, which brought forth Cain and, with him, the fall of man. Quoting the booklet, the pastor said to me, "Eve is truly Satan's queen" because "Satan, the serpent, got to Eve before Adam got to her. . . . So he beguiled her, see; so Satan, the serpent, was the husband of Eve before Adam ever knew" (Branham 2004, 20). Rather than eat from the Tree of Knowledge, the pastor explained, Eve had sex with the serpent. Moreover, he said, Eve's original sin of the flesh continues until today in the "sexuality" of contemporary women. Again quoting from the pamphlet he said, "It was Eve that Satan used to make Adam sin by her power of lust. Now the same . . . bobbed hair, painted face, sexually dressed . . . things contrary to the Word of God. To cut her hair, makes her a dishonorable woman, a prostitute. To wear shorts . . . sexy dresses . . . makes her a prostitute . . . because the lust of Satan . . . She causes her Adam to lust for her" (21).

In Congolese churches, crusades against "loose" female sexuality have become commonplace (Pype 2012, 278). But the pastor's specific evocation of the abhorrent union between Eve and the serpent *in* the Garden of Eden also struck a chord with a stubborn rumor in the CTI concession. It was indeed well known that a serpent-like creature resided alongside the forest camp bungalows, either in a muddy pool near the path connecting the expat quarters to the work site or in the rivulet leading to the labor compound. This water spirit—a beautiful white woman with the tail of a fish—was notorious for her affluence and power. Several people told us she was married to Michel through a mystical love contract, according to which she gave him material wealth in return for sexual fidelity. Was it not true, one of our neighbors asked, that Michel, contrary to his colleagues, rarely had sexual relations with Congolese women? Was not his occult marriage the reason behind his seemingly abnormal sexuality? And was his water spirit not why he had become rich?

As in other parts of Central and West Africa, people called this serpent/mermaid Mami Wata (Bastian 1997; Biaya 1988; Drewal 2008a; Frank 1995; Jewsiewicki 2003). Possibly originating from fifteenth-century images of mermaids on the bows of Portuguese ships, Mami Wata is indeed a well-known figure of the colonial encounter (Drewal 2008b). In the CTI concession, she literally occupied the threshold between the expat quarters and the labor camp. Pablo's cook, for instance, claimed he had seen a beautiful rich lady (*dame riche*) when returning to the labor compounds at night. As a hybrid creature with explicitly European looks and signaling a characteristically "Western" erotics—by displaying naked breasts rather than buttocks—she physically embodied occult power through an alluring whiteness (Jewsiewicki 2008, 117). Much like Eve in the doctrine of the serpent seed, Mami Wata was indeed a seducing immoral figure, operating outside or against normative marriage and kinship relations (Bernault 2019, 26–68).

In the logging concession people generally referred to this hybrid woman/snake/fish as *la sirène* (the siren). They described her as fatally beautiful but extremely vain, procuring riches and power for her "husbands" at the expense of their health or in return for sacrificing their relatives. As such, she both embodied modernity and set its horrible price (Jewsiewicki 2008, 113). "When you don't respect the terms of her contract," a villager from Mombwassa said, "she takes revenge on you and makes you fall sick. She can even kill you." Michel's skinny body, for instance, was said to be a sign of the physical toll of their arrangement; his remarkable abstinence, a consequence of his consumed fertility. It was not for nothing that villagers had nicknamed Michel *le chat* (the cat).

According to CTI workers, some of their Congolese managers also possessed a "rich lady," which explained their apparent access to power, authority, and money within the company. But Michel's Mami Wata was special. She was even more powerful, dangerous, and unpredictable than others. One of the oldest prospectors claimed that Michel, upon his arrival in the concession in the late 1980s, had installed the siren himself in the small Mamoissa River. Indeed, had I not seen the huge green mamba (*Dendroaspis angusticeps*) that people had warned me about in that marshy pool not far from his bungalow? Normally, any snake that size close to living areas would immediately be killed, but Michel had apparently forbidden his workers from doing so because he wanted to "protect nature."

Yet what was most troubling about Michel's siren was not her physical threat to passersby but her notorious, murderous jealousy. A bulldozer driver told us that, a few years back, Michel had taken the habit of picking up the younger sister of one of his colleagues in the labor camp to spend the night in the Garden of Eden. Because Mami Wata could not know about this, the worker claimed, the girl had to undergo three painful abortions to cover up their relationship. One day, however, when Michel's girlfriend took a bath in the Mamoissa River, the mermaid appeared. "She waved her long, wet hair," the bulldozer driver said, "and some water drops touched the girl's body. The next day, she fell very ill." Michel had indeed told me about a sick girl he had once sent to Congo-Brazzaville for treatment. Unfortunately, she had passed away in the hospital several weeks later. Some whispered that she died of AIDS.

Many compound residents seemed to know this story, but I only heard about it after another sad event. One evening, an eight-year-old boy drowned in the Mamoissa River. Apparently he had left his parents' house to take a bath but had not returned by nightfall. His older brother set out to look for him and later told people he had found his brother "mystically hovering" in a squatted position above a bizarre vortex in the water. Freddy and I attended the boy's funeral. It was a dreadful evening, and many people speculated about his death. It was difficult to believe that someone could drown in such a shallow river, even a small boy. Had we not often seen him swim with his friends? During the funeral, suspicions quickly settled on the boy's own father, a contract worker who had recently lost his job. Perhaps he had sacrificed his son to get his position back. The next day the local police commander officially charged the father with "dereliction" and made him pay a fine. But everyone knew what was at stake. That night, the father simply disappeared. Some said he fled to Kisangani.

A few weeks later a new element turned up. Apparently a young woman, a paternal cousin of the boy, had tried to seduce Michel in order to steal money from him. I had seen them talking on the road heading to the expat quarters. Some concluded Michel had taken revenge on her family by poisoning the Mamoissa River and killing the bathing boy. Had one of the guards in the Garden of Eden not told us that the water reservoir, which supplied the expat bungalows, had run over and spilled its content back into the river on the very day of the boy's death? Others said the girl's sexual audacity had aroused the jealousy of Michel's Mami Wata, who claimed the boy's life as a price for avenging her anger.

Yet Michel's siren was not merely a source of personal enrichment. She was also suspected of being a means for the logging company to achieve its aims. When CTI had to carry out a population census for its new management plan, for instance, village after village refused to collaborate out of fear that its agents were making lists of potential victims whose spirit (*elimo*) or life force (*nguya ya bomoi*) the company would sacrifice in return for profits. Papa Esibo, the bulldozer operator discussed in chapter 5, also told me that, on multiple occasions, villagers from the south had sabotaged his machine because they assumed the road he was building was being "paid for" with local lives.

As a central figure in these stories, rumors, and suspicions, Mami Wata firmly inscribed the European loggers in a subsurface system of extraction, where the random souls of innocent residents were consumed as raw material for the company's operations.[3] CTI was indeed thought to participate in what Jean Comaroff and John Comaroff (1999, 297) call an "occult economy," that is, in "the deployment of magical means for material ends or, more expansively, the conjuring of wealth by resorting to inherently mysterious techniques [that] are neither transparent nor explicable in conventional terms [and that] often involve the destruction of others and *their* capacity to create value." Occult economies, which are often read as popular commentaries on "modernity," effectively seem to be a globally recurring dimension of contemporary capitalism (Comaroff and Comaroff 2000, Geschiere 1997).

In the CTI concession, however, the occult powers of expat managers were clearly localized and materialized in the landscape. Mami Wata, for instance, was explicitly said to live in or near the Mamoissa River, and the European living quarters were situated just below its source. The river then flowed from the Garden of Eden toward the labor camp and neighboring settlements, passing by places where residents took drinking water, bathed, or washed their clothes and kitchenware. As such, the expats found themselves *upstream* of workers and villagers—a spatial setup the former had deliberately planned so as to assure a continuous supply of fresh water that was "uncontaminated" by discharge from the labor camp. For many workers and villagers, however, this upstream position clearly constituted political control. Rivers were devices for possible manipulation: had Mobutu not "dumped tons of 'mystical products' into the River Congo" to keep his subjects loyal and quiescent (Schatzberg 2001, 133)?

In the Itimbiri region, flowing water indeed expressed ancestral influence. Considered as streams of vital energy, rivers literally divided the landscape, whereby elders metaphysically occupied the higher ground. As a result, ancestors could control their descendants' lives by either blocking or releasing energetic flows. Mbudza villagers told us, for instance, how traditional wrestling matches used to require the blessing of the *atulu* ritual whereby young wrestlers were first washed at an upriver site in the forest and then made to crawl between their elders' legs in returning to the village downstream. As among the Sakata of the Mai-Ndombe region, this washing ritual was like a childbirth that opened up the flux of life, which originated from the ancestors and streamed through the elders to the next generation (Bekaert 2000, 295–96).

These old rituals illustrate a widespread hydraulic metaphysics of control whereby flowing water symbolized and materialized occult influence. From this perspective, CTI occupied an upriver position of relative power that, in popular cosmologies, was reserved for the ancestors. But while ancestral control was usually seen as morally good (*ya malamu*)—either in a protective or corrective sense—white control was considered essentially bad (*ya mabe*). Although both were qualified as mystical—and could therefore be rejected as satanic by Pentecostal opponents of tradition—white hydraulic control was clearly an immoral application of technologies of power. It was therefore no coincidence that Michel had installed his Mami Wata in or along the Mamoissa River. As a threshold figure, she corrupted and diverted the flow of life from socially approved ends to antisocial objectives. But this position of control came with its own toll and Michel's thinning body was taken as physical proof that *one could not eat without being eaten*.

Compagnie Kitunga

The CTI concession was not the only place about which such rumors were told. The sleepy town of Aketi to the east of the logging concession was another central site in the rich repertoire of stories about white men secretly consuming black lives. Freddy and I often traveled to this former railway town in the company of the father of one of the CTI prospectors, himself a retired railway worker who had grown up in Aketi. In the logging camps he had already told us about the Cercle Vicicongo, the clubhouse of the later Chemins de fer des Uele, where Belgians organized concerts, balls, and *Paris soir* dinner parties. Later we learned that this modern building of ambiance also hid a terrifying reality beneath its dance floor.

The old man indeed told us that "the Belgians in Aketi used to bring people there and chain them to the walls and the ceiling of the basement. Then, they fattened them and slaughtered them. Some of them were eaten. Others were sent to restaurants in Europe as corned beef." For this reason, he said, "As children, we were afraid of the Belgians. When we heard a car approaching, especially when it was getting dark, we immediately jumped into the high grasses to hide." Only after independence, the man continued, could Congolese finally enter these basements. "Some said there was blood on the floor, metal hooks on the walls, and small cages for keeping prisoners." He hesitated. "I don't know," he said. "Maybe it was pig's blood. . . . But, later, children climbed in a pit and found a large number of empty food cans."

In the CTI labor camps we had heard similar stories about other places. Congolese truck drivers from the Huileries du Congo Belge, for instance, were said to crisscross the region in the 1950s to kidnap children for their European bosses at the oil palm plantation. And around the town of Bumba, employees from the Congo Tobacco Company—later, British American Tobacco—were notorious for searching for young women at night. They were known as *Beleli* and would have worked for a white man who went by the same nickname, which meant "lover of women" (Likaka 2009, 118).

All these stories invariably mentioned an organization known as Compagnie Kitunga, Lingala for woven basket. This was said to be a secret network of white colonial agents whose employees had to kidnap Congolese (children, women, and, to a lesser extent, men) in delivery vans and pickup trucks in order to slaughter them and sell their flesh. Such stories had a long history. Rik Ceyssens (1975), for instance, tracks the origin of the similar *mutumbula* myth to memories of the slave trade in the Belgian Congo (see also Shaw 2002 and Thornton 2003). And Nancy Rose Hunt (1999, 182–85) mentions colonial *tokwakwa* tales of whites turning black people into tinned food in the Congolese rainforest. On a more national scale, the historian Isidore Ndaywel è Nziem (1998, 225) notes how Congolese used to mobilize widespread ideas of Europeans killing and devouring black bodies in order to account for the forced recruitment of colonial workers.

In an influential book, Luise White (2000) analyses "vampire stories" from East and Central Africa in which vampiric firemen, or *wazimamoto*, attack Africans to drain their blood at night. White, however, suggests that scholars should not take such rumors as mere metaphors for colonial exploitation, as this would only "reduce them to African misunderstandings of colonial interventions" (5). Instead, she shows how stories about black blood-draining employees were "ways for working men to express the subtle and contradictory anxieties that might accompany their good fortune at finding gainful employment" (123). Rather than an allegory of colonial extraction, she argues, these stories were really about the specific experience of skilled laborers and their intimacy with new technology. White (1993, 33) thereby particularly emphasizes the *closed* nature of "cars out of place [that were] used for unintended purposes." Such weird vehicles, she claims, having no windows or lights, literally "veiled" colonial labor and made it an "object of scrutiny and speculation" (36). These rumors therefore seemed to express "African concerns about mechanization," as a new class of workers came to possess knowledge that was inaccessible to most but "bonded a few select Africans to specialized procedures" (37, 38).

White's analysis is strikingly similar to Compagnie Kitunga stories. People indeed frequently emphasized the inaccessible, locked, and opaque aspect of vehicles and places inside of which "nobody knew what was going on." Perhaps the name *kitunga* or woven basket referred to the enclosed nature of cars, vans, hotels, restaurants, clubhouses, basements, and prisons (Bernault 2003, 27). Moreover, as White also suggests, these stories seemed to be about the performance of skilled labor. Some CTI employees effectively recycled old rumors on white cannibalism to create an atmosphere of strategic secrecy around their special status as a worker in intimate contact with the white world. It is not unthinkable that they retold them—for Freddy and me but also for other listeners—to this effect. Other workers, by contrast, loudly dismissed such stories as "mistaken beliefs" of ordinary villagers. Either way, commentators deliberately positioned themselves as men "who really knew."

As such, Compagnie Kitunga stories clearly contributed to maintaining a worker identity in a largely post-labor milieu of generalized unemployment. Yet, at the same time, these stories were also a means of making political statements about contemporary neocolonialism and expressing current experiences of violence and injustice. Their dark moral point was indeed the primary reason why, fifty years after the formal end of colonialism, they had reemerged from the oral archive as a popular critique of racialized extraction. Some workers might have doubted the historical veracity of these rumors or maintained that they were just "stories people make up." Others nonetheless insisted they were true.[4] What matters is that the debates they triggered contributed to their ongoing circulation and maintained at least the possibility that CTI might have been familiar with the cannibalistic practices of its predecessors.

Inverting the problematic trope of cannibalism from its Western stereotype about black anthropophagic savages to an equally terrifying notion of white, man-eating companies, these rumors effectively reinscribed the CTI expats into an occult economy they themselves qualified as "superstition." Although the European loggers were rarely accused of witchcraft (*kindoki*)—an otherwise common form of occult eating practices—they were effectively suspected of partaking in hidden transactions through other, more literal, means. Indeed, because witchcraft usually presupposed a close relationship between witch and victim, it mainly occurred within families—as what Peter Geschiere (2003, 2013) calls the "dark side of kinship." Cannibalism, on the other hand, did not suppose such intimacy between perpetrator and victim. To the contrary, cannibalism seemed very much the opposite of kinship.[5] Because cannibals are supposed to be outsiders, white colonizers and European loggers could be suspected of cannibalism exactly *because* of their distance and foreignness.

Just like the rumors about Michel's Mami Wata, cannibal stories thus translated popular memories about colonial violence into a neocolonial context of industrial logging. As such, they were a way to "remember the present" by unveiling the immoral economy on which it was based (Fabian 1996). Articulating widespread critical sentiments about a starkly racialized mode of extraction and accumulation, they expressed profound suspicions about white presence in the region and uncovered its hidden reality of violence as another "darkness" beneath a surface of affluence and wealth—not as the Conradian tune the expats liked to sing to themselves, but as a troubling occult dynamic.

Marx in the Rainforest

While different inhabitants of the logging concession told similar stories about white occult practices, in the case of CTI employees, they also had an immediate physical counterpart in their everyday experiences on the work floor. Operating in difficult and sometimes dangerous conditions, many employees indeed complained about generalized fatigue. "We are always tired," they said. Tree fellers and machine operators in particular experienced work as a direct attack on their bodies or as a theft of their bodily capacity (Tonda 2005, 134–36). As we saw in chapter 2, they explicitly conceived of logging as a struggle (*lutte*) or combat (*etumba*) between workers and trees. Moreover, fierce shocks and sudden movements of chainsaws, bulldozers, skidders, and loaders continually weakened their bodies (Rolston 2013). Long hours operating heavy machinery led to frequent health problems, such as lower back pain, hernias, or hemorrhoids—ailments that were, not coincidentally, situated in a part of the body that was also thought to contain one's sexual energy. Returning from the forest, many CTI agents effectively claimed that work reduced their sexual potency and sapped their male strength. "If I don't eat a piece of kola nut after work," one of the fellers laughingly admitted, "my wife complains!"

It is important to note that forest workers described the gradual destruction of their bodies through the same idiom of *being eaten*, as discussed above. Bulldozer and skidder operators, for instance, said their machines "ate" their bodies—almost as a necessary counterpart to the ways in which they also "ate" the forest. In general, *kolia* (eating) was a common verb to refer to all kinds of relationships whereby one side was said to grow *at the expense of* the other (Bayart 1989; Harms 1981). As such, it expressed a zero-sum theorization of politics in which every increase in power necessarily entailed a consumption of power elsewhere (Bekaert 2000, 84–85). While Central African histories have often led to political cosmologies in which power effectively *is* the "capacity to consume" (Schatzberg 2001, 40), this eating should be understood as both physical and metaphysical (Bernault 2019, 168). Whether a cannibal eating human flesh, a witch eating a victim, a chief eating the tribute of his people, or politicians eating the money of the state, eating occurred both in this world (*monde oyo*) and in the invisible realm of the second world (*deuxième monde*).

Anthropologists of natural resource extraction have long pointed at the broad register of eating as a way of rendering experiences of work under capitalism. In *We Eat the Mines and the Mines Eat Us* (1979), for instance, June Nash famously describes how Bolivian tin miners pointed to a similar equation. And in the Alaskan timber industry, Native American loggers often referred to their jobs as the "kind of work [that] will eat you up and spit you out" (Dombrowski 2002, 133). In the CTI concession, the tired and bruised bodies of workers eaten by machinery also expressed an acute awareness of exploitation. Rather than prisoners of "false consciousness," CTI workers were very much aware that the secret of capitalist profit-making lay in the exploitation of their own labor power. Without therefore wanting to reduce the popular idiom of eating to nothing but a vernacular version of Marxist critique, it is at least striking to note the similarity between workers' occult imagery and Marx's vocabulary in *Das Kapital* (Taussig 1980). Indeed, if, according to Marx (1990, 342), capital "is dead labour which vampire-like lives only by sucking living labour, and lives the more, the more labour it sucks," what else is capitalism, if not an organized system of eating and being eaten?

Yet in the CTI concession this common imagery of workers being eaten by capital also took another turn. Villagers and workers alike indeed suspected that the *trees* CTI exported to Europe were being processed into canned food—such as corned beef or tinned sardines—which was then re-exported to the DRC. Even skilled CTI employees with a great deal of experience in the logging sector, who knew that trees were sold as timber for construction, carpentry, and paneling, occasionally took me aside to ask whether there was any truth in such rumors. I replied that, to the best of my knowledge, I had never seen any proof of their suspicions. But my answer never fully reassured. "Had I ever been *inside* those factories where meat was tinned?" they asked. Of course, I hadn't.

This latest iteration of older stories about white cannibalistic practices reflected deep-seated uncertainties about the ulterior motives and objectives of global capitalism. The assumed transformation of trees—rather than human bodies—into commodified industrial food indeed expressed a certain alienation from processes of production that could never be entirely known. Suspicious of the products of their own labor, workers effectively entertained the possibility that the corned beef and tinned sardines they bought in the labor compounds might very well contain timber they had themselves produced.

No one could be certain about what was pressed into those small metal cans. Just as with the older Compagnie Kitunga stories, opacity troubled.

Zombie Labor

To further understand these vernacular critiques of the exploitation of labor power, we need to look at a last set of rumors that circulated through the concession area. The events and stories mentioned thus far have traced a profoundly racialized occult economy based on expat dealings with Mami Wata, suspicions about white cannibalism, and the international transformation of trees into canned food. But the immorality of capitalist labor relations was not limited to instances of black workers toiling for white bosses. Exploitation was a much larger question that concerned *all* forms of work.

Forest residents for instance talked about a specific technique for occult enrichment that was known as *ponoli*: a particular medicine (*nkisi* or *fétiche*) that enabled its practitioners to turn people into zombies (*babutwa* or *revenants*). Ponoli masters who used or "touched" this medicine were thereby said to capture the spirits of recently deceased persons or attack living individuals in order to reverse their breath (*kobalola mpema*). Their victims thereby lost their free will and could thus be put to work. Many were said to hunt or cultivate. Others had to fish in the middle of the Congo River. Some were forced to help out in small businesses, shops, and boutiques. In any case, the products of their labor directly entered into the hands of their masters, who, though leading a seemingly normal life, had been initiated into the secret ponoli association (*association ya ponoli*)—usually in return for sacrificing a family member.

Ponoli victims who had once disappeared in the forest but returned to the CTI labor camp invariably expressed their experiences as episodes of profound disorientation. One ponoli victim, for instance, described how a sudden noise—"as if an airplane flies over"—struck him deaf and numb (*baba*) so that he no longer knew where he was and started to wander around. After some time he arrived at a spot in the forest where he was strapped to a tree. His ears were filled with leeches (*mikute*), and his mouth was closed so that he could not call for help. People who passed by were unable to see him. Later he was put to work in a huge maize field.

When Freddy asked him how he had been able to return to the world of the living, he replied he did not know. One day, he said, he simply woke up on a garbage heap behind his house. Another man, however, told us that he had managed to escape from his master after stealing salt. He claimed zombies were only allowed to eat unsalted food and described how, as soon as his tongue touched the salt, a whirlwind transferred him back to the forest camp. The ponoli association immediately started looking for him with airplanes and helicopters, but he was well hidden, he said, and they were unable to find him.

Scarce references in the literature attest to similar stories in the wider region. Among the Wagenia people near Kisangani, for instance, André Droogers (1980, 58) refers to *fónólí* practices as a nonhereditary form of sorcery that could be learned through apprenticeship with a specialist—a *moto wa fónólí*—who belonged to a "guild of sorcerers." Hunt (1999, 189) also mentions "contemporary fonoli tales of disappeared people who live on as invisible slaves" in the Congolese rainforest. And T. K. Biaya (1988) refers to fonoli as a form of confusion provoked by the mythical serpent Monama, attributing the origins of fonoli to the Lokele and Topoke peoples in Orientale Province.

Yet, ponoli rumors are also a regional variation on a more widespread genre of stories in Central and Southern Africa. In colonial and postcolonial Cameroon, for instance, Cyprian Fisiy and Peter Geschiere (1991) analyzed how and why new forms of zombifying witchcraft arose with new economic inequalities. And Jean Comaroff and John Comaroff (1999, 285) described how the rural north of "post-apartheid" South Africa came under the grip of "a burgeoning fear . . . that some people, usually old people, were turning others into zombies; into a vast virtual army of ghost workers, whose lifeblood fueled a vibrant, immoral economy." As such, the Comaroffs understand zombification as an illustration of the rise in occult economies during what they call the "millennial capitalism" of the 1990s—"capitalism in its messianic, salvific, even magical manifestations" (Comaroff and Comaroff 2000, 293).

Ponoli magic is indeed a paradigmatic example of the "promise to deliver almost preternatural profits, to yield wealth *sans* perceptible production, value *sans* visible effort" (Comaroff and Comaroff 1999, 281). In the CTI labor compounds, direct and open accusations were rare, but inhabitants somehow took it for granted that their most well-to-do neighbors might very well be ponoli practitioners. Although those suspected of wealth medicine were not always the most affluent, rumors about ponoli practices contained a clear moral critique of the immorality of excessive accumulation in a context of scarcity and generalized unemployment (Niehaus 2001). Indeed, while accusations of witchcraft (*kindoki*) were usually directed against the relatively poor and socially marginalized, ponoli practitioners were generally thought to be rich men, such as Congolese staff, team overseers, or successful traders.

Suspicions about ponoli were clearly about how people amassed their wealth (Englund 1996). But they were also a direct commentary on labor. The popular idea of an army of unpaid zombie slaves indeed spoke to the everyday concerns of workers who felt "eaten" away by harsh work in return for a meager salary. In a milieu where wage work was rare and insecure, the terrifying image of the zombie, sapped from all humanizing vitality, seemed to occupy the extreme end of a lived spectrum of extraction and exploitation. Moreover, ponoli stories also contained ecstatic dimensions. Many workers talked about ponoli as a kind of madness (*liboma* or *folie*) that made people lose their way and lose their minds in the first place—its victims but also its supposed masters.

Although I never heard the expat managers being directly accused of ponoli magic—perhaps because the technology of "traditional" medicine was supposedly beyond their reach—rumors about zombie labor nevertheless partook in a much larger occult system in which some got rich at the expense of others. They contributed to the same invisible economy in which the European loggers also participated, albeit through different means. In fact, as Florence Bernault (2019) recently illustrated, ponoli stories contributed to a "transactional" field of deals, fluxes, and exchanges that had a long history in Equatorial Africa and was *co*produced by Europeans and Africans alike. As a collective form of social action, propagating rumors, stories, and gossip about CTI's occult practices thereby strengthened the popular drive to hold the company accountable for its acts and contributed to a tense—indeed, ecstatic—social landscape in which discontented villagers so quickly blocked logging roads to claim their fair share (Kirsch 2006).

Reweaving Paranoia

Not surprisingly, my own research project was also vulnerable to being drawn into such suspicions about white presence. For instance, when Freddy and I visited villages or towns in and around the CTI concession to construct an archive of stories about colonial companies, we were often confronted with questions and misgivings. Why exactly were we so interested in these companies' remains? What were we after? And what were we going to do with the stories we collected? Especially when people discovered that my maternal grandfather used to be a colonial army officer, I was regularly assumed to be looking for my grandparents' stuff (*biloko na bakoko na ye*).

In a way, people were of course right. We crisscrossed the landscape to trace old ruins and asked people about them.

Only time, respect, and unobtrusiveness could somehow ease suspicions. Nonetheless, in several places we heard about how the Belgians had left secret signposts (*signes secrets*) in the forest upon Congolese independence. In the 1960s, many plantation owners, factory bosses, and state agents had indeed hurriedly left the country and been unable to take all of their belongings with them. For this reason, it was said that they had hidden treasures in the forest and marked them with signs "only they could read." This deliberate concealment implied that, despite formal independence, colonialism "was not over yet." "Someday," a woman in her sixties told us, "the Belgians will return to take what is theirs."

CTI too had no choice but to operate in this climate of suspicion. Had it not replaced former colonial companies? Did it not know how to decode the numbers on overgrown concrete posts that served as old landmarks in the forest? And had it not left its own bizarre marks inscribed on wooden poles wherever it went? Ever since its appearance, CTI had followed in the footsteps of earlier companies, using old maps, reopening colonial roads, and "discovering" well-trodden paths (Fabian 2000, 48–51). With their survey technology, the company also had extensive knowledge of forest resources that was off-limits to most Congolese. And rumor had it that CTI was actually interested in diamonds rather trees. Logging activities, it was said, were merely the visible side of its covert operation. In the middle of the 1990s, for instance, when the then site manager requested permission to deepen the Itimbiri River to make it navigable year-round, local authorities sent inspectors to investigate if the operation was not an undercover search for diamonds.

Again, such rumors were not new. The notorious Cercle Vicicongo clubhouse in Aketi—the head office of Compagnie Kitunga—was equally known as a place from where Europeans smuggled diamonds through a long tunnel that was said to connect its basements with the Itimbiri River. Diamonds were supposed to be the "real source" of white wealth. The grit and gravel they left behind still glittered on Aketi's roads, people said. And, in the early 1990s, the rediscovery of diamonds to the east of the concession, and the subsequent emergence of artisanal mining, only confirmed old suspicions that the Belgians had always known more than what they disclosed to the Congolese (see also Turner 1978).

In several ways, secrecy and concealment thus seemed essential to rainforest capitalism, from its colonial past to the contemporary moment. There literally was an "occult" dimension to the presence of white men: a hidden aspect of industrial extraction that was deeply disturbing. Yet, at the same time, it was nothing out of the ordinary. In fact, it simply was how things worked. People—Europeans and Congolese alike—kept stuff from one another and protected their sources of enrichment. The so-called occult was therefore often stunningly banal. Women kept money hidden from husbands. Girls tried to keep lovers a secret from their parents. Visitors were deliberately vague about their objectives. And many people were known by different names. Being fully transparent was simply naive and possibly dangerous. And as long as one shared what one gained, nobody really objected.

Moreover, the vital need to constantly look for the "underneath of things"—as Mariane Ferme (2001) so aptly put it in her ethnography of the Mende in war-torn Sierra Leone—is not only a characteristic of African epistemologies; it is also a fundamental drive of the social sciences. Indeed, what else is social analysis if not an attempt "to understand how the visible world . . . is activated by forces concealed beneath the surface of discourse, objects, and social relations" (2)? What else, for instance, is "millennial capitalism" if not an occult force arranging, without fully determining, the world (Comaroff and Comaroff 2000)? And what difference does it make to a "hermeneutics of suspicion" whether it exposes witches, cannibals, or zombies rather than neoliberalism, heteronormativity, or the production of surplus value (Ricoeur 1965)? Is not, in both cases, the "skill to see beyond the visible phenomenon and to interpret deeper meanings . . . a culturally valued and highly contested activity" (Ferme 2001, 3)?

Suspicion is indeed central to both popular epistemologies and critical theory. Or, to put it differently, "paranoid" attitudes seem to characterize social sciences and witch-finding alike (West 2007). They are both hyper-vigilant forms of probing, invested in finding and exposing hidden forces that operate behind the surface of things and which ordinary people are unable to discern on their own. Both are, furthermore, also continuously vulnerable to accusations of being complicit with what they expose: witch-finders are always potential witches, and social theory is eagerly scanned for moments that would prove that it remains unconsciously entangled in what it criticizes.

So, how to take seriously the widespread suspicion and paranoia we encountered in the logging concession as part of an ethnography that nonetheless announced itself as a *post*-critical account of timber production (Felski 2015)? Perhaps we can draw inspiration from Mariane Ferme's insistence that Mende "strategies of concealment" and their "cultural order of dissimulation" also imply an "aesthetics of ambiguity" that is characterized by an "absence of ideals of transparency" (Ferme 2001, 1, 9, 6). In other words, rather than *unveil* illusion and show the real, Mende hermeneutics actively *maintain* ambiguity. In a similar way, when dealing with vernacular conspiracy theories and suspicions about occult forces, we should perhaps not aim to expose any final truth that would invalidate them as mere rumors but try to retell these stories in a format "that adds reality rather than taking it away" (Love 2017, 66).

This chapter indeed tries to think *with* the occult forces our interlocutors described. But maybe we can also go further and engage the popular suspicions this chapter evokes through what Eve Sedgwick (2003) calls "reparative" reading practices that counterbalance the hegemonic "paranoid" stance of critical theory. In her inspiring essay, Sedgwick explicitly calls on "the reparatively positioned reader" to reorganize "the fragments and part-objects she encounters or creates" (146). This reparative *reorganizing* is strikingly similar to what many Central African healing practices and cults aim for when they "re-knot" or "re-weave" the "threads of life" (De Boeck 1991; Devisch 1993). Healing, in this sense, is about mending what was broken and unblocking what was blocked (Bekaert 2000).

Yet while healers and diviners are meant to repair the physical, social, and cosmological body, they are also—and by necessity—experts in the same occult forces they redirect. As the history of therapeutic cults in the region suggests, healing indeed entails a certain violence (Eggers 2015). Reading Sedgwick *from* Central Africa therefore creates ample room for reparative practices not only against or alongside but also *within* paranoid and violent economies of thought (Comaroff and Comaroff 2015). It suggests the existence of a third stance, beyond the alternatives of paranoid versus reparative hermeneutics: a perspective that is not above suspicion but instead transforms it. Healers and diviners effectively rechannel hidden forces everyone suspects but that they alone can "do business with." As such, Central African healing practices do not *undo* the occult but *do* it in a different—and ideally reparative—way.

Can this chapter on occult contracts, cannibalism, and ponoli magic be a similar reweaving or reknotting of what was and often remains hidden? Taking seriously our interlocutors' suggestions that capitalism is nothing but an inherently occult system, such strategies of redoing indeed allow one to reproduce stories and experiences without simply repeating hegemonic forms of paranoid critique or assuming a naive position from which to impose reparation. If capitalism is another form of witchcraft holding all of us in its grip, one should not therefore conclude, as Phillipe Pignarre and Isabelle Stengers suggest in *La sorcellerie capitaliste* (2005), that it necessarily renders the imagination of other worlds impossible because "there is no alternative." The apparent fatalism of capitalism-as-witchcraft is internally countered by an always-possible redoing. The omnipresence of occult practices in and around the CTI concession effectively show that "we are all in it." Yet the possibility of alternative arrangements is not so much dependent on breaking the spell of capitalism as on rechanneling it. In other words, the banality of the occult requires one to (learn to) live *with* one's witches (Geschiere 2013). It calls for an art to transform the paranoid relationship between the visible and the invisible into a more reparative one—a *suturing* practice that can only ever be re-begun (De Boeck and Baloji 2016).

So, how to keep both paranoid and reparative dimensions on board when thinking about rumors of white cannibalism? And how to accurately represent the horrifying conspiracy of white men eating black flesh without foreclosing reparative possibilities? The previous sections illustrate a strong moral critique that was viscerally expressed through popular occult imagery. But they also argue that white cannibalism was in itself nothing extraordinary as it partook in a much larger trophic economy of eating and being eaten. As such, our fieldwork suggests that the *ur*-paranoid suspicion that "we are all already in it" contains reparative pathways. Indeed, the very realization that, in the last instance, we are all complicit in a supposed system— that is, that we all *live* through hierarchical relationships that simultaneously sustain and limit us—foregrounds a certain commonality that is both terrifying and reassuring.

Achille Mbembe (1992, 10; 2019, 29) describes this commonality as the "conviviality" of power that seemed so characteristic of postcolonial politics: a "dynamics of domesticity and familiarity, which inscribed the dominant and the dominated in the same episteme" and linked them "in one and the same bundle of desire." While Mbembe (1992, 25) mainly understands this cohabitation of people and the elite from a largely paranoid position, as a ruse for postcolonial states to "capture" their subjects in intimate "traps [that] are so interconnected that they become a unitary system of ensnarement," he nevertheless also recognizes that this same system allows for reparative possibilities. At the very least, it enables "myriad ways in which ordinary people guide, deceive and actually toy with power instead of confronting it directly" (25).

But intimate proximity with the "system of ensnarement" is also a necessary condition for trapping power and redirecting it. Moreover, folk theories of eating and being eaten suggest that the act of (licit or illicit) commensality contains a reparative possibility—an eating *together*—that holds a particularly affective and political charge. As we saw in chapter 4, popular actions against the logging company were indeed aimed at repairing a torn or broken commensality and bringing CTI back to the negotiating table—which was also, often literally, a lunch table. In the same way, propagating rumors and gossiping about occult practices in the expat Garden of Eden entrapped CTI in a moral economy of the "rightful share" over which it had little control (Ferguson 2015).

In this context, the reparative possibilities *within* paranoia depend on the very suspicion that "we are all cannibals" (Lévi-Strauss 2013). Obviously, no one in the logging concession admitted to being a cannibal, sorcerer, or witch—and many, as good Christians, firmly opposed occult practices. But it was nonetheless implicitly understood that *in order to live* one needed to participate in the give and take of life. This pragmatic attitude was forged by a violent history that included everyone in more or less occult transactions and that forced us all to inventively deal with what was hidden.

In a recent essay, Francis Nyamnjoh (2018, 2, 68) provocatively argues that cannibalism is indeed a ubiquitous and "normal way of being human" and explores the ethical consequences of the banal fact of eating and being eaten as a "universal reality and preoccupation." How, Nyamnjoh asks, can we "go about the business of putting together an ethics and moral order sanctioned by the understanding that every hierarchy is cannibalistic, wittingly and unwittingly" (68)? As an answer, he suggests that the "awareness that cannibalism and cannibalisation are, in one form or another, the only game in town" calls for an "ethics of conviviality," which requires a fundamental recognition of the necessary and vital entanglements between people (4), an ethics that takes seriously the "continuous (and indeed unstoppable) cannibalistic flow of bodily substances into and through individual bodies" (72).

From this perspective, it is important to emphasize that the accusations, rumors, and stories about white occult practices targeting black victims in the CTI concession were not only a means for emphasizing the violence and horror of capitalist extraction—though they were certainly that. They were also a way to incorporate strangers into a trophic economy. In contrast to the Western man-eating myth, Congolese memories and whispers about white cannibalism were not, essentially, about *ex*cluding the cannibal other

(Arens 1979). On the contrary, they were about *including* the other in a common though always potentially violent humanity.

In short, suspicions that we are all cannibals are both paranoid *and* reparative. On the one hand, they suggest a system to which there is no outside: "a vision of the world that is threatening and anxiogenic, one that grants primacy to logics of suspicion, and indeed to all that which is secret" (Mbembe 2019, 48). On the other hand, this same world can also always be redone to rebalance shifting power relations and inequalities. It is a world in which "everything is arranged, arrangeable and rearrangeable," and where the power to eat is never total, but always reversible and itself subject to ruses and rechannelings (Bekaert 2000, 111). Hence, as power can be trapped only *because* of its voracity, it is never entirely what it seems nor fully in control. For these reasons, this book suggests, any analysis of power remains incomplete as long as it ignores the ecstasis it generates at its core.

Making a contract with Mami Wata, for instance, is an ecstatic technique for acquiring power, as it simultaneously implies relinquishing autonomy and subjecting oneself to her whims. Occult technologies make one do things despite oneself and often against one's intimates. Zombies are literally outside themselves—but their owners are equally bound by the contracts of their magic. And ponoli victims experience a form of profound disorientation that repeats or announces their masters' madness. Again, the examples in this chapter suggest how accessing power actually entails forsaking control. Perhaps this is the postcritical lesson we can learn from staying with paranoid stories in a less suspicious mode. In a world where trees continuously left the forest to feed a hungry global economy, the paranoid suspicion that we are all cannibals suggests a reparative potential of shared complicities "in fields of power already traversed by dynamics of mutual influence and cross-fertilizing" (Bernault 2019, 59).

Worker posing with a skidder

Men and Trees

WE WERE SITTING ON A PILE OF LOGS, waiting for the truck to come and pick us up at the side of the road. The truck driver was late. It was getting dark. Bosco took out his knife and started to carve his name in the bark of a sipo tree (*Entandrophragma utile*). He was one of the younger assistant conductors in the skidding team, and we had grown quite close. He carefully added his name to the production numbers CTI clerks had hammered into the wood. "This way, my name will travel," he said. "Bosco RF will walk here and there, over the river to Kinshasa, to Matadi, to Europe, America, China, the whole world!" "Bosco RF?" I asked. "*Roi de la forêt*," he said, smiling. "Isn't Paul the king of the forest?" I asked, winking.[1] "He is a false king [*faux roi*]," Bosco laughed.

Rumor had it that exported trees were transformed into canned food through occult pathways. And yet this international destination was also an opportunity to send one's name into the world. A way of reaching out and connecting. Another form of centrifugality. Of hope, perhaps. A chance for workers to make themselves known and leave a mark. To literally inscribe their presence in a process *that was also theirs*. A reparative counter-script to alienation and to CTI's tracking system. Often they used nicknames—Bosco, for instance, was not the name his parents had given him. Or epithets that emphasized their strength: *homme fort, makasi, kilo*. Reclaiming autonomy in the face of a world that otherwise erased their presence.

Bosco shared a small hut in one of the forest camp's squatter neighborhoods. He was still waiting for a company house. Underneath his bed he kept a photo album with pictures of himself in different poses and outfits. One picture showed him in a blue CTI overall in front of a new skidding machine; another showed him in a perfectly ironed suit and well-polished leather shoes after Sunday service in Bumba. There was also a photograph of his sister's marriage. And a picture of his dead grandmother in an open coffin—he was ten when she passed away. There were more photographs on the back of his door. A girlfriend in a school dress. His best friend. "He left for Kisangani," Bosco said. "We were born on the same day." Some pictures of him flexing his muscular torso. Intimate portraits.

Many compound inhabitants kept similar pictures. Photographs that captured fleeting lives in an uncertain world, giving some proof of temporary arrival and achievement. Traces from which to reconstruct biographies. Fragments from which to conjure a whole. A way to look at oneself and to show others what one wanted them to see. A tool for self-creation and self-reflection (Behrend 2002). And a way to tend to wounds and remember lost family and friends.

In the logging camps, several young men made money by taking photographs on demand. There was even a small photo studio where people had their pictures taken in front of an assemblage of the same colorful Chinese posters that workers also put up in their living rooms. A closed, windowless dream cell where camp inhabitants dressed up in different styles, experimented with new selves, and fantasized about migration. Grandstanding and showboating (*frimer*). Or just playing around (*kosakana, s'amuser*). Another way to travel (Weiss 2009).

Carved names and photographs asserted one's presence. The first were sent into the world to create global circulation. The second were kept close, often to reaffirm one's status as a salaried worker. As such, they reestablished some autonomy in the midst of dependencies. Strong masculinities in a profession that could break one's back. Manifestations of pride despite all suffering. "Kings of the forest" rather than zombies sapped of their energy. Sharp and mobile men who knew how to make money.

Praise names and self-portraits created gendered selves. This chapter describes these self-making practices and focuses on the performance of masculinity in a complex relational field in which men had to craft themselves with and against others: workers in relation to employers, traders and smugglers in relation to CTI agents, autochthonous inhabitants in relation to people from elsewhere, and men in relation to women. As we will see, the ecstatogenic logging camps bred multiple masculinities, and yet they also reproduced a hegemonic idea of male strength in an often disturbingly misogynist environment.

The first section of this chapter shows how CTI workers tried to maintain ideals of male breadwinner independence while simultaneously acknowledging and even foregrounding their reliance on the logging company as a provider. The chapter then explores the surprising relationship between worker and villager masculinities through the story of a rare wildcat strike in which a fortifying ancestral Mbudza tree came to play a remarkable role. This is followed by a closer look at how nonworkers presented alternative masculinities that contested workers' salaries with fend-for-yourself strategies of resilience. In particular, it foregrounds the deliberate blurring of boundaries between youth and adulthood and contextualizes the central role of transgression in the performance and negotiation of masculinities. The last section sketches the tension-ridden field of camp sexuality in a milieu saturated with anxieties over derision and concludes with a reflection on the paradoxical nexus between masculinity, self-making, and ecstasis.

Children of the Company

We have already seen how new CTI workers used kinship to frame their relationship to those who initiated them, with apprentices calling their teachers work father (*papa ya mosala*). But CTI employees also talked about their relationship *to the company* in explicitly kinship terms. "CTI is our father [*tata ya biso*]," many insisted. "We are the children of CTI [*toza bana ya CTI*]." As such, workers used the ethics of kinship to create and emphasize moral obligations of sustenance, protection, and responsibility, which they felt their employer held toward them. This idea of CTI as a caring father drew not only on idealized memories of late-colonial paternalism but also on a "cultural logic of legitimacy" that extended to private companies "the tacit normative idea that government stands in the same relationship to its citizens as a father does to his children" (Schatzberg 2001, 1).

This self-infantilization of workers who otherwise considered themselves strong and independent men aptly expresses the lived contradictions of labor. In a context of generalized unemployment, dependency on (and of) wage work indeed enabled a simultaneous deployment of autonomy. Workers effectively prided themselves as family men able to support their wives and children in difficult times. But this male breadwinner role directly depended on their position as metaphorical children of the company, as CTI provided the necessary salaries, work bonuses, housing, health care, and schooling with which to craft their housefather reputation. Wage work was therefore "a highly valued kind of dependence" (Ferguson 2015, 159).

Yet the framing of employment in kinship terms also had its limits. Whereas Congolese staff usually accepted the metaphorical father position toward those they had introduced into the company, the forging of more personalized kin-like relationships with expat managers was far more difficult. Generally the latter bluntly refused to fulfill a caring role. In contrast to villagers who—as we saw in chapter 4—were able to trap CTI in moral obligations toward their well-being, workers rarely succeeded in getting anything beyond the monthly wages and benefits to which they were contractually entitled. To the contrary, any overt "declaration of dependence" (Ferguson 2015, 141), by which workers claimed to be rightful beneficiaries of a more general morality of care, was counterproductive. It was indeed met with profound irritation and impatience by the European loggers. "I am not their father!" Jens often said. In contrast to their counterparts in idealized colonial companies, the CTI expats did not consider their responsibilities to reach much further than the strict labor contract. The idea of CTI as a father to whom one "belonged" was therefore profoundly jeopardized, and many workers felt "abandoned" (Dibwe dia Mwembu 2001).

Despite this discourse of abandonment, however, having a job at CTI still made a huge difference for young men in their quest for adulthood. In particular, having a house of one's own was a necessary condition to start one's own life. Although compound houses were of a poor quality and usually only occupied for as long as one had a job, they nevertheless enabled young men to achieve a crucial sign of male adulthood and deliver on widespread "expectations of domesticity" (Ferguson 1999, 169). Yet, for this very reason, as one of our neighbors explained, "Children in the camp [also] become men too quickly [*mbangumbangu*]" as if their salaries and houses enabled them to precociously attain adult status or gave them access to resources with which to "*play* at being adult" (Masquelier 2019, 13). To a certain extent this jumping of age messed up conventional relationships of respect and assistance based on seniority (Meiu 2015). As we saw in chapter 5, the logging camps were indeed perceived as places of relative freedom and "ambiance" where one could get *away* from kinship obligations.[2]

Workers' metaphorical childhood in relation to the company effectively enabled the (precocious) attainment of adulthood. But, at the same time, salaries and premiums hardly sufficed to meet their dependents' needs. And while many employees—especially those who came from farther away—had fled their extended families, the latter almost always found ways to claim a part of their sons' apparent wealth. Workers' households therefore frequently included uncles, nephews, sisters-in-law, and "brothers from the village" who counted on the financial and material support of their relatives, while faraway kin continuously sent messages asking for money.

A regular salary and a company house thus rendered one both strong and vulnerable at the same time. Dependency on an employer indeed enabled a form of *in*dependence that confirmed one's status as a "big man" accumulating "wealth in people" (Guyer 1993). But resources were never really enough to take proper care of one's dependents. "How can I ever give my children the education they need?" Olivier, the chainsaw mechanic, asked me. Like others, he worried that he would remain unable to give his offspring the opportunities he had himself enjoyed when growing up on a plantation. Vice versa, children reproached their parents for "eating their inheritance." Rather than invest in our future, "our fathers just spend their money uselessly," a twenty-year-old student said. In turn, CTI employees deplored the ingratitude of their kin. The salaries that helped them build families and maintain peaceful relationships were therefore also a permanent source of conflict and frustration.

Moreover, the brutal reality of layoffs, shutdowns, and dismissals further emphasized the precarity of the nexus between masculinity and wage labor. Workers who got fired sometimes fell sick from feelings of inadequacy and humiliation. When dismissed, they immediately had to leave their houses and make space for others. Such evacuations were painful scenes. One day the wife of a former worker attacked the new occupants with a machete. The next day, she was in jail. The whole affair was extremely shameful (*ya nsoni*), our neighbors said.

Wives of CTI workers were keenly aware of the vulnerability of their husbands' status and did not spare ridicule and critique when necessary. The spouse of an assistant tree feller, for instance, claimed that "all CTI employees are married to [the logging company]," whereby the latter would occupy the position of husband in relation to its workers. "*They* are the wives of the company," she said—not without visible amusement. "The whites have paid their bride price, and now they have to work for them!" Undermining the very basis of worker masculinity, she thus pointed at the contradictory nature of building male autonomy on precarious and often demeaning wage labor. "And what do we get out of this?" she asked. "Often it is *me* who has to support *him!*"

In the logging camps, where harmonious social reproduction frequently gave way to generational and gender conflict, the worker ideal of respectable bourgeois masculinity was a strong but contested and ultimately impossible dream. Working for CTI effectively made one's manhood. But dependency on the company—as its "child" or even "wife"—simultaneously troubled boastful claims to inflated strength and autonomy. Whereas workers often presented themselves as *real* men, their wives—and, as we will see, other camp residents—did not so easily take their claims at face value.

The Mbudza Tree of Resistance

Workers depended on the logging company for their autonomy. But they also—and perhaps surprisingly—relied on local inhabitants of the region to *resist* the company. Employees rarely took action against their managers and usually endured their bosses' insults, outbursts, humiliations, and constant affirmation of white superiority with a stoic silence or, at most, an uncomfortable mumble. Speaking back to Europeans could effectively lead to being fired. Yet, at some moments, conflicts did erupt. The following paragraphs tell the story of such a rare act of open resistance. What is remarkable is that, during this event, CTI workers explicitly came to mobilize autochthonous resources to bolster their agency. A specific tree with indigenous powers, which grew on the threshold between the forest camp labor compounds and the work site, thereby came to play a striking role in the unfolding of workers' resistance.

In 2006 a strike broke out. For some time the then site manager had neglected to pay his workers' overtime. According to testimonies Freddy and I gathered four years later, discontent about low wages had been building up since CTI reopened its concession in 2003 after the war. But demands for wage increases and the payment of overtime fell on deaf ears. So, when their colleagues from the lumber mills in Kinshasa spontaneously stopped working, voices rose to do the same in the concession. One day the employees assembled before their bosses' offices and called for the site manager to resign. They presented a written request in which they asked the European mother company to replace their manager with someone who would live up to his responsibility and behave "as a good father to his employees."

The next day, a group of five loggers occupied the entrance to the work site in order to stop their colleagues from going to work. Yet, afraid to lose their jobs, most initially ignored the loggers' actions. As a result, the strike president (*président de grève*), a middle-aged Mbudza man who had worked as a tracker before the war, called for a ritual specialist (*nganga*) from a nearby village to perform a ritual that would prevent all employees from entering the work site. "In the evening, a *féticheur* arrived," one of the strikers told us, "and buried alive a white rooster under the big eleko tree to mystically block the company gate." As many later confirmed, this ritual seemed effective: strikebreakers became scared, and the forest camp workers effectively managed to halt logging activities.

At first the CTI expats decided to send labor union representatives to convince workers to abandon what they called the illegal wild strike (*grève sauvage*). But, despite their position, these men did not possess the moral authority to mediate such a conflict. "Our representatives are all corrupt," a striker told us. "They just do what the whites tell them to." Union representatives were effectively elected on lists that needed to be preapproved by CTI. And because they had shown themselves weak and ineffective in previous talks, many workers contested the very rationale of paying their union dues (*cotisations syndicales*).

The arrival of union representatives therefore only made things worse, and the blockade of the company gate continued. After three days the site manager appealed to Bumba's administrateur de territoire to send a police force and break the blockade. When the police arrived, company trucks were forced to drive into the labor compounds and pick up workers as quickly as possible. Several strike organizers were arrested. Some told us that later that evening the European site manager arrived with his own ritual specialist who went to the eleko tree and broke the spell. The next morning the blockade indeed seemed lifted, and work restarted as if nothing had happened.

Yet why were these rituals held beneath *this* specific tree? Of course, the tree was ideally situated: just next to the company gate separating the labor camp from the work site. But why did it stand at this exact location? And why was only this tree standing while the compounds were otherwise devoid of large trees? The majestic eleko indeed dominated its surroundings and was a remarkable sight. Many people called it the big tree (*nzete monene*) or the great Tali (*le grand Tali*).[3] The foresters knew it by its scientific name, *Pachyelasma tessmannii*. But the tree was also of special significance for the Mbudza people.

When CTI began building the forest camp labor compounds back in 1994, it had asked its workers to clear the area of all trees in order to prevent damage from tropical storms. At that time, Michel, the French overseer, stayed in the old hunting camp near the Mamoissa River belonging to a dominant Mbudza clan of the village of Yambili. Together with some bulldozer drivers and tree fellers, he left the hunting camp each morning to construct the new work site. One night, however, Eyenga—the local hunter we met at the beginning of chapter 3—warned the loggers not to cut a particular tree at the center of the future camp. He called this tree "eleko" and said anyone who harmed it would be struck by his ancestors' wrath. The CTI workers, most of whom did not originate from the area, therefore decided to leave the tree standing. "This was *their* forest," one of them later told us. "So, we had to be careful."

Michel, however, claimed that the eleko tree was only spared because of its exceptional size and beauty. "It would be a pity to cut such a tree down," he said. But for the CTI workers, the tree became synonymous with autochthonous magic (*la magie des autochtones*), and many who had to pass daily beneath its branches knew it had secret powers. The tree was indeed gigantic but leafless—apparently dead but very much alive.

Called *eleko* in Embudza or *ende* in Kibaati, villagers in and around the CTI concession considered this particular tree species an emblem of chiefly authority (see also De Boeck 1994). Mbudza elders told us that palavers were held at its foot and that its bark was used in traditional medicine (*nkisi ya bakoko*). In particular, it was used in therapeutic rituals to treat epilepsy, convulsions, and muscle pain. Eleko was also thought to be a spirit who could inhabit traditional healers as well as a name given to young boys. Others who were less well informed about local customs regularly confused it with other healing trees, such as *gbukulu/bokuma* (*Ceiba pentandra*), *moika/ndande* (*Garcinia epunctata*), or *wokombo*, the Mbudza tree of "origin." Some simply took it as a generic tree of the ancestors (*nzete ya bakoko*).

For the many non-Mbudza residents in the forest camp, it was clear that the eleko in their midst could only be fully understood and controlled by people from the area. "It is *their* ancestral tree," they said. Yet, regardless of ethnic background, many still pragmatically mobilized eleko in daily practices of protection and healing. Workers and villagers alike stripped pieces of its bark for use as treatment against inguinal hernia or as a male aphrodisiac. Several tree fellers and machine operators took small injection bottles with eleko bark into the forest as a fortifier against back pain, fatigue, and the loss of sexual energy. Literally ingesting eleko to cure their bodies from the emasculating effects of work, they inscribed this Mbudza tree in an "incessant quest for strength" (Bekaert 2000, 357). Originating in local traditions but co-opted by other inhabitants, eleko effectively stood for both traditional authority and male strength. As a huge tree, it materialized firmness and uprightness, qualities that supposedly characterized both the famous Mbudza wars against colonial implantation and dominant ideas of manhood.

Because of its role in traditional therapeutics, however, several churches firmly rejected eleko as a tree of witchcraft (*nzete ya kindoki*). For Pentecostals in particular, ancestral powers were satanic forces from which true Christians had to break free (Meyer 1999). They said its naked branches appeared dead to the uninitiated but were actually very much alive "for those who could really see." Men of God preached that the tree was a "parabolic antenna" for making contact with the invisible world and a place where witches held their nightly gatherings. One pastor even claimed to have received a spiritual map (*plan spirituel*) that revealed eleko to be a "mystical airport and dock" where planes and boats arrived at night to deliver motorcycles or television sets for those in the labor camp who practiced occult sciences.

This eleko tree was indeed odd. Why had it not fallen, even though it had long seemed dead? Why had even the Europeans refrained from cutting it down? And why had they placed the company gate exactly at its foot? Some suggested that the tree manifested a secret alliance between CTI and traditional Mbudza chiefs—a profit-sharing deal that was struck unbeknownst to ordinary workers and villagers. But, more frequently, the tree was seen as a pillar of continuing autochthonous control over the area despite the invasion of foreigners.[4] Proudly remaining erect while others went down, its story bespoke resistance. Literally standing up against chainsaws, the eleko was indeed taken as a phallic symbol of indigenous strength.

It should therefore come as no surprise that CTI workers, many of whom were not Mbudza-speaking, resorted to traditional Mbudza rituals for blocking access to the work site and to an ancestral tree for curing back problems and male impotence. Although loggers sometimes called their unemployed neighbors *basendji*—a Lingala term of abuse derived from the French racial slur *singe* (monkey)—and considered themselves civilized (*civilisés*) rather than mere farmers, they still relied on tradition to support their cause. As if they had to tap into the legendary history of Mbudza anticolonial resistance to stage their own revolt. As if they needed the ancestral eleko to bolster their potency. As if they depended on the power of traditional masculinity to withstand a foreign company to whom they were otherwise bound.

Masculinity and Transgression

While CTI workers thus mobilized substances and ideas of traditional strength to boost their masculinity, contractual work for the logging company was still a highly desired means of constructing a sense of male autonomy and responsibility. In a largely post-labor context of generalized unemployment, the old bourgeois ideal of the wageworker as breadwinner effectively remained a common ambition (Cornwall 2003). But it was not the only model—and certainly not *the* hegemonic idea of what it meant to be a man. Beyond the notion of traditional resistant masculinity evoked above, the logging camps also produced alternative strategies for constructing male selves, outside or even against wage labor. Different models for and trajectories to manhood existed side by side. Some explicitly contested the status on which CTI workers built their reputation.

Most fuel smugglers, for instance, could easily outperform many company employees in conspicuous consumption (Cuvelier 2017; De Boeck 1998b). As self-identified *ambianceurs*, they explicitly flaunted their money by buying large quantities of beer in forest camp bars—both for themselves and for others who praised their generosity. Kaddafis also introduced the latest gadgets, clothes, music, and videos in the labor compounds and embodied a certain cosmopolitanism that was highly attractive to men and women alike. Some dressed as stylish businessmen and explicitly "employed" younger aides (so-called *petits*) who executed their orders on flashy motorcycles. For smugglers, they were indeed remarkably visible. Deliberately so. "I am a real *patron*," one of them often said.

Other traders, who owned shops or market stalls in the logging camps, also contested the bourgeois ideal of wage work. "CTI employees," a boutique owner once laughed, "have to work long hours, but they only make others rich!" Openly ridiculing wage laborers for their reliance on meager salaries received from a foreign company, traders by contrast presented as entrepreneurial and self-made men (Ndjio 2012). Proud of their independence, they strongly invested in the art of *débrouillardise* (coping or making do), which Mobutu had famously raised to the level of an unwritten article of the constitution (Ayimpam 2014; De Villers, Jewsiewiecki, and Monnier 2002; Trefon 2004). They had indeed called their formal association for mutual assistance the Association des Débrouillants du Camp Forêt (Make-do association of the forest camp) and strategically turned a context of poverty and isolation into a ground for self-esteem. Identifying as combatants (*combattants*) and courageous men (*bacourageux*), they deliberately deflated the image of ideal masculinity that workers so eagerly tried to embody.

Hence, social and moral oppositions between workers and nonworkers were troubled by claims and counterclaims to relative independence and by the sheer fact that many CTI employees earned substantially less money than several of their so-called unemployed neighbors. But alongside smugglers and traders, there was also a third and more heterogeneous group of less well-to-do men who directly contested workers' respectability. They did so through what was frequently described as looking for trouble (*koluka mobulu*)—a practice that explicitly highlights the centrality of *transgression* in debates and contests about masculinity in the timber camps.

As we saw in chapter 5, the rowdy behavior of troublemakers was simultaneously admired and disapproved of. In that chapter we also contextualized their transgressions as ecstatic strategies to create temporary sovereignty in a context of boredom and lacking opportunities (see also Groes-Green 2010). Let us now look at the ambiguous importance of *youth* and *generation* for this group of agitators. Indeed, although some of their members were already in their early thirties, they explicitly described themselves as youngsters (*bajeunes*), and many camp residents referred to them as the children of trouble (*bana ya mobulu*) (Durham 2004). The twenty-six-year old nephew of one of the company cartographers was often seen as their leader. "Yes, I am trouble," he proudly confirmed to us after leaving prison for yet another time. He and his friends were known to start fights and harass girls, and the right mixture of alcohol and music frequently made them dance in what others described as obscene ways—sometimes suggestively with each other.

Such behavior strongly resembles what Jeroen Cuvelier (2014) describes as a particular "trouble-making style" among young artisanal miners in Katanga. Copper and cobalt miners refer to this style as *kivoyou*—from the French *voyou* for villain or gangster—which denotes "an extensive register of acts and types of conduct such as swearing, wearing eccentric or expensive clothes, cross-dressing, drinking excessively [and] being disrespectful towards senior members of society" (Cuvelier 2014, 12; see also Rubbers 2013). Yet while Cuvelier (2014, 15) analyzes such deviant masculinity as a way for young miners to "distinguish themselves from other men in Katangese society, including their fathers and grand-fathers," in the more socially mixed logging camps, the public performance of social or sexual transgression was not strictly limited to youthful masculinities.

On the contrary, it was not uncommon for older men to applaud, support, or even participate in the staging of debauchery. "Often, the young ones start. But then even old *papas* join in," Freddy once remarked after another row in a loggers' bar. Several middle-aged employees and big-bellied kaddafis indeed assured me that, "deeply within" they were even bigger daredevils (*aventuriers*) than the camp youth—implying that a certain antinormativity was central to the performance of masculinity itself. As such, one should not reduce deliberate rowdiness to a form of adolescent protest or a transgressive mode of masculinity that would simply characterize youth as a liminal life stage (Johnson-Hanks 2002). Transgression indeed infected "respectability" and circulated back and forth between masculinities (Demetriou 2001). Transgressive behavior could thus be a paradoxical resource for building reputation and accumulating symbolic capital (Hendriks 2016, 2021). Although adults were generally supposed to contain and manage their emotions, the very absence of daring and risk-taking was unthinkable for a *real* man. In the logging camps, as in other postcolonial fields of "ambiance," the public display of social and moral defiance was therefore a common battleground for making and breaking masculinities (Biaya 1996).

Not all men, however, young or old, conformed to such transgressive ideals in their everyday performances of self. Men (and women) who tried to walk with Jesus (*kotambola na Yesu*), for instance, explicitly criticized the camp for allowing and celebrating transgression. For them, the apparent immorality of the camp environment was a challenge they could only face and overcome by relying on God and the Bible. And it was exactly the hedonistic dimension of camp life that allowed them to show perseverance and craft a resistant masculinity based on (moral) strength and upright behavior.

Moreover, the old colonial ideal of the bourgeois breadwinner and the more recent counter-ideal of the rowdy rascal were not mutually exclusive. Filip De Boeck (1998b, 797) notes that for diamond smugglers in the borderlands between Angola and the DRC, masculinity involved "two opposing aspects—that of singularized, autonomous manhood, a model which seems to be idealized by many youngsters—and a second aspect of social responsibility, highlighting the elders' capacity to . . . give a tangible form to ties of reciprocity and solidarity." In the CTI compounds, however, the interpenetration of both axes of masculinity partially blurred the division between respect and transgression. Older employees boasting of their "rascal-within" indeed seemed to question the very "desirability of becoming an adult" (Pype 2012, 207, 227).

Hence, with elders mimicking youngsters and young men playing at being adult, "youth" and "adulthood" seemed to be conscious styles rather than clearly separated life stages (Masquelier 2019, 162). Self-identifying as young (at heart), for instance, was a stylized way of navigating a camp environment in which being a responsible housefather/breadwinner was difficult, *despite* one's salary and the hopes it generated. Contrary to the widespread idea that being young always equals being dependent, claiming youth was also a way to claim *in*dependence and to disconnect from kinship obligations. Age was therefore a matter of self-conscious performativity and contestation that "index[ed] shifting relationships of power and authority, responsibility and capability, agency and autonomy" (Durham 2004, 589).

This blurring of (the value of) youth and adulthood and the interpenetration of different modes of becoming a man in the logging camps makes it difficult to speak of one "hegemonic" masculinity that could be clearly situated in a relation of superiority toward others (Connell 2005). Although there was a clear struggle between masculinities, power relations were dynamic, revertible, and context dependent. The models of masculinity this chapter foregrounds are therefore not static (ideal) types, but processual, relational, and mutually influencing constructs (Connell and Messerschmidt 2005). Moreover, single individuals also related simultaneously to multiple models of masculinity in different ways, thereby both reproducing and changing them (Miescher and Lindsay 2003; Ratele 2008). Becoming a man was therefore not so much about choosing between mutually exclusive models as it was a practice of pragmatic composition that produced what Emily Wentzell (2013, 26) calls *composite* masculinities: "contingent and fluid constellations of elements that men weave together into masculine selfhoods."

And yet, notwithstanding its multiplicity and composite nature, men and women in the logging camps still associated masculinity (*kimobali*) with the key signifier of strength (*bokasi*). Whether as a worker, smuggler, trader, teacher, pastor, hunter, or troublemaker, men were invariably expected to be strong (*makasi*). This explicit association between masculinity and strength is of course nothing special—and arguably reflects a widespread ideology of gender. Katrien Pype (2007, 258), for instance, shows how, in contemporary Kinshasa, a model of the strong man (*moto ya makasi*) underlies most, if not all, valued concretizations of masculinity, whether as "the physically muscled man, the wealthy man [or] the spiritual strong man."

This obsession with male strength has a long history. In an insightful study, Didier Gondola (2016, 7) describes how the quest for manhood among young city dwellers in colonial Léopoldville led to forms of hypermasculinity that were based on a "cult and culture of performative violence" in a context of colonial emasculation (see also M. Hendriks 2018). Through new subcultural movements such as Billism—a Congolese reappropriation of iconic Hollywood images of rugged cowboys during the 1950s and 1960s—the idea of the *Yankee* as a strong "macho man" thereby became a common Lingala term and the "yard-stick against which all men . . . are measured" (Gondola 2016, 93, 198). Drawing on Michael Herzfeld (1985, 16), Gondola (2016, 92) aptly describes Yankee masculinity as a form of "performative excellence" that implies not so much "being a good man," but "being *good at* being a man."

Gondola's research thereby unearths a social and cultural genealogy of masculinity-as-strength that continues to manifest in the widespread fascination with and celebration of transgression in contemporary popular culture (Hendriks 2019). In this respect, the logging camps were not unlike Congo's cities in their performance of transgression as a necessary quality in the "quest for the [true] incarnation of the 'yankee'" (Pype 2007, 264). Ideals of the bourgeois worker/breadwinner, the entrepreneurial self-made man, the fend-for-yourself combatant, and the rowdy rascal were indeed all based on an underlying ideology of male strength attested to by participation in brazen performances of transgression that created fleeting but real experiences of autonomy and control.

Hence, if there was one undercurrent to masculinities, it was their generally assertive nature: the assumption that one had to build one's status *against others* and to promote oneself at their expense (Barber 2007, 114). Workers, traders, and troublemakers alike indeed constantly worried about being despised or laughed at and wanted to avoid being perceived as worthless men (*bato pamba*) or good for nothing (*mpambalampambala*). As we have seen, women accused their husbands and lovers of "not being men enough," and among friends, teasing someone about one's apparent "uselessness" simultaneously confirmed and deflated the latent threat of ridicule.

The judgment of others—real or imagined—could therefore make or break one's reputation. Especially for men, a general fear of being found out as weak characterized everyday gender games. Moreover, as the opposite of strength, weakness (*bolembu*) came in many forms: a lack of endurance, intelligence, rhetorical ability, resistance, flexibility, courage, vision, style, or money. A man who was too easily intoxicated, for instance, was considered weak. A man who ejaculated too soon was described as "good for nothing." Becoming and remaining a man was therefore accompanied by deep anxieties, and hence the constant search for substances and other means of increasing strength, whereby eleko was only one of the fortifiers and aphrodisiacs people prepared, sold, and consumed in the logging camps.

The popular ideology of male strength produced a series of masculinities that, each in their own way, seemed partial manifestations of a similar idea, as camp inhabitants invariably used the strong versus weak opposition to judge reputations.[5] This taken-for-granted idea of male strength was therefore hegemonic without resulting in one monolithic hegemonic masculinity. Moreover, men who were considered weak in one respect could actively claim strength in another. Our seventeen-year old neighbor, for instance, a boy whose feminine walk and features sometimes provoked insults and derision from his peers, was still admired for the courage and strength he performed in his quotidian resistance *against* so-called normal masculinity (Hendriks 2018). And despite remarks about his gender dissidence, most camp inhabitants simply accepted his presence as the way he was (*ezaleli na ye*). Strength, in other words, came in multiple—and sometimes queer—forms.

The Minefield of Heterosexuality

It always surprised me how, after work and during weekends, a sizable minority of CTI workers still mustered the energy and willpower to participate in weightlifting sessions. Bosco, for instance, was one of those who rebuilt their bodies with great perseverance. No matter how tired or bruised he felt after a day of work, he claimed that physical exercising "gave me strength." As we saw at the beginning of this chapter, he kept intimate pictures of himself to minutely monitor his development and discussed each sign of weakness with friends who discreetly shared remedies and advice. Because of his well-developed muscles, camp inhabitants called him *pomba* or tough guy (Cuvelier 2014, 17; Gondola 2016, 28, 97–98).

Weightlifters indeed seemed to cure their bodies from traces of exploitation by lifting scrap metal and the spare parts of bulldozers or skidders that "ate" their physique in the first place. Their inflated muscles were material proof of self-fashioning and resistance in a hard world of logging that otherwise sapped male strength (Masquelier 2019, 140). But the surprising occurrence of weightlifting in a logging camp also shows how, in a context where money was rarely enough to impress and care for women and girls, the male *body* took on an erotic importance that was carefully cultivated by some (Groes-Green, 2009).

This section therefore looks at the ways in which Congolese loggers tried to present themselves as attractive partners for women and girls—but often failed in their endeavor. The timber camps were widely known for their financial opportunities, and many women tried their luck in catching current or future CTI employees for shorter or longer lasting relationships. Yet, upon closer examination, gender relations in the labor compounds were often strained and conflictual. And it was exactly the tightly knotted nexus of money and sexuality that accounted for such tensions.

CTI employees knew very well that their wages made them attractive to women and girls on the lookout to tap into multiple sources of support. But they also knew that their financial resources were frustratingly uncertain. As a result, they invariably complained about what they viewed as women's greedy materialism and thirst of money (*mposa ya mbongo*). "Women just see your salary," an older CTI worker told us. "They only love you for your money." Money was indeed essential for dating women and girls. And it was a constant provocation that some well-to-do kaddafis had more resources to flaunt "their" girls than many loggers.

But money was even more important when it came to marriage. In order to marry a woman, a man was first expected to provide his future in-laws with money and drinks so as to *kokanga lopangu* (literally, to close the compound) of the girl's family to his competitors. Then the respective families started negotiations about the bridewealth or bride price (*likonza*). Although the particulars of marriage transactions varied—depending on the specific customs (*coutumes*) that families applied and the dynamics of patrilineal or matrilineal kinship ideologies—bridewealth was always transferred from the man's family to the woman's family. Most bridewealth "lists" comprised money and goods, such as imported fabrics, bicycles, sewing machines, televisions, HiFi sets, goats, chickens, and beer. After courtship, men first usually paid a precursor to the bridewealth—the so-called *prédot*—to officially become engaged to their fiancée, while the bridewealth itself was later transferred during a customary marriage (*marriage coutumier*), which was sometimes followed by a religious ceremony in one of the compound's churches—though the latter often had to be postponed for lack of funds.

Yet even after the official transaction of bridewealth, in-laws frequently continued to claim money and gifts. Bosco, for instance, stated that marriage was "a garbage bin [*poubelle*] that could never be filled." As a result, official marriages were accessible only to more well-to-do men in the labor compounds. For this reason, many family arrangements were, in practice, the outcome of what people described as a fait accompli, a matter of irreversible fact. Several young workers, for instance, simply made their girlfriends pregnant and preferred to deal with the consequences later.

Such tactics were risky. Families could always accuse their daughters of prostitution (*kindumba*) or prosecute their lovers for stealing their girls, thereby rendering useless the daughters in whom they had invested. One of our neighbors had been imprisoned for more than a month until families arranged the matter through a fine. Everyone knew, however, that such arrangements did not lead to fully recognized marriages. Families-in-law indeed continued to claim bridewealth and threatened to take back wives and children.[6] Because marriages—and, especially, offspring—were a necessary condition for reaching full adulthood, the insecurity of such family arrangements continued to compromise the status of both spouses—but particularly that of the husband, who was seen as incapable of properly "paying" for his wife.

A tree feller in his early thirties therefore aptly described (hetero)sexuality as a "minefield" when we discussed the latest events in an ongoing saga of passion and jealousy that had unfolded between him and a girl from Bumba. He said that, whatever he did, "the field is mined" (*terrain eza miné*). Not only did he need to maneuver carefully because of other contenders, he also felt he no longer understood girls. Women, he said, have a "hacked" or "pirated nature" (*basi baza na nature pirate*). "She even forces me to lie!" he continued. "If I speak the truth, she doesn't believe me, but when I tell her a lie, she does." As a result, he claimed, "It's better to tell a woman you're a rich man, even if you're not, because then she will fight for you; but if you just tell her the truth and say you love her, she will ignore you." He said his girlfriend therefore drove him crazy and provoked heartsickness (*mpasi ya motema*).

The general idea that there was "no romance without finance" in the CTI labor compounds was a considerable source of frustration (Cornwall 2003, 240). Many men had gone through painful experiences and were profoundly disappointed (*découragé*) in women, whom they saw as inherently greedy and untrustworthy. In times of difficulty, girlfriends had indeed left for partners who could better provide for them. Hence, the true love (*bolingo ya solo*) that popular music so often sang about seemed impossible to find (Cole and Thomas 2009; Trapido 2010). Moreover, did not the traditional Mbudza song and dance—known as *Engundele*—urge men to "protect" themselves against the seductive force of women "who dye their hair all day" and have the power "to make men fall" (see also Hendriks 2021)? As a result, several workers came to consider sexuality as a "game" in which girlfriends were only a "means of distraction" to unwind. Hostile comments about women became blunt weapons to reclaim manhood. And infidelity was proof, as one worker said, that a man was like a "wasp stinging its sting in different places without getting killed."

The quotidian misogyny that characterized the logging camps' hypermasculine work culture was truly disturbing. While men could publicly boast about their sexual adventuring because it would increase their transgressive capital, women were ostracized for being loose women or prostitutes (*bandumba*) or for their parading around (*kotambolatambola*). Although many men treated their partners with kindness and respect, physical violence and abuse were not unheard of. But wives and girlfriends also proudly claimed to know how to "deal" with men. They for instance shared and sold substances for controlling their partners, as medicines (*nkisi*) they secretly put in the men's food. And, in cases of conflict, wives would stop fulfilling household tasks or refuse sexual intercourse. Because bridewealth was often left unpaid, others simply left the labor camps and returned to their families.

The construction of male selves was therefore based on an idea of control that had become quite impossible to realize (Miescher and Lindsay 2003, 20). Due to the generalized uncertainty of camp life, male strength was always a fragile achievement, constantly under attack and subject to gossip. As a result, it had to be permanently reclaimed and, ideally, confirmed by others. Indeed, despite all their boasting and misogynist comments, men deeply relied on their wives and girlfriends not only for domestic and sexual labor but also for reconfirming their masculinity. Verbal and physical violence against women was perhaps the reverse side of an acute male dependence on women and their emasculating powers. So, while men often attributed women's materialism to their assumed female nature, the "political economy of misogyny" in the logging camps seemed very much a product of the precarity and insufficiency of wage labor (Ferguson 1999, 197).

Being a man in the CTI logging camps was indeed a challenge. Workers tried to perform tough masculinities and present themselves as strong men who knew how to "see clearly" in the hard world of timber production. But although they flashed their salaries and work contracts in the face of traders and smugglers, they were nonetheless still beaten in contests of competitive consumption. While they emphasized their distinction from "mere villagers," they were forced to recognize their therapeutic reliance on traditional sources of resistant masculinity. And while they might want to impress women and girls, they could not but lament the absence of love without money. Some literally rebuilt their bodies as compensation for what CTI had eaten away. Others claimed to be young in an attempt to negotiate the double bind of desiring *both* breadwinner and daredevil status. Many resorted to public performances of transgression—or violence—to reassert their manhood in the midst of a simultaneously desired and deplored dependency on a foreign company. Is it any surprise, therefore, that in such paradoxical circumstances homosocial relations between men sometimes appeared as a relatively safe space, away from the minefield of heterosexuality—despite the jealousy and conflicts that also occurred between friends (Boulton 2019)?

This chapter shows how and why the "strong" logger masculinity that CTI workers tried to effect was a fragile construct. Claims to autonomy were based on multiple dependencies, and self-making was a rather insecure undertaking. Perhaps all human existence is a never-ending search for balance between autonomy and dependency (Jackson 2012). But the daily quest for manhood in the logging camps aptly illustrates the strikingly *ecstatic* dimension of self-making, in which the very means of attaining control could also push people off-balance. Money, for instance, was a tool for crafting and asserting the self but also an intoxicating force that could make one lose it (Cuvelier 2017, 210). A regular salary might center men as breadwinners but also pull them in different directions through kinship networks. And in a competitive environment where social, sexual, and romantic agency seemed to "revolve around an idea of 'overpowering' the other," one was always at risk of *being* overpowered (Trapido 2010, 136).

The importance of the performance of transgression at the center of masculinities shows the complexity of their ecstatic dynamics. Indeed, the transgression of moral and sexual orders was equally a transgression of the "self" created by these orders. But, paradoxically, these same acts were also a means of *gaining* autonomy and control. Moreover, is it not striking that, in order to fight against dependency on CTI money, workers relied on Mbudza traditions for gaining courage and strength, using as a resource of resistance the eleko tree, itself a well-known medicine for treating the paradigmatically ecstatic condition of epilepsy? The state of ecstasis was therefore both what one reacted against *and* the means of reacting, both the problem and the cure. The paradox lay in the fact that ecstatic tools to fight ecstasis were themselves risky and prone to undo what they aimed to accomplish.

Yet transgression and ecstasis were not specific to masculinities in the labor compounds. The next chapter shows how and why they were equally central to the slippery trajectories of sexuality and desire among CTI expats.

Logs waiting for transport to Kinshasa

Women and Chainsaws

"BUT THESE WHITE GUYS were really there to fuck black women, right?" This is the kind of question that often pops up spontaneously whenever friends or colleagues at home imagine the expat loggers. The image of a small group of single white men living and working in a remote place in the rainforest easily arouses fantasies of interracial sex in the Western imagination. People often push me for more details, avidly awaiting juicy stories that can only confirm what they already seem to know: that white men go to Africa to have lots of sex. As if out-of-the-way places allow for the expression of a "true" sexuality that would otherwise remain repressed. As if "the" Congo is still that "place where one [can] look for sexual experiences unobtainable in Europe" (Said 1978, 190).

Whether transmitting disgust or a barely concealed fascination with "wild" sexualities, such questions themselves participate in the reproduction of old stereotypes that exoticize, feminize, and sexualize Africa as a space to be conquered and penetrated by white men. Such assumptions, images, and taken-for-granted truths have a history (Gilman 1985; Young 1995). They specifically participate in what Anne McClintock (1995, 22) calls the "porno-tropics"—a "long tradition of male travel as an erotics of ravishment"—that was a crucial dimension of imperialist and colonial projects. Her book *Imperial Leather: Race, Gender and Sexuality in the Colonial Contest* argues:

> For centuries, the uncertain continents—Africa, the Americas, Asia—were figured in European lore as libidinously eroticized. Travelers' tales abounded with visions of the monstrous sexuality of far-off lands, where, as legend had it, men sported gigantic penises and women consorted with apes, feminized men's breasts flowed with milk and militarized women lopped theirs off. Renaissance travelers found an eager and lascivious audience for their spicy tales, so that, long before the era of high Victorian imperialism, Africa and the Americas had become what can be called *a porno-tropics for the European imagination*—a fantastic magic lantern of the mind onto which Europe projected its forbidden sexual desires and fears. . . . By the nineteenth century, popular lore had firmly established Africa as the quintessential zone of sexual aberration and anomaly. (22; my emphasis)

Little has changed. The avid interest in and explicit questions about the intimate lives of European loggers still betray a widespread curiosity about interracial sex that has lost none of its obsessions. Under colonialism, questions about sexual relations between white men and native women were indeed at the center of imaginations, policies, and anxieties, and the management of sexuality was a device for securing white bourgeois identities. Ann Stoler's (2002, 43) work, for instance, illustrates how "observers and participants in the imperial enterprise appear to have had unlimited interest in the sexual interface of the colonial encounter." In these uncertain worlds, she argues, sex mattered because imperial security relied on and "required managed passions, self-discipline over unruly drives and the education of sentiment and desire" (130).

Even today the Belgian ex-colony continues to evoke uncomfortable memories and barely disavowed fantasies about interracial sex (Ceuppens 2003), as if everyone still knows what was "really" going on there. In her groundbreaking study, the historian Amandine Lauro (2005) describes how interracial concubinage in the Congo Free State (1885–1908) was, at first, largely accepted as a quasi-institutionalized relationship between colonial officers and their so-called *ménagères*, or housekeepers. Ménagères were even thought to be necessary for the colonial undertaking, Lauro argues, as they would absorb the sexual drives of Europeans in the absence of white women—and thus help prevent "congolitis," a form of tropical psychosis characterized by depression, apathy, and fits of anger. Gradually, however, ménagères became increasingly criticized as policy makers thought they "decivilized" colonial agents and revealed the actual weakness of their authority. By the time the Belgian government took over in 1908, a new moral wind generally disapproved of the institution.[1] In an attempt to reinforce racial boundaries, the administration therefore encouraged European women to join their men. And, especially after World War II, colonial agents were supposed to marry before they started their careers.

It is therefore not surprising that the mere idea of single white men being isolated and removed from their wives and family immediately arouses suspicion. Congo is indeed still imagined as an "ethnosexual frontier," where sexual opportunities are easily available or can be simply taken by those with power or money (Nagel 2003). As such, the old porno-tropics are alive and well, not only for friends and colleagues eager to hear more about "sex in the forest" but also for the CTI expats themselves, who frequently talked about their adventures and relationships with black women as though a strong and essentialized interracial sex drive was an inherent characteristic of their sexuality that needed flaunting in self-exoticizing performances of their "darkened" masculinity.

This chapter takes an ethnographic look at how specific articulations of race, sex, and desire affected the lives of European managers in the CTI concession (Hendriks 2014b). As such, it describes a complex erotic field that was deeply conditioned by history and illustrates how and why sex, gender, and desire need to be taken into account in any analysis of racial capitalism (Robinson 1983). Yet, while illustrating the enduring force of the porno-tropic tradition, it also shows how industrial rainforest logging produced an erotic economy that cannot simply be reduced to a hydraulic model where "white men fuck black women" to release excess energy. The porno-tropic tradition and the racial/sexual stereotypes it fostered were more complex. On the one hand, interracial sex was at least as much about *talking* as it was about *doing*. And, on the other hand, the racialized dynamics of desire equally comprised white women and black men—alongside white men and black women—as fetishized figures of the porno-tropic imagination. Although rather absent in McClintock's account, these figures played a fundamental role in expat sexual fantasies. And, as we will see, their physical and imaginary presence unleashed unpredictable (and possibly queer) dynamics of desire that constitute yet another aspect of the ecstasis this book is tracing.

Hence, as a complement to the previous chapter's evocation of Congolese loggers' gendered practices of self-making, the following sections show how—*also* for their European bosses—masculinity and sexuality were strikingly ecstatic processes, albeit in profoundly different ways. Even more so than in the previous chapter, we will have to get closer to the explicitly sexual and even pornographic. I can only hope that this closeness and the possible discomfort it might provoke help the reader comprehend the situations I found myself involved in. Rather than sensationalize or exoticize expat sex, this chapter presents a careful picture that demonstrates both its banality and ecstatic vulnerability.

Studying sexual practices and desires is, however, notoriously difficult and requires a creative use of ethnographic methods. This chapter therefore approaches its subject matter in two (more oblique) steps. It first reconstructs expat *discourses* on sex. Then, it proposes a contextualized reading of two sets of erotic *images* that emerged during fieldwork. As we will see, these readings, which actualize pathways of desire that might otherwise remain virtual, offer a rare way into the porno-tropics and its complex dynamics of interracial competition and identification, which so often resist fine-grained empirical analysis.

The first reading presents an iconic calendar that was distributed each year by a global chainsaw manufacturing company. Depicting scantily dressed white women playing with heavy machinery, its images directly confirmed the hypermasculine status of the logger and the phallic nature of logging. Moreover, because European managers strongly believed their own workers were trying to steal these calendars from expat offices and bungalows, their soft-erotic pictures also played up white fears about the unstoppable appetite that black men purportedly had for white women.

The second reading takes these anxieties a step further. It focuses on the iconography of a particular porn site the expats showed me during fieldwork: a genre of hard-core pornography that explicitly staged white women as "naughty daughters" who were "addicted" to well-endowed black men. As a topic of laughter, gossip, fascination, and arousal, the surprising appearance of this kind of pornography in the European Garden of Eden manifested a complex economy of fear and desire that recycled expat anxieties about race, gender, and sexuality. We will see how the European loggers' eager visual consumption of fetishized black masculinity articulated fantasies that somehow queered their position of mastery and control—suggesting that the racialized erotics of the porno-tropics might perhaps be less *straight*forwardly heterosexual than is generally assumed.

Sex in the Forest

The sleazy title of this section is of course a tongue-in-cheek reference to the avid curiosity about white loggers' sex lives in the rainforest. The following paragraphs do not, however, intend to cheaply satisfy voyeuristic desires. They simply set the scene for what will follow by evoking expat discourses on race, sex, and gender and offer a matter-of-fact account of the actual sexual and romantic relationships the European foresters tended to have.

At the time of our fieldwork, three of the CTI expats were married or had girlfriends in Europe, but they were all living on their own, and their wives rarely visited, if ever. Moreover, although some had been in past relationships with African women, new Congolese girlfriends never seemed to stay for long. In contrast to other "enclaves" of extractive capitalism, where the physical presence of expat wives "mobilizes white heteronormative marriage to communicate industry morality," the European loggers led mostly "single" and "lonely" lives (Appel 2019a, 82). As we saw in chapter 6, the Europeans therefore told each other stories that exoticized and "darkened" their *masculinity* as a means of resolving the resulting tensions and frustrations. Yet, as we will see below, these same stories also molded and brought into circulation fears and desires that reproduced a largely shared discourse on essentialized "white" and "black" *sexualities* (Holland 2012).

The following, for instance, is an excerpt from a conversation that occurred between Jens, Julien, and Roger at a crossroads in the middle of the forest a week after a European Greenpeace team had organized a workshop on sustainable logging in Bumba. The activists had visited the concession unannounced, and the expat managers had discussed their "trespassing" for weeks.

When they saw Roger's jeep speeding in their direction, Jens and Julien stopped talking. Roger parked in the middle of the road, got out, and slowly walked toward us with his characteristic limp. We all knew the story about his leg and the terrible accident with a logging truck back in Congo-Brazzaville.

"Did you see that hole in the road farther down towards Mombwassa?" he shouted. "One of these days we'll have an accident with one of my trucks!"

"Yeah . . . I already sent the road grader," Jens said, "but she's [the grader's] still working at the other side."

"It'll be fine," Julien said.

Roger didn't look very convinced. He knew he worried too much, but another broken truck would mean yet another delay. Meanwhile, the Mombwassa people were really getting impatient about their new school. He lit a cigarette and took a spot beside Julien, who was leaning against the hood of the jeep.

"So . . . those Greenpeace bastards finally left us," Julien said.

"Yes! What fools these guys are," Roger said. "They come here only as tourists . . . but we, we're in shit every day! Did you see that sissy who came along with them? I think it's the first time he ever came to a place like this."

"No, I haven't seen him," Julien said. "It doesn't interest me."

"And those girls!" Jens interjected. "They were soooo ugly! If they'd been beautiful, I would have invited them to our place to spend a nice evening together."

Roger and Julien sniggered, responding to the idea of them having fun with Greenpeace activists who had just accused them of illegal logging. Fucking them would certainly teach them a lesson. And show them who was really in charge in this godforsaken place. Roger seemed to like the idea.

"But the little one had a nice figure all the same, hadn't she?" he said.

Jens waved it away.

"Yes, she did!" Roger said. "You can't find something like that in these dirty villages over here!"

Jens looked at him and shook his head. "You know you've to go to Bumba for that," he said. "You'll find really beautiful girls there."

"I know . . . but those girls are morons!" Roger said. "They're just lying there with their mouth open, and it's only eee, eee, eee. No, it's not worth the trouble. If I want to fuck, it's easier to give two thousand francs to a slut in one of these villages and it's over; all the rest is not worth the trouble."

Julien nodded in silence. It was true. Difficult to find nice girls here. Only farmer girls, looking for money. Roger often bored us with stories about his former girlfriend in Cameroon. How different she was. And how much he missed her.

A little farther down the road a young girl appeared on her way to sell food at a nearby logging site. Julien pointed at her.

"But what about that one?" he asked.

He teasingly turned toward me. "Thomas, what do you think? You have to get 'integrated' right?"

I smirked a little, tried to avoid the subject and then heard myself saying in my most masculine voice, "Bwa . . . I don't really know."

I did not want to be found out to be a "sissy" like the Greenpeace activist. But neither did I want to be seen as one of the expat loggers. Slowly but surely my forced performances of straightness began to bother me.

"Oh, but Thomas is still thinking about his wife in Belgium," Jens said.

"Yes, I really miss her," I sheepishly replied, hoping Jens's remark had saved the day.

In conversations like this, expat loggers liked to present themselves as tough no-bullshit men who did what needed to be done in order to make money and bring development to a poor country. They pictured themselves as the exact opposites of the "sentimental" environmentalists who—they supposed—were only on the lookout to harm their reputation. Sex talk was a way to re-confirm their lumberjack masculinity in contrast to the "effeminate" activists who "didn't have the balls" to actually "come and live here in the forest."

Commenting on women's buttocks and boasting about one's sexual ad-ventures was indeed a favorite expat pastime, a game in masculinity to which I was invited to play but often failed to convince. I sometimes wondered whether the expat managers deliberately exaggerated their racism and mi-sogyny in my presence—perhaps to shock the shy bourgeois boy I must have been in their eyes. But the stubborn insistence with which their nasty ste-reotypes reappeared in many conversations indicated they must have been deeply engrained.

Chatting about sex effectively reproduced old commonplaces about race, gender, and sexuality. On the one hand, these European loggers depicted black women as "mute," "stupid," and "stinking" lumps of flesh, reducing their sexuality to the sheer reception of frustrated male energy looking for a way out and with "no better options" available. In this respect, they boasted about "shooting their load" wherever they pleased, "just to clear their mind." On the other hand, the expat managers talked about black women as sexually "insatiable creatures" who were capable of offering erotic delights unavailable in Europe. Perceiving Congolese women as alternat-ingly repulsive and irresistible, they situated the CTI concession in an old geography of racialized and sexualized essences. White women, by contrast, were seen as aesthetically more "pleasing" but ultimately also more "boring." While some expats missed the "civilization" and "style" of the sexual and ro-mantic milieu back home, they usually compared white women unfavorably to the more "passionate" and "unbridled" nature of "local girls."

European loggers sometimes debated the apparent accuracy of their own stereotypes, alternatingly confirming and refuting racist and misogynist commonplaces with examples and counterexamples drawn from experiences or stories they heard from colleagues. Yet, race always remained a prime marker of sexuality. The expats indeed rarely questioned the overarching black/white opposition. As "the most visible of fetishes," skin color was an obsessive focus in stories about erotic adventures, romantic experiences, or sexual turnoffs (Bhabha 1994, 112). The stereotype of the "black Venus" could thereby quickly turn into its mirror image of the "stinking Negro" (Hendriks 2014b)—or make way for the idealized white woman in a porno-tropic structure from which she initially was erased.

Boastful stories and discourses about race and sex do not, however, allow for easy conclusions in terms of sexual practices. There are considerable gaps and differences between what people *say* they do and what they actually do behind closed doors. In fact, contrary to the image the expats cultivated in their own self-exoticizing stories, actual sexual contact seemed rather limited. As we will see, the European loggers' sex lives consisted more of downloading, watching, and sharing porn from the internet than actual bodily contact.

Yet this is not to say the expats never interrupted their single lives with short-term relationships or occasional one-night stands. While some of them were notorious for their sexual abstinence, others were indeed known for their erotic appetites. Although the latter often preferred to send drivers to fetch young women from Bumba, they also occasionally received girls from the labor compounds. Job seekers sometimes promised or offered expat managers women in the hope of increasing their chances of getting hired.[2] And women knew very well with whom they could develop relationships in exchange for money and gifts and who, on the other hand, were too "stubborn" to take them up on such an offer.

Girls who managed to access the small expat circle, either on their own account or through the mediation of others, often exchanged advice and anecdotes about the Europeans' individual habits, tastes, and eccentricities as well as potential dangers involving them—stories that rapidly spread through the labor compounds. Despite their internal rivalries, these women seemed to team up in small groups and sometimes even share sources of revenue. While camp inhabitants occasionally accused them of prostitution, most people claimed these girls only tried to benefit from white men in order to "pay for their school fees" or "help out their families."

From their side, too, the expats shared dirty stories about individual girls and discussed their sexual skills in great detail. Occasionally they asked women to bring along "sisters" or "cousins" to pass on to colleagues. Hence, although some women were deemed special and kept secret, some expats ended up sharing the same girls over time. While this gave rise to slumbering jealousies and, more rarely, open conflicts, sharing girls (or, more frequently, *stories* about girls) created a strong sense of an expat "we"—a naughty-boy identity through which white masculinity could be rated and judged. This chapter unpacks the complexity of this erotic subject position. But, first, we need another snippet of conversation from my field notes to introduce more stories into the mix.

Pinup Girls and Thieves

Julien almost ran over Monga, the old cook who had just put a tuna salad in the fridge for when Pablo got back from the forest. Entering the bungalow, he threw something on the table.

"Here you go," he said. "One for you and one for Pablo."

I looked up from my laptop and took the two calendars in my hands. "Thank you," I said. "I'll give it to him."

"The pictures are really nice this year, really good-looking chicks." Julien took a calendar from me and paged through it. "See, this one is great, really beautiful figure, don't you think? Those legs—"

I looked at a photograph of a dark-haired woman in black underwear kneeling down and holding a leaf vacuum machine between her legs. She pointed the tube of the machine in the direction of a blond woman, whose white dress was lifted up, revealing her underwear.

"Oh, cool" I said. "Looks like Marilyn Monroe."

"Yeah . . . but be careful not to let them lie around though. You know, these niggers around here, they just can't be trusted. Especially when they see a beautiful white woman like this," Julien said, smirking. "Keep them somewhere safe; don't let them lie here on the table."

He turned toward the door. "Anyway, I am off again, too much work. . . . Maybe I'll be back next week for coffee."

"Ok," I said. "Take care."

Julien got back to his car, and I heard old Monga making some noise in front of the kitchen outside. I could not imagine Monga to be particularly interested in these calendars. I put them on the coffee table. Later, I discovered Pablo had indeed hidden his copy in the drawer of his bedside table.

Calendars like these are sent annually to forestry-related businesses all over the world. Their presence in offices, garages, workshops, and expat bungalows is part of a global lumberjack culture. Since 1973, the German chainsaw manufacturer Stihl has used such soft-erotic calendars as a marketing strategy, and despite early protests over their "pornographic" nature, its calendars quickly attained a cult status, following the example of the more glamorous Pirelli calendars distributed by the Italian tire manufacturer of the same name. From blonde, 1970s girls posing with chainsaws in Southern Germany forests to 1980s models having fun with machinery in traditional villages in the Alps to 1990s girls holidaying in southern Europe with their gear to twenty-first-century urban fashion shoots, the popularity of the Stihl calendar only grew: production rose from forty-five thousand copies in the 1970s to one million in 2010 (Anonymous 2009; Belser 2009).

The expat managers at CTI eagerly looked forward to each new issue. Commenting on the women in these calendars allowed them to highlight and lament their "misery" in a region where "clean and sexy girls are unfindable." They jealously guarded issues from previous years and some decorated their desks with cutouts. Cracking dirty jokes about these calendars was simply part of being a logger. The Stihl calendar indeed confirmed the paradigmatic idea of the *forestier* as the ultimate masculine man and visualized the phallic nature of logging gear. Most pictures showed women caressing chainsaws between their legs or otherwise playing with "dangerous" tools, as if to emphasize their risk-taking naughtiness. Maybe the classic iconography of women adoring cars—or, in this case, chainsaws—somehow sanitizes and heterosexualizes male viewers' own fascinations with and desires for phallic machinery?

In any case, the objectifying depiction of sexy women playing with purported boy toys seems to be a successful strategy for marketing products to predominantly male clients. Yet the 2010 calendar that arrived during our fieldwork also wanted to be a little different. This edition was produced by Esther Haase, a German fashion photographer and only the second woman to work for Stihl. Through her €200,000 photo shoots, Haase claimed to produce "spontaneous" images of "strong women" using logging machines as tools in games of domination and submission, sometimes in an implicitly s/m or lesbian setting (Anonymous 2009). The photo for March, for instance, showed a woman as a dominatrix in a black leather dress "riding" a heavy machine. June's depicted a woman in tiger print posing on an antique desk with a chainsaw between her legs. And September's page eroticized a girl, sweaty and seemingly exhausted after having performed heavy labor with Stihl machinery.

Moreover, five months out of twelve also depicted male models. Often they remained in the background as iconic, working-class youth with lean bodies looking at the women in the foreground. But the July page explicitly reversed the gendered direction of the gaze and its scopophilic pleasures, as it showed a woman floating on an air mattress in a swimming pool looking at the thick muscles of the man sleeping by her side. With his head literally cut out of the frame, his physical body was explicitly presented as an *object* of female desire.

For the CTI expats, however, these photographs were still, first and foremost, about "sexy girls" whose beauty strongly contrasted with "local" women. Commenting on their bodies in the starkest macho terms, the European loggers seemed rather unaffected by Haase's attempt to realize a more feminist politics of representation. But, more importantly, these calendars reintroduced white women into a highly racialized economy of desire, despite or beyond their physical absence in the concession. As such, their photographed bodies partially shifted McClintock's reading of the pornotropics as an affair between predominantly white men and *black* women to a more complex triangle. Indeed, unlike colonial imaginations of white women as guardians of morality who were largely devoid of their sexuality, the Stihl models appeared as explicitly eroticized objects (Stoler 2002, 71). As such, these calendars literally repositioned white women in a broader field of racialized sexuality—as sexual *objects* and no longer as desexualized "wives" or "mothers" expelled from male ethno-erotic drives.

Moreover, the very jealousy with which expat loggers protected their calendars also reveals the looming presence of yet another figure in the pornotropic imagination. Indeed, the Stihl calendars operated equally as material carriers for the imagined sexual threat of *black men*. Although Jens sometimes used them as business gifts for Congolese state agents, Julien's remark about workers trying to steal these calendars from expat bungalows reveals a deep concern about black masculinity and its assumed craving for white women. The intensively discussed erotic appeal of the provocative Stihl girls was said to be simply "irresistible" to Congolese workers. And the nervous protection of white women (and their images) from male residents hinted at widespread cultural anxieties about black men trying to steal, rape, or seduce white women.[3] As equally essentialized porno-tropic figures, black men indeed seemed to point at an obsessive interracial competition for white women as objects of desire. But their real and imaginary presence also set in motion a more complex dyanmic of *identification*.

Encountering Pornography

It was one of those Saturday nights when we gathered at Roger's bungalow on the shore of the Itimbiri River. Michel and I had just arrived from the forest camp when Jens approached. He had already told us he would invite a new girl from Bumba to come over for dinner.

"This is the girl I've been talking about. She's not bad, is she?" he said. The young woman smiled nervously, and Michel graciously took her hand and kissed it. "Madame, it's a real pleasure to meet." I tried to say hello, but Jens had already pushed her forward.

Roger was in the kitchen. "Let me open these bottles of wine and check on the roast in the oven," he said. "This time, I'll do it myself!" Roger always complained about his cook, Marcel. Two months before, a similar dinner had ended in a row about overcooked food. And Roger wanted everything "just is it was in Europe."

Marcel brought in the starters from the kitchen, and Jens made the girl serve us. "Sit next to me," he ordered.

Roger then presented a small tin of caviar from his latest trip to France. "Do you like caviar?" he asked the girl. "Fish eggs." He took a spoon, dipped it in the tin, and put it in her mouth. Everyone laughed at the disgusted look it elicited.

During dinner Julien twice tried to put his hand on the girl's thighs, but Jens kept a close watch over her. "Are you not too cold?" Michel asked—the air-conditioning was blasting through the dining room at maximum level. She looked down. "No," she said, though clearly she was shivering.

Later that night Jens told the girl to take place behind the bar and serve us drinks. "Do something sexy," he said.

After the bottles of red wine, we started with whiskey and cognac. Roger had her drink a full glass. We were all getting pretty drunk. Julien pulled her to the sofa. "Would you not prefer to come to my place instead of spending the night with old Jens?" he asked.

Next thing I knew, Roger called us from behind his computer. "Come and have a look at this," he said. "A friend from Kinshasa sent me this link." As I came closer, I realized he was showing us a scene from a porn website—a black man violently penetrating a young white girl. The staging was ridiculous. I didn't know whether to laugh or leave. The others seemed to find it quite amusing though. Someone grabbed the girl from Bumba from behind and made her watch. "Look at the size of that cock," he said. "You like that, don't you?" The girl laughed uneasily.

All of a sudden, Jens got up. "Time to go to bed," he said, smiling. He pulled the girl to the door. The others pleaded for her to stay. As she left, I clumsily tried to apologize.

Several months later I accidentally ran into the young woman at a bar in Bumba. She asked me about the whites from CTI and why they no longer called on her. I said I didn't know. I tried to explain how uncomfortable I had felt and asked her whether she had gotten home all right. She looked at me with eyes that seemed to mock me for my concern. Who was I to think she needed pity? She turned around and went to a man on the dance floor whom I knew as a fuel smuggler. After a slow rumba, they disappeared into the night.

I vividly remember how, lying on my bed after that dinner party, my head turned with booze and pulsating questions. How to write about this in my notebook? The next morning, I thought it best to ignore what had happened. Yet, a week later, Roger asked me whether I had looked at the porn site again. I would certainly find it very interesting, he winked. He forwarded me the link. That evening, I opened it on my laptop in Pablo's bungalow. How unpredictable fieldwork was. I had never expected pornography to become a serious object of attention in this already serendipitous story about rainforest logging.

Phallic Obsessions

The website Roger had shown us that night was called Watching My Daughter Go Black. After the obligatory warning about its "explicit adult material," the site described itself as providing movies in which "fathers watch in horror as their young daughters get defiled by huge black cocks" (DogfartNetwork 2012).[4] In itself, this focus on white girls having sex with black men was not very different from dominant imagery in the quickly growing field of so-called interracial porn. But the explicit presence of *white men* as "fathers" who "watch their daughters go black" was remarkable. Why would this specific triangle of black men, white girls, and white men captivate the attention of expat loggers in the Congolese rainforest? How could this specific kind of porn trigger and arouse? Browsing through the videos, I quickly realized that they strongly resonated with racial and sexual stereotypes that circulated in dominant expat discourses and fantasies.

The website was part of the DogfartNetwork that comprised twenty interracial porn sites—such as Interracial BlowBang, Interracial Pickups, and Blacks on Blondes—of which thirteen featured black men and white women in different sexual activities. The main webpage invites viewers to take a tour of the available videos that depict "anguished heartbroken fathers" who see "their precious daughters defiled by a black man right before their eyes," and to look at "spoiled suburban white girls" who "can't get enough thick meaty black cock to satisfy." Each video is also introduced by a short description written from the perspective of one of its protagonists.

When describing scenes from the position of the so-called father, Watching My Daughter Go Black graphically spells out ethno-sexual fears. The father figure is invariably scripted as a decent, hard-working, lower-middle-class white man who cares for his daughter but realizes that all she is interested in is "messing around" with black men. The website's imagery and narratives moreover explicitly depict fathers as victims of their own daughters, as if the girls deliberately want to hurt their feelings. In one video, for instance, a father comes home from a day of hard work only to catch his daughter with a "big black guy." Afraid the latter might "kick his ass," the father admits he has no choice but to obey his daughter's command to watch her as she gets "violated in his own home." The father then complains about his daughter being "just like her mother"—nothing but another "black-cock slut." Realizing he has "lost" both women in his life, he finally bursts into tears.

Descriptions from the "daughter" perspective confirm that white girls are indeed addicted to "black mammoth dicks." Notwithstanding their innocent schoolgirl looks, white daughters are staged as "sluts" or "bitches" who live only for sex with black men. At the same time, many girls claim they look for "love" and describe their relationships as "romantic." Yet, because of the enduring taboo against interracial relationships in suburban America, they realize their quest for exotic sex, love, and romance is badly perceived. For this reason, they frame their racial transgressions as a deliberate *choice* to shock—and belittle their fathers for their fears and prejudices.

From the black man's perspective, however, relationships with white girls are presented as "casual"—nothing serious, just another sexual occasion in their already "promiscuous" life. Their gangsta clothes, da hood origins, language, postures, and carefully staged genitality reproduce long-standing stereotypes that, as Kobena Mercer (1994, 133–34) argues, circulate "a rigid set of racial roles and identities which rehearse scenarios of desire [and] trace the cultural legacies of slavery, empire and imperialism [that are] still in existence." Black men are indeed depicted as sexual brutes on the lookout to steal white daughters. And, in contrast to the white, usually fat, and rather ridiculous father figures, they are athletic and strong. Moreover, in the fictive descriptions beneath the videos, black men seem perfectly aware of the power of their genitals and strategically mobilize their "irresistible" attraction. At the same time, however, they also voice fears about white fathers' angry reactions and echo memories of lynching.

In this notable melodrama of racialized taboo and transgression, the website invariably and obsessively zooms in on the black penis, which is consistently filmed so as to stress its "massive" size. Its scripted narratives furthermore present the black phallus as an explicit "threat to the secure identity of the white male ego" (Mercer 1994, 134). In itself, this is nothing unusual for the genre. Many interracial porn scenes seem to "promise the punishment of naughty white teens and their over-protective fathers," even though the latter usually remain "absent from the mise-en-scene" (Bernardi 2006, 233). Watching My Daughter Go Black, however, deliberately stages the father figure as a reluctant observer *before* the camera. And, more importantly, the website casts daughters as punishing, rather than punished, figures. Instead of an alleged rape victim, the white teen is indeed presented as a conscious solicitor of interracial sex and thus stands in a relative position of power—punishing her father by making him watch. Hence, rather than castigate the apparently transgressive desires of "daughters," the scripts and imagery primarily seem to punish "fathers" for *their* pervert pleasures.[5]

White men on the website invariably strike explicitly horrified poses to show their disgust toward their daughters' behavior—as if they frantically want to express their abhorrence of interracial sex. But the overacted and almost parodying nature of their performances simultaneously subverts their staged horror. As a result, the website suggests that fathers know only too well what forbidden pleasures are elicited by breaking sexual and racial taboos. While exaggeration is a common stock-in-trade in pornography, where sex acts are often overacted, the exaggerated looks of fathers "watching their daughters go black" express both a repugnance of, and fascination with, the black male genitals they are "forced" to watch. As such, their gaze further fetishizes the black phallus, reproducing old stereotypes that reduce African men to their sexual parts (Spronk 2014). As Frantz Fanon famously wrote in *Black Skin, White Masks* (1967), this visual economy of scale stimulates a position from where "one is no longer aware of the Negro but only of a penis" (130).

This particular porn site thus clearly draws from a specifically North American context and history where, as bell hooks (1992, 34) observes, "It is the *young black male body* that is seen as epitomizing [a] promise of wildness, of unlimited physical prowess and unbridled eroticism. It was this black body that was most 'desired' for its labor in slavery, and it is this body that is most represented in contemporary popular culture as the body to be watched, imitated, desired, possessed" (emphasis added). Yet, even in the middle of the Congolese rainforest, the European loggers must have experienced the iconography of this particular website as sufficiently titillating to consume (and share with others). The surprising appearance of this kind of porn was not a coincidence. On the one hand, the expat managers' sexualized ideas of whiteness and blackness were directly informed by globally circulating media products. And, on the other hand, the website's scripts and narratives firmly resonated with personal experiences and emotions.

On several occasions during our fieldwork I had indeed heard European managers talk about the superior strength and appeal of black men, thereby almost avowing the comparative *un*desirability of their own (pale) bodies. In everyday sex talk they compulsively repeated references to black male genitality with such phrases as "hung like a Negro" or "fuck like a Negro." Hence, as a symbol of sexual potency, the black penis constituted both a fetish and a threat for white men anxious to satisfy their sexual partners with a body of at least equal merit. Jens, for instance, told me about one of his nieces who had broken off her relationship with her Danish boyfriend after she was "seduced" by a "beach boy" during a holiday in The Gambia. And Julien and Roger often made fun of a colleague from Kinshasa who seemed to have lost his wife to her "black dance teacher" in France.

Told and retold, such stories expressed deep fears of losing (real or imagined) sexual partners to better endowed and physically superior black men. Moreover, because they assumed that women were always inadvertently attracted to black male bodies, the European loggers could also experience their own workers' presence as threatening or emasculating (Fanon 1967, 122). In order to somehow compensate for their experienced insufficiency, some tried to keep in good shape. But jogging or weightlifting in a tropical climate is not easy. And, on the work floor, they often could not but recognize the superior physique and condition of many of their employees.

The iconography of Watching My Daughter Go Black thus strikingly visualized a *dialectic of competition and desire* that informed everyday games in masculinity between white lumberjacks and black workers in the logging concession. By re-visualizing the white woman as a "daughter" who, just as on the Stihl calendar, needs to be protected from a threatening black male sexuality, the website foregrounded the emasculatory power of black men as sexual competitors. Yet, perhaps in contrast to colonial fears about interracial rape, the website explicitly eroticized such anxieties. The hallucinating potency of the black phallus—a stereotype "as anxious as it is assertive"— was indeed framed as both an object of fear as well as desire (Bhabha 1994, 100). As a product marketed to presumably white male consumers, the website's scripts and imagery thus seemed to punish "white fathers" for their own perverted pleasures of looking at hypersexualized black men. As such, their deliberately overacted performances of disgust *both covered up and allowed for* the white viewer to act on his own transgressive fascination for the spectacle of black male genitality.

Mimetic Desires

If, as porn scholar Laura Kipnis (2006, 119) argues, the general aim of pornography is to "hold us in the thrall of its theatrics of transgression, its dedication to crossing boundaries and violating social strictures," an ethnographic reading of Watching My Daughter Go Black suggests that its desired and desire-producing transgression is both a violation of taboos against interracial sex *and* an implicit crossing of normative heterosexuality. Yet, how to understand this tentative observation in the macho environment of the logging camps? How to think the website's particular dynamics of identification and desire in the context of our fieldwork?

The explicit eroticization of the black man at the heart of a predominantly heterosexual porno-tropic structure shows how and why fears and anxieties about competition were always already intertwined with what René Girard (1966) called "mimetic desire." Exploring the imitative structure of desire in Western literature, Girard indeed showed how desire often arises through the mediation of "models" that protagonists strive to mimic. In his view, a subject therefore desires an object primarily because the latter is *already desired* by a model the subject wants to emulate. Hence, rather than an autonomous linear movement from subject to object, desire turns out to be a more complex triangular process.

In *Between Men* (1985), Eve Sedgwick explicitly mobilized Girard's concept to foreground the potentially queer implications of the ubiquitous love triangles between two men and a woman that one encounters in many English novels. She thereby emphasized that the bond between male competitors is often as strong as, and even precedes, the bonds between either of them and the woman. For Sedgwick, this male bond expresses a homo*social* desire between men whose longings "to be like the other" cannot be openly expressed for fear of being read as homo*erotic*. Because emulation thus expresses both rivalry and admiration, "identification"—Sedgwick suggests—is a form of desire *to be like* that can always become a desire *for*. Yet, unlike for women, this slippery continuum between male homosociality and homoerotics is radically disrupted in contexts of hegemonic homophobia. For this reason, "heterosexual" desire—that is, a desire for the woman who is equally desired by the other man—seems *a way out* of the very impossibility of the homoerotic, as "a place where that potentially homosexual encounter is relayed, suspended, and contained" (Butler 2004, 139).

Both the Stihl calendars, which were said to be so coveted by black workers that they would try to steal them from expat bungalows, and the porn site, which explicitly pictured white women as objects of interracial male competition, illustrate the triangular dynamics of desire whereby a subject (a white man) desires the object (a white woman) of another subject (a black man)—and, by the same movement, expresses largely unspoken desires *for* the black man as a model of masculinity. As such, both sets of images point at a profoundly racialized libidinal economy *between men* in the logging concession that complicates and supplements white men's porno-tropic fantasies of black women on a feminized African continent. Indeed, white women and black men were equally part of this "fantastic magic lantern of the mind" (McClintock 1995, 22). And legacies of empire and colonialism were equally present in the interplay of "mimesis and alterity" between men (Taussig 1993).

Yet, while Watching My Daughter Go Black explicitly puts a fetishized black phallus at the center of its scripts and imagery, and while it feeds on a triangular structure of desire with homoerotic possibilities, neither the expat fascination for the black phallus nor the mimetic desires it produced automatically implies a closeted homosexuality for the assumedly white male viewer. Indeed, the previous readings do not "out" supposedly straight consumers of interracial porn as repressed homosexuals who secretly desire black men—as, for instance, Frantz Fanon (1967, 121) suggested in his notorious psychoanalysis of the "negrophobic" white man in the colonies (see also Young 1996, 96). In fact, such a paranoid reading would completely misrepresent the erotic economy on which this pornography was built (Jenkins 2006; Waugh 2001). On the contrary, the white expats' heterosexual identity was the point of departure from which the porn site was experienced. And heterosexuality was the very place where male-male erotic potentials emerged.

The previous readings thus largely confirm Sedgwick's insight that there is always a possibility for homo*erotic* effects of male homosocial desire in even the most homophobic of contexts. Occasionally the expats themselves even alluded to a possible queerness through jokes, offhand remarks, suggestive comments, and brief gestures, as if flirting with sexual dissidence would provide further proof of their masculinity. The homoerotics at work at the very center of the phallocentric institutions of heterosexuality, Sedgwick (1985, 89) argues, "is not most importantly an expression of the psychic origin of these institutions in a repressed or sublimated homosexual genitality [but] the coming to visibility of the normally implicit terms of a coercive double bind." It is indeed out of such a double bind, between hegemonic heterosexuality and homoerotic transgression, that male-male desire in seemingly straight pornography seems to arise.

These transgressions and ambiguities do not mitigate the blunt racism that was mobilized in, and reproduced by, interracial pornography and its visual consumption. Although film scholar Linda Williams (2004) argues that the transgression of racial boundaries in interracial porn makes its content always "subversive," Watching My Daughter Go Black did not diminish the enduring strength of ethnosexual stereotypes. Pornographic subversion does not prevent the reproduction of racism. For the European loggers, the eroticized obsession with interracial sex between black men and white women—rather than white men and black women—reconfirmed taken-for-granted stereotypes about black phallic superiority (Bernardi 2006). And while interracial mimetic desires effectively seemed to open up subversive pathways that, one might argue, potentially queered white masculinities, they did not query the racial fetishism on which they fed (Hendriks 2014a).

During their visits to the logging concession, executives from CTI's mother company seemed very much aware of their colleagues' racism, sexism, and misogyny. Although they would never publicly admit it, they were indeed concerned about the "racist impulses" and "macho culture" that rainforest work seemed to produce among their expats. Some therefore called for the organization of workshops to sensitize their employees and teach them a more "modern" and "respectful" attitude toward women and Congolese. Others thought the problem would spontaneously disappear as older Europeans retired and younger folk replaced them. Some proposed diversity as a solution (Ahmed 2012).

But no one really recognized the extent to which race, sex, and gender were essential features of rainforest capitalism. No one took rumors of white cannibalism seriously as stories about structural racism. No one acknowledged that corporate and lumberjack masculinities were essential to the quest for profit. And no one was prepared to face the racialized economy of desire and its less straightforwardly straight fetishes and phobias. But how could they? Were they not blinded by the system in which they found themselves? Does it not take a paranoid observer—an anthropologist, for instance—to analyze and name the realities they could not see?

From the perspectives of the expat loggers, critiquing racism and sexism from the sideline was all too easy. Their "politically correct" bosses did not have to live in the rainforest. The concession managers even claimed that their superiors' apparently "progressive" attitude was nothing but hypocrisy. *They*, by contrast, did not cover up what they really thought. They assumed their opinions. In fact, the expats said, they were perhaps the "least racist men on earth." They "loved" Africa and its people. They, at least, *did* something for them. Racism and sexism? That's just locker room talk—only men joking. Aren't we allowed to have some fun?

But still. Racism was a crack in the image CTI wanted to present of itself. And the articulations of race and desire were among those "uncontrolled and uncontrollable elements" that made for the ecstasis of rainforest logging (Fabian 2000, 87). Race was indeed an issue where the company was not in control and where its managers did not control themselves. As Achille Mbembe (2019, 133) observes, racism "produce[d] and redistribute[d] all sorts of miniaturized madnesses." Although, at first sight, racism seemed to create a reassuring sense of order and familiarity in a strange world—by assigning people to their "proper" places and thus "externalizing our loss of control" (Gilman 1985, 20)—it never succeeded. It only manufactured others who threatened to re-turn and destabilize the fragile self, hence, as Homi Bhabha (1994, 106) suggests, the need to compulsively *repeat* stereotypes so as to temporarily disavow their constant failure.

Yet the stubborn process of othering, or, as Stuart Hall (1997, 48) puts it, "the attempt to expel the other to the other side of the universe," was also "always compounded by the relationships of love and desire." Longing, identification, fascination, lust, and "mimetic yielding" indeed messed with the leaky divisions between self and other that came into being as they were anxiously defended (Mazzarella 2017, 5–7). As we have seen, European loggers effectively produced a racialized other as an anti-self but then reappropriated that "black" other as if it were a source of wild power to heal themselves from civilization whenever they posed as "forest whites" or "the last of their kind" in a long history of colonial violence (Taussig 1987). As such, strategies of self-exoticization created a "dark" drive within, which unsettled any clean oppositional logic that defined the "white self" by what the "black other" was *not* and vice versa.

As a deconstructing supplement, this interior darkness thus set in motion complex identifications, resonating with racist fantasies of blackness as "closer to nature" and of the black phallus as "an at once totally affirmative and transgressive force that no prohibition holds in check" (Mbembe 2019, 136). Such productive slippages between a constructed interior "darkness" and an imagined outside "blackness" reveal mimetic desires that complicated the libidinal economy between the expat quarters and the labor compounds. Expat self-making indeed entailed a process through which whiteness was reproduced in self-exoticizing confessions of a "dark" interior, which were set in a dialectic of competition and identification with imagined blackness. The CTI expats' attempts to outdo their workers' masculinity—through performances of toughness and sexual prowess or the disciplined practice of bodybuilding—as well as their occasional avowals of white insufficiency could barely hide a fascination for black masculinity. Largely unspoken desires "to be black" thereby coexisted with nervous affirmations of whiteness. As such, racism came across as a profoundly ambiguous mode of *attachment*—a slippery affair of love and hate, disgust and desire (Ahmed 2014). As a legacy of long and violent histories, racism produced an intimate double bind of mimesis and abjection. Identification and dis-identification.

The expats said they loved Congo but hated its people. Yet they *also* said they loved the people but hated the country. They were in both paradise and hell. They maintained they were not racist but also claimed the freedom *to be* racists. They valued whiteness over blackness, and blackness over whiteness. They found African women both highly attractive and repulsive. They thought their men both weak and strong. They upheld white authority while also engaging in contests of sexual blackface to temporarily embody a phantasmagoric masculinity and reaffirm their superiority. Expat discourses, practices, imaginations, and fantasies were full of contradictions.

How to prevent one from losing one's mind when things were never what they seemed or felt? Among the expat loggers, the carefully nurtured and, without a doubt, exaggerated darkness was certainly a strategy of power. But, at the same time, it also *undermined* ideologies of male autonomy and control—not least because it put into the open their ecstatic dependency on others. Perhaps this self-exoticization reveals an existential paradox of the human condition, what Judith Butler (2004, 137) calls "a self that is *ekstatically* involved in the Other, decentered through its identifications" (my emphasis). Perhaps this darkness suggests that we are all already "outside of ourselves [and] motivated by an elsewhere whose full meaning and purpose we cannot definitively establish" (15). Perhaps it translates the all-too-human realization that any membrane between "inside" and "outside"—"us" and "them"—is always porous and vulnerable. That the other is intimately *in*folded within the self—a process Lacan called "extimacy" (Miller 1994).

The affective world that rainforest logging brought into being strikingly amplified this ecstatic dimension of human existence. We have seen how for CTI expats—but also for many inhabitants of the labor compounds—the headlock between mimesis and alterity could push "oneself in a trajectory of desire in which one [was] *taken out* of oneself" (Butler 2004, 25; emphasis added). Yet, because ecstasis also allows the self to be "transformed through its encounter with alterity, not in order to return to itself, but to become a self it never was" (148), one would be justified in hoping that the ecstatic might equally contain *reparative* possibilities that allow for a coming together across racialized and class boundaries. In the conclusion, however, we will see how the constant repetition of stereotypes and the quotidian violence of racial fetishism largely prevented the emergence of more reparative and less paranoid relations between European and Congolese inhabitants of the CTI logging concession.

Two skidders at work

Conclusion
Capitalism and Ecstasis

But what would the colony be, if not a place where the European, freed not only of inhibitions but of any need to keep watch on his or her imagination, reveals his or her "other" self? What would the colony be, if no longer the site of sudden shouts, abrupt gestures, a place where time is abolished yet flows inexorably by, while the White man, besieged by a mob of Negroes, drowned in alcohol and stricken with fever, wonders, "Have I gone mad?" What would the colony be, if not a place where all sorts of mythical fabrications could be unleashed, the place of unbridled and crazy *delirium*?—Achille Mbembe, *On the Postcolony*

THE PREVIOUS CHAPTERS ILLUSTRATE how ecstasis in the CTI logging concession manifested in details of quotidian existence as well as in larger affective structures. From labor, political economy, and history, over everyday camp life and self-making, to the darker aspects of wealth, race, and sex, they show how rainforest capitalism produced an uncomfortable, ecstatogenic, and often violent world.

But how different was this world from Achille Mbembe's captivating lines on "the colony"? Was a certain "madness" not also palpable in CTI's practices of extraction as well as in the imaginaries, fantasies, and desires they triggered? Postcolonial studies have amply documented the multiple afterlives of empire and colonialism. Yet few have faced the lingering effects of colo-niality as a Fanonian factory of *madness* in today's racial capitalism.

While in this book multiple madnesses emerged in implicit as well as explicit terms, one cannot simply take "madness" for granted as a straight-forward descriptor of the reality it appears to denote. The very invocation of madness is itself part of what it describes. And the colonial obsession with "going mad" is nothing but an aspect of the very madness it brings into being—through self-diagnosis. How, then, to pay ethnographic attention to what this madness is and does without accepting its explanatory power but also without explaining it away as merely delusion? How to listen to what it has to say without reducing it to what we think we already know (Foucault 1961)? And how to do an anthropology of what it can*not* say?

Mbembe's rendering of the "colony" would certainly strike a chord among CTI's expat managers. They loved to depict their world in nostal-gically Conradian strokes. For them, the African postcolony was indeed a time capsule back into the heart of darkness. A place of delirium where only certain men could survive. Their often-repeated avowal that one needed to be "crazy" in order to endure the life they had chosen was a way of creating a mold of madness in which to refashion their selves. As we have seen, this craziness was part of a deliberate trick of self-exoticization—an old product of colonialism.

Can one therefore simply disqualify such "craziness" as misguided de-lusion? Or sanitize and rationalize it as a cunning strategy to save expat masculinity? Rather than explaining madness away, this book takes it as an index of broader affective currents of rainforest capitalism—that is, as an-other manifestation of *ecstasis*. The previous chapters have indeed illustrated how, in the CTI concession, ecstasis emerged from multiple angles and per-spectives as well as in different degrees. Self-avowed madness was only one of its forms.

Ecstasis was, for instance, visible when expat managers engaged in risky 4×4 racing on bumpy dirt roads. Or when one of them, in a choleric reac-tion against his own powerlessness, smashed up the interior of the bungalow he so painstakingly tried to make into a real home. Or when his colleague recited Conrad's mantra "The horror! The horror!" in an ironic performance of his own darkness. It was equally traceable in expat dreams of freedom and adventure, racist paranoia, sexual fantasies, mimetic structures, and a highly fetishized economy of desire. Or in European loggers' attempts to save their masculinity in a world they both loved and hated.

But ecstasis was also palpable among CTI workers and other camp inhabitants. In boredom, drinking, and deliberate troublemaking. In desires to seize flashes of opportunity. In the realization that imagined futures would always remain beyond reach and prospects deeply racialized. In frustrating experiences of stasis in the midst of frantic movement. In church services that announced the coming reversal of the world. In the relative freedom to escape village moralities and kinship obligations. In transgressive and risk-taking masculinities. In oneiric displacements, centrifugal homemaking, performances of dependency, and contested claims of autonomy. But, also, in experiences of danger on the work floor. When workers fought trees and destroyed their backs. And when they joked, played, sang, or dozed off in the forest.

Beyond the logging camps, ecstasis was perhaps more intermittent but not less notable. It was felt, for instance, when new opportunities for advancement and development slipped away. When intoxicated villagers set up roadblocks and police violently broke them up. When acts of sabotage triggered reactions that ran out of control. When fuel smugglers extracted energy from CTI and were celebrated for reestablishing some justice in a starkly unequal world. Or when regional rumors about white cannibalism and zombie labor reemerged in a landscape scattered with traces of past extraction.

These examples show a broad range of phenomena. It has not been this book's intention to smother their differences under the weight of one overarching concept. But the notion of ecstasis offered a way to think (and feel) how extraction unleashed desires, affects, memories, mobilities, and expectations that derailed CTI's carefully elaborated policies and rational planning. Rather than an enclave disconnected from its surroundings, the concession was a vulnerable actor, itself obliged to *make concessions* to material, discursive, and affective forces beyond its control. It was a place entangled in regional histories and moral economies that frustratingly curtailed its room for maneuver, and where, in the wake of a global financial crisis, logging produced frantic accelerations, potential violence, unpredictability, opacity, and nervous possibilities that generated a particular atmosphere that deeply affected the company—and those who had to live with its activities.

As noted in the introduction, the concept of ecstasis, with which to think these circulating affects, was drawn primarily from *Out of Our Minds* (2000), Johannes Fabian's remarkable study of reason and madness in the colonial exploration of the Congo Basin. Rather than coin its "own" concept and make the expected academic gesture of inventing yet another newish metaphor as a token of originality, *Rainforest Capitalism* reads, transmits, and transforms Fabian's concept—which was never entirely his to start with. Cherishing the queer genealogies by which ideas become inheritances, this book is therefore deeply indebted to Fabian—and not merely to his earlier and better-known critique of ethnographic knowledge production (Fabian 1983).

Yet, in the end, ecstasis was nothing but a device for crafting a true story. Other devices were of course possible. Moreover, ecstasis was not always and everywhere present. This book is by no means a definitive account of industrial rainforest logging, but it is a necessary one. Strategically forwarding Fabian's concept from early colonialism to the first decades of the twenty-first century, it extends the heuristic productivity of ecstasis. This concluding chapter takes stock of the accumulated ethnographic material and invites the reflection on rainforest capitalism to go a little further. It thereby shows how and why the idea of ecstasis does not negate the actual powers of extractive industries or corporations, but rather proposes *a different relationship to power*.

This chapter first returns to Fabian's original conceptualization of ecstasis and shifts his primarily epistemological analysis to a more existential perspective so as to propose ecstasis as a non-romanticized commonality from which to think the human condition. The next section compares ecstasis with what Nancy Rose Hunt calls "nervousness" and rethinks its relationship with power and control. The final section suggests a way of studying capitalism that approaches corporate power from situations of vulnerability. Opening up the idea of weakness, it refuses the masculinist gold standard of "strength" in critical analysis and proposes to think capitalism differently— beyond its supposedly totalizing reach and mastery and through the more fragile, uncontrollable, and queer productivity of ecstasis.

Tricky Common Ground

When studying places like rainforest logging concessions, one can be struck by their uncanny similarities with earlier modes of extraction. The contemporary moment of neoliberal capitalism effectively seems a partial return to a pre-paternalist age of "old-style laissez-faire liberalism" (Ferguson 2010, 173). As we have seen, CTI indeed tried (but largely failed) to *disentangle* itself from social responsibilities and moral economies. It operated in a strange mixture of frontier fantasies, development speak, corporate social responsibility, fend-for-yourself neoliberalism, and ghostly reminders of modernist ideologies and bourgeois worker domesticity. As a reappearance of multiple pasts in the present, CTI messed up linear temporalities, replaying Conradian tunes of madness in the afterlives of empire, paternalism, decolonization, and postcolonial authoritarianism.

For this reason, picking up Fabian's notion of ecstasis was helpful to approach a contemporary world that is both similar and different to an earlier epoch. In *Out of Our Minds*, Fabian indeed unpacks the issue of madness at the center of colonial reason and proposes ecstasis as a concept for tackling the apparent irrationality of imperial exploration. Without thereby reproducing old stereotypes of explorers as victims of their own madness, Fabian shows how they "frequently overcame [their] intellectual and existential problems by *stepping outside*, and sometimes existing for long periods outside, the rationalized frames of exploration" (8; emphasis added). Yet, as historians of empire have shown, the "inherently contradictory" and "anarchic" nature of colonial encounters had to be anxiously "concealed or, better, negated by projecting to the world images of a purposeful *oeuvre civilisatrice*" (4). By deliberately foregrounding ecstasis within the imperial project, Fabian therefore calls for a "radical critique [of] the very concept of rationality [itself and] especially the built-in tendency of that concept to present itself as outside and above historical contexts" (4).

Fabian however insists that ecstasis is *not* simply "nonrational, erratic, escapist [or] enthusiastic behavior" (8). In his nontrivial understanding of the term, ecstasis is rather "a dimension or quality of human action and interaction—one that creates a common ground for encounters" (8). As such, he explicitly redefines ecstasis as an *epistemological* rather than a psychological concept: "a 'condition of possibility' for the meetings between Europeans and Africans to result in anything more than physical collision" (8). Moreover, as he sees it, ecstasis is not only inevitable but also a "prerequisite for, rather than an impediment to, the production of ethnographic knowledge" (8).

Whereas *Out of Our Minds* restricts itself to the archival study of European explorers and their writings, our fieldwork suggests that, in the CTI concession, ecstasis was not limited to the lives of its expat managers. It was equally—but differently—present in labor compounds and neighboring villages. To account for its multiple manifestations, this book therefore had to broaden its reach. It proposed ecstasis not only as an inherent dimension of human *interaction* but also as a slumbering potential of human *existence*, activated in all kinds of situations when people are confronted with their limits, realize their capture, and try to take back control. Ecstasis thereby turned from an epistemological notion into a more existential one. As such, rather than formulate a radical *critique* of knowledge production, *Rainforest Capitalism* provides a more *post*critical exploration of the affective circuits of power and vulnerability.[1]

The introduction already defined this broadened notion of ecstasis as a name for complex feelings of vulnerability, penetrability, and relative impotence in the face of larger forces, structures, and histories, as well as for the frustration, anger, and resistance these generate. While the Greek *ékstasis* is usually translated as rapture or trance, this redefinition extended the concept beyond publicly visible forms and spectacular moments of frenzy and included less spectacular and more mundane waves, lingering moods, and pervasive emotions that, as the word implies, make one "step outside oneself." From this broadened perspective, ecstasis became a useful tool to write about the world that rainforest logging brought into being, as it allowed for particular stories but also for a broader tale on the human condition.

Having gone through its ethnographic illustration, what should we now make of the concept of ecstasis? What did it allow for? And where were its dangers and limitations? The notion of ecstasis was especially helpful to realize the surprising *commonality* of feelings that pushed otherwise differentiated people together. Strikingly similar moods, affects, and atmospheres indeed infected the lives of workers, expat managers, job seekers, smugglers, villagers, and the odd anthropologist. Despite otherwise diverging perspectives, interests, projects, and moral evaluations, something quite similar was felt and talked about, though rarely adequately worded and often beyond linguistic expression, something that stitched us all into a common fabric and created "a common ground for encounters" (Fabian 2000, 8).

In the previous pages, ecstasis effectively emerged as that which seemed to hold in common otherwise different worlds. In the midst of the opacities, uncertainties, sudden possibilities, and disappointments of rainforest logging, ecstasis was the spectacular as well as mundane manifestation of a largely shared "economy of affect"—a shimmering power grid of contagious currents (Ahmed 2004). At the same time, ecstasis was also a strategy for *approaching* that commonality; not exactly as a "method," but as the existential ground from which we all started attempts to make sense of each other. As such, it became a heuristic device for describing the "co-constitution of worlds where before we saw separate populations, dynamics and problematics" (Povinelli 2006, 19).

Ecstasis is therefore both the condition of possibility and the explicit topic of this book. It was both *what* was held in common and the very *ground* for approaching this commonality—a recursive ambivalence that turned out to be ethnographically productive. But although ecstasis stitched worlds together beyond their differences and power differentials, it did not fuse them into one. Ecstasis is not so much an intersubjective merging of perspectives as it is the mutual recognition of limitation and impossibility as a temporary common ground from which communication takes off and meanings are forged. And it is primarily in this negative way that it allows us to feel and think *with* (rather than merely about) others.

While Fabian (2000, 279) holds on to a rather optimistic and explicitly "utopian" view on the potential of ecstasis to lead to a "meeting of the West and Africa on equal terms," our fieldwork suggests a less rosy reality. Although ecstasis was actively performed and maintained in both expat living quarters and labor compounds in order to make life in the concession possible, this surprising commonality was not therefore an avenue for transcending racist prejudices or enabling communication beyond mutual misunderstandings. On the contrary, it was often in ecstatic moments that racist stereotypes were intensified. When Congolese and Europeans came together—for instance, when expats screamed at workers or when intoxicated villagers threatened Europeans—ecstatic moments were scenes of violence rather than motors of commonality. As such, the circulation of affects and moods did not undermine the racial segregation that structured everyday life. While ecstasis produced "constitutive resonances" and "congruent imaginaries," it also reproduced racism, violence, and misogyny (Bernault 2019).

It is therefore important not to romanticize ecstasis as a guarantee to resolve differences and reach common understanding. Infectious moods and contagious feelings do not automatically produce a single space of shared experience and imagination (Ahmed 2014). Ecstasis equally generates mutual *mis*understandings and distorted reflections "where assumed meanings [meet] with assumed meanings to form strange codependencies" (Taussig 1987, 109). While ecstatic processes take us "outside of ourselves" and suggest the possibility that we are always already other than what we are, there is no guarantee that they will repair the paranoid production and reduction of otherness (Hage 2012). As our fieldwork suggests, ecstasis might as easily lead to a proliferation of racialized stereotypes and fetishized essences in which selves attract and reject others in intimate choreographies of difference and desire.

Neither should we exoticize the notion of ecstasis as a mystic journey to knowledge for hero-anthropologists who are able to get "out of their minds" and yet somehow return from "going native" (Fabian 2000, 281).

It is rather an *ordinary* aspect of human existence in circumstances where people—deliberately or by accident, consciously or unconsciously—step outside the very ordinariness of life itself. Ecstasis is not and should not be the overt aim of fieldwork. But it allows the ethnographer to reproduce moments, moods, events, rumors, and stories without assuming or taking control. It allows one to write while recognizing how much "they" have taken us in and how much "we" are "from the start, and by virtue of being a bodily being, already given over, beyond ourselves, implicated in lives that are not our own" (Butler 2004, 22).

Power and Control

To understand the significance of ecstasis, we need to investigate in some more detail its relationship to power. Given the ethnographic material presented in the previous pages, how should we see the relationship between power and ecstasis in the context of extractive capitalism?

To some extent, ecstasis resembles what Nancy Rose Hunt calls the "nervousness" of power (Hunt 2016). In her vibrantly written account of violence and affect in the Congo Free State and later Belgian Congo, Hunt indeed argues that one cannot understand colonial power without grasping its *nervous* dimension. She thereby qualifies the colonial state as a "nervous state" that was characterized by a "fearful, jumpy mode of presence" as it was "edgy, agitated, restless, [and] grew more paranoid with time" (8). This nervousness, she argues—"a kind of energy, taut and excitable" (5)—not only characterized colonial interventions but also infiltrated among colonial subjects, as it sparked insurgencies and healing movements.[2] Focusing on the larger rainforest area in which CTI would later come to operate, Hunt describes how "tension, edginess, and volatility were pervasive in colonial Equateur, where rubber bonuses once fed terrible, nervous excess" (6).

At the time of our fieldwork, such nervousness again seemed to characterize natural resource extraction in the Itimbiri region as an effect of a volatile export economy. CTI indeed operated on the verge of failure and continued its production as long as doing so was less costly than simply shutting down. As timber prices increased after the 2008 financial crisis, the company frantically tried to accelerate its activities, though roadblocks, a regional traffic in stolen company fuel, and exceptionally long periods of rainfall frequently brought logging to a standstill. In this context, expat managers were often "on edge with suspicion, paranoia, insomnia, and nightmares" (Hunt 2016, 235). But nervous feelings also infected their workers, as they tried to keep their jobs, worried about the future, and negotiated the rhythm of camp life with its long stretches of boredom mixed with sudden possibilities. And nervousness equally affected village politics, wherein logging fueled old suspicions about white cannibalism and people grew anxious about missing another opportunity to benefit from CTI's uncertain presence.

One might therefore recalibrate much of what this book has illustrated through the parallel framework of *nervousness*. Hunt's work indeed shows that nervous feelings have a long, troubling, and unfinished history in the Congolese rainforest. Yet nervousness is not entirely the same as ecstasis. The first entails a certain alertness, whereas the second denotes a loss of control. Nervousness is also a more or less conscious feeling, while ecstasis is a less conscious movement that leads one outside of oneself. And although they might be conceptualized as kindred states on a spectrum, we have redefined the ecstatic in a broad way so as to account for the multiple feelings it generates—some of which might very well resemble nervousness while others do not.

Hunt's account of colonial affects nevertheless helps us think the complex relationship between power and ecstasis. Hunt indeed explicitly conceptualizes nervousness as the *other* side of the biopolitical rationality of state power. She (2016, 5) thereby notes how nervousness combines "vigor, force and determination with excitation, weakness, timidity." In a similar vein, Fabian's ecstasis nervously shifts between agency and impotence, autonomy and anxiety, feelings of grandeur and frustration. Both nervousness and ecstasis should therefore be recognized as related aspects of—and supplements to—power.

Rather than opposites, power and ecstasis are indeed intimately related. In fact, ecstasis cannot exist *but* in relation to larger forces that are conjured up and experienced in mundane as well as spectacular forms—powers to which the ecstatic subject is bound and subjected but also engaged in desperate revolt against. As such, ecstasis seems to create what it rebels against: a force, a situation, a milieu that overpowers the individual. Rather than fixate power as the taken for granted "attribute" of the always already powerful logging company, the *dialectic* of power and ecstasis allows for a more dynamic analysis, which accounts for the drama of human existence as it tries to control the world and must recognize its failure in doing so (Jackson 2005).

For the European loggers, this dialectic between power and ecstasis—of being "in" and "out" of control—was part of a broader liberal ideology, with its strong dichotomy between freedom and constraint. CTI expats indeed liked to present themselves as determin*ing* rather than determined agents who believed in their "ability to control the world" (Ouroussoff 1993, 293). At the same time, they also avowed to feeling "lost" and taken over by conditions beyond their control. Telling stories about how "impossible" it was to get things done thereby set the scene for a tough lumberjack masculinity that enabled them to transform failure and vulnerability into a self-described strength to face circumstances that might otherwise drive one mad. Yet anxious performances of toughness also remained an index of their own impotence (Henriet 2021). And attempts to *take back* control often produced further slippage.

A similar dialectic of power and ecstasis was palpable among inhabitants of the labor compounds. The previous chapters show how CTI workers alternated between claims of dependency and declarations of independence. How youngsters stirred up trouble in order to produce agency in a world where they felt immobilized. How men aspired autonomy yet refused the frustrating responsibilities of adulthood through performances of transgression. How brittle forms of status were dependent on the recognition of others and the avoidance of derision. And how the power that people accumulated—occultly or otherwise—always stood "on fragile, and temporary, foundations" (Ferme 2001, 6).

Hence, when thought from the logging concession, ecstasis is not an "alternative" to power—it *is* power, but in a different mode. Describing how CTI failed to control the environment in which it got itself entangled is not to downplay its sometimes violent activities on the ground, but rather to approach them as symptoms of the ecstatic nature of corporate power. Strategically foregrounding the ecstasis of rainforest logging does not deny, ignore, or minimize CTI's power to cut trees, build roads, impose deadlines, exploit workers, or break roadblocks by force. It rather shows how the company had to—and was often able to—make money *without* assuming a position of total control.

Moreover, the previous chapters equally suggest how power itself might already be ecstatogenic. Concession inhabitants indeed knew very well that the apparently powerful expat loggers were consumed by the same occult forces that enabled their power. And that one could not assume control without some form of payment. Power was never in control of itself, and no one seemed to control the powers they had acquired. Nothing would be easier than to tell the story of industrial rainforest logging as one of rational resource extraction and management, of large-scale control over space and time, of the violent commodification of nature or the imposition of a global capitalist system to the detriment of local people. But such stories would overlook the messy entanglements we have followed as well as underestimate the ecstatic dynamic of corporate power, at least in certain milieus and conjunctures. Recognizing the importance of ecstasis is a way to trouble such clean stories.

Foregrounding ecstasis is thus a way to undo what William Mazzarella (2017, 167) calls the usual "opposition between capture (power) and escape (resistance)." Ecstasis does not promise any freedom *from* power—it is essential *to* power and its captivating magic. From its perspective, the problem is "that too many analyses of power and ideology are set up as a zero-sum game between agents of domination that are bent on co-opting us completely and heroically resistant subjects whose complex interiorities and intentions will always elude full capture" (167). Our fieldwork showed more complex realities. In chapter 7, for instance, we encountered a very different zero-sum game in popular political theories that rendered the occult as an ordinary dimension of power. Their vernacular analytic was not so much a game of power versus resistance, but an *ecology of eating relations* in which we were all captured as participants—and thus "all vulnerable, but not equally so" (Povinelli 2006, 73). Their zero-sum dimension implied that all possible gains over here equaled losses over there. As such, it posed the question of a *fair distribution* of gains and losses rather than the possibility of any heroic "outside" to power. And it made for a politics in which what makes one strong is also what makes one weak.

A Weak Theory

Whereas CTI generally presented its activities as rational exercises in planning, mapping, and auditing, ecstasis enables us to see how it was actually confronted with stubborn realities that could be said to "control the [company] rather than the other way around" (Fabian 2000, 42): roadblocks and angry villagers, stolen company fuel and kaddafi smugglers, specters of political instability and company closure, nervous possibilities to make money; choleric outbursts, blunt racism, misogyny and logger machismo; boredom, drinking, masculine bravura, drugs and daydreaming, uncanny attempts to create a home in temporary labor camps and expat bungalows; stress, frustration, depression, fear, self-destruction, paranoia and delusions; lofty development ambitions, rumors of occult accumulation and popular critiques of exploitation; the impossibility of oversight and control in the forest; sudden eruptions of violence and overzealous attempts to take back control; a highly fetishized erotic economy of interracial desires and its unexpectedly queer pathways.

All of this troubles the idea of forestry as a rational endeavor. While trees *were* of course logged, and money *was* made, production was not the outcome of an ordered management process. It was rather experienced and perceived as the always-vulnerable, almost magical result of a continuous fight against uncertainty and opacity. Given its many faces, forms, and dimensions, how should we therefore think the relationship between ecstasis and extractive capitalism? And, first of all, at what level?

While the previous chapters illustrated the surprising commonality of ecstasis at the level of individual and collective experiences, thoughts, and feelings, they do not automatically imply ecstasis at higher levels. As usual, anthropology is confronted with a problem of *scale*. At what scale should we think ecstasis? And can we simply scale up from ecstatic individuals to higher level entities—such as the camp, the concession, the corporation, the logging sector, resource extraction, capitalism, the global economy, or even the human condition? The scale of our analysis immediately affects our critical capacities and political investments. As Gabrielle Hecht (2018, 114) notes, scale is "about categories: what they reveal or hide, the ways in which they do (or do not) nest. And it is about orientation: how we position ourselves, what we position ourselves against, and what comparisons such locations do (or do not) authorize."

Contemporary ethnography frequently finds itself working on "awkward" scales (Comaroff and Comaroff 2003). While we should think twice before *jumping* scale—especially if we aim for higher level causes behind lower level effects—scales cannot be easily kept apart or neatly separated. They are fictions of our own analysis that carve up messy realities. One way to deal with this challenge is to realize the fractal nature of our problematics and track "partial connections" between them (Strathern 2004). Ecstasis would then reappear at whatever scale we position ourselves. Another way is to follow our interlocutors when *they* assume the existence of scales so that scales become outcomes of concrete projects and processes of scale-making (Tsing 2000).

If ecstasis thereby becomes the effect or property of a *system*, it is important to acknowledge that this system is itself the outcome of an ecstatic process whereby individuals create a higher level reality in the act of conceding to and/or resisting it. Yet, at the same time, ecstasis remains notoriously difficult to track as a mood or atmosphere. Its causes remain opaque. Our interlocutors often blamed the "world," the "economy," the "conjuncture," "racism," "poverty," or "solitude" for what this book describes as ecstatic behavior. Its relationship to capitalism is thereby suggested rather than demonstrated.

One should therefore keep in mind that, although ecstasis seemed to run through industrial logging as a "nervous system," it is not therefore the "true" nature of capitalism (Taussig 1992). Ecstasis is not a hidden secret we can only discover by digging deep. Nor is it what we find upon penetrating into what Marx (1990, 279–80) called "the hidden abode of production on whose threshold there hangs the notice 'No admittance except on business.'" While this book is obviously affected by popular modes of paranoid hermeneutics that perceive hidden forces behind the surface of things—whether it be workers and villagers suspecting occult realities beneath the visible world or European expats perceiving conspiracy or hypocrisy behind Congolese performances of gratitude—ecstasis operated very much at skin level, electrifying life in flashing moments.

As an ethnography of logging-in-action, *Rainforest Capitalism* is therefore not so much invested in opening up the black box of industrial timber production and finding out what *really* goes on inside. On the contrary, ecstasis is a highly visible and visceral economy of affect, operating at the very surface of everyday life. Ecstasis is not another master concept for explaining capitalism by laying bare its carefully hidden irrationality. It denotes an affective economy with a long history of sticky feelings that were reproduced in and through industrial logging (Ahmed 2014). Rather than the end product—the aha! moment—of ethnography, it has slowly grown into a heuristic device affected by what people say and do. A tool for writing about the intimacies of power and the affective life of dependency. A way to describe how powers were both productive *and* possessive: how they possessed people while enabling agency and how they contained possibilities as well as excess.

Too slippery to be grabbed by the throat, ecstasis cannot be easily held in place so as to fully describe its characteristics. As an analytic concept, it is akin to what Eve Sedgwick (2003) and Kathleen Stewart (2008) have called "weak theory." It "comes unstuck from its own line of thought to follow the objects it encounters, or becomes undone by its attention to things that don't just add up but take on a life of their own as problems for thought" (Stewart 2008, 72). As we tracked its manifestations and effects in the CTI concession, the idea of ecstasis indeed accumulated meanings that enriched its tentative definition. Some might see this as a weakness. Perhaps it is. But rather than force the concept of ecstasis to become stronger than what it tries to describe, we need to allow for it to respect the multiplicity of what it encounters.

Yet ecstasis is also a weak concept in the sense of a "reparative" antidote to dominant scholarly practices of paranoid reading that so often produce "strong" theory (Sedgwick 2003, 133). While ecstasis is a writing device that has to repeat and replicate what it tries to understand—in the sense that thinking about ecstasis cannot avoid becoming ecstatic thinking—the deliberate weakening of ecstasis as a theory is a way to protect this text from the paranoid stories it cannot but retell. "Traced through the generative modalities of impulses, daydreams, ways of relating, distractions, strategies, failures, encounters, and worldings of all kinds" (Stewart 2008, 73), ecstatic theory is theory that lives with its own weaknesses in the paranoid search for forces, systems, and explanations.

Third, ecstasis is also a weak theory inasmuch as it refuses to hold its object accountable for the strength it seems to lack. The discovery of ecstasis at the heart of capitalism is not an accusation that the latter is, in reality, not as strong as it pretends to be, as if the explicit foregrounding of ecstatic dynamics in an ethnographic account of extraction would be a warlike move intending to deflate the power of capitalism by unveiling the weaknesses it tries to cover up. It is indeed important to realize that the choice to tell the story of CTI as a vulnerable rather than powerful actor—and mapping the fears, desires, and excesses that drove its managers "out of their minds"—can easily become another strategy for identifying the failures and blind spots within capitalism as a system we set out to oppose.

The latter is a well-known tactic among critical scholars. In *The End of Capitalism (As We Knew It)*, for instance, J. K. Gibson-Graham (1996, xxiv) explicitly aims to "cut capitalism down to size (theoretically) and refuse to endow it with excessive power." These scholars indeed strive to "disarm and dislocate the naturalized dominance of the capitalist economy" and to refuse the ways in which, in anticapitalist writings, capitalist globalization often implicitly figures as a kind of "rape" whereby multinational corporations "penetrate" non (or not yet) capitalist spaces so as to impose their will (xii). Companies are thereby inevitably thought to behave "like the man of the rape script . . . inherently strong and powerful" (127). Given such widespread metaphors and images, they provocatively ask, how can we "get globalization to lose its erection?" (127). In other words, how to emasculate capitalism?

This book owes a great deal to such feminist critiques of capitalism—especially when it comes to realizing that anticapitalist politics is, more often than not, emotionally invested in the idea of a strong and phallic capitalist monster we love to hate. But, at the same time, I do not think that foregrounding the ecstasis of capitalism is only a big punch in the balls.[3] As long as one prevents ecstasis from growing into a "strong" theory, the strategic illustration of weakness, failure, excess, and madness within capitalism is not necessarily an emasculating gesture. Neither is it a complaint about phallic power not being powerful enough. Dwelling in and on ecstatic dynamics within industrial logging is not a way of simply trying to reveal that, in reality, power was never as powerful as it pretended to be—or to hold the logging company accountable for weaknesses it failed to cover up. On the contrary, as weak theory, ecstasis deliberately *refuses strength* as a standard. In this way, it builds on but also goes beyond feminist analyses of capitalism that either deliberately weaken its power or reconfirm its strength by attributing its surprising resilience to its makeshift and heterogeneous character (Bear at al. 2015).

For the same reason, the previous chapters substantially differ, for instance, from Alex Golub's (2014, 207) call for a strong and courageous ethnography of big corporations that is not "overawed" by them or "trembles at their sights, but . . . ready, willing, and able to sport with leviathans." Golub indeed describes his account of a mining corporation in Papua New Guinea as the "thoroughgoing and self-confident decomposition of the beast back into its constituent networks" (206). Our project is less Olympian. Ecstasis is not so much a powerful tool with which to *critique* capitalism as it is a weak concept that does not rejoice in its castrating powers. Rather than hold CTI and its managers accountable for not living up to standards of masculinity, it searches for oblique departures and possibilities to deal with powers in all their fragility. A queering move, perhaps, rather than an emasculating one.

The previous pages indeed slowly cultivated a queer mode of attention that lingered at both CTI's fragility and its heroic machismo. *Queer* thereby needs to be understood more capaciously than as a simple synonym for the nonheterosexual or the antinormative.[4] Queer is rather an orientation to what lies beyond the binary of strength versus weakness. Although the explicit foregrounding of ecstasis obviously troubles the phallic mastery of timber companies, it does not play out vulnerability or penetrability as a weakness in an ideology of strength (see also Butler, Gambetti and Sabsay 2016). It enables a different relationship *with* power—rather than against it. And it supplements opposition with engagement, resistance with reparation. Telling and retelling stories of ecstasis alongside and through tales of power do not therefore intend to break the spell of capitalism. If, as Philippe

Pignarre and Isabelle Stengers (2005, 93) suggest, capitalism is akin to a system of witchcraft that captures us all, the aim is not to free oneself from its hegemonic reach in order to think outside it. It requires practices of protection *from within* rather than from without—loosening, deflecting, and redoing rather than undoing its spell.

In contemporary Congo, Pentecostal ideologies and imaginaries often depict the protection from witchcraft as part of a Manichean fight of God against Satan. And yet, as discussed in chapter 7, many Central African therapeutics teach us that in order to reroute witchcraft one actually needs to play along. Healing and witchcraft use the same forces and techniques but to different ends. Both partake in an ecstatic game of power where no one is permanently in control. The reality of witchcraft requires one to live *with* one's witches, as an ongoing pragmatic exercise of maintaining a precarious balance between production and destruction, life and death. In a similar way, the inhabitants of the CTI concession were not trying to do *without* the logging company or capitalism, but *with* them—though differently. Learning from them, this book therefore proposes a postcritical analysis of extractive capitalism that explores ways of living with its violence.

Dealing with extractive capitalism was really about negotiating and trading with its powers. "Like all pragmatics," such "commerce requires confidence, not in the other but in the relationship that is made possible" (Pignarre and Stengers 2005, 159; my translation). It is primarily in this sense that recognizing ecstasis allows for thinking and doing capitalism differently, without harboring any "illusions about the work theory does in the world" (Appel 2019a, 282). Approaching capitalism not as an all-powerful machine monolithically imposing its will wherever it operates, but as a "nervous system" in which we all partake—especially when we try to trap its powers and redirect them elsewhere (Taussig 1992). The *ur*-paranoid suspicion that we are all "always already" part of what we wish to undo contains reparative possibilities as a result of the commonality and intimacy it presupposes. Indeed, as Mbembe (2019, 142) writes about Fanonian politics, "every authentic act of curing presumes the reconstitution . . . of something that is common to us."

Because ecstasis shows how and why playing-with-power always somehow implies forsaking control, it allows for imagining alternative arrangements based on the humble recognition that we all happen to find ourselves, for shorter or longer periods, "out of our minds." Perhaps it might thereby inspire alternative tactics and strategies for those of us who deal with multinational corporations, sometimes to better resist and fight and sometimes to come to pragmatic deals, awkward alliances, temporary deviations, or new attachments.

This book ultimately had to *trade* with ecstasis. And, like all trading and dealmaking, it was not without risks. Textually foregrounding ecstasis can open up possibilities for thinking them anew. But it can also bind us even more to the uncontrollable powers we ecstatically evoke and reproduce. As such, it raises the methodological and epistemological issue of *complicity*. During our fieldwork, ecstasis stubbornly imposed itself in different forms. But what if the central place of ecstasis in these chapters is the result of taking CTI managers all too seriously? What if my weak theory of ecstasis is complicit in expat self-representations I uncritically repeat? Even more, what if the white loggers' confessions to "lose control" were a deliberate strategy to cover up their real powers? Companies are indeed not unknown to tactically present themselves as vulnerable when it is in their interest to do so (for instance, when lobbying for fiscal exemptions or special protections).

In other words, what if ecstasis were only a cunning company performance? It should be noted that such questions—though legitimate—reproduce the paranoid stance of critical analysis this book has tried to supplement with a more generous postcritical attitude. Even without considering the impossibility of separating the *real* from the merely *performed*—or pointing at the always performative nature of social life—do we not, in the end, need to "believe" our interlocutors if we want them to believe us? Such an ethnographic attitude does not imply blind naivety. Neither does "the collapse of critical distance" necessarily lead to "unscrutinized belief" (Robbins 2017, 374). It rather enables new possibilities for thinking and acting (Pandian and McLean 2017). Ethnography is such a slow method because it takes time for deliberate misrepresentations to become disentangled. As they untie, they give rise to new tricks but also to a precarious reality that slowly grows as it is coproduced with others. Such is the poiesis of fieldwork.

Ecstasis was a name for this growing reality. For this structure of feeling and affective atmosphere from where thinking grew and to which it returned. Ecstasis triggered participation during fieldwork, as it produced "moments of freedom, abandonment and surrender" (Fabian 2000, 278). But it also imposed itself in writing, as it could only be re-presented by extending the dynamics it inherited—albeit in a different and seemingly calmer form. As such, ecstasis never tires to foreclose any position of sanity or rationality from where one can pretend to see things "as they are" and from where to simply denounce ecstasis as the ultimate madness of a capitalist system. Such is the risk of a postcritical anthropology that takes people seriously when "out of their minds" and thinks and writes with their words and actions (Jensen 2014). But such is also the *promise* of conceding to ecstasis: "it makes us vulnerable to violence, but also to another range of touch" (Butler 2004, 23).

———————

While writing this book, an extended and reworked notion of ecstasis turned out to be a fertile concept for understanding the affective world of industrial logging in the north of the Congolese rainforest. Perhaps it can also be of use in other analyses of extractive capitalism. Drawn from Fabian, refracted through ethnographic particulars, rubbed alongside postcolonial, feminist, and queer theory, confronted with Central African diagnostics and therapeutics, and supplemented with a postcritical attitude, ecstasis can tell us something else and something more about extraction. About how life itself is already extractive because it depends on multiple outsides. And about how we might try to live with its inherent violence.

Workers posing with a truck

EPILOGUE

It was only when Filip, my doctoral supervisor, came to visit me from Belgium that Michel, the French forest overseer, finally found the courage to join us for drinks in the labor camp. I had often encouraged Michel to come and see Freddy and me in our new house. But although he repeatedly promised that he would visit us, he had never done so. Most evenings we saw only his jeep speeding by. Sometimes he blew the horn. Rarely did he stop for a brief chat. But he never came out of his vehicle. He only spoke a few words, while hanging out of his car window.

Great was our surprise, therefore, when late that afternoon Michel parked his jeep on the side of the main forest camp avenue, closed the door, and walked toward us. "Gentlemen, can I join you?" he asked, smiling.

Of course, he could. Filip had just bought us some beers, and we were chatting around a small table: Freddy; our two housemates, Patrick and Xavier; Doris, a bulldozer driver; and Benjamin, a fuel smuggler and occasional day worker. Monique, Freddy's fiancée, was talking to one of our neighbors in the kitchen.

When Michel arrived, he stood still for a few seconds, unsure what to do. Doris got up to offer him his plastic chair. "Please *patron* have a seat," he said.

He then called one of the boys who had assembled to see what was happening. "Quickly! Go and fetch a cold Turbo King beer for *monsieur*," he commanded. He gave the boy five hundred francs. "Tell André [the forest engineer] that I will pay the rest later," he added—more quietly this time.

"Oh, that's really not necessary," Michel replied. But Doris insisted. Never before had he shared a drink with one of his white bosses.

Waiting for the beer, our joking and gossiping died out. Doris tried to make some conversation, but Michel was visibly out of his comfort zone. Even Freddy, who was usually so apt at small talk, could not unfreeze the situation.

"Do you often visit Thomas while he's here in the camp?" Filip finally asked. It only made things worse.

Luckily, the boy soon arrived with a large brown bottle of beer. "It's not cold though," he whispered. Doris took the bottle and lifted the cap with his teeth. "That's how we do things in the forest," he laughed. He then decided to nonetheless wipe the bottle neck clean with his sleeve.

"Monique, bring us a glass," Freddy shouted to the back of the parcel. But Michel told us not to worry. In a couple of gulps, he drank half of the bottle. "Nice fieldwork," he winked. Another long silence.

Michel put the beer on the table. "I think I must be going," he said. And before we knew it, he was back on his feet, mumbled an excuse, went to his jeep, and drove back home. It left us all perplexed.

A week later, Michel told me he had actually wanted to stay but did not see how he could. I was glad he thought he could say such things to me. It was both touching and sad to hear a man his age and experience express such inaptitude at having, what he called, "normal relations" with people among whom he spent most of his adult life. I confessed to him that, although I was supposed to be an anthropologist, I also often felt awkward.

Michel and I *did* drink together. But always at his house, on the terrace of his bungalow, a place of safe conventions for a self-declared libertarian who had initially come to the rainforest to get away from all conventionality.

Johannes Fabian (2000, 69) writes that alcohol was one of the main ecstatic elements that encouraged European explorers to transcend psychological, social, and cultural boundaries, insisting on its capacity to foster "communication relatively free of the exercise of power and control." He also speculates about "moments of truth" and the "unguarded meeting of minds" when Africans and Europeans "enjoyed drinking together" (74). Yet he also recognizes that such moments were always "rare and short" (74) and that "sacrifices for the comforts of conformity too often and too quickly replaced the gains in freedom and insight travelers made when they went beyond themselves in the field" (253).

Again, it was eerie to read these lines during my fieldwork. As if nothing had changed. The tiniest details of quotidian life propelled me back and forth between the early days of imperial exploration and the contemporary realities of extractive capitalism in the Congolese rainforest.

But Michel's brief visit, no matter how awkward, had broken an unwritten rule of segregated leisure. As such, it contained the seeds of another world. A possibility that was already there. This book is the stubbornly hopeful product of a long encounter with violence and injustice that is itself part of the ecstatic world of logging it describes. And part of what that world can become.

Main road into the logging concession

NOTES

INTRODUCTION

1. Over the past few decades, critique has come under significant pressure. Bruno Latour (2004) notoriously argued that it has "run out of steam." In anthropology, scholars such as Talal Asad and Saba Mahmood have investigated alternatives to the Eurocentric bias of critique as a modern genre and disposition (Asad et al. 2013). In queer studies, Eve Sedgwick's (2003) search for "reparative reading" has continued to inspire postcritical experiments. And, in the humanities, the broader turn toward *affect* partially overlaps with the turn away from critique.

2. In their analysis of an apparent postcritical turn in recent ethnographic studies of elites, Paul Gilbert and Jessica Sklair (2018, 2) question the ways in which some anthropologists have come to see "critique as an anti-ethnographic move that *curtails* one's ability to . . . produce sensitive, rich ethnographic work." They rightfully reject the view that critique automatically implies a distance from one's participants or that ethnographic intimacy forecloses the possibility of critique. Yet Gilbert and Sklair all too easily deny the progressive potential of postcritical experiments that do not seem to fit into their idea of class analysis and political economy as "good" politics. If anything, this book shows how Marxist and postcritical dispositions *can* go together.

3. In her superb ethnography of offshore oil production in Equatorial Guinea, Hannah Appel (2019a) makes a similar argument but stops short of calling for a postcritical ethos in the anthropology of capitalism. Indeed, rather than try to deconstruct capitalist fictions and show the real-life contingency and complexity they try to cover up, Appel takes the as ifs of capitalism as her ethnographic objects and tracks the ways in which they become real. As such, she admirably shows how and why the oil industry became "robust and durable, *despite* the contingencies of their making processes" (29; emphasis added).

4. For Georges Bataille (1943, 1957), erotic and mystic ecstasy was about (re)encountering a lost continuity in and through *transgression*: a movement that was not aimed toward God, but was itself a sacred, never-ending dynamic of limit-experiences and dissolution in which true sovereignty could be found.

5. Martin Heidegger (1995), for instance, uses ecstasis to point at how *Dasein* is always "thrown" out of the past and projected into the future.

6. Drew Leder (1990), for instance, gives a phenomenological account of the lived body as always already ecstatic in nature, away from itself, and beneath the reach of personal control.

7. See also Carlo Ginzburg's (1991) historical evocation of a Eurasian substratum of shamanism to explain the ecstatic features of popular imaginations about the witches' sabbath in Renaissance Europe.

8. Yet see Mazzarella (2017) for a Durkheimian rereading of ecstatic vital energy *beyond* extraordinary moments and circumstances.

9. For a fascinating study of another example of a foreign company's relative lack of agency and power in relation to its political environment, see Miriam Driessen's (2019) recent ethnography of Chinese roadbuilding companies in Ethiopia.

10. For a description of the queer dimension of this experiment beyond its sporadic attention to the nonheterosexual, see the conclusion.

11. Yet although the ecological impacts of selective rainforest logging are far less drastic than those of large-scale clear-cutting, selective practices are not, therefore, inherently sustainable or ecologically sound. Road construction, soil compaction by heavy machinery, and the selective pressure on certain tree species do affect forest ecologies. And although secondary growth usually fills in forest gaps and abandoned logging roads rather quickly, selective logging leaves behind skimmed-off forests that, because of their diminished economic value, are more vulnerable to being converted into ranches or plantations.

12. Oil production also requires its own forms of mobility. Onshore drillers, for instance, move from frack site to frack site, and even offshore rigs are surprisingly mobile for their massive size. As Appel (2019a, 47) notes, they are indeed frequently moved to different seas, thereby producing "fitful and unpredictable temporalities" that can make them "seem fleeting and spectral."

13. Note that *onshore* oil and gas rigs or wells also use the same land as subsistence farmers or large-scale ranchers.

14. At least in the Democratic Republic of the Congo, logging also differentiates itself from most mining and oil because of its shorter commodity chains, less complex corporate structures, little to no subcontracting, less state involvement, and, above all, its lower macroeconomic importance and political weight.

15. The anthropologist Ade Peace (1996, 1999), for instance, writes about the practices and discourses of Australian timber workers, Brendan Sweeney and John Holmes (2008) give a thick description of work cultures in Canadian tree-planting camps, and Kirk Dombrowski (2002) provides an interesting account of the everyday lives of Native American workers in the Alaskan timber industry. From a more historical perspective, Robert Ficken (1983) looks into the organization of American lumbermen along the Pacific Northwest coast, Adam Tomczik (2008) deals with lumberjack work cultures in Maine and Minnesota,

and Charles Menzies and Caroline Butler (2001) focus on Native American labor in the history of commercial forestry in British Columbia.

16. See, for instance, Van Klinken (2008) or Wadley and Eilenberg (2005). A recent article by Morten Nielsen and Mikkel Bunkenborg (2020) offers interesting insights into the collaborations between Chinese loggers and local tree scouts in Northern Mozambique.

17. For a useful review article, see Charnley and Poe (2007).

18. For historical studies on state, politics, and forestry, see, for instance, Barton (2002), Gray and Ngolet (2012), Rajan (2006), Sivaramakrishnan (1999), and Vandergeest and Peluso (2006).

19. For studies on peasant resistance against commercial forestry, see Guha (2000), Peluso (1992), and Tsing (1993, 2005). For the link between forestry police and poverty, see Larson and Ribot (2007). For an inspiring study on environmentalism, green neoliberalism, and forest labor, see Sodikoff (2012).

20. See, for instance, Christopher Barr's (1998) description of oligopoly in the Indonesian timber commodity chain or Patrick Johnston's (2004) account of the political economy of timber in Liberia.

21. The information presented in this and the following paragraphs is based primarily on information and statistics that circulate within the gray literature on logging in the DRC: Debroux et al. (2007), De Wasseige et al. (2009), De Wasseige et al. (2012), and Partenariat pour les Forêts du Bassin du Congo (2006).

22. For historical studies on concessions in French Equatorial Africa— focusing on both their systemic violence and pragmatic improvisations—see Coquery-Vidrovitch (1972) and Cantournet (1991).

23. Today this is the border between the Mongala and Bas-Uele provinces, as they were created as part of the 2015 decentralization campaign that raised the number of Congolese provinces from eleven to twenty-six.

CHAPTER ONE. AWKWARD BEGINNINGS

1. When CTI managers traveled from Kinshasa to the logging concession, they often referred to their trip as *descendre sur le terrain* (descending to the field). The fiction of fieldwork is as fundamental for foresters as it is for anthropologists. For a critique of its assumptions, see Gupta and Ferguson (1997).

2. See Pratt (1986) for a critique of arrival stories and their fictional authorization of ethnography.

3. The Forest Stewardship Council (FSC) is a well-known certification scheme that carries out inspections and audits of logging companies seeking a green label to certify the ecologically, socially, and economically sustainable provenance of their timber.

4. The agreement defined "confidential matters and circumstances" formulaically as: (a) operating and business secrets relating to the company, to the associated companies, or the shareholders, business partners or customers of the company; (b) objects and other documents produced by the company containing

specific information on its activities; and (c) oral information given by company staff. The agreement, however, explicitly *excluded* from its scope: (d) data and information gathered from my personal research observations and notes; and (e) data and information gathered from third parties through ethnographic research methods, in particular interviewing.

5. Until a young Spanish forest engineer arrived, I was the only university-trained European in the CTI concession.

6. For a contrasting strategy, see Kirsch (2014b).

7. I guaranteed all interlocutors and interviewees that their contributions would remain anonymous and that I would use fictive names in all my academic writings.

8. The possibility of slipping from ethnographic empathy to (more political) sympathy is indeed what worries some scholars of corporate capitalism (Salverda 2019) and global elites (Gilbert and Sklair 2018). See also Carrier (2016).

9. For a critical questioning of this promise, see Berlant (2011), Hemmings (2005), and Wiegman (2014).

10. Note that Fabian's deliberate association of critique with "madness" points at the ecstatic dimension of the critical position. Critique is indeed "associated with the way it enables us to reflexively *move outside of ourselves*" (Hage 2012, 287; emphasis added).

CHAPTER TWO. FOREST WORK

1. The influence of village chiefs and local elites in the recruiting process was surprisingly limited. In contrast to other extractive companies in the DRC that often give chiefs a quota of temporary jobs to "sell" to their population, direct collaboration between CTI and local elites was rare (e.g., Edmond and Titeca 2019). The practical monopoly of senior Congolese staff in deciding who gets hired was therefore a great source of frustration for villagers in the concession (see chapter 4).

2. Although Marina Welker's (2014) book draws predominantly from (interviews with) public relations officers and executives, ordinary workers too can be said to "enact" the corporation, both internally—that is, toward one another—as well as externally—that is, toward nonworkers.

3. "The king of the forest" is also a well-known sobriquet of Werrasson, a musician from Kinshasa who was extremely popular during the time of our fieldwork and whose most popular song will be discussed in the following section.

4. Tola, or *Gossweilerodendron balsamiferum*, was a recurrent commercial tree species.

5. For another exploration of the interaction between gendered resources and gendered subjects see the work of Emma Ferry (2011) on Mexican miners.

6. Timothy Mitchell (2009) makes a similar but broader argument about the relationship between forms of labor in the coal and oil industries and the material affordances of their resources.

1. For a detailed analysis of the eleko, or *Pachyelasma tessmannii*, in popular healing practices, see chapter 8.

2. Reliable ethnographic and historical studies on the Itimbiri region are scarce. Apart from chapters in *Paths in the Rainforest* (1990), Jan Vansina's seminal work on the political history of Equatorial Africa, and his *Introduction à l'Ethnographie du Congo* (1966), an earlier ethnographic survey, this section is largely based on interviews carried out with Mbudza and Bati village elders but also draws from two romanticized ethnographies by Lolo missionaries: Van den Bergh (1933) and de Mey and Gevaerts (1948). More recent material is taken from interviews and triangulated with information drawn from Ndaywel è Nziem (1988) and Gondola (2002). For more general histories of the provinces of Mongala and Bas-Uele see, respectively, Ambwa et al. (2015) and Akude et al. (2014).

3. I use the spelling *Mbudza* rather than *Mbuja* because the former better approaches how people in the CTI logging concession actually pronounced it. Also, Mbudza intellectuals themselves often preferred this spelling (e.g., Gbema 1976).

4. Dikpo was said to be the son of Liambi, the first son of Salaka, who was the fourth and last son of Mbudza.

5. The creation of a Congolese proletariat nevertheless also generated anxiety about the development of a more socially conscious working class that would be receptive to emerging anticolonial ideas.

6. Only after World War II did the colonial administration roll out the agricultural scheme of *paysannats indigènes*, whereby farming families received land titles in exchange for producing a surplus for the market. Yet these schemes never produced a separate social category of planteurs and often required continued coercion by Belgian agronomists and their Congolese counterparts (Loffman 2019, 205–10). Moreover, the returns collected by Congolese farmers—even those who specialized in selling food to industrial and plantation workers—were meager (Jewsiewicki 1979).

7. Patrice Lumumba was elected as Congo's first prime minister in 1960 but was ousted from power by President Joseph Kasa-Vubu. He was murdered in January 1961 with the active support of the Belgian government.

8. The so-called Simba rebellion was an insurrection directed against the central Congolese government by Lumumbist politicians, such as Christophe Gbenye, Gaston Soumaliot, and Antoine Gizenga.

9. Between 1967 and 1997, Joseph-Désiré Mobutu was president of the country that in 1971 he renamed Zaire.

CHAPTER FOUR. SHARING THE COMPANY

1. See Schouten (2020) for the longer history of roadblock politics as a source of political power in Central Africa.

2. These paragraphs are based on personal observations in CTI offices during the described events as well as on testimonies collected afterward. To protect its protagonists, the name of the village is not mentioned.

3. If and when they were co-opted, local elites were whimsical allies at best, and corruptible village chiefs were often unable to control their populations (see also Geenen and Verweijen 2017).

4. My criticism of Ferguson's generalizations on enclave capitalism does not, however, preclude admiration. The previous chapter is indeed profoundly indebted to his earlier work on connection and disconnection in the Zambian Copperbelt (Ferguson 1999). More recently, Ferguson (2010, 2015) also partially revised his monolithic story of enclave capitalism in contemporary Africa and even questioned the analytic use-value of the concept of neoliberalism itself. Moreover, his later work has been of great help to think the CTI logging concession. This chapter has, for instance, mobilized his analytic of the "share" to better understand village roadblocks. And chapter 8 will employ his preoccupation with performances of *dependency* as a socially valorized state to account for worker masculinities.

CHAPTER FIVE. OUT OF HERE

1. For the intersections among boredom, unemployment, precarity, capitalism, and neoliberalism, see Jeffrey (2010), Mains (2007, 2017), Masquelier (2013, 2019), O'Neill (2014, 2017), Ralph (2008), and Van den Berg and O'Neill (2017). While these ethnographies describe how boredom often emerges in cities in the absence of job opportunities, this chapter shows how the face of boredom also extends beyond the conventionally urban.

2. The idea of "centrifugality" came out of a conversation with my friend and colleague Peter Lambertz during a conference panel we organized together. For a complementary reading of transnational appropriation as centripetal rather than centrifugal, see Lambertz (2018, 64, 259).

3. These *libaku* signs were implicitly gendered. The right foot—*na loboko ya mobali* (literally, at the side of the man's hand)—was associated with men and was considered strong enough to deal with obstacles. The left foot—*na loboko ya mwasi* (literally, at the side of the woman's hand)—was not.

4. Although Jens often asked me for data from the census Freddy and I had conducted, as well as for detailed maps and lists of houses within both the official and unofficial camp quarters, I refused to give CTI any information that might contribute to evicting so-called illegal camp residents.

CHAPTER SIX. A DARKER SHADE OF WHITE

1. The expat managers rarely ate local or African food and greatly dreaded times when European ingredients were out of stock and not flown in on time. See also Fabian (2000, 71).

2. For Freud (2003), the uncanny comprises both the secret familiarity of the strange and the sudden strangeness of the familiar.

3. For another striking example, see Penny Harvey and Hannah Knox's account of how road engineers in Peru humorously self-characterized as a "tribe" (Harvey and Knox 2015, 107).

4. The expats confessed their ecstatic darkness only to fellow whites and not to their Congolese workers. In relation to their employees, weaknesses had to be very much concealed. Indeed, the *appearance* of "self-control was generally understood as a prerequisite for the control of others" (Fabian 2000, 59).

5. Note that *mundele*, the common Lingala word for white person (plural *mindele*), was not reserved for people whose skin color was classified as white. Mundele was also used for people who were rich, lived in or had traveled to *mpoto* (the West), or occupied positions of political authority. The administrateur de territoire in Bumba, for instance, was often called *mundele mboka* (literally, the white man of the town). Mundele was therefore not a simple racial category and referred as much to class, culture, power, and nationality as to pigmentation.

6. For exceptions, see Butler (2015) and Appel (2019a).

CHAPTER SEVEN. CANNIBALS AND CORNED BEEF

1. William Branham was a key figure in the evangelical revival that swept across the United States in the 1950s and was the charismatic founder of a Pentecostal church known in the DRC as the Tabernacle du Temps de la Fin (Tabernacle of the end times).

2. All page references to *L'Eden de Satan* are to the French translation I was given during fieldwork, but the English text is taken from the original transcriptions, as found on the *Living Word Broadcast* website, accessed April 14, 2012, https://www.livingwordbroadcast.org/LWBWBTextfiles/gettf.php?lang =en&textfile=65-0829.htm.

3. Lesley Braun (2015) offers an insightful analysis of similar rumors about Chinese laborers capturing Mami Wata in order to install underwater optic fiber cables in Kinshasa.

4. Compagnie Kitunga stories indeed seem based on all-too-real practices. A recent article on surgery and autopsy in the Belgian Congo, for instance, describes how colonizers used to "cut off, extract and send away blood, lumbar fluid, tumours and so forth, consuming them in the process of medical research" (Au 2017, 311; see also Bernault 2019).

5. In many Central African oral histories witches are often supposed *to hand over* their intimates to strangers to be eaten (Peter Geschiere, personal communication).

CHAPTER EIGHT. MEN AND TREES

1. As noted in chapter 2, Paul, the general supervisor of the prospection teams, was often called "king of the forest"—a nickname borrowed from the popular Congolese singer Werrasson.

2. To a certain extent this is similar to what Joseph Tonda (2005) calls "un-kinning" or *déparentalisation* in camp contexts.

3. Tali is a commercial tree species of the *Erythrophleum* genus that CTI exported.

4. CTI workers generally assumed that autochthonous villagers—rather than the logging company—controlled the forest. For instance, unlike Jessica Rolston's (2013) miners who criticized their management for unsafe working conditions, CTI employees usually attributed work floor accidents to the (occult) influence of angry concession residents.

5. It should be noted that a strong/weak opposition was also used for women, albeit with different connotations. For female "yankees," see especially Gondola (2016, 136–41) and Pype (2007, 266).

6. In contrast to the "free marriages" people in Kinshasa call *yaka tofanda*—which means "come and let's live together"—*fait accompli* arrangements were not a mutual agreement between lovers to cohabitate and have children, but the result of a boy getting a girl pregnant, with or without her consent (Pype 2012, 204). Moreover, unlike urban forms of *concubinage*, marriages "by theft" usually led to temporary family arrangements, though the ultimate payment of official bride-wealth frequently remained a promise.

CHAPTER NINE. WOMEN AND CHAINSAWS

1. The issue of so-called mixed-race children in particular became a colonial obsession (Jeurissen 2003).

2. This strategy was also effective with Congolese staff who had a say in hiring procedures.

3. Such fears directly reproduced colonial "Black Peril" scares that had been instrumental in the construction and maintenance of white settler communities across Africa (e.g., Anderson 2010; McCulloch 2000).

4. All references to texts, images, and videos were taken from the website as it was during fieldwork in 2010 (www.watchingmydaughtergoblack.com).

5. Note that the daughter's "punishment" of her father allows for masochistic pleasures in the (middle-aged, white, male) viewer. Daughters indeed mediate their fathers' desires to hurt themselves, "as the Negro would if . . . he were in [their] place, if he had the opportunity" (Mbembe 2019, 136; Fanon 1961).

CONCLUSION

1. At the end of his book, Fabian (2000, 279) suggests that there might indeed be an "existential" dimension to the interplay between ecstasis and self-control.

2. Frantz Fanon already (1961, 1967) famously foregrounded the idea of colonialism as a "neurosis" that characterizes both colonizers and colonized.

3. The psychoanalytic theorist Alenka Zupančič even suggests that there is a "hysterical" dimension to the never-ending critical act of breaking the illusion of

power by revealing its failures. Although her (paranoid) diagnosis of feminist critique as a form of "hysteria" is problematic in itself, there is indeed much to learn from the observation that, as critics, we are often "much more revolted by the weakness of power than by power itself, and the truth of [our] basic complaint about the master is usually that the master is not master enough" (Zupančič 2006, 165; quoted in Mazzarella 2017, 167–68).

4. As I argue elsewhere (2016, 2019, 2021), *queer* can indeed entail a more oblique relationship to norms and their powers in which seduction, complicity, and imitation trouble the clear-cut oppositional logic of resistance and antinormativity. See also Wiegman and Wilson (2015).

REFERENCES

Achebe, Chinua. 1977. "An Image of Africa." *Massachusetts Review* 18, no. 4: 782–94.

Agamben, Giorgio. 1998. *Homo Sacer: Sovereign Power and Bare Life*. Stanford, CA: Stanford University Press.

Ahmed, Sara. 2004. "Affective Economies." *Social Text* 22, no. 2: 117–39.

Ahmed, Sara. 2012. *On Being Included: Racism and Diversity in Institutional Life*. Durham, NC: Duke University Press.

Ahmed, Sara. 2014. *The Cultural Politics of Emotion*. Edinburgh: Edinburgh University Press.

Akude, Jean de Dieu, Elodie Stroobant, Charles K. Sita, Mathieu Z. Etambala, Jean O. Tshonda, Edwine Simons, Joris Krawczyk, and Mohamed Laghmouch. 2014. *Bas-Uele: Pouvoirs locaux et economie agricole, héritages d'un passé brouillé*. Tervuren, Belgium: Musée Royale de l'Afrique Centrale.

Ambwa, Jean-Claude, Elodie Stroobant, Jérôme Mumbanza mwa Bawele, Jean O. Tshonda, Joris Krawczyk, and Mohamed Laghmouch. 2015. *Mongala: Jonction des territoires et bastion d'une identité supra-ethnique*. Tervuren, Belgium: Musée Royale de l'Afrique Centrale.

Anderson, Ben. 2009. "Affective Atmospheres." *Emotion, Space and Society* 2, no. 2: 77–81.

Anderson, David M. 2010. "Sexual Threat and Settler Society: 'Black Perils' in Kenya, c. 1907–30." *Journal of Imperial and Commonwealth History* 38, no. 1: 47–74.

Angé, Olivia, and David Berliner. 2014. *Anthropology and Nostalgia*. New York: Berghahn.

Anker, Elizabeth S., and Rita Felski. 2017 *Critique and Postcritique*. Durham, NC: Duke University Press.

Anonymous. 2009. "Wenn schöne Mädchen mit Motorsägen hantiere." *Welt*, July 17. http://www.welt.de/lifestyle/article4117917/Wenn-schoene -Maedchen-mit-Motorsaegen-hantieren.html.

Appadurai, Arjun. 1996. *Modernity at Large: Cultural Dimensions of Globalization*. Minneapolis: University of Minnesota Press.

Appel, Hannah. 2012a. "Offshore Work: Oil, Modularity, and the How of Capitalism in Equatorial Guinea." *American Ethnologist* 39, no. 4: 692–709.

Appel, Hannah C. 2012b. "Walls and White Elephants: Oil Extraction, Responsibility, and Infrastructural Violence in Equatorial Guinea." *Ethnography* 13, no. 4: 439–65.

Appel, Hannah. 2019a. *The Licit Life of Capitalism: US Oil in Equatorial Guinea.* Durham, NC: Duke University Press.

Appel, Hannah. 2019b. "To Critique or Not to Critique? That Is (perhaps not) the Question . . ." *Journal of Business Anthropology* 8, no. 1: 29–34.

Appiah, Kwame A. 1990. "Racisms." In *Anatomy of Racism*, edited by David T. Goldberg, 3–17. Minneapolis: University of Minnesota Press.

Arendt, Hannah. 1969. *On Violence.* New York: Harcourt, Brace.

Arens, William. 1979. *The Man-Eating Myth: Anthropology and Anthropophagy.* New York: Oxford University Press.

Arondekar, Anjali. 2003. "Lingering Pleasures, Perverted Texts: Colonial Desire in Kipling's Anglo-India." In *Imperial Desire: Dissident Sexualities and Colonial Literature*, edited by Philip Holden and Richard R. Ruppel, 65–89. Minneapolis: University of Minnesota Press.

Asad, Talal, Wendy Brown, Judith Butler, and Saba Mahmood. 2013. *Is Critique Secular? Blasphemy, Injury, and Free Speech.* New York: Fordham University Press.

Au, Sokhieng. 2017. "Cutting the Flesh: Surgery, Autopsy and Cannibalism in the Belgian Congo." *Medical History* 61, no. 2: 295–312.

Augé, Marc. 1992. *Non-lieux: Introduction à une anthropologie de la surmodernité.* Paris: Seuil.

Ayimpam, Sylvie. 2014. *Économie de la débrouille à Kinshasa: Informalité, commerce et réseaux sociaux.* Paris: Karthala.

Barber, Karin. 2007. "When People Cross Thresholds." *African Studies Review* 50, no. 2: 111–23.

Barchiesi, Franco. 2011. *Precarious Liberation: Workers, the State, and Contested Social Citizenship in Postapartheid South Africa.* Albany: State University of New York Press.

Barr, Christopher M. 1998. "Bob Hasan, the Rise of Apkindo, and the Shifting Dynamics of Control in Indonesia's Timber Sector." *Indonesia*, no. 65 (April): 1–36.

Barton, Gregory A. 2002. *Empire Forestry and the Origins of Environmentalism.* Cambridge: Cambridge University Press.

Bastian, Misty L. 1997. "Married in the Water: Spirit Kin and Other Afflictions of Modernity in Southeastern Nigeria." *Journal of Religion in Africa* 27, no. 2: 116–34.

Bataille, Georges. 1943. *L'expérience intérieure.* Paris: Gallimard.

Bataille, Georges. 1957. *L'érotisme.* Paris: Minuit.

Bataille, Georges. 1967. *La part maudite: Précédé de la notion de dépense.* Paris: Minuit.

Bayart, Jean-François. 1989. *L'état en Afrique: La politique du ventre.* Paris: Fayard.

Bayart, Jean-François, and Stephen Ellis. 2000. "Africa in the World: A History of Extraversion." *African Affairs* 99, no. 395: 217–67.

Bear, Laura, Karen Ho, Anna Tsing, and Sylvia Yanagisako. 2015. "Gens: A Feminist Manifesto for the Study of Capitalism." *Cultural Anthropology*, March 30. http://www.culanth.org/fieldsights/652-gens-a-feminist-manifesto-for-the-study-of-capitalism.

Behdad, Ali. 1994. *Belated Travelers: Orientalism in the Age of Colonial Dissolution*. Durham, NC: Duke University Press.

Behrend, Heike. 2002. "'I am like a movie star in my street': Photographic Self-Creation in Postcolonial Kenya." In *Postcolonial Subjectivities in Africa*, edited by Richard P. Werbner, 44–62. London: Zed.

Bekaert, Stefan. 2000. *System and Repertoire in Sakata Medicine: Democratic Republic of Congo*. Uppsala, Sweden: Acta Universitatis Upsaliensis.

Belser, Marko. 2009. "40 Jahre Stihl-Kalender: Mädchen und Maschinen." *Schwarzwälder Bote*, August 19. https://www.schwarzwaelder-bote.de/inhalt.40-jahre-stihl-kalender-maedchen-und-maschinen.647a587e-68a3-4723-a931-45569fe87d6e.html.

Benson, Peter, and Stuart Kirsch. 2010. "Capitalism and the Politics of Resignation." *Current Anthropology* 51, no. 4:459–86.

Berlant, Lauren. 2011. *Cruel Optimism*. Durham, NC: Duke University Press.

Bernardi, Daniel. 2006. "Interracial Joysticks: Pornography's Web of Racist Attractions." In *Pornography: Film and Culture*, edited by Peter Lehman, 220–43. New Brunswick, NJ: Rutgers University Press.

Bernault, Florence. 2003. "The Politics of Enclosure in Colonial and Postcolonial Africa." In *A History of Prison and Confinement in Africa*, edited by Florence Bernault, 1–53. Portsmouth, NH: Heinemann.

Bernault, Florence. 2019. *Colonial Transactions: Imaginaries, Bodies, and Histories in Gabon*. Durham, NC: Duke University Press.

Bhabha, Homi. 1994. *The Location of Culture*. London: Routledge.

Biaya, T. K. 1988. "L'impasse de crise Zaïroise dans la peinture populaire urbaine, 1970–1985." *Canadian Journal of African Studies* 22, no. 1: 95–120.

Biaya, T. K. 1996. "La culture urbaine dans les arts populaires d'Afrique: Analyse de l'ambiance Zaïroise." *Canadian Journal of African Studies* 30, no. 3: 345–70.

Biaya, T. K. 1998. "La mort et ses métaphores au Congo-Zaïre, 1990–1995." In *Mort et maladie au Zaïre*, edited by Jan-Lodewijk Grootaers, 89–127. Paris: L'Harmattan.

Bissell, William C. 2005. "Engaging Colonial Nostalgia." *Cultural Anthropology* 20, no. 2: 215–48.

Boulton, Jack. 2019. "I Only Relax with My Friend and My Wife." *Etnofoor* 31, no. 1: 85–98.

Bourdieu, Pierre. 1977. *Outline of a Theory of Practice*. Translated by Richard Nice. New York: Cambridge University Press.

Branham, William M. 2004. *L'éden de satan*. Kinshasa: Shekinah.

Braun, Lesley. 2015. "Cyber Siren: What Mami Wata Reveals about the Internet and Chinese Presence in Kinshasa." *Canadian Journal of African Studies* 49, no. 2: 301–18.

Burawoy, Michael. 1979. *Manufacturing Consent: Changes in the Labor Process under Monopoly Capitalism*. Chicago: University of Chicago Press.

Butcher, Tim. 2008. *Blood River: The Terrifying Journey through the World's Most Dangerous Country*. New York: Grover.

Butler, Judith. 2004. *Undoing Gender*. London: Routledge.

Butler, Judith, Zeynep Gambetti, and Leticia Sabsay, eds. 2016. *Vulnerability in Resistance*. Durham, NC: Duke University Press.

Butler, Paola. 2015. *Colonial Extractions: Race and Canadian Mining in Contemporary Africa*. Toronto: Toronto University Press.

Callon, Michel, and Bruno Latour. 1981. "Unscrewing the Big Leviathan: How Actors Macro-structure Reality and How Sociologists Help Them to Do So." In *Advances in Social Theory and Methodology: Toward an Integration of Micro- and Macro-sociologies*, edited by Karin Knorr-Cetina and Aaron V. Cicourel, 277–303. London: Routledge and Kegan Paul.

Cantournet, Jean. 1991. *Des affaires et des hommes: Noirs et blancs, commerçants et fonctionnaires dans l'Oubangui du début du siècle*. Paris: Société d'Ethnologie.

Carrier, James. 2016. *After the Crisis: Anthropological Thought, Neoliberalism, and the Aftermath*. London: Routledge.

Ceuppens, Bambi. 2003. *Congo Made in Flanders? Koloniale Vlaamse Visies op 'Blank' en 'Zwart' in Belgisch Congo*. Ghent, Belgium: Academia.

Ceyssens, Rik. 1975. "Mutumbula, mythe de l'opprimé." *Cultures et Développement* 7, nos. 3–4: 483–550.

Charnley, Susan, and Melissa R. Poe. 2007. "Community Forestry in Theory and Practice: Where Are We Now?" *Annual Review of Anthropology* 36, no. 1: 301–36.

Cole, Jennifer, and Lynn M. Thomas. 2009. *Love in Africa*. Chicago: University of Chicago Press.

Comaroff, Jean, and John L. Comaroff. 1999. "Occult Economies and the Violence of Abstraction: Notes from the South African Postcolony." *American Ethnologist* 26, no. 2: 279–303.

Comaroff, Jean, and John L. Comaroff. 2000. "Millennial Capitalism: First Thoughts on a Second Coming." *Public Culture* 12, no. 2: 291–343.

Comaroff, Jean, and John L. Comaroff. 2003. "Ethnography on an Awkward Scale: Postcolonial Anthropology and the Violence of Abstraction." *Ethnography* 4, no. 2: 147–79.

Comaroff, Jean, and John L. Comaroff. 2015. *Theory from the South: Or, How Euro-America Is Evolving toward Africa*. Abingdon, UK: Routledge.

Connell, R. W. 2005. *Masculinities*. Cambridge: Polity.

Connell, R. W., and James W. Messerschmidt. 2005. "Hegemonic Masculinity: Rethinking the Concept." *Gender and Society* 19, no. 6: 829–59.

Conrad, Joseph. 2006. *Heart of Darkness*. Norton Critical Edition. New York: W. W. Norton.

Cooper, Frederick. 1992. "Colonizing Time: Work Rhythms and Labor Conflict in Colonial Mombassa." In *Colonialism and Culture*, edited by Nicholas B. Dirks, 209–46. Ann Arbor: University of Michigan Press.

Coquery-Vidrovitch, Catherine. 1972. *Le Congo au temps des grandes compagnies concessionnaires, 1898–1930*. Paris: Mouton.

Cornwall, Andrea A. 2003. "To Be a Man Is More Than a Day's Work: Shifting Ideals of Manliness in Ado-Odo, Southwestern Nigeria." In *Men and Masculinities in Modern Africa*, edited by Lisa A. Lindsay and Stephan F. Miescher, 230–48. Portsmouth, NH: Heineman.

Côte, Muriel, and Benedikt Korf. 2018. "Making Concessions: Extractive Enclaves, Entangled Capitalism and Regulative Pluralism at the Gold Mining Frontier in Burkina Faso." *World Development* 101 (January): 466–76.

Coumans, Catherine. 2011. "Occupying Spaces Created by Conflict: Anthropologists, Development NGOs, Responsible Investment, and Mining." *Current Anthropology* 52, no. S3: S29–S43.

Cross, Jamie. 2011. "Detachment as a Corporate Ethic." *Focaal: Journal of Global and Historical Anthropology*, no. 60 (June): 34–46.

Cuvelier, Jeroen. 2014. "Work and Masculinity in Katanga's Artisanal Mines." *Africa Spectrum* 49, no. 2: 3–26.

Cuvelier, Jeroen. 2017. "Money, Migration and Masculinity among Artisanal Miners in Katanga (DR Congo)." *Review of African Political Economy* 44, no. 152: 204–19.

De Boeck, Filip. 1991. "From Knots to Web: Fertility, Life-Transmission, Health and Well-Being among the Aluund of Southwest Zaire." PhD diss., KU Leuven University.

De Boeck, Filip. 1994. "Of Trees and Kings: Politics and Metaphor among the Aluund of Southwestern Zaire." *American Ethnologist* 21, no. 3: 451–73.

De Boeck, Filip. 1998a. "Beyond the Grave: History, Memory and Death in Postcolonial Congo/Zaïre." In *Memory and the Postcolony: African Anthropology and the Critique of Power*, edited by Richard Werbner, 21–57. London: Zed.

De Boeck, Filip. 1998b. "Domesticating Diamonds and Dollars: Identity, Expenditure and Sharing in Southwestern Zaire (1984–1997)." *Development and Change* 29, no. 4: 777–810.

De Boeck, Filip. 2005. "The Apocalyptic Interlude: Revealing Death in Kinshasa." *African Studies Review* 48, no. 2: 11–32.

De Boeck, Filip. 2008. "Dead Society in a Cemetery City: The Transformation of the Burial Rites in Kinshasa." In *Heterotopia and the City: Public Space in a Postcivil Society*, edited by Michiel Dehaene and Lieven De Cauter, 297–308. London: Routledge.

De Boeck, Filip. 2011. "Inhabiting Ocular Ground: Kinshasa's Future in the Light of Congo's Spectral Urban Politics." *Cultural Anthropology* 26, no. 2: 263–86.

De Boeck, Filip, and Sammy Baloji. 2016. *Suturing the City: Living Together in Congo's Urban Worlds*. London: Autograph.

Debroux, Laurent, Terese Hart, David Kaimowitz, Alain Karsenty, and Guiseppe Topa. 2007. *Forests in Post-conflict Democratic Republic of Congo: Analysis of a Priority Agenda*. Bogor, Indonesia: CIFOR/World Bank/CIRAD.

Demetriou, Demetrakis Z. 2001. "Connell's Concept of Hegemonic Masculinity: A Critique." *Theory and Society* 30, no. 3: 337–61.

De Meulder, Bruno. 1996. *De kampen van Kongo: Arbeid, kapitaal en rasveredeling in de koloniale planning.* Amsterdam: Meulenhoff and Kritak.

de Mey, Godfried, and Nicolaes Gevaerts. 1948. *Tussen Uele en Itimbiri.* Tongerlo, Belgium: St. Norbertus-Boekhandel.

De Villers, Gauthier, Bogumil Jewsiewiecki, and Laurent Monnier. 2002. *Manières de vivre: Économies de la "débrouille" dans les villes du Congo/Zaïre.* Paris: L'Harmattan.

Devisch, Renaat. 1993. *Weaving the Threads of Life: The Khita Gyn-eco-logical Healing Cult among the Yaka.* Chicago: University of Chicago Press.

De Wasseige, Carlos, Didier Devers, Paya De Marcken, Richard Eba'a Atyi, Robert Nasi, and Philippe Mayaux. 2009. *Les forêts du bassin du Congo: État des forêts 2008.* Luxembourg City, LU: Office des Publications de l'Union Européenne.

De Wasseige, Carlos, Paya De Marcken, Nicolas Bayol, François Hiol H., Philippe Mayaux, Baudoin Desclée, Robert Nasi, Alain Billand, Pierre Defourny, and Richard Eba'a Atyi. 2012. *Les forêts du bassin du Congo: État des forêts 2010.* Luxembourg City: Office des Publications de l'Union Européenne.

Dibwe dia Mwembu, Donatien. 2001. *Bana Shaba abandonnés par leur père: Structures de l'autorité et histoire sociale de la famille ouvrière au Katanga, 1910–1997.* Paris: L'Harmattan.

DogfartNetwork. n.d. "Watching My Daughter Go Black." Accessed January 25, 2012. http://www.watchingmydaughtergoblack.

Dolan, Catherine, and Dinah Rajak. 2016. *The Anthropology of Corporate Social Responsibility.* New York: Berghahn.

Dombrowski, Kirk. 2002. "Billy Budd, Choker-Setter: Native Culture and Indian Work in the Southeast Alaska Timber Industry." *International Labor and Working-Class History*, no. 62 (Fall): 121–42.

Douglas, Mary. 1966. *Purity and Danger: An Analysis of Concepts of Pollution and Taboo.* London: Routledge.

Drewal, Henry J. 2008a. *Mami Wata: Arts for Water Spirits in Africa and Its Diasporas.* Seattle: University of Washington Press.

Drewal, Henry J. 2008b. "Mermaids, Mirrors, and Snake Charmers." *African Arts* 21, no. 2: 38–45.

Driessen, Miriam. 2019. *Tales of Hope, Tastes of Bitterness: Chinese Road Builders in Ethiopia.* Hong Kong: Hong Kong University Press.

Droogers, André. 1980. *The Dangerous Journey: Symbolic Aspects of Boys' Initiation among the Wagenia of Kisangani, Zaire.* The Hague: Mouton.

Dunn, Kevin. 2003. *Imagining the Congo: The International Relations of Identity.* New York: Palgrave Macmillan.

Durham, Deborah. 2004. "Disappearing Youth: Youth as a Social Shifter in Botswana." *American Ethnologist* 31, no. 4: 589–605.

Durkheim, Émile. 1912. *Les formes élémentaires de la vie religieuse: Le système totémique en Australie.* Paris: Presses universitaires de France.

Dyer, Richard. 1997. *White*. London: Routledge.

Edmond, Patrick, and Kristof Titeca. 2019. "Corporate Social Responsibility and Patronage: Effects on Popular Mobilisation in DRC's Oilfields, Muanda." In *Conjonctures de l'Afrique Centrale*, edited by Sara Geenen, Aymar N. Bisoka, and An Ansoms, 127–56. Paris: L'Harmattan.

Eggers, Nicole. 2015. "Mukombozi and the Monganga: The Violence of Healing in the 1944 Kitawalist Uprising." *Africa* 85, no. 3: 417–36.

Englund, Hari. 1996. "Witchcraft, Modernity and the Person: The Morality of Accumulation in Central Malawi." *Critique of Anthropology* 16, no. 3: 257–79.

Fabian, Johannes. 1978. "Popular Culture in Africa: Findings and Conjectures." *Africa* 8, no. 4: 315–44.

Fabian, Johannes. 1983. *Time and the Other: How Anthropology Makes Its Object*. New York: Columbia University Press.

Fabian, Johannes. 1996. *Remembering the Present: Painting and Popular History in Zaire*. Berkeley: University of California Press.

Fabian, Johannes. 1998. *Moments of Freedom: Anthropology and Popular Culture*. Charlottesville: University Press of Virginia.

Fabian, Johannes. 2000. *Out of Our Minds: Reason and Madness in the Exploration of Central Africa*. Berkeley: University of California Press.

Fabian, Johannes. 2003. "Forgetful Remembering: A Colonial Life in the Congo." *Africa* 73, no. 4: 489–504.

Fanon, Frantz. 1961. *Les damnés de la terre*. Paris: Maspéro.

Fanon, Frantz. 1967. *Black Skin, White Masks*. New York: Grove.

Favret-Saada, Jeanne. 2012. "Being Affected." *Hau: Journal of Ethnographic Theory* 2, no. 1: 435–45.

Felski, Rita. 2015. *The Limits of Critique*. Chicago: University of Chicago Press.

Ferguson, James. 1999. *Expectations of Modernity: Myths and Meanings of Urban Life on the Zambian Copperbelt*. Berkeley: University of California Press.

Ferguson, James. 2005. "Seeing Like an Oil Company: Space, Security, and Global Capital in Neoliberal Africa." *American Anthropologist* 107, no. 3: 377–82.

Ferguson, James. 2006. *Global Shadows: Africa in the Neoliberal World Order*. Durham, NC: Duke University Press.

Ferguson, James. 2010. "The Uses of Neoliberalism." *Antipode* 41, no. 1: 166–84.

Ferguson, James. 2015. *Give a Man a Fish: Reflections on the New Politics of Distribution*. Durham, NC: Duke University Press.

Ferme, Mariane. 2001. *The Underneath of Things: Violence, History, and the Everyday in Sierra Leone*. Berkeley: University of California Press.

Ferry, Elizabeth. 2011. "Waste and Potency: Making Men with Minerals in Guanajuato and Tucson." *Comparative Studies in Society and History* 53, no. 4: 914–44.

Ficken, Robert E. 1983. "The Wobbly Horrors: Pacific Northwest Lumbermen and the Industrial Workers of the World, 1917–1918." *Labor History* 24, no. 3: 325–41.

Fisiy, Cyprian F., and Peter Geschiere. 1991. "Sorcery, Witchcraft and Accumulation: Regional Variations in South and West Cameroon." *Critique of Anthropology* 11, no. 3: 251–78.

Foster, Hal. 2012. "Post-critical." *October*, no. 139 (Winter): 3–8.

Foucault, Michel. 1961. *Folie et déraison: Histoire de la folie à l'âge classique*. Paris: Plon.

Foucault, Michel. 1975. *Surveiller et punir: Naissance de la prison*. Paris: Gallimard.

Foucault, Michel. 1984. "Des espaces autres (conférence au Cercle d'études architec-turales, 14 mars 1967)." *Architecture, Mouvement, Continuité* 5 (October): 46–49.

Foucault, Michel. 1997. *Il faut défendre la société: cours au Collège de France, 1976*. Paris: Seuil.

Frank, Barbara. 1995. "Permitted and Prohibited Wealth: Commodity-Possessing Spirits, Economic Morals, and the Goddess Mami Wata in West Africa." *Ethnology* 34, no. 4: 331–46.

Freud, Sigmund. 2003. *The Uncanny*. Translated by David McLintock. London: Penguin.

Fuss, Diana. 2017. "But What about Love?" PMLA 132, no. 2: 352–55.

Gardner, Katy. 2012. *Discordant Development: Global Capitalism and the Struggle for Connection in Bangladesh*. London: Pluto.

Gardner, Katy. 2015. "Chevron's Gift of CSR: Moral Economies of Connection and Disconnection in a Transnational Bangladeshi Village." *Economy and Society* 44, no. 4: 495–518.

Gbema, L. M. 1976. "Les sacrifices des Mbudza et les sacrifices bibliques." MA thesis, l'Institut Supérieur Théologique de Bunia.

Geenen, Sara, and Judith Verweijen. 2017. "Explaining Fragmented and Fluid Mobilization in Gold Mining Concessions in Eastern Democratic Republic of the Congo." *Extractive Industries and Society* 4, no. 4: 758–65.

Geertz, Clifford. 1972. "Deep Play: Notes on the Balinese Cockfight." *Daedalus* 101, no. 1: 1–38.

Geissler, Paul W., Guillaume Lachenal, John Manton, and Noémi Tousignant. 2016. *Traces of the Future: An Archaeology of Medical Science in Africa*. Bristol, UK: Intellect.

Geschiere, Peter. 1997. *The Modernity of Witchcraft: Politics and the Occult in Post-colonial Africa*. Charlottesville: University of Virginia Press.

Geschiere, Peter. 2003. "Witchcraft as the Dark Side of Kinship: Dilemmas of Social Security in New Contexts." *Etnofoor* 16, no. 1: 43–61.

Geschiere, Peter. 2009. *The Perils of Belonging: Autochthony, Citizenship, and Exclusion in Africa and Europe*. Chicago: University of Chicago Press.

Geschiere, Peter. 2013. *Witchcraft, Intimacy, and Trust: Africa in Comparison*. Chicago: University of Chicago Press.

Gibson-Graham, J. K. 1996. *The End of Capitalism (As We Knew It): A Feminist Critique of Political Economy*. Minneapolis: University of Minnesota Press.

Gilbert, Paul R., and Jessica Sklair. 2018. "Introduction: Ethnographic Engage-ments with Global Elites." *Focaal: Journal of Global and Historical Anthro-pology*, no. 81 (June): 1–15.

Gilberthorpe, Emma, and Dinah Rajak. 2017. "The Anthropology of Extraction: Critical Perspectives on the Resource Curse." *Journal of Development Studies* 53, no. 2: 186–204.

Giles-Vernick, Tamara. 2002. *Cutting the Vines of the Past: Environmental Histories of the Central African Rainforest*. Charlottesville: University of Virginia Press.

Gilman, Sander. 1985. *Difference and Pathology: Stereotypes of Sexuality, Race, and Madness*. Ithaca, NY: Cornell University Press.

Ginzburg, Carlo. 1991. *Ecstasies: Deciphering the Witches' Sabbath*. Chicago: University of Chicago Press.

Girard, René. 1966. *Deceit, Desire, and the Novel: Self and Other in Literary Structure*. Baltimore, MD: Johns Hopkins University Press.

Giskeødegård, Marte F. 2016. "O Organization, Where Art Thou? Tracing the Multiple Layers of Ambiguous and Shifting Boundary Processes in a Formal Organization." *Journal of Business Anthropology* 5, no. 1: 116–36.

Global Witness. 2015. *Exporting Impunity: How Congo's Rainforest Is Illegally Logged for International Markets*. London: Global Witness.

Golub, Alex. 2014. *Leviathans at the Gold Mine: Creating Indigenous and Corporate Actors in Papua New Guinea*. Durham, NC: Duke University Press.

Gondola, Ch. Didier. 2002. *The History of Congo*. Westport, CT: Greenwood.

Gondola, Ch. Didier. 2016. *Tropical Cowboys: Westerns, Violence, and Masculinity in Kinshasa*. Bloomington: Indiana University Press.

Gray, Christopher, and François Ngolet. 2012. "Lambaréné, Okoumé and the Transformation of Labor along the Middle Ogooué (Gabon), 1870–1945." *Journal of African History* 40, no. 1: 87–107.

Groes-Green, Christian. 2009. "Hegemonic and Subordinated Masculinities: Class, Violence and Sexual Performance among Young Mozambican Men." *Nordic Journal of African Studies* 18, no. 4: 286–304.

Groes-Green, Christian. 2010. "Orgies of the Moment: Bataille's Anthropology of Transgression and the Defiance of Danger in Post-socialist Mozambique." *Anthropological Theory* 10, no. 4: 385–407.

Guha, Ramachandra. 2000. *The Unquiet Woods: Ecological Change and Peasant Resistance in the Himalaya*. Berkeley: University of California Press.

Gupta, Akhil, and James Ferguson. 1997. *Anthropological Locations: Boundaries and Grounds of a Field Science*. Berkeley: University of California Press.

Guyer, Jane I. 1993. "Wealth in People and Self-Realization in Equatorial Africa." *Man* 28, no. 2: 243–65.

Hadot, Pierre. 1993. *Plotinus or the Simplicity of Vision*. Translated by Michael Chase. Chicago: University of Chicago Press.

Hage, Ghassan. 2012. "Critical Anthropological Thought and the Radical Political Imaginary Today." *Critique of Anthropology* 32, no. 3: 285–308.

Hall, Stuart, dir. 1996. *Race, the Floating Signifier* (videotape lecture). Northampton, MA: Media Education Foundation.

Hall, Stuart 1997. "Old and New Identities, Old and New Ethnicities." In *Culture, Globalization, and the World-System: Contemporary Conditions for the Representation of Identity*, edited by Anthony D. King, 41–68. Minneapolis: University of Minnesota Press.

Hannerz, Ulf. 1998. "Other Transnationals: Perspectives Gained from Studying Sideways." *Paideuma* 44: 109–23.

Hansen, Karen T. 2005. "Getting Stuck in the Compound: Some Odds against Social Adulthood in Lusaka, Zambia." *Africa Today* 51, no. 4: 3–16.

Haraway, Donna J. 1988. "Situated Knowledges: The Science Question in Feminism and the Privilege of Partial Perspective." *Feminist Studies* 14, no. 3: 575–99.

Haraway, Donna J. 2016. *Staying with the Trouble: Making Kin in the Chthulucene*. Durham, NC: Duke University Press.

Hardin, Rebecca, 2002. "Concessionary Politics in the Western Congo Basin: History and Culture in Forest Use." *Environmental Governance in Africa Working Papers*, no. 6. Washington, DC: World Resources Institute.

Hardin, Rebecca. 2011. "Concessionary Politics: Property, Patronage, and Political Rivalry in Central African Forest Management." *Current Anthropology* 52, no. s3: s113–s125.

Harms, Erik, Shafqat Hussain, Sasha Newell, Charles Piot, Louisa Schein, Sara Shneiderman, Terence Turner, and Juan Zhang. 2014. "Remote and Edgy: New Takes on Old Anthropological Themes." *Hau: Journal of Ethnographic Theory* 4, no. 1: 361–81.

Harms, Robert. 1981. *River of Wealth, River of Sorrow: The Central Zaire Basin in the Era of the Slave Trade*. New Haven: Yale University Press.

Harrison, Robert P. 1992. *Forests: The Shadow of Civilization*. Chicago: University of Chicago Press.

Harvey, David. 2003. *The New Imperialism*. Oxford: Oxford University Press.

Harvey, Penny, and Hannah Knox. 2015. *Roads: An Anthropology of Infrastructure and Expertise*. Ithaca, NY: Cornell University Press.

Headrick, Daniel R. 1981. *The Tools of Empire: Technology and European Imperialism in the Nineteenth Century*. Oxford: Oxford University Press.

Hecht, Gabrielle. 2018. "Interscalar Vehicles for an African Anthropocene: On Waste, Temporality, and Violence." *Cultural Anthropology* 33, no. 1: 109–41.

Heidegger, Martin. 1995. *The Fundamental Concepts of Metaphysics: World, Finitude, Solitude*. Translated by William McNeill and Nicholas Walker. Bloomington: Indiana University Press.

Hemmings, Clare. 2005. "Invoking Affect: Cultural Theory and the Ontological Turn." *Cultural Studies* 19, no. 5: 548–67.

Hendriks, Maarten. 2018. "The Politics of Everyday Policing in Goma: The Case of the Anti-gang." *Journal of Eastern African Studies* 12, no. 2: 274–89.

Hendriks, Thomas. 2014a. "Queer Complicity in the Belgian Congo: Autobiography and Racial Fetishism in Jef Geeraerts's (Post)colonial Novels." *Research in African Literatures* 45, no. 1: 63–84.

Hendriks, Thomas. 2014b. "Race and Desire in the Porno-Tropics: Ethnographic Perspectives from the Postcolony." *Sexualities* 17, nos. 1–2: 213–29.

Hendriks, Thomas. 2015. "Ethnographic Notes on 'Camp': Centrifugality and Liminality on the Rainforest Frontier." In *Borderities: The Politics of*

Contemporary Mobile Borders, edited by Anne-Laure Amilhat Szary and Frédéric Giraut, 155–70. New York: Palgrave Macmillan.

Hendriks, Thomas. 2016. "SIM Cards of Desire: Sexual Versatility and the Male Homoerotic Economy in Urban Congo." *American Ethnologist* 43, no. 2: 230–42.

Hendriks, Thomas. 2017. "A Darker Shade of White: Expat Self-Making in a Congolese Rainforest Enclave." *Africa* 87, no. 4: 683–701.

Hendriks, Thomas. 2018. "'Erotiques Cannibales': A Queer Ontological Take on Desire from Urban Congo." *Sexualities* 21, nos. 5–6: 853–67.

Hendriks, Thomas. 2019. "Queer(ing) Popular Culture: Homo-erotic Provocations from Kinshasa." *Journal of African Cultural Studies* 31, no. 1: 71–88.

Hendriks, Thomas. 2021. "'Making Men Fall': Queer Power beyond Anti-normativity." *Africa* 91, no. 3: 398–417.

Hendriks, Thomas, and Dominique Malaquais. 2016. "Sammy Baloji's Kolwezi: Imag(in)ing the Congo-China Nexus." In *Afrique-Asie: Arts, Espaces, Pratiques*, edited by Dominique Malaquais and Nicole Khouri, 213–28. Mont Saint Aignan, France: Presses Universitaires de Rouen et du Havre.

Henriet, Benoît. 2021. *Colonial Impotence: Virtue and Violence in a Congolese Concession (1911–1940)*. Berlin: De Gruyter.

Herzfeld, Michael. 1985. *The Poetics of Manhood: Contest and Identity in a Cretan Mountain Village*. Princeton, NJ: Princeton University Press.

Higginson, John. 1989. *A Working Class in the Making: Belgian Colonial Labor Policy, Private Enterprise, and the African Mineworker, 1907–1951*. Madison: University of Wisconsin Press.

Ho, Karen. 2005. "Situating Global Capitalisms: A View from Wall Street Investment Banks." *Cultural Anthropology* 20, no. 1: 68–96.

Ho, Karen. 2009. *Liquidated: An Ethnography of Wall Street*. Durham, NC: Duke University Press.

Hochschild, Adam. 1998. *King Leopold's Ghost: A Story of Greed, Terror, and Heroism in Colonial Africa*. Boston: Houghton Mifflin.

Holland, Sharon P. 2012. *The Erotic Life of Racism*. Durham, NC: Duke University Press.

hooks, bell. 1992. *Black Looks: Race and Representation*. Boston: South End.

Hunt, Nancy R. 1999. *A Colonial Lexicon: Of Birth Ritual, Medicalization, and Mobility in the Congo*. Durham, NC: Duke University Press.

Hunt, Nancy R. 2016. *A Nervous State: Violence, Remedies, and Reverie in Colonial Congo*. Durham, NC: Duke University Press.

Jackson, Michael. 1998. *Minima Ethnographica: Intersubjectivity and the Anthropological Project*. Chicago: University of Chicago Press.

Jackson, Michael. 2005. *Existential Anthropology: Events, Exigencies and Effects*. New York: Berghahn.

Jackson, Michael. 2012. *Lifeworlds: Essays in Existential Anthropology*. Chicago: University of Chicago Press.

Jeffrey, Craig. 2010. "Timepass: Youth, Class, and Time among Unemployed Young Men in India." *American Ethnologist* 37, no. 3: 465–81.

Jenkins, Henry. 2006. "'He's in the Closet but He's not Gay': Male-Male Desire in Penthouse Letters." In *Pornography: Film and Culture*, edited by Peter Lehman, 133–53. New Brunswick, NJ: Rutgers University Press.

Jensen, Casper B. 2014. "Experiments in Good Faith and Hopefulness: Toward a Postcritical Social Science." *Common Knowledge* 20, no. 2: 337–62.

Jervis, Lori L., Paul Spicer, Spero M. Manson, and the AI-SUPERPFP Team. 2003. "Boredom, 'Trouble,' and the Realities of Postcolonial Reservation Life." *Ethos* 31, no. 1: 38–58.

Jeurissen, Lissia. 2003. *Quand le métis s'appelait mulâtre: Société, droit et pouvoir coloniaux face à la descendance des couples eurafricains dans l'ancien Congo belge*. Louvain-La-Neuve, Belgium: Academia Bruylant.

Jewsiewicki, Bogumil. 1976. "La contestation sociale et la naissance du proletariat au Zaire au cours de la première moitié du xxe siècle." *Canadian Journal of African Studies* 10, no. 1: 47–70.

Jewsiewicki, Bogumil. 1979. "Le colonat agricole européen au Congo-belge, 1910–1960: Questions politiques et économiques." *Journal of African History* 20, no. 4: 559–71.

Jewsiewicki, Bogumil. 1986. "Collective Memory and the Stakes of Power: A Reading of Popular Zairian Historical Discourses." *History in Africa* 13: 195–223.

Jewsiewicki, Bogumil. 1991. "Peintres de cases, imagiers et savants populaires du Congo, 1900–1960: Un essai d'histoire de l'esthétique indigène." *Cahiers d'études Africaines* 31, no. 3: 307–26.

Jewsiewicki, Bogumil. 1992. *Art pictural Zaïrois*. Sillery, Québec: Editions du Septentrion.

Jewsiewicki, Bogumil. 1995. *Chéri Samba: The Hybdridity of Art*. Westmount, Québec: Galerie Amrad African Art.

Jewsiewicki, Bogumil. 2003. *Mami Wata: La peinture urbaine au Congo*. Paris: Gallimard.

Jewsiewicki, Bogumil. 2008. "Residing in Kinshasa: Between Colonial Modernization and Globalization." *Research in African Literatures* 39, no. 4: 105–19.

Jobson, Ryan C. 2019. "Black Gold in El Dorado: Frontiers of Race and Oil in Guyana." *SSRC Items*, January 8. https://items.ssrc.org/race-capitalism/black-gold-in-el-dorado-frontiers-of-race-and-oil-in-guyana.

Johnson-Hanks, Jennifer. 2002. "On the Limits of Life Stages in Ethnography: Toward a Theory of Vital Conjunctures." *American Anthropologist* 104, no. 3: 865–80.

Johnston, Patrick. 2004. "Timber Booms, State Busts: The Political Economy of Liberian Timber." *Review of African Political Economy* 31, no. 101: 441–56.

Kabamba, Patience. 2010. "'Heart of Darkness': Current Images of the DRC and Their Theoretical Underpinning." *Anthropological Theory* 10, no. 3: 265–301.

King, Anthony D. 1984. *The Bungalow: The Production of a Global Culture*. London: Routledge and Kegan Paul.

Kipnis, Laura. 2006. "How to Look at Pornography?" In *Pornography: Film and Culture*, edited by Peter Lehman, 118–29. New Brunswick, NJ: Rutgers University Press.

Kirsch, Stuart. 2006. *Reverse Anthropology: Indigenous Analysis of Social and Environmental Relations in New Guinea*. Stanford, CA: Stanford University Press.

Kirsch, Stuart. 2014a. "Imagining Corporate Personhood." *PoLAR: Political and Legal Anthropology Review* 37, no. 2: 207–17.

Kirsch, Stuart. 2014b. *Mining Capitalism: The Relationship between Corporations and Their Critics*. Oakland: University of California Press.

Kneas, David. 2016. "Subsoil Abundance and Surface Absence: A Junior Mining Company and Its Performance of Prognosis in Northwestern Ecuador." *Journal of the Royal Anthropological Institute* 22, no. s1: s67–s86.

Kneas, David. 2018. "Emergence and Aftermath: The (Un)becoming of Resources and Identities in Northwestern Ecuador." *American Anthropologist* 120, no. 4: 752–64.

Lakoff, George, and Mark Johnson. 1980. *Metaphors We Live By*. Chicago: University of Chicago Press.

Lambek, Michael. 2015. "Both/And." In *What Is Existential Anthropology?*, edited by Michael Jackson and Albert Piette, 58–83. New York: Berghahn.

Lambertz, Peter. 2018. *Seekers and Things: Spiritual Movements and Aesthetic Difference in Kinshasa*. New York: Berghahn.

Larson, Anne M., and Jesse C. Ribot. 2007. "The Poverty of Forestry Policy: Double Standards on an Uneven Playing Field." *Sustainability Science* 2, no. 2: 189–204.

Latour, Bruno. 2004. "Why Has Critique Run Out of Steam? From Matters of Fact to Matters of Concern." *Critical Inquiry* 30, no. 2: 225–48.

Lauro, Amandine. 2005. *Coloniaux, ménagères et prostituées au Congo belge (1885–1930)*. Loverval, Belgium: Éditions Labor.

Leder, Drew. 1990. *The Absent Body*. Chicago: University of Chicago Press.

Leonard, Pauline. 2010. *Expatriate Identities in Postcolonial Organizations: Working Whiteness*. Surrey, UK: Ashgate.

Lévi-Strauss, Claude. 2013. *Nous sommes tous des cannibales, précédé de le père Noël supplicié*. Paris: Seuil.

Lewis, Ioan M. 1989. *Ecstatic Religion: A Study of Shamanism and Spirit Possession*. London: Routledge.

Li, Tania Murray. 2019. "Politics, Interrupted." *Anthropological Theory* 19, no. 1: 29–53.

Likaka, Osumaka. 1997. *Rural Society and Cotton in Colonial Zaire*. Madison: University of Wisconsin Press.

Likaka, Osumaka. 2009. *Naming Colonialism: History and Collective Memory in the Congo, 1870–1960*. Madison: University of Wisconsin Press.

Loffman, Reuben. 2019. *Church, State and Colonialism in Southeastern Congo, 1890–1962*. London: Palgrave Macmillan.

Loffman, Reuben, and Benoît Henriet. 2020. "'We Are Left with Barely Anything': Colonial Rule, Dependency, and the Lever Brothers in the Belgian Congo, 1911–1960." *Journal of Imperial and Commonwealth History* 48, no. 1: 71–100.

Love, Heather. 2010. "Truth and Consequences: On Paranoid Reading and Reparative Reading." *Criticism* 52, no. 2: 235–41.

Love, Heather. 2017. "The Temptations: Donna Haraway, Feminist Objectivity, and the Problem of Critique." In *Critique and Postcritique*, edited by Elizabeth S. Anker and Rita Felski, 50–72. Durham, NC: Duke University Press.

Lovell, Nadia. 1998. *Locality and Belonging*. London: Routledge.

Lund, Christian. 2006. "Twilight Institutions: An Introduction." *Development and Change* 37, no. 4: 673–84.

MacGaffey, Wyatt. 1983. *Modern Kongo Prophets: Religion in a Plural Society*. Indianapolis: Indiana University Press.

Mains, Daniel. 2007. "Neoliberal Times: Progress, Boredom, and Shame among Young Men in Urban Ethiopia." *American Ethnologist* 34, no. 4: 659–73.

Mains, Daniel. 2017. "Too Much Time: Changing Conceptions of Boredom, Progress, and the Future among Young Men in Urban Ethiopia, 2003–2015." *Focaal: Journal of Global and Historical Anthropology*, no. 78 (June): 38–51.

Malaquais, Dominique. 2006. "Douala/Johannesburg/New York: Cityscapes Imagined." In *Cities in Contemporary Africa*, edited by Martin J. Murray and Garth A. Myers, 31–52. New York: Palgrave Macmillan.

Marcus, George E. 1995. "Ethnography in/of the World System: The Emergence of Multi-sited Ethnography." *Annual Review of Anthropology* 24, no. 1: 95–117.

Marx, Karl. 1990. *Capital: A Critique of Political Economy. Volume 1: The Process of Capitalist Production*. Translated by Ben Fowkes. London: Penguin.

Masquelier, Adeline. 2013. "Teatime: Boredom and the Temporalities of Young Men in Niger." *Africa* 83, no. 3: 470–91.

Masquelier, Adeline. 2019. *Fada: Boredom and Belonging in Niger*. Chicago: University of Chicago Press.

Mauss, Marcel. 2012. *Essai sur le don: Forme et raison de l'échange dans les sociétés archaïques*. Paris: Presses universitaires de France.

Mazzarella, William. 2017. *The Mana of Mass Society*. Chicago: University of Chicago Press.

Mbembe, Achille. 1992. "Provisional Notes on the Postcolony." *Africa* 62, no. 1: 3–37.

Mbembe, Achille. 2001. *On the Postcolony*. Berkeley: University of California Press.

Mbembe, Achille. 2002. "African Modes of Self-Writing." *Public Culture* 14, no. 1: 239–73.

Mbembe, Achille. 2019. *Necropolitics*. Durham, NC: Duke University Press.

McClintock, Anne. 1995. *Imperial Leather: Race, Gender and Sexuality in the Colonial Contest*. New York: Routledge.

McCulloch, Jock. 2000. *Black Peril, White Virtue: Sexual Crime in Southern Rhodesia, 1902–1935*. Bloomington: Indiana University Press.

Meiu, George P. 2015. "'Beach-Boy Elders' and 'Young Big-Men': Subverting the Temporalities of Ageing in Kenya's Ethno-erotic Economies." *Ethnos* 80, no. 4: 472–96.

Mélice, Anne. 2012. "La désobéissance civile des Kimbanguistes et la violence coloniale au Congo belge (1921–1959)." *Les Temps Modernes* 658–59, nos. 2–3: 218–50.

Menzies, Charles R., and Caroline F. Butler. 2001. "Working in the Woods: Tsimshian Resource Workers and the Forest Industry of British Columbia." *American Indian Quarterly* 25, no. 3: 409–32.

Mercer, Kobena. 1994. *Welcome to the Jungle: New Positions in Black Cultural Studies*. London: Routledge.

Meyer, Birgit. 1999. *Translating the Devil: Religion and Modernity among the Ewe in Ghana*. Edinburgh: Edinburgh University Press for the International African Institute.

Mezzadra, Sandro, and Brett Neilson. 2017. "On the Multiple Frontiers of Extraction: Excavating Contemporary Capitalism." *Cultural Studies* 31, nos. 2–3: 185–204.

Miescher, Stephan F., and Lisa A. Lindsay. 2003. "Introduction: Men and Masculinities in Modern African History." In *Men and Masculinities in Modern Africa*, edited by Lisa A. Lindsay and Stephan F. Miescher, 1–29. Portsmouth, NH: Heineman.

Miles, Robert. 1993. *Racism after "Race Relations."* London: Routledge.

Miller, Jacques-Alain. 1994. "Extimité." Translated by Françoise Massardier-Kenney. In *Lacanian Theory of Discourse: Subject, Structure, Society*, edited by Mark Bracher, Marshall W. Alcorn Jr., Ronald J. Corthell, and Françoise Massardier-Kenney, 74–87. New York: New York University Press.

Mitchell, Timothy. 2009. "Carbon Democracy." *Economy and Society* 38, no. 3: 399–432.

Mosse, David. 2006. "Anti-social Anthropology? Objectivity, Objection, and the Ethnography of Public Policy and Professional Communities." *Journal of the Royal Anthropological Institute* 12, no. 4: 935–56.

Musharbash, Yasmine. 2007. "Boredom, Time, and Modernity: An Example from Aboriginal Australia." *American Anthropologist* 109, no. 2: 307–17.

Nader, Laura. 1969. "Up the Anthropologist: Perspectives Gained from 'Studying Up.'" In *Reinventing Anthropology*, edited by Dell Hymes, 284–311. New York: Pantheon

Nagel, Joane. 2003. *Race, Ethnicity, and Sexuality: Intimate Intersections, Forbidden Frontiers*. Oxford: Oxford University Press.

Nash, June. 1979. *We Eat the Mines and the Mines Eat Us: Dependency and Exploitation in Bolivian Tin Mines*. New York: Columbia University Press.

Navaro-Yashin, Yael. 2009. "Affective Spaces, Melancholic Objects: Ruination and the Production of Anthropological Knowledge." *Journal of the Royal Anthropological Institute* 15, no. 1: 1–18.

Ndaywel è Nziem, Isidore. 1998. *Histoire générale du Congo: De l'héritage ancient à la république démocratique*. Paris: De Boeck and Larcier.

Ndjio, Basile. 2012. *Magie et enrichissement illicite: La feymania au Cameroun*. Paris: Karthala.

Nelson, Samuel H. 1994. *Colonialism in the Congo Basin, 1880–1940*. Athens: Ohio University Press.

Niehaus, Isak. 2001. "Witches and Zombies of the South African Lowveld: Discourse, Associations and Subjective Reality." *Journal of the Royal Anthropological Institute* 11, no. 2: 191–210.

Nielsen, Morten, and Mikkel Bunkenborg. 2020. "Natural Resource Extraction in the Interior: Scouts, Spirits and Chinese Loggers in the Forests of Northern Mozambique." *Journal of Southern African Studies* 46, no. 3: 1–17.

Northrup, David. 1988. *Beyond the Bend in the River: African Labor in Eastern Zaire, 1865–1940.* Athens: Ohio University Center for International Studies.

Nyamnjoh, Francis B. 2018. "Introduction: Cannibalism as Food for Thought." In *Eating and Being Eaten: Cannibalism as Food for Thought*, edited by Francis Nyamnjoh, 1–98. Bamenda, Cameroon: Langaa RPCIG.

O'Neill, Bruce. 2014. "Cast Aside: Boredom, Downward Mobility, and Homelessness in Post-communist Bucharest." *Cultural Anthropology* 29, no. 1: 8–31.

O'Neill, Bruce. 2017. "The Ethnographic Negative: Capturing the Impress of Boredom and Inactivity." *Focaal: Journal of Global and Historical Anthropology*, no. 78 (June): 23–37.

Ortner, Sherry. 2016. "Dark Anthropology and Its Others: Theory since the Eighties." *Hau: Journal of Ethnographic Theory* 6, no. 1: 47–73.

Ouroussoff, Alexandra. 1993. "Illusions of Rationality: False Premises of the Liberal Tradition." *Man* (n.s.) 28, no. 2: 281–98.

Pandian, Anand, and Stuart McLean. 2017. *Crumpled Paper Boat: Experiments in Ethnographic Writing.* Durham, NC: Duke University Press.

Partenariat pour les Forêts du Bassin du Congo (PFBC). 2006. *Les forêts du bassin du Congo: État des forêts 2006.* Kinshasa: PFBC.

Peace, Ade. 1996. "'Loggers Are Environmentalists Too': Towards an Ethnography of Environmental Dispute, Rural New South Wales 1994–1995." *Australian Journal of Anthropology* 7, no. 3: 43–60.

Peace, Ade. 1999. "Anatomy of a Blockade: Towards an Ethnography of Environmental Dispute (Part 2), Rural New South Wales 1996." *Australian Journal of Anthropology* 10, no. 2: 144–62.

Peluso, Nancy L. 1992. *Rich Forests, Poor People: Resource Control and Resistance in Java.* Berkeley: University of California Press.

Pierre, Jemima. 2013. "Race in Africa Today: A Commentary." *Cultural Anthropology* 28, no. 3: 547–51.

Pietz, William. 1985. "The Problem of the Fetish, I." *Res: Anthropology and Aesthetics* 9, no. 1: 5–17.

Pignarre, Philippe, and Isabelle Stengers. 2005. *La sorcellerie capitaliste: Pratiques de désenvoûtement.* Paris: La Découverte.

Posel, Deborah. 2001. "Race as Common Sense: Racial Classification in Twentieth-Century South Africa." *African Studies Review* 44, no. 2: 87–114.

Povinelli, Elizabeth. 2006. *The Empire of Love: Toward a Theory of Intimacy, Genealogy, and Carnality.* Durham, NC: Duke University Press.

Pratt, Mary L. 1986. "Fieldwork in Common Places." In *Writing Culture: The Poetics and Politics of Ethnography*, edited by James Clifford and George E. Marcus, 27–50. Berkeley: University of California Press.

Pype, Katrien. 2007. "Fighting Boys, Strong Men and Gorillas: Notes on the Imagination of Masculinities in Kinshasa." *Africa* 77, no. 2: 250–71.

Pype, Katrien. 2012. *The Making of the Pentecostal Melodrama: Religion, Media and Gender in Kinshasa*. Oxford: Berghahn.

Rajak, Dinah. 2011. *In Good Company: An Anatomy of Corporate Social Responsibility*. Stanford, CA: Stanford University Press.

Rajan, S. Ravi. 2006. *Modernizing Nature: Forestry and Imperial Eco-development 1800–1950*. Oxford: Oxford University Press.

Ralph, Michael. 2008. "Killing Time." *Social Text* 26, no. 4: 1–29.

Ranger, Terence. 2007. "Scotland Yard in the Bush: Medicine Murders, Child Witches and the Construction of the Occult: A Literature Review." *Africa* 77, no. 2: 272–83.

Ratele, Kopano. 2008. "Analysing Males in Africa: Certain Useful Elements in Considering Ruling Masculinities." *African and Asian Studies* 7, no. 4: 515–36.

Richardson, Tanya, and Gisa Weszkalnys. 2014. "Introduction: Resource Materialities." *Anthropological Quarterly* 87, no. 1: 5–30.

Ricoeur, Paul. 1965. *De l'interprétation: Essai sur Freud*. Paris: Seuil.

Robbins, Bruce. 2017. "Not So Well Attached." PMLA 132, no. 2: 371–76.

Robinson, Cedric J. 1983. *Black Marxism: The Making of the Black Radical Tradition*. Chapel Hill: University of North Carolina Press.

Roda, Jean-Marc, and Katrin Erdlenbruch. 2003. "Analyse des conditions de reprise économique du secteur forestier en République Démocratique du Congo." *Rapport d'appui à la revue économique du secteur forestier*. Kinshasa: La Banque Mondiale et Ministère de l'Environnement de la RDC.

Rogers, Douglas. 2012. "The Materiality of the Corporation: Oil, Gas, and Corporate Social Technologies in the Remaking of a Russian Region." *American Ethnologist* 39, no. 2: 284–96.

Rolston, Jessica S. 2013. "The Politics of Pits and the Materiality of Mine Labor: Making Natural Resources in the American West." *American Anthropologist* 115, no. 4: 582–94.

Rubbers, Benjamin. 2013. *Le paternalisme en question: les anciens ouvriers de la Gécamines face à la libéralisation du secteur minier Katangais (RD Congo)*. Paris: L'Harmattan.

Rubbers, Benjamin. 2019. "Mining Towns, Enclaves and Spaces: A Genealogy of Worker Camps in the Congolese Copperbelt." *Geoforum* 98 (January): 88–96.

Said, Edward. 1978. *Orientalism*. New York: Pantheon.

Salverda, Tijo. 2019. "Conflicting Interpretations: On Analyzing an Agribusiness' Concerns about Critique." *Journal of Business Anthropology* 8, no. 1: 4–24.

Schatzberg, Michael G. 2001. *Political Legitimacy in Middle Africa: Father, Family, Food*. Bloomington: Indiana University Press.

Schouten, Peer. 2020. *Roadblock Politics: The Origins of Violence in Central Africa.* Cambridge: Cambridge University Press.

Scott, James C. 1985. *Weapons of the Weak: Everyday Forms of Peasant Resistance.* New Haven: Yale University Press.

Scott, James C. 1990. *Domination and the Arts of Resistance: Hidden Transcripts.* New Haven: Yale University Press.

Sedgwick, Eve K. 1985. *Between Men: English Literature and Male Homosocial Desire.* New York: Columbia University Press.

Sedgwick, Eve K. 2003. "Paranoid Reading and Reparative Reading, or, You're so Paranoid, You Probably Think This Essay Is about You." In *Touching Feeling: Affect, Pedagogy, Performativity,* 123–51. Durham, NC: Duke University Press.

Seibert, Julia. 2011. "More Continuity Than Change? New Forms of Unfree Labor in the Belgian Congo, 1908–1930." In *Humanitarian Intervention and Changing Labor Relations: The Long-Term Consequences of the Abolition of the Slave Trade,* edited by Marcel Van der Linden, 369–86. Leiden, NL: Brill.

Shaw, Rosalind. 2002. *Memories of the Slave Trade: Ritual and the Historical Imagination in Sierra Leone.* Chicago: University of Chicago Press.

Sidaway, James D. 2007. "Enclave Space: A New Metageography of Development?" *Area* 39, no. 3: 331–39.

Sivaramakrishnan, Kalyanakrishnan. 1999. *Modern Forests: Statemaking and Environmental Change in Colonial Eastern India.* Stanford, CA: Stanford University Press.

Slater, Candace. 2002. *Entangled Edens: Visions of the Amazon.* Berkeley: University of California Press.

Sodikoff, Genese M. 2012. *Forest and Labor in Madagascar: From Colonial Concession to Global Biosphere.* Indianapolis: Indiana University Press.

Sontag, Susan. 2009. *Against Interpretation and Other Essays.* London: Penguin.

Spronk, Rachel. 2014. "The Idea of African Men: Dealing with the Cultural Contradictions of Sex in Academia and in Kenya." *Culture, Health and Sexuality* 16, no. 5: 504–17.

Stengers, Isabelle. 2003. *Cosmopolitiques.* 7 vols. Paris: La Découverte.

Stengers, Jean. 1989. *Congo, mythes et réalités: 100 ans d'histoire.* Paris: Editions Duculot.

Stengers, Jean, and Jan Vansina. 1985. "King Leopold's Congo." In *The Cambridge History of Africa. Volume 6: From 1870 to c. 1905,* edited by Roland Oliver and G. N. Sanderson, 315–58. Cambridge: Cambridge University Press.

Stewart, Kathleen. 1991. "On the Politics of Cultural Theory: A Case for 'Contaminated' Cultural Critique." *Social Research* 58, no. 2: 395–412.

Stewart, Kathleen. 1996. *A Place on the Side of the Road: Cultural Poetics in an 'Other' America.* Princeton, NJ: Princeton University Press.

Stewart, Kathleen. 2007. *Ordinary Affects.* Durham, NC: Duke University Press.

Stewart, Kathleen. 2008. "Weak Theory in an Unfinished World." *Journal of Folklore Research* 45, no. 1: 71–82.

Stewart, Kathleen. 2017. "In the World That Affect Proposed." *Cultural Anthropology* 32, no. 2: 192–98.

Stirrat, Roderick L. 2008. "Mercenaries, Missionaries and Misfits: Representations of Development Personnel." *Critique of Anthropology* 28, no. 4: 406–25.

Stoler, Ann L. 1995. *Race and the Education of Desire: Foucault's History of Sexuality and the Colonial Order of Things*. Durham, NC: Duke University Press.

Stoler, Ann L. 2002. *Carnal Knowledge and Imperial Power: Race and the Intimate in Colonial Rule*. Berkeley: University of California Press.

Stoler, Ann L. 2013. *Imperial Debris: On Ruins and Ruination*. Durham, NC: Duke University Press.

Strathern, Marilyn. 2004. *Partial Connections*. Walnut Creek, CA: Altamira.

Svendsen, Lars. 2005. *A Philosophy of Boredom*. London: Reaktion.

Sweeney, Brendan, and John Holmes. 2008. "Work and Life in the Clear-Cut: Communities of Practice in the Northern Ontario Tree Planting Industry." *Canadian Geographer/Le Géographe Canadien* 52, no. 2: 204–21.

Taussig, Michael. 1980. *The Devil and Commodity Fetishism in South America*. Chapel Hill: University of North Carolina Press.

Taussig, Michael. 1987. *Shamanism, Colonialism, and the Wild Man: A Study in Terror and Healing*. Chicago: University of Chicago Press.

Taussig, Michael. 1992. *The Nervous System*. New York: Routledge.

Taussig, Michael. 1993. *Mimesis and Alterity: A Particular History of the Senses*. New York: Routledge.

Thompson, Edward P. 1967. "Time, Work-Discipline, and Industrial Capitalism." *Past and Present*, no. 38 (December): 56–97.

Thornton, John. 2003. "Cannibals, Witches, and Slave Traders in the Atlantic World." *William and Mary Quarterly* 60, no. 2: 273–94.

Thrift, Nigel. 2005. *Knowing Capitalism*. London: Sage.

Tomczik, Adam. 2008. "'He-men Could Talk to He-men in He-man Language': Lumberjack Work Culture in Maine and Minnesota, 1840–1940." *Historian* 70, no. 4: 697–715.

Tonda, Joseph. 2005. *Le souverain moderne: Le corps du pouvoir en Afrique centrale (Congo, Gabon)*. Paris: Karthala.

Trapido, Joseph. 2010. "Love and Money in Kinois Popular Music." *Journal of African Cultural Studies* 22, no. 2:121–44.

Trefon, Theodore. 2004. *Reinventing Order in the Congo: How People Respond to State Failure in Kinshasa*. London: Zed.

Trefon, Theodore. 2006. "Industrial Logging in the Congo: Is a Stakeholder Approach Possible?" *South African Journal of International Affairs* 13, no. 2: 101–14.

Trefon, Théodore. 2008. "La réforme du secteur forestier en République Démocratique du Congo: Défis sociaux et faiblesses institutionelles." *Afrique Contemporaine* 227, no. 3: 81–93.

Trefon, Theodore. 2016. *Congo's Environmental Paradox: Potential and Predation in a Land of Plenty*. London: Zed.

Tsing, Anna L. 1993. *In the Realm of the Diamond Queen: Marginality in an Out-of-the-Way Place*. Princeton, NJ: Princeton University Press.

Tsing, Anna L. 2000. "The Global Situation." *Cultural Anthropology* 15, no. 3: 327–60.

Tsing, Anna L. 2003. "Natural Resources and Capitalist Frontiers." *Economic and Political Weekly* 38, no. 48: 5100–5106.

Tsing, Anna L. 2005. *Friction: An Ethnography of Global Connection*. Princeton, NJ: Princeton University Press.

Tsing, Anna L. 2015. *The Mushroom at the End of the World: On the Possibility of Life in Capitalist Ruins*. Princeton, NJ: Princeton University Press.

Turner, Harold W. 1978. "The Hidden Power of the Whites: The Secret Religion Withheld from the Primal People." *Archives des Sciences Sociales des Religions* 46, no. 1: 41–55.

Turner, Victor. 1967. *The Forest of Symbols: Aspects of Ndembu Ritual*. Ithaca, NY: Cornell University Press.

Turner, Victor. 1969. *The Ritual Process: Structure and Anti-structure*. New Brunswick, NJ: Transaction.

Van den Berg, Marguerite, and Bruce O'Neill. 2017. "Introduction: Rethinking the Class Politics of Boredom." *Focaal: Journal of Global and Historical Anthropology*, no. 78 (June): 1–8.

Van den Bergh, E. 1933. *Bij de Budja's*. Postel, Belgium: Norbertijner Abdij.

Vandergeest, Peter, and Nancy L. Peluso. 2006. "Empires of Forestry: Professional Forestry and State Power in Southeast Asia, Part 1." *Environment and History* 12, no. 1: 31–64.

Vangroenweghe, Daniel. 1985. *Rood rubber: Leopold II en zijn Congo*. Brussels: Elsevier.

Van Klinken, Gerry. 2008. "Blood, Timber, and the State in West Kalimantan, Indonesia." *Asia Pacific Viewpoint* 49, no. 1: 35–47.

Vansina, Jan. 1966. *Introduction à l'ethnographie du Congo*. Kinshasa: Editions universitaires du Congo.

Vansina, Jan. 1990. *Paths in the Rainforest: Toward a History of Political Tradition in Equatorial Africa*. Madison: University of Wisconsin Press.

Van Wolputte, Steven, and Mattia Fumanti. 2010. "Beer and the Making of Boundaries: An Introduction." In *Beer in Africa: Drinking Spaces, States and Selves*, edited by Steven Van Wolputte and Mattia Fumanti, 1–25. Berlin: LIT Verlag.

van Zyl-Hermann, Danelle, and Jacob Boersema. 2017. "Introduction: The Politics of Whiteness in Africa." *Africa* 87, no. 4: 651–61.

Vidler, Anthony. 1992. *The Architectural Uncanny: Essays in the Modern Unhomely*. Cambridge, MA: MIT Press.

Wadley, Reed L., and Michael Eilenberg. 2005. "Autonomy, Identity, and 'Illegal' Logging in the Borderland of West Kalimantan, Indonesia." *Asia Pacific Journal of Anthropology* 6, no. 1: 19–34.

Waugh, Thomas. 2001. "Homosociality in the Classical American Stag Film: Off-Screen, On-Screen." *Sexualities* 4, no. 3: 275–91.

Weiss, Brad. 2009. *Street Dreams and Hip Hop Barbershops: Global Fantasy in Urban Tanzania*. Bloomington: Indiana University Press.

Welker, Marina. 2014. *Enacting the Corporation: An American Mining Firm in Post-authoritarian Indonesia*. Berkeley: University of California Press.

Welker, Marina. 2016a. "No Ethnographic Playground: Mining Projects and Anthropological Politics: A Review Essay." *Comparative Studies in Society and History* 58, no. 2: 577–86.

Welker, Marina. 2016b. "Notes on the Difficulty of Studying the Corporation." *Seattle University Law Review* 39: 397–422.

Wentzell, Emily A. 2013. *Maturing Masculinities: Aging, Chronic Illness, and Viagra in Mexico*. Durham, NC: Duke University Press.

West, Harry G. 2007. *Ethnographic Sorcery*. Chicago: University of Chicago Press.

White, Luise. 1993. "Cars Out of Place: Vampires, Technology, and Labor in East and Central Africa." *Representations*, no. 43 (Summer): 27–50.

White, Luise. 2000. *Speaking with Vampires: Rumor and History in Colonial Africa*. Berkeley: University of California Press.

Wiegman, Robyn. 2014. "The Times We're In: Queer Feminist Criticism and the Reparative 'Turn.'" *Feminist Theory* 15, no. 1: 4–25.

Wiegman, Robyn, and Elizabeth A. Wilson. 2015. "Introduction: Antinormativity's Queer Conventions." *Differences* 26, no. 1: 1–25.

Williams, Linda. 2004. "Skin Flicks on the Racial Border: Pornography, Exploitation, and Inter-racial Lust." In *Porn Studies*, edited by Linda Williams, 271–308. Durham, NC: Duke University Press.

Williams, Raymond. 1977. *Marxism and Literature*. Oxford: Oxford University Press.

Young, Crawford, and Thomas Turner. 1985. *The Rise and Decline of the Zairian State*. Madison: University of Wisconsin Press.

Young, Lola. 1996. "Missing Persons: Fantasizing Black Women in *Black Skin, White Masks*." In *The Fact of Blackness: Frantz Fanon and Visual Representation*, edited by Alan Read, 86–97. London: Institute of Contemporary Arts.

Young, Robert J. C. 1995. *Colonial Desire: Hybridity in Theory, Culture and Race*. London: Routledge.

Zupančič, Alenka. 2006. "When Surplus Enjoyment Meets Surplus Value." In *Jacques Lacan and the Other Side of Psychoanalysis: Reflections on Seminar XVII*, edited by Justin Clemens and Russell Grigg, 155–78. Durham, NC: Duke University Press.

INDEX

cotton cultivation: colonialist imposition of, 79–80; postcolonial legacy of, 94–95

counting teams, work of, 58

critique of capitalism: emasculation and, 243–44; overview of, 2–5

Cuvelier, Jeroen, 197–98

dark anthropology: capitalist exploitation and, 2–5; self-exoticization of European managers and, 153–56

darkness: colonialism and cannibalism and, 174–75; Conrad and, 156–59; European self-exoticization and, 156–58, 209, 226–27, 259n4

Das Kapital (Marx), 176

day workers, logging industry reliance on, 54–55

De Boeck, Filip, 198

débrouillardise (coping or making do), 196–97

deforestation, logging and cultivation linked to, 30–31

Democratic Republic of Congo (DRC): burials in, 131; forest code established for, 19–20, 100–103; mediatized stereotypes of, 156–57; natural resources in, 17–18; timber production in, 17–21, 254n14

dendrology, prospectors' knowledge of, 59

diamond smuggling, 180, 198

Dikpo (Mbudza chief), 79–80, 275n4

discipline and control: camp architecture and, 122; ecstasis and, 9–11, 237–40; hydraulic metaphysics of, 171–72; of logging workers, 68–73

Droogers, André, 178

eating metaphor: corruption and, 102; paranoid and reparative readings of, 182–85, 240; work under capitalism and, 174–77

ecstasis: alcohol and drugs and, 129–31, 250–51; anthropology of extraction and, 11–15; cannibalism and, 185; defined, 9; ethnographic research and, 37–40, 236–37; in expat quarters, 148, 151–52,

156, 158–59, 210, 227–28, 231; game playing and, 128–29; human existence and, 205, 227–28, 234–37; in logging camps, 54, 135–41, 197–98, 205, 232; memory and, 96; occult technologies and, 179, 185; philosophy and anthropology and, 7–11; power and, 237–40; in timber production, 66, 69, 73, 232; transgression and masculinity and, 205, 210; violence and, 105, 110, 118, 236; weak theory and, 241–47; writing and, xxi, 44, 232–33

Eden, Garden of, as timber industry metaphor, 35, 143–51, 162, 164–68

eleko tree, 75; as resistance symbol, 192–95, 200, 205

enclaving: as capitalist extraction model, 114–18, 232, 258n4; as feeling, 25, 82, 100

End of Capitalism (As We Knew It), The (Gibson-Graham), 243–44

Engundele (traditional Mbudza song and dance), 203–4

entrepreneurship: roadbuilding impact on, 111; in timber industry families, 122–26

ethics: in ethnographic research, 33–34; research autonomy and dependence and, 41

ethnicity: forest workers and, 24, 120–22; Mbudza, 77

ethnic tensions, near Bumba, 83–84, 105

European loggers: attitudes toward expat work among, 145–48; diamond smuggling by, 180; discipline and control by, 69–73; ecstasis in fieldwork with, 34–37, 39–40; neglect of logging camps by, 137–40; occult practices of, 169–72, 179; pornography and, 217–19; power and ecstasis for, 238–39; roadbuilding and, 111; segregated housing for, 149–51; self-exoticization of, 153–56; sexuality and, 207–15; social responsibility contracts and, 102–6; soft-erotic calendars for, 215–17; workers relations with, 53–56, 165–67

existential anthropology, ecstasis and, 9–10, 205, 238

extractive capitalism: anthropology of, 11–15, 176–77; in Democratic Republic of Congo, 78–84; ecstasis and capitalism of, 1–2, 233–37, 241–47; occult technologies and, 170–79; race, sex, and gender in, 225–28; whiteness as fixture in, 155–56

Fabian, Johannes, 8–9, 37–38, 134, 158, 232–36, 250, 256n10
family life: of Congolese workers, 48–49, 120–26; marriage and, 202–4; self-infantilization of workers and, 189–92; wives of workers, 191–92
Fanon, Frantz, 221, 224, 260n2
felling operations, xv–xvii, 56, 64–66
Felski, Rita, 5
feminist theory, critique of capitalism in, 2–5, 243–47, 260n3
Ferguson, James, 109–10, 115–17, 258n4
Ferme, Mariane, 181–82
field research: agreement on boundaries of, 255n4; ecstasis and, 37, 236–37; friendship and, 37–40; negotiating access to logging enterprises, 32–34; queerness and, 40; on transnational corporations, 40–46
Fisiy, Cyprian, 178
fónólí practices, sorcery and, 178–79
forest code (DRC): establishment of, 19–20, 100–103; socioeconomic obligations of, 101–6
forestry research, blind spots in, 15–17
Forest Stewardship Council (FSC), certification of logging operations and, 30–32, 104, 255n3
forest wives (basi ya zamba), 60
friendship, ethnographic research and, 37–40
fuel smuggling, 111–14; consumption and, 196–201; fight against, 113–14; logging camp culture and, 125–26, 130–31, 138; masculinity and, 196
funerals, social interactions at, 130–31
Fuss, Diana, 6

Gaddafi, Muammar al-, 112
game playing: as anti-boredom strategy, 126–29; forest work as, 68
garage operations, 56
Geertz, Clifford, 128
gender: colonial stereotypes and, 207–9, 213; conflict in logging camps over, 191–92; dissidence and, 201; in felling operations, 65–66; hunting and, 62; libaku signs and, 258n.3; logging camp culture and, 57, 123–24, 130, 201–4; logging gear and, 215–17; natural resources and, 256n.5; pornography and, 217–25; in prospecting, 60–61; in roadbuilding, 64; tracking and, 61–63
general services operations, 56
genre paintings, Congolese home decoration and, 134–35
Geschiere, Peter, 174, 178
Gibson-Graham, J. K., 3, 243
gift giving, logging concessions and, 20, 98–100, 102, 104, 108–9
Gilbert, Paul, 253n.2
Girard, René, 223
Golub, Alex, 13, 116, 244
Gondola, Didier, 199–200
Greenpeace movement, 32, 35–36, 211–12

Haase, Esther, 216–17
Hall, Stuart, 226
Haraway, Donna, 157
Hardin, Rebecca, 16–17, 108
Harvey, David, 12
Harvey, Penny, 106, 259n.3
Heart of Darkness (Conrad), 18, 156–58, 231
Hecht, Gabrielle, 241
Herzfeld, Michael, 200
heterochronic environment, forest camp as, 128, 131–36
heterosexuality: challenge of, 201–4; machinery and, 215–17; queer dimensions of, 210, 223–25
homemaking practices: of European managers, 149–53; in forest camps, 132–36
homoeroticism, mimetic desire and, 223–25

masculinity: Congolese history of violence and, 199–201; European managers' framing of, 154–56, 207–15, 238–39; ideals of strength and, 156, 187–88, 194–95, 199–201, 204; in logging camps, 188–89, 192–95, 204–5; mimetic desires and, 223–25; queering and, 244; race and, 219–23, 227; transgression and, 196–201; wage earning linked to, 80, 190–92

Masquelier, Adeline, 128

Mazzarella, William, 240

Mbembe, Achille, 135, 147, 183–84, 226, 230–31, 245

Mbudza people: *atulu* ritual of, 171; contemporary ethnic mobilization of, 83; ethnography of, 21–22, 77–80, 257nn.2–3; farming and, 124; labor resistance and, 192–95; logging operations and, 24; reputation for resistance of, 31, 78, 192–95, 205; war magic and, 65; as workers, 93

McClintock, Anne, 207–8

memories: of dispossession, 109; of violence, 81, 84, 173–74; of wage work, 72, 80–81, 87–96, 117, 122–23, 189

Mercer, Kobena, 220–21

mimetic desire: self-exoticization and, 226–27; sexuality and, 223–25

mining companies, differences between logging and, 13–15, 105, 115, 117, 244, 254n14

missionaries, in Congo, 21, 78–79, 92, 257n2

Mobutu, Joseph-Désiré, 19, 81–84, 171, 196, 257n9

Mouvement pour la Libération du Congo (MLC), 83

multi-sited ethnography, 43

mutual instrumentalization, in ethnographic research, 33–34

Nader, Laura, 41

Naipaul, V. S., 18

Nash, June, 176

Navaro-Yashin, Yael, 96

Ndaywel è Nziem, Isidore, 173

neoliberal capitalism: corporate social responsibility and, 105–6, 108–9; investment enclaves and, 115–18, 258n4; race aversion in scholarship on, 155–56

non-intentional communication, in fieldwork, 36–37

Nyamnjoh, Francis, 184–85

occult practices: exploitation of workers and, 176–79; female sexuality and, 168–72; Mbudza resistance and, 110, 192–195, 260n.4; paranoia and, 180–85; power and ecstasis and, 239–40; rainforest capitalism and, 100, 165; whiteness and, 165, 167, 172–75, 185–86; working conditions and, 175–77

oil companies, differences between logging and, 13–15, 105, 115, 117, 244, 254nn12–14

oil palm industry, 80–81, 88–94

Oneness, ecstasis as, 8

Ortner, Sherry, 2–3

Outline of a Theory of Practice (Bourdieu), 69

Out of Our Minds (Fabian), 8–9, 232–36

paranoia: in ethnographic research, 33, 43–44, 179–82; in logging concession, 84, 144; reparative strategies and, 44–46, 182–85, 243–46

Parti du Peuple pour la Reconstruction et la Démocratie (PPRD), 83

paternalism, capitalism and, 84, 88–90, 189

patronage, timber industry and, 16–17, 98–101, 106–11

performativity: corporate social responsibility and, 98, 108; of dependency, 109, 189–92, 258n4; ecstasis and, 246; ethnography on corporations and, 42–43; of labor, 86–87, 173; of masculinity, 188–89, 197–201, 204–5, 239; pornography and, 221–22

personal identification number (*numéro de matricule*), worker status tied to, 52–56, 63

phallic imagery: in pornography, 219–23; in soft-erotic calendars, 215–17 photography by timber workers, 187–89

Pierre, Jemima, 155–56

Pignarre, Phillipe, 183, 244–45

plantation history, Congolese colonialism and, 80–82, 87–90, 92–94

Plantations Lever au Zaire (PLZ), 82–84, 88–90

Plotinus, 8

pointer teams, work of, 58–59

ponoli practices, 177–79, 185

pornography: ethnographic fieldwork and, 210; European loggers and, 217–19; mimetic desires and, 223–25; phallic obsessions and, 219–23. *See also* porno-tropics tradition

porno-tropics tradition (McClintock), 207–9, 214, 217

postcritical ethnography: ecstasis and, 245–47; paranoia and, 181–82; rainforest capitalism and, 5–7; recent trends in, 253nn1–2; reparative reading and, 44–46

post-labor environment, memories and ideologies of wage work and, 87, 132, 174, 196

power: cannibalism and, 184–85; Central African concepts of, 175–76; of corporations, xvii–xviii, 3–4, 6–7, 12–13, 69–73, 105, 254n9; ecstasis and, 9–11, 73, 233, 237–40, 242–47; ensnarement and, 184; ethnographic research and role of, 41–43; in labor camp, 140–41; Mbembe on, 183–84; nervousness of, 237–38; paranoia and, 183–85, 260n3

precarity of industrial logging, 1–2, 7, 9, 13, 15, 43

prospectors in timber industry, 56–61

protocoles d'accord, CTI negotiations over, 102–6

Pype, Katrien, 199

queerness: ecstasis and, 11, 233; ethnography and dissimulation and, 40, 145; heterosexual masculinity and, 210, 223–25; as transgressive sexuality, 60, 130, 201; as weak/strong binary alternative, 244, 261n4

race and racism: black men as sexual threat and, 217, 222–23, 260n3; capitalist extraction and, 13, 155–56; colonialism and cannibalism and, 174; ecstasis and, 226, 236; ethnographic research and, 37–40; in expat culture, 146–48, 225–28; interracial sex and, 207–10, 225; lack of worker mobility and, 53–54; mimetic desires and, 223–27; in pornography, 219–23; religion in Africa and, 161–66; segregated housing of European managers and, 149–51; sexualized stereotypes of whiteness and, 208–9, 221–22; whiteness as ideology and domination mechanism, 144, 155–56; workers' reactions to, 68–69, 192

railways, 90–92

Rajak, Dinah, 13, 105–6, 108–9

real forester (*vrai forestier*) status, 57, 59, 137

recruitment of workers, Congolese gatekeepers and, 55–56, 256n1

religion: Black assumption of power and, 161–64; as escape from boredom, 129–31; female sexuality and, 167–68; logging camp culture and, 49, 125, 132, 161–64; white-Congolese relations and, 166–67; witchcraft and, 195, 245. *See also* churches

reparative strategies: cannibalism and, 182–85; ecstasis and, 228, 243, 251; ethnographic research and, 44–46, 243–47; photography as, 187–88; postcritique and, 253n1; racism and, 144

research autonomy and dependence, corporate power structure and, 41

resource-specific materiality, anthropology of extraction and, 14–15

reverse anthropology, 165

roadblocks: company reactions to, 114–18; history of, 257n1; protests over infrastructure and, 106–11

roadbuilding operations, 56, 63–64; villages as beneficiaries of, 111–12

Royaume des Cieux sur la Terre (Kingdom of heavens on earth), 162–64 rubber industry, colonialism and, 17, 79–80, 92–94

work in, 56–69, 71–73; salaries, contracts, and work bonuses in, 52–56; size
and composition of workforce in, 51, 121;
skidding and loading operations in, 56,
66–69; statistics office in, 70–71; tracking operations in, 56, 61–63; villagers'
attitudes toward, 98–101; village-timber
firm demarcation and, 120–22; violent
power of, 45–46
time management, in timber industry,
72–73
tracking operations, 56, 61–63
trailing teams, work of, 57–58
transgression: ecstasis and, 253n4; masculinity and, 60, 131, 196–201, 205, 223
transnational corporations: Congolese
timber industry and, 21; ethnographic
research on, 40–43; investment enclaves
of, 115–18; power of, 7, 13
transport operations, 56
tree symbolism: gender and, 57, 64, 66;
labor resistance and, 192–95
tropical rainforests: material-ecological
specificity of, 14–15; residents' vs. corporate perspectives on, 75–77; romantic
view of, 18–19, 145–46
trouble in logging camps: camp management and, 136–40; masculinity and,
197–98; as reaction to boredom, 130–31
Tsing, Anna, 3
Turner, Victor, 62

unions, timber industry and, 84–87, 192–93
upward mobility: cruel optimism about,
126; race and, 53–54

"vampire stories," in Central Africa, 173–74
Van den Bergh, E. (Father), 21–22
Vansina, Jan, 77, 257n2
villages (Itimbiri region): confrontation
between timber industry and, 84,
106–11, 258n3; DRC forest code and, 20,
101–6; history of, 77–84; relations with
logging camps, 120–26; roadbuilding
impact on, 111–12; timber industry
relations with, 23–24, 256n1

violence: colonialism and, 17–18, 87–90,
96, 157–59, 174, 237; ecstasis and, 117–18,
158–59, 236, 245–47; by European managers, 152–53; extraction and, 12; in felling operations, 65–66; against squatters
in labor camps, 138–41; against villagers,
107–8, 116–17; against women, 204

wage labor ideology, 80–81, 86–87, 132;
gender relations and, 201–4; rejection
of, 196–201
wages of logging workers, 52–56
war metaphors, in logging operations,
65–68
Watching My Daughter Go Black website,
219–25
water symbolism, in Itimbri region,
171–72
Way International Church, the, 49
weak theory, ecstasis and, 242–47
We Eat the Mines and the Mines Eat Us
(Nash), 176
weightlifting: by European loggers, 222; in
logging camps, 201
Welker, Marina, 13, 42–43, 116, 256n2
Wentzell, Emily, 199–201
Werrasson (Congolese musician), 62,
256n2
White, Luise, 173–74
whiteness: ethnographic research and role
of, 36–37, 39–40; as ideology and mechanism of domination, 144; mundele
classifications of, 259n5; occultist practices and, 165, 167–68, 172–75; segregated
housing of European managers and,
149–51; self-exoticization of, 153–56, 227;
sexuality and, 207–9, 211–15; visibility in
Congolese timber industry of, 155–56
Williams, Linda, 225
witchcraft: African Christianity and, 131,
161; capitalism and, 17, 182–85, 244–45;
CTI accused of, 100, 167, 174; eleko tree
linked to, 195; exploited workers and,
177–79; in village life, 75; whiteness
linked to, 167
Wokombo (Mbudza ancestor), 78–79, 194

women: churches and sexuality of, 168; exclusion from negotiations, 99, 102; forest workers relations with, 66, 111; in logging camps, 123–24, 130, 138–40, 161, 181, 200–204; logging machismo and stereotypes of, 211–15; in pornography, 217–21; porno-tropic tradition and, 207–209, 224, 227; in soft-erotic calendars, 215–17

work bonuses, in logging enterprises, 52–53, 65, 69

working conditions: colonialism and, 80–81, 173–74; discipline and control and, 69–73; for expat managers, 143–44; in logging camps, 48–51; physical toll of, 175–77; for prospectors, 57–61; for roadbuilders, 63–64; for skidders and loaders, 66–69; for tracking crews, 61–63; for tree fellers, 64–66; wage work vs. false labor, 86–87

Yankee, Congolese concept of, 200, 260n5

youth: adulthood and, 197–99; exclusion from negotiations, 99, 102; Mbudza nationalism and, 83; the performativity of, 199

Zaireanization campaign (Democratic Republic of Congo), 19, 82

zombie labor: in Central Africa, 177–79; ecstasis and, 185

Zupančič, Alenka, 260n3